Handbook of Research on Artificial Intelligence and Soft Computing Techniques in Personalized Healthcare Services

AAP Advances in Artificial Intelligence and Robotics

Handbook of Research on Artificial Intelligence and Soft Computing Techniques in Personalized Healthcare Services

Edited by

Uma N. Dulhare, PhD
A. V. Senthil Kumar, PhD
Amit Datta, PhD
Seddik Bri, PhD
Ibrahiem M. M. El Emary, PhD

APPLE
ACADEMIC
PRESS

First edition published 2024

Apple Academic Press Inc.
1265 Goldenrod Circle, NE,
Palm Bay, FL 32905 USA

760 Laurentian Drive, Unit 19,
Burlington, ON L7N 0A4, CANADA

CRC Press
2385 NW Executive Center Drive,
Suite 320, Boca Raton FL 33431

4 Park Square, Milton Park,
Abingdon, Oxon, OX14 4RN UK

Library and Archives Canada Cataloguing in Publication

Title: Handbook of research on artificial intelligence and soft computing techniques in personalized healthcare services / edited by Uma N. Dulhare, PhD, A.V. Senthil Kumar, PhD, Amit Datta, PhD, Seddik Bri, PhD, Ibrahiem M. M. El Emary, PhD.
Names: Dulhare, Uma N., editor. | Senthil Kumar, A. V., 1966- editor. | Dutta, Amit, 1971- editor. | Bri, Seddik, 1968- editor. | El Emary, Ibrahiem M. M., editor.
Series: AAP advances in artificial intelligence and robotics.
Description: First edition. | Series statement: AAP advances in artificial intelligence and robotics | Includes bibliographical references and index.
Identifiers: Canadiana (print) 20230495753 | Canadiana (ebook) 2023049580X | ISBN 9781774913383 (hardcover) | ISBN 9781774913390 (softcover) | ISBN 9781003371250 (PDF)
Subjects: LCSH: Artificial intelligence—Medical applications. | LCSH: Soft computing. | LCSH: Medical care—Technological innovations.
Classification: LCC R859.7.A78 H36 2024 | DDC 610.285/63—dc23

Library of Congress Cataloging-in-Publication Data

....

CIP data on file with US Library of Congress

....

ISBN: 978-1-77491-338-3 (hbk)
ISBN: 978-1-77491-339-0 (pbk)
ISBN: 978-1-00337-125-0 (ebk)

AAP ADVANCES IN ARTIFICIAL INTELLIGENCE AND ROBOTICS

The book series AAP Advances in Artificial Intelligence & Robotics will provide detailed coverage of innovations in artificial life, computational intelligence, evolutionary computing, machine learning, robotics, and applications. The list of topics covers all the application areas of artificial intelligence and robotics such as: computational neuroscience, social intelligence, ambient intelligence, artificial life, virtual worlds and society, cognitive science and systems, computational intelligence, human-centered and human-centric computing, intelligent decision making and support, intelligent network security.

With this innovative era of simulated and artificial intelligence, much research is required in order to advance the field and also to estimate the societal and ethical concerns of the existence robotics and scientific computing. The series also aims that books in this series will be practically relevant, so that the results will be useful for managers in leadership roles related to AI and robotics, researchers, data analysts, project managers, and others. Therefore, both theoretical and managerial implications of the research need to be considered.

The book series will broadly consider the contributions from the following fields:

- Artificial Intelligence Applications in Security
- Artificial Intelligence in Bioinformatics
- Robot Structure Design and Control
- Artificial Intelligence in Biomedical and Healthcare
- Multi-Robot Intelligent Aggregation Mechanisms and Operation Platforms
- Artificial Intelligence and Learning Environments
- Advances in AI-Driven Smart System Designs
- Robot Navigation, Positioning, and Autonomous Control
- Robot Perception and Data Fusion
- Advances in Artificial Intelligence research
- Advances in AI-Driven Data Analytics and Innovation
- Application of Intelligent Systems for Solving Real-World Problems

- Hybrid Systems Design and Applications Using AI
- Robot Grabbing and Operation
- Robot Behavior Decision and Control
- Robot Motion and Path Planning
- Applications of Intelligent Systems and Computer Vision

For additional information, contact:
Book Series Editor: Subhendu Kumar Pani
Professor & Research Co-ordinator
Dept. of Computer Science and Engineering
Orissa Engineering College, Bhubaneswar, India
Email: pani.subhendu@gmail.com

BOOKS IN THE SERIES

Advancements in Artificial Intelligence, Blockchain Technology, and IoT in Higher Education: Mitigating the Impact of COVID - 19
Editors: Subhendu Kumar Pani, PhD, Kamalakanta Muduli, PhD,
Sujoy Kumar Jana, PhD, Srikanth Bathula, PhD, and
Golam Sarwar Khan, PhD

The Fusion of Artificial Intelligence and Soft Computing Techniques for Cybersecurity
Editors: M. Ajabbar, PhD, Sanju Tiwari, PhD, Subhendu Kumar Pani, PhD,
and Stephen Huang, PhD

Incorporating AI Technology in the Service Sector: Innovations in Creating Knowledge, Improving Efficiency, and Elevating Quality of Life
Editors: Maria Jose Sousa, PhD, Subhendu Pani, PhD,
Francesca dal Mas, PhD, and Sergio Sousa, PhD,

Handbook of Research on Artificial Intelligence and Soft Computing Techniques in Personalized Healthcare Services
Editors: Uma N. Dulhare, PhD, A. V. Senthil Kumar, Amit Dutta, PhD,
Seddik Bri, PhD, and Ibrahiem M. M. EI Emary, PhD

Fusion of Artificial Intelligence and Machine Learning for Advanced Image Processing, Data Analysis, and Cyber Security
Editors: Rashmi Gupta, PhD, Sharad Sharma, PhD, Ahmad A. Elngar, PhD,
Arun Rana, PhD, and Sachin Dhawan, PhD

ABOUT THE EDITORS

Uma N. Dulhare, PhD
Professor & Head, Computer Science & Artificial Intelligence Department, Muffakham Jah College of Engineering and Technology, Hyderabad, India

Uma N. Dulhare, PhD, is currently working as a Professor and Head of the Computer Science and Artificial Intelligence Department, Muffakham Jah College of Engineering and Technology, Hyderabad, India. She has 20+ years of teaching experience. She received her PhD from Osmania University, Hyderabad. Her research interest includes data science, big data analytics, machine learning, IoT, cloud computing, biomedical image processing. She has published more than 30 research papers in reputed national and international journals and 8 book chapters and edited 3 books. She is a member of the editorial board for various national and international journals in the field of computer science and program committee member/reviewer for various international conferences.

A. V. Senthil Kumar, PhD
Director & Professor, Department of Research & PG in Computer Applications, Hindusthan College of Arts and Science, Coimbatore, India

A. V. Senthil Kumar, PhD, is working as a Director and Professor in the Department of Research and PG in Computer Applications, Hindusthan College of Arts and Science, Coimbatore. He has to his credit 11 book chapters, 250 papers in international journals, 15 papers in national journals, 25 papers in international conferences, 5 papers in national conferences, and edited 8 books (IGI Global, USA). He is the editor-in-chief for international journal titled *International Journal of Data Mining and Emerging Technologies, International Journal of Image Processing and Applications, International Journal of Advances in Knowledge Engineering and Computer Science, International Journal of Advances in Computers and Information Engineering,* and *International Journal of Research and Reviews in Computer Science.* He is also a key member of Machine Intelligence Research Lab (MIR Labs), India. He is an editorial board member and reviewer for various international journals.

Amit Datta, PhD

Deputy Director, All India Council for Technical Education, New Delhi, India

Amit Datta, PhD, is currently working as a Dy. Director at AICTE, New Delhi. He has more than 20 years of teaching, research, and administration experience. He published four books on C++, Data Mining Techniques, Neural Networks, and A Practical Solution Data Structure. He has published 23 research papers in international and national journals. He is an editorial board member of a number of international journals such as *International Journal of Scientific and Engineering Research* (IJSER), India, *International Journal of Scientific Knowledge (Computing and Information Technology)* (IJSK), *International Journal of Data Mining Techniques and Applications*, India. He obtained his Doctor of Philosophy in Artificial Neural Networks from Barkatullah Vishwavidyalaya, Bhopal.

Seddik Bri, PhD

Professor, Electrical Engineering Department, High School of Technology (ESTM), Moulay Ismail University, Meknes, Morocco

Seddik Bri, PhD, is a Professor in the Electrical Engineering Department at High School of Technology (ESTM), Moulay Ismail University, Meknes, Morocco. His scientific work is in the application of microwaves in security in communications systems. He has published 150 journal papers, over 160 papers at internationals conferences, ten books, and several book chapters. He is a referee for the *International Journal of Microwaves Applications, International Journal of Network Security, International Journal of Science and Applied Technology, International Journal of Electronics*, and many others. Dr. Bri has worked on integrated action projects and is a member of the scientific committee of about 60 international conferences. He has completed several research projects at Moulay Ismail University and was an Expert Evaluator with the National Center for Scientific and Technical Research (CNRST). He has supervised over 30 PhD students and has been examiner of over 70 PhD theses.

Ibrahiem M. M. El Emary, PhD

Professor of Computer Science and Engineering, King Abdulaziz University, Jeddah, Kingdom of Saudi Arabia

Ibrahiem M. M. El Emary, PhD, is a Professor of Computer Science and Engineering at King Abdulaziz University, Jeddah, Kingdom of Saudi Arabia. His former positions include assistant professor of computer sciences at different faculties and academic institutions in Egypt and visiting professor of computer science and engineering in two universities in Jordan. His research interests cover various analytic and discrete event simulation techniques, performance evaluation of communication networks, application of intelligent techniques in managing computer communication networks, and performing comparative studies between various policies and strategies of routing, congestion control, and subnetting of computer communication networks. He has published more than 150 articles in various refereed international journals and conferences in the areas of computer networks, artificial intelligence, expert systems, software agents, information retrieval, e-learning, case-based reasoning, image processing and pattern recognition, wireless sensor networks, cloud computing, and robotic engineering. He has participated in publishing seven book chapters in three international books and has also edited two books from international publishers. Dr. El Emary received his PhD in from the Electronic and Communication Department, Faculty of Engineering, Ain Shams University, Egypt.

CONTENTS

CONTRIBUTORS

Srinivas Aluvala
Department of Computer Science and Engineering, SR Engineering College, Warangal Urban, Telangana, India

Asha Ambhaikar
Professor and Dean Student Welfare, Kalinga University, Naya Raipur, Chhattisgarh, India,

Niket Amoda
Department of Electronics and Telecommunication Engineering, Thakur College of Engineering and Technology, Mumbai, Maharashtra, India

Areefa
Department of Computer Science and Engineering, SR Engineering College, Warangal Urban, Telangana, India

Jagdish R. Baheti
Kamla Nehru College of Pharmacy, Butibori, Nagpur, Maharashtra, India

Vishakha Bansod
PhD Scholar, Kalinga University, Naya Raipur, Chhattisgarh, India

Neeraj Bhargava
Department of Computer Science, School of Engineering and System Science, MDS University, Ajmer, Rajasthan, India

Ritu Bhargava
Sophia Girls' College, Ajmer, Rajasthan, India

Mrudul Bhatt
Department of Engineering and Physical Science, Institute of Advanced Research, Gandhinagar, Gujarat, India

Kapil Chauhan
Assistant Professor, Aryabhatta College of Engineering and Research Center, Ajmer, Rajasthan, India

Aruna Deoskar
ATSS College of Business Studies and Computer Application (CBSCA), Affiliated to SP Pune University, Pune, Maharashtra, India

Disha M. Dhabarde
Kamla Nehru College of Pharmacy, Butibori, Nagpur, Maharashtra, India

Uma N. Dulhare
Muffakham Jah College of Engineering and Technology, Hyderabad, Telangana, India

Vishal Dutt
Assistant Professor, Department of Computer Science, Aryabhatta College, Ajmer, Rajasthan, India

Kiran L. N. Eranki
Associate Professor, School of Computer Science and AI, SR University, Warangal, Telangana, India

Sunil Gautam
Department of Computer Science and Engineering, Institute of Technology, Nirma University, Ahmedabad, Gujarat, India

S. Geetha
Faculty, School of Computer Science and Engineering, Vellore Institute of Technology, Chennai, Tamil Nadu, India

Maniza Hijab
Computer Science and Engineering Department, Muffakham Jah College of Engineering and Technology, Hyderabad, Telangana, India

Lochan Jolly
Department of Electronics and Telecommunication Engineering, Thakur College of Engineering and Technology, Mumbai, Maharashtra, India

Marta Kadłubek
Department of Logistics and International Management, Czestochowa University of Technology, Czestochowa, Poland

A. Sampath Kumar
Assistant Professor, Department of Computer Science and Engineering, Dambi Dollo University, Ethiopia

A. V. Senthil Kumar
Hindusthan College of Arts and Science, Coimbatore, Tamil Nadu, India

Ambeshwar Kumar
School of Computing, SASTRA Deemed University, Tamil Nadu, India

B. Sateesh Kumar
Professor, Department of Computer Science & Engineering, JNTUH-College of Engineering, Jagitial, Telangana, India

S. Praveen Kumar
Department of Computer Science and Engineering, SR Engineering College, Warangal Urban, Telangana, India

N. Kumaran
Assistant Professor, DCSE, Sri Chandrasekharendra Saraswathi Viswa Mahavidyalaya (SCSVMV), Enathur, Tamil Nadu, India

Walunjkar Gajanan Madhavrao
Research Scholar, Computer Science and Engineering, Vel Tech Rangarajan Dr. Sagunthala R&D Institute of Science and Technology, Chennai, Tamil Nadu, India; Assistant Professor, Army Institute of Technology, Pune, Maharashtra, India

P. Malathi
Head of Department, Department of Electronics and Telecommunication Engineering, D.Y. Patil College of Engineering, Akurdi, Pune, Maharashtra, India

Monika P. Maske
Kamla Nehru College of Pharmacy, Butibori, Nagpur, Maharashtra, India

B. K. Mishra
Department of Electronics and Telecommunication Engineering, Thakur College of Engineering and Technology, Mumbai, Maharashtra, India

J. S. Shyam Mohan
Assistant Professor, Department of CSE, GITAM University, Bangalore, Karnataka, India

Rahul Reddy Nadikattu
Research Scholar, University of Cumberland, USA

Shilpa Parab
CMF College of Physiotherapy, Maharashtra, India

Shubhangi Patil
ATSS College of Business Studies and Computer Application (CBSCA), Affiliated to SP Pune University, Pune, Maharashtra, India

K. Pragathi
Department of Computer Science and Engineering, SR Engineering College, Warangal Urban, Telangana, India

S. Kanaga Suba Raja
Professor, Department of Computer Science and Engineering, Easwari Engineering College, Tamil Nadu, India

Manikandan Ramachandran
School of Computing, SASTRA Deemed University, Tamil Nadu, India

V. Srinivasa Rao
Professor, Vel Tech Rangarajan Dr. Sagunthala R&D Institute of Science and Technology, Chennai, Tamil Nadu, India

Shaik Rasool
Methodist College of Engineering and Technology, Hyderabad, Telangana, India

Pramod Singh Rathore
Assistant Professor, Aryabhatta College of Engineering and Research Center, Ajmer, Rajasthan, India

K. Rishitha
Department of Computer Science and Engineering, SR Engineering College, Warangal Urban, Telangana, India

Kundankumar Rameshwar Saraf
PhD Research Scholar, Department of Electronics and Telecommunication Engineering, D.Y. Patil College of Engineering, Akurdi, Pune, Maharashtra, India

Hitesh V. Shahare
Shriman Sureshdada Jain College of Pharmacy, Chandwad, Nashik, Maharashtra, India

Kiran Sharma
Assistant Professor, KIET School of Pharmacy, KIET Group of Institutions, Delhi-NCR, Meerut Road (NH-58), Ghaziabad, Uttar Pradesh, India

Pavika Sharma
Assistant Professor, Bhagwan Parshuram Institute of Technology (BPIT), Rohini, Delhi, India

Kaushal Singh
School of Engineering, P.P. Savani University, Surat, India

Mohammad Sirajuddin
Research Scholar, Department of Computer Science & Engineering, JNTU, Hyderabad, Telangana, India

K. Sridevi
Computer Science and Engineering Department, Muffakham Jah College of Engineering and
Technology, Hyderabad, Telangana, India

Murugan Subramanian
Assistant Professor, Department of Computer Science and Engineering,
Sri Aravindar Engineering College, Tamil Nadu, India

G. Sunil
Department of Computer Science and Engineering, SR Engineering College, Warangal Urban,
Telangana, India

Fahmina Taranum
Computer Science and Engineering Department, Muffakham Jah College of Engineering and
Technology, Hyderabad, Telangana, India

Tvisha Trivedi
Student, School of Computer Science and Engineering, Vellore Institute of Technology, Chennai,
Tamil Nadu, India

Arun Velu
Director Equifax, Atlanta, USA

Pawan Whig
Dean Research, Vivekananda Institute of Professional Studies, New Delhi, India

ABBREVIATIONS

ABIDE	autism brain imaging data exchange
ACLS	advanced cardiac life support
ADHD	attention deficit disorders
ADMET	absorption, distribution, metabolism, excretion, and toxicity
AE	auto-encoder
AF	atrial fibrillation
AGRE	autism genetic resource exchange
AI	artificial intelligence
AIoMT	AI-enabled IoMT
AMD	automated medical diagnosis
ANN	artificial neural networks
API	application program interface
ASD	autistic spectral disorder
ASICs	applied explicit incorporated circuits
AUC	area under curve
B2B	business-to-business
B2C	business-to-client
BERT	bidirectional representations from transformer
BPM	beats per minute
BPM	business process management
CBFCM	case based fuzzy cognitive map
CCS	connectome computation system
CMS	Centers for Medicare and Medicaid Services
CNN	convolution neural networks
CPS	cyber-physical system
CRUD	create, read, update, delete
CSS	cascading style sheets
CVDs	cardiovascular diseases
DDoS	distributed denial-of-service
DL	deep learning
DNNs	deep neural networks
DP	differential privacy
DR	diabetic retinopathy

DSPs	digital signal processors
DTRs	dynamic treatment regimens
EDF	earliest deadline first
EHRs	electronic health records
EMR	electronic medical record
EVM	Ethereum virtual machine
FCFS	first come first serve
fMRI	function magnetic resonance imaging
FPGAs	field-programmable gate arrays
GA	genetic algorithm
GDPR	general data protection regulation
GPS	global positioning system
GRU	gated recurrent units
gTTS	google text to speech
HC	healthy control
HIE	health information exchange
HO	Harvard-Oxford
ICT	information and communication technology
IIIT-B	Indian Institute of Information Technology-Bhagalpur
IoMT	internet of medical things
IoT	internet of things
ITS	intelligent tutoring systems
ITSI	IT service intelligence
IVR	interactive voice response
KB	knowledge base
KDS	Khoja–Durrani–Scott
KNN	K-nearest neighbor
LAN	local area network
LDA	latent Dirichlet analysis
LRN	local response normalization
LSTM	long short-term memory
LVQ	learning vector quantization
M&S	models and simulations
M2M	machine-to-machine
ML	machine learning
MLP	multilayer perceptron
MRI	magnetic resonance imaging
NIAK	neuro-imaging analysis kit
NIC	network interface card

NLP	natural language processing
OR	operating room
PBFT	practical byzantine fault-tolerance
PBT	path-based fund transfer
PCA	principal component analysis
PHI	personal health information
PHR	personal health record
PI	perfusion index
POEM	peroral endoscopic myotomy
PPM	patient pathway manager
PRISMA	preferred reporting items for systems analysis and meta-analyzes
PSO	particle swarm optimization
RBM	restricted Boltzmann machine
ReLU	rectified linear unit
ResNet	residual neural network
RF	random forest
RL	reinforcement learning
RMSE	root mean square error
RNN	recurrent neural network
ROC	receiver operating characteristics
RPA	robotic process automation
RPM	remote patient monitoring
RR	round-robin
SAR	search and rescue
SARS	severe acute respiratory syndrome
SGD	stochastic gradient descent
SJF	shortest job first
SLP	single-layer perceptron
SRS	social responsiveness scale
SRT	shortest remaining time
SVM	support vector machine
TCP	transmission control protocol
TDM	therapeutic drug monitoring
TLC	thought, language, and communication
UDP	user datagram protocol
WAN	wide-area network
WBAN	wireless body area network
WHO	World Health Organization

PREFACE

The rapid growth in technology over the last few years has contributed to the enormous data generation required by the changing face of healthcare services. This has led to the emergence of artificial intelligence (AI) and soft computing for next generation solutions to achieve sustainable healthcare ecosystems. Enhanced and sophisticated models built using the application of AI and ML algorithms can deliver excellent personalized healthcare services.

Today, healthcare systems have started integrating AI technology in every service. Personalized healthcare services is a broad framework for care that unifies predictive technologies with an engaged patient to coordinate care with the aim of promoting health and preventing diseases. Personalized healthcare increases the effectiveness of medical treatment through: active monitoring of treatment response and disease progression, early detection of disease at the molecular level when treatment can be most effective, genetic testing to reveal predisposition to disease, targeted treatment to improve outcomes and reduce side effects, accurate diagnosis to enable development and implementation of effective and individual treatment strategy and more.

Assistance of AI algorithms in healthcare can reduce diagnostic errors and provide the most up-to-date research and resources to support decision-making. Data focused on patient behavior risk factor, can enable AI to automatically identify risky behavior and predisposition to certain conditions so that doctors can proactively and confidently recommend the best lifestyle. Three main principles for adoption of AI in healthcare include data and security, analytics and insights, and shared expertise.

Today, the healthcare system is so computer-dependant, that it cannot progress a single step without soft computing which is highly related to artificial intelligence. Soft computing techniques may be used as an efficient method to assist doctors in monitoring the data of their patients with various healthcare issues and to diagnose by leveraging state of the art treatment. These approaches have the ability to adapt themselves according to the problem.

Soft computing approaches like particle swarm optimization (PSO), genetic algorithm (GA); ANN (artificial neural networks) is effectively used for diagnosing and prediction of disease from healthcare data of genetics, physiology, radiology, and cardiology and neurology disciplines. AI and soft computing can be used to make smart personalized healthcare services to build next generation ultra-digital hospitals with complete AI methodology, robotic surgery, 5G infrastructure for remote assistance, etc. The scope of this book covers not only background related to AI but also state-of-the-art applications in AI and soft computing to achieve intelligent personalized healthcare services.

Chapter 1 covers how remote health monitoring systems can help patients get advice related to the required treatment from doctors. The first part of the module gives a brief idea and demonstration of systems with the help of an experimental setup using LabVIEW. The later part of the module covers how AI-IoMT can assist doctors in prescribing medicines in accordance with the patient's critical parameters. This module also assesses numerous IoT security, privacy characteristics, various cyber threat models and attack classification.

Chapter 2 discusses the use of huge biomedical things data with emerging cloud and edge computing technologies to identify diseases with high accuracy. Chapter 3 emphasizes the accurate identification and diagnosis of disease using artificial intelligence and machine learning in today's unpredictable world environment.

Chapter 4 presents an approach for accessing patient records using blockchain. This chapter deals with ways to enhance data-sharing application of the health sector and pharmacy that are built on concepts of hyper ledger fabric and practical Byzantine fault tolerance consensus. Chapter 5 discusses the various security issues and intelligent solutions for IoMT-enabled healthcare systems. This chapter covers a variety of security, privacy issues, and various attacks on smart devices, intrusion detection systems and intelligent solutions such as malware identification for safeguarding healthcare data.

Chapter 6 proposes a paradigm which integrates an AI-driven distribution of resources with a personalized healthcare system, offering medical services to both the hospital and the patient. It also explores strategies for optimizing the error rates, expenditure, processing period, patient wellbeing and productivity is a multi-response methodology.

Chapter 7 presents a novel CNN architecture to address autism infliction disorders. The chapter provides insights on the performance of the improved CNN model on fMRI datasets. Proposed work in the chapter will assist autism researchers to improve the quality of data sets and data acquisition procedures.

Chapter 8 provides insight to researchers on how reinforcement learning can be used in future automated medical diagnosis. Chapter 9 exhibits the capacity of deep learning to analyze and recognize information in surgical videos. This capability could be used to aid in accurate planning of future surgical operations.

Chapter 10 discusses about the deep learning model deployed in various wearable sensor-based devices that helps in real time monitoring of patient's health by the caretaker. Chapter 11 elaborates on personalized physio-care system and how the technology has impacted the physiotherapy treatments. It emphasizes how tele-rehabilitation has made it possible to support all patient's physio treatment through distant location as well as the challenges faced in the adoption of such a system.

Chapter 12 provides an introduction to genetic algorithm (GA) and how multilevel techniques of GA carried out in various clinical regions including cardiology, medical procedure, radiology, radiotherapy, irresistible infections, nervous system science, and pharmacotherapy. Chapter 13 deals with the significance of telehealth and various technologies used to implement artificial intelligence in virtual health management systems.

Chapter 14 is about the trending use of AI in healthcare with the integration of robotics and IoMT to benefit patients, physicians, hospitals, researchers, etc. It also discusses its application for providing medical facilities in remote areas. Chapter 15 demonstrates the use of Splunk for implementation of smart and secure online medication system against the unwanted cyber-attacks. It also explores the effective integration of cyber physical components to treat the remotely located patient.

Chapter 16 introduces an audio bot known as DurBhashan, which is a healthcare-guiding booth used for connecting rural people with healthcare facilities through interaction and guiding them in their local language. Chapter 17 presents the issues of identifying the conditions and structure of the online pharmacy branches in Poland and logistic solutions supporting the management areas of the analyzed industry.

Chapter 18 proposes and analyzes an optimized reinforcement learning method in a disaster scenario and how this method is applied to reduce the loss of human life by ensuring timely communication and transportation among various units. Chapter 19 discusses the model for scheduling and allocation of healthcare resources as per patient's physical activity needs. The model can be utilized to apply different scheduling algorithms and select the efficient ones to reduce waiting time of a patient.

We would extend our gratitude to everyone who has contributed directly or indirectly to the book. We express our sincere gratitude to all authors who have been committed to completing this book even in the pandemic situation. We would like to thank to the publisher AAP Press for accepting our proposal.

—*Editors*

PART I

Internet of Medical Things and Cloud Technologies in Healthcare

CHAPTER 1

ARTIFICIAL INTELLIGENCE-ENABLED IOMT FOR MEDICAL APPLICATION

LOCHAN JOLLY, NIKET AMODA, and B. K. MISHRA

Department of Electronics and Telecommunication Engineering, Thakur College of Engineering and Technology, Mumbai, India

ABSTRACT

The present pandemic has put the whole of humanity under threat of getting infected by a deadly coronavirus. Remote health monitoring systems can help such patients to get advice related to the required treatment from doctors at remote locations.

The first part of the module gives a brief idea about a simple system that will sense using medical sensors and send information to the cloud using the internet and provide assistance to the patients after processing the data collected on the cloud as per the levels of the critical parameters under consideration. Internet of medical things (IoMT) is the name given to this system. The illustration for the same is done for demonstration with the help of an experimental setup using LabVIEW.

The later part of the module covers IoMT using AI which allows the doctors to prescribe medicines in accordance with the patient's critical parameters analysis. A comparative study of a simple IoMT with AI-enabled IoMT (AIoMT) for medical application will be provided for enhancing the understanding of the impact and application of IoMT and AIoMT.

From a healthcare perspective, this module assesses numerous IoT security and privacy characteristics, as well as various cyber threat models and attack classification.

Handbook of Research on Artificial Intelligence and Soft Computing Techniques in Personalized Healthcare Services, Uma N. Dulhare, A. V. Senthil Kumar, Amit Datta, Seddik Bri, Ibrahiem M. M. EI Emary, (Eds.)
© 2024 Apple Academic Press, Inc. Co-published with CRC Press (Taylor & Francis)

1.1   INTRODUCTION

IoT is a system with the potential to connect a wide range of medical devices, neurologists, and healthcare professionals to supply the best healthcare services in remote and rural locations. This has reduced the risk of physicians getting infected by potentially infected patients and healthcare costs along with improved patient safety and access to healthcare services [1].

IoT improves and transforms the way healthcare facilities are delivered with existing connected technologies [1]. IoT allows users to set up a central network of connected IoT devices that can generate and exchange useful information within an autonomous network. All the information can be tracked and collected in real-time. This is an advanced system where all data can be tracked and managed simultaneously. Healthcare has better IoT performance than any other field. In terms of improving medical and healthcare facilities, this means that a general hospital can be transformed into a smart hospital.

IoMT is an IoT-based application for medical and health-related applications for data collection, research analysis, monitoring, and timely assistance. IoMT is called "intelligent healthcare," as this technology can create a computerized healthcare system, connect medical services and health services. Therefore, it is a platform that can establish communication between patients and physicians in remote areas [2].

The use of IoMT will have significant benefits such as health monitoring, personal care, access to new preventive treatment, and disease control and diagnosis. The main idea of it is to provide remote healthcare services to people living in remote areas, especially where there are no healthcare facilities. In addition, it also aims to reduce the burden of overcrowded hospitals.

1.2   BACKGROUND

1.2.1   IOMT FRAMEWORK

An IoMT framework integrates the benefits of IoT technology and cloud technology in the area of healthcare. It is also responsible for transferring patient information from multiple medical sensors integrated with medical infrastructure to a given healthcare network. The topology used in IoMT is a geometrical representation of the various sensors and hardware components connected in a healthcare network [2].

IoMT system mainly consists of these three elements: publisher, vendor, and subscriber:

1. **Publisher:** It consists of a network of sensors and other medical hardware connected in such a way that can work alone or in collaboration with each other to record important patient data. This data may include blood pressure, RBC, heart rate, blood glucose random, temperature, blood glucose random, oxygen saturation, ECG, bacteria, blood urea, and so on. The publisher may continue to send this information via a network to the vendor. So, in this way, data is uploaded on the cloud [2].

2. **Vendor:** It is responsible for processing data that is collected on the cloud into meaningful information and storing it on the cloud for future reference. During processing, relevant data is filtered out, cleansed, and various AI algorithms are applied to ensure data accuracy and precision. The processed data is then subjected to multiple machine learning (ML) and deep learning (DL) algorithms to make predictions [3] and medical recommendations.

3. **Subscriber:** It is responsible for the steady observation and monitoring of patient information that can be viewed on a tablet, smartphone, computer, etc.

    At the receiving end, the subscriber can process the data and provide feedback after detecting any deterioration of the patient's health. This is done with the help of AIML algorithms.

The success of the IoMT application depends upon how well it meets the needs of healthcare services. Since each disease requires a complex process of healthcare services, the topology must follow some medical rules and steps in the diagnostic process. Figure 1.1(a) gives an example of the IoMT framework and Figure 1.1(b) is IoMT system [4].

1.2.2 IOMT WEARABLE DEVICES

IoMT devices will revolutionize the whole healthcare sector. Statistics show that the Global IoT Medical Devices Market to Top of $62 Billion by 2025. As humans and animals are mobile, smart IoMT wearable devices are becoming popular nowadays [5].

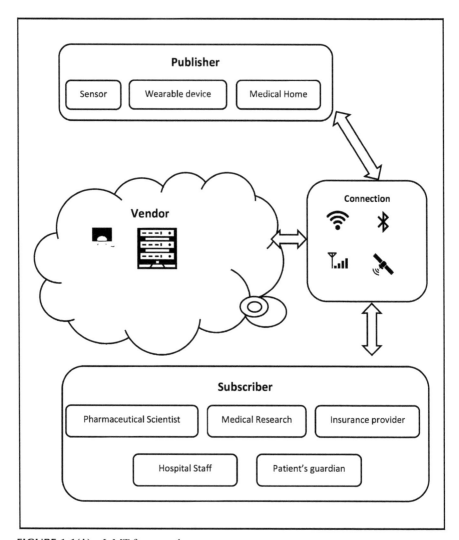

FIGURE 1.1(A)   IoMT framework.

The IoMT wearable device is a compact system that can continuously monitor the patient. It can collect and transmit the data on the move and simultaneously receive the data for making more refined decisions. Figure 1.2 shows the configuration of an IoMT wearable device.

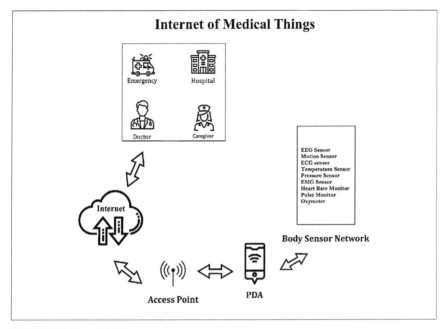

FIGURE 1.1(B). IoMT system.

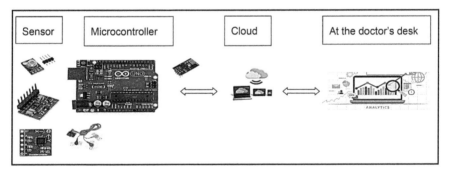

FIGURE 1.2 IoMT wearable devices configuration.

The simple wearable sensors are easy to configure as it only consists of sensors, microcontroller, and a Wi-Fi module. Figure 1.2 shows a simple setup that can be made using Arduino in a laboratory [5].

IoMT wearable devices can be worn on as an external accessory on the human body, embedded in clothes or garments, or even tattooed or stuck on the skin. These devices are capable of being connected to the internet to collect, transmit, and receive the data that can be useful for making smart decisions. Researchers and Scholars are working on the development of these accessories for more specialized and practical applications. Smart wearables can coordinate with various devices like tablets, smartphones, computers, etc., where computation can be done for making decisions. The developments in the field of low-power mobile networks have considerably decreased the size of sensors and actuators that are used in smart wearable devices. For example, body straps, smartwatches, smart eyewear, and smart jewelry are some wearable devices that have been developed so far for different applications [6, 7].

Having understood an IoMT system, let us now explore ways to demonstrate these concepts and principles in a classroom environment using Virtual instrumentation.

1.3   EXPERIMENTATION

With the understanding of a simple IoMT we tried to simulate an IoMT setup for continuously monitoring the critical parameters of a patient. The setup can be divided into four parts [8]:

- Hardware setup for sensing real-time data from the sensors attached to the microcontroller and viewing on the cloud;
- Sending patient data on the cloud and continuously monitoring it using a Virtual instrument in LabVIEW;
- Fetching data from the cloud continuously at remote locations using Virtual instruments in LabVIEW; and
- Integration of hardware and virtual instruments to sense data through hardware and display using virtual instruments in LabVIEW.

Illustration of these simple IoT applications for healthcare is done using LabVIEW software, ThingSpeak cloud, and Arduino board.

1.3.1   SENSE AND SEND USING HARDWARE INSTRUMENTS

A setup was made to make a wearable device to measure Temperature and pulse rate and upload on the cloud. The block diagram for the wearable device is shown in Figure 1.3. The wearable gadget will be worn by the patient with a temperature and pulse rate sensor [8]. The input from the sensor will be given to the microprocessor which will generate SMS under emergency conditions and send it to the caretaker or doctor and through Wi-fi module upload data on the cloud through the internet.

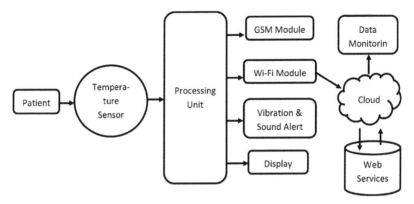

FIGURE 1.3   Block diagram of wearable device.

A sensor is connected in this arrangement, which will perceive the data and send it to the controller for further processing. All the data will be displayed on LCD as shown in Figure 1.4(a). Simultaneously all data strings will be sent to the server via a Wi-Fi module [8]. If measured parameters are greater than the threshold value, emergency actions will be taken like the buzzer will be switched on and a message will be sent to the caretaker or doctor as shown in Figure 1.4(b). And if the parameters measured are normal, then the cycle will continue, and continuous monitoring will be done.

Thing Speak chart field which gives a graphical analysis of temperature, which is monitored continuously as shown in Figure 1.4(c). A doctor or any caretaker can analyze the patient's health from any remote location, and they can provide better action if required. The Thing Speak application provides secure data communication. All the data which are analyzed by the graph can be stored as an excel file that contains all the information of the patient, and it can be used in the future if required [8].

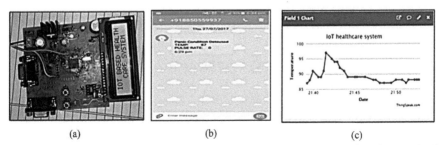

| (a) | (b) | (c) |

FIGURE 1.4   (a) Main board of IoMT wearable device; (b) SMS alert; and (c) data on cloud through system.
Source: Reprinted with permission from Ref. [8].

1.3.2   SENSE AND SEND USING VIRTUAL INSTRUMENT

A simulation setup to upload the heart rate parameter value on the cloud using a virtual instrument in LabVIEW was made. LabVIEW provides us the platform to upload the data from lab view to the cloud. In this setup, we are taking the input from the heart rate meter, which is the input terminal, and using the "Data communication" handles, this data is uploaded on the cloud continuously. This will not only create a platform for the monitoring of patients about the condition of heart rate but also keep a continuous monitoring chart for the doctor for future reference in case of emergency. Figures 1.5(a) and 1.5(b) shows block diagram and front panel of the setup for the heart rate monitor on LabVIEW, respectively [9].

Figure 1.5(c) shows that the heart rate from the system is correctly uploaded on the cloud. This will be beneficial when the doctor needs to monitor patients' history of the various parameters and make correct decisions regarding the medication and special assistance.

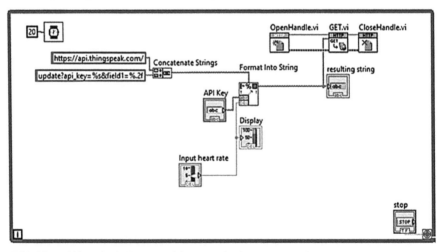

FIGURE 1.5(A)   Block diagram of the setup for heart rate monitor.

1.3.3   FETCHING DATA USING VIRTUAL INSTRUMENTS

A simulation setup was prepared to get the Heart Rate from the cloud at the receiver end using LabVIEW. In this setup we are taking the input from the cloud and using the "Data communication" handles to fetch it from the cloud continuously and display it at the receiver end. This will not only create a platform for the monitoring of patients at the doctor's end about the

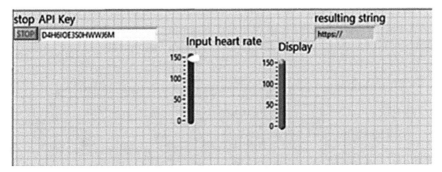

FIGURE 1.5(B)   Front panel of the setup for heart rate monitor.

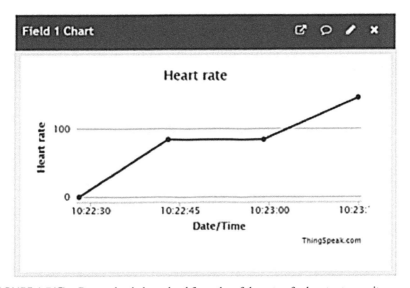

FIGURE 1.5(C)   Data uploaded on cloud from the of the setup for heart rate monitor.

condition of heart rate. This setup will take input parameters being collected at the remote location of the patient, which is heart rate which could be the input from the cloud and display at the location of the doctor for monitoring in case of emergency treatment for the patient. Figure 1.6(a) gives the block diagram of a virtual instrument to fetch data from the cloud [10].

Figure 1.6(b) gives the information about the parameter data uploaded on the cloud from a remote location which is to be fetched by the doctor at another location and Figure 1.6(c) gives the virtual instrument on the Front Panel to display data on the cloud which could be at the doctor's location [11].

The data on the system is the replica of the data on the cloud and hence clearly shows that the setup is capable of remotely accessing the data of the patient from anywhere on the cloud without the use of hardware instruments [11].

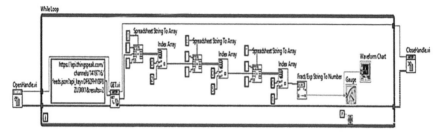

FIGURE 1.6(A)   Block diagram of the setup on LabVIEW to fetch heart rate from cloud.

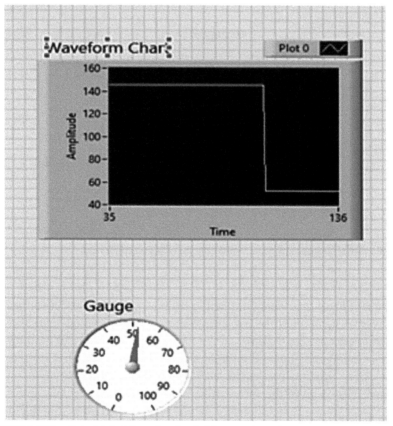

FIGURE 1.6(B)   Data fetched from the cloud at the remote system.

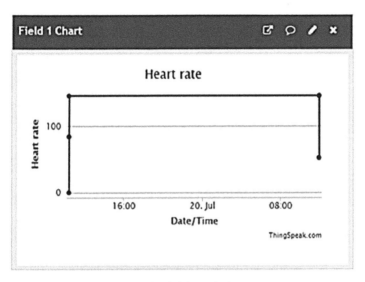

FIGURE 1.6(C)   Data on the cloud uploaded from the heart rate sensor.

1.3.4   SENSE AND SHARE DATA USING A COMBINATION OF HARDWARE AND SOFTWARE

A combination of hardware and software systems was designed to take the actual data from the hardware sensor and share it on a virtual instrument on LabVIEW. This setup will reduce the hardware requirements and will be able to upload the sensor data from Arduino to the LabVIEW front panel. This will create a platform for the monitoring of patients' conditions at remote locations and use the setup to continuously monitor the patients by doctor end. This setup will take the input parameter that is sensor data which could be the input from the Arduino and display it on the LabVIEW terminal. This data can be uploaded on the cloud using a previous setup which can be used for monitoring by a doctor when required. Figures 1.7(a) and (b) show block diagram and front panel, of the setup on LabVIEW to sense and display data from Arduino board, respectively.

Figure 1.7(a) gives the block diagram of a virtual instrument to fetch data from the Arduino board. Figure 1.7(b) displays the data on the virtual instrument on the Front Panel which is at the sender's Figure 1.7(c) gives the information about the sensor data on the serial monitor of the Arduino.

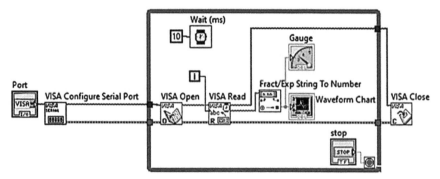

FIGURE 1.7(A)   Block diagram of the setup on LabVIEW to sense data from Arduino board.

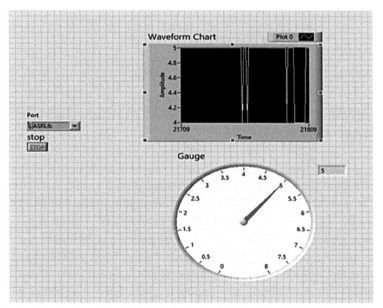

FIGURE 1.7(B)   Front panel displaying data sensed from sensor.

The front panel shows the variation like the variation on the serial monitor. Thus, it clearly shows that we can design wearable devices that could be a combination of actual hardware sensors and software [12]. Sensors and Arduino can collect actual data and virtual instruments on LabVIEW can display it for processing at the patient end and if required can take some primary decisions and further this will not need Wi-Fi Module to upload data on the cloud.

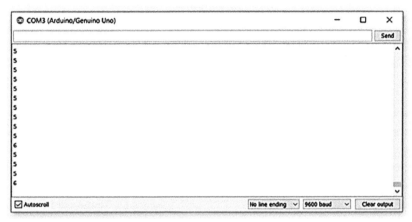

FIGURE 1.7(C)   Serial monitor displaying data sensed from sensor.

These simple demonstrations can be used in the classroom and laboratory to develop an understanding of IoMT and make designs to enhance the user experience. These setups perform sense and send operations. If the IoMT system is integrated with artificial intelligence (AI) it gives efficient and optimized performance. AI enabled IoMT is called AIoMT. It is covered in detail in the next section [13].

1.4   AIOMT

1.4.1   INTRODUCTION TO AIOMT

The evolving collaboration between AI and IoMT promises us an astute future. AI and IoMT are self-sustaining bodies capable of doing extraordinary things. The convergence of AI and the IoMT can alter the way medical assistance can be provided to critical patients when the whole system has a crunch of medical doctors and support staff. It is evident that AI and IoMT together will steer the medical assistant world soon. This blend will create machines credible enough to make smart decisions on their own without any interference from humans with the help of AI assistants [14].

AIoMT is a combination of IoT and AIML as shown in Figure 1.8. IoT will sense information and synchronize with other devices and send sensed data to the cloud (storage). Cloud will handle data and would learn with ML. AI and ML algorithms will predict and give recommendations regarding timely assistance to the patients.

The recommendations will be based on initially given inputs, i.e., threshold levels for various parameters under observation and training of the system based on learnings obtained from decisions taken in the past. This continuous process of learning and training from every decision that the system takes its performance keeps on refining for future predictions [15]. These features are making AIoMT popular among people for medical assistance as this has resulted in affordable and quality healthcare to rural populations and people in remote locations. New possibilities are emerging during this pandemic in the field of healthcare because of AI which was not there earlier [15]. Table 1.1 shows a comparison of AIoMT and IoMT.

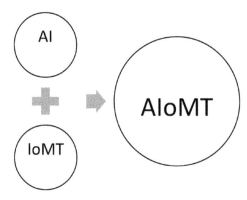

FIGURE 1.8   AIoMT system.

TABLE 1.1   Comparison of IoMT and AIoMT

IoMT	AIoMT
IoMT is an internet-connected network of integrated medical sensing devices.	AIoMT is an area of computer science devoted to the development of machines that can make intelligent judgments based on enormous volumes of medical data collected via sensors.
The purpose is to allow objects to send and receive data over the internet with minimal or no human intervention.	The purpose is to simulate human behavior and intelligence in machines to make them act more humanly.
Applications of IoMT include fitness trackers, health monitoring devices, hospital digitization, smart wearables, etc.	AIoMT's applications include machine learning-based predictive medicine, reasoning, natural language processing, and more.

When considering the practical implementation of IoT for any application, particularly medical, there is a problem: as the number of devices in an IoT network grows exponentially, the size of medical data on the cloud grows exponentially as well, resulting in medical big data. So, to make any decision, there is a need to manage and process this medical big data. In the next section, we will understand medical big data, its management, and analysis using AI [16].

1.4.2   MEDICAL BIG DATA

In the Healthcare sector, huge amounts of medical data are generated. Figure 1.9 shows that, medical data can be from the following sources [16]:

- Patient's medical history;
- Patient's genetic information;
- Generic data of the patient;
- Wearable devices;
- Smart devices;
- Handheld devices;
- Medical imaging reports;
- Healthcare routine documentation, etc.

Medical big data is the outcome of the exponential development in the size of healthcare medical data. Medical big data is slightly different from the big data coming from other areas. It is difficult to access it frequently, as it may have legal issues and require various levels of approval for access.

Patient's medical history
Patient's genetic information
Generic data of the patient
Wearable devices
Smart devices
Handheld devices
Medical imaging reports
Healthcare routine documentation

FIGURE 1.9   Composition of medical big data.

This medical big data isn't just kept for the sake of keeping records; it also contains vital information that may be studied to learn more about the illness's 'concept or fundamental cause.' [17]. This can bring major advancements in the field of healthcare, for the diagnosis, prevention, and cure of the disease. With the evolution of high-performance computing, medical big data can be analyzed faster to draw reliable conclusions regarding the health of the patient. This extracted information can be visualized for better understanding. Predictions of the occurrence of diseases in the future can be done based on these results [17].

Medical big data also has characteristics like volume, velocity, variety, value, etc. The medical data records are huge in terms of volume due to ever-increasing patient data. The data is streaming at a rate of MBPS or GBPS so we can say that data is being transmitted and received at high velocity for example constant monitoring of patient data like age, pulse, blood pressure, sugar, RBC, bacteria, and many more based on the patient's illness. The data which is being received is in various formats, not necessarily in a particular format as the origin of data is from multiple sources. Thus, the data has a component of variety in it. Among the various characteristics, perhaps the value is most important. It doesn't matter how fast the data is generated or received, what matters most is that it should be valid and reliable for processing. If the data is not reliable then processing such data will generate inaccurate results which will lead to poor diagnosis and cure of the patient.

After having understood medical big data and its characteristics, the next task is about developing an application for patient assistance using AI algorithms. The next section covers the role of AI assistance in healthcare.

1.4.3   AI ASSISTANT IN HEALTHCARE

With the population explosion in the present situation, the world is having inadequate healthcare personnel, and this gap is increasing continuously. According to the World Health Organization (WHO), there is going to be a shortage of about 13 million healthcare professionals by the year 2035. An ecosystem needs to be developed for handling the practical challenges of the shortage of medical professionals, especially in rural and remote areas. AI is evolving with state of art technological developments in the field of Medical Healthcare for providing solutions to practical challenges by identifying and managing gaps in the field of healthcare services. It is more inclined towards using the customized AI-enabled architecture with application support like medical decision support, patient disease diagnosis and predicting probable disease that may happen in the future, drug discovery, etc. [17].

All these advancements in IoMT with the inclusion of AI has the following advantages:

1. **Upliftment of Customer Satisfaction:** The machine automatically reduces manual interference and enhances the consumer's end-to-end experience.

2. **Improved Risk Management:** IoT devices help every patient to get assistance from an expert doctor when in an emergency. As per the analysis of various types of health parameters under consideration, alerts are generated for the concerned to provide immediate medical help. This reduces medical fatalities and risks.

3. **Eliminating the Unplanned Downtime:** This enables one to predict whether a healthcare setup requires any maintenance or thereby ensuring proper steps are taken to correct the failure without causing any hindrance to the normal functioning of the healthcare ecosystem.

4. **Helps in Real-Time Monitoring:** It displays real-time assistance reducing the time to assist patients in an emergency.

As the healthcare sector is transforming at a rapid rate, some current trends in the field of AIoMT are as follows:

i.   AIoMT healthcare model has already been modern Hospitals to the diagnosis of critical diseases like:
  a.   Detection of lung cancer;
  b.   CT Scans are used to detect strokes;
  c.   Using ECG and MRI reports to predict the risk of sudden heart attacks or other heart illnesses;
  d.   Determining the skin infection in skin images;
  e.   Discovering symptoms of diabetic retinopathy (DR) in eye images.

  AIoMT is reliable and provides accurate results for the detection of the disease at an early stage. All India Institute of Medical Sciences-Patna (AIIMS-P) is now collaborating with the Indian Institute of Information Technology-Bhagalpur (IIIT-B) to perform research and use AI for giving a boost to the healthcare system. The institutes will also develop new software for the easy detection of diseases [18].

ii. AIoMT is extensively used in Medical Data Mining using various AI-enabled cloud services like Google AI, Microsoft Azure, Amazon Web Services, etc. Figure 1.10 shows the various steps to extract knowledge from the data. Medical Data Pre-processing block does preprocess of raw data in order to ensure that the data is available in a required format for mining. Association rules, classification, clustering, and outlier detection blocks are the ways of filtering the unwanted data before mining so that we can get rid of the unwanted data for mining.

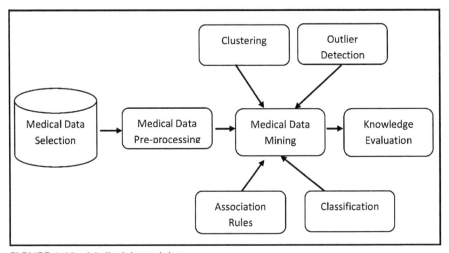

FIGURE 1.10   Medical data mining.

iii. AIoMT-based chatbots are providing value-added services as healthcare assistants. In some cases, it is found that chatbots are scheduling healthcare appointments with doctors, provide medication reminders, and coordinating with caregivers.

iv. AIoMT-based surgical robots are in the developmental phase by many technological giants by making use of IBM Watson. Deploying AI-enabled robots' capabilities can result in more accurate surgeries causing less damage and speedy recovery of the patient.

   a. AIoMT is equally useful in in-patient drug discovery. It can be used to detect different parts of drugs including their chemical composition. It can be used for determining drug activity, toxicity, bioactivity, reaction yield, etc.

v. Today AIoMT is widely used in conducting medical trials in which various data streams are of healthcare data in various algorithm-based models. Using these models' doctors can identify patient's responses to the AIoMT based medical treatment [18].

vi. Today, new technologies such as cognitive computing and DL are playing an increasingly important role in the field of healthcare, and AIoMT is contributing to current research and development efforts to prevent, halt, delay, or reverse the early aging phenomena. The main goal is to create medicine for the prevention of serious diseases associated with aging phenomena like Parkinson's Disease, Alzheimer's Disease, and cardiovascular diseases (CVDs).

In the next section, we propose the AIoMT model based on the study presented above for improved patient experience.

1.4.4   AIOMT PROPOSED MODEL

The advancement in technology has provided us with a platform to predict medication for patients to prevent them from getting infected with major diseases. This platform will assist by recommending changes w.r.t. to lifestyle and medication. We propose a predictive medical assistant AIoMT system. In this system, AIML will make the system act like humans. Advanced AI algorithms allow machines to gather, process, and analyze information with almost no errors and make predictions accordingly in real-time. Predictive analysis will be done using a set of rules which is defined by the programmer, according to the predictive ML algorithmic model for analysis for medical big data [19].

The proposed AIoMT-based platform will drastically refine the process of diagnosis and cure by verifying the medical data and patient's data. The system can compare the patient's medical test based on various algorithms and provide expert advice for the cure based on the patient's previous records with similar symptoms. This will improve the efficiency of doctors to deliver more accurate results and minimize errors [19].

The flowchart for the proposed AIoMT system is shown in Figure 1.11. A detailed explanation of the flowchart is given below:

i. The first block shows the basic operation to sense and sends data. The sensor network will help to sense all the parameters including medical images required for detection from the patient and send them to the cloud for storage. The medical data stored on the cloud could be structured or unstructured.

ii.   The second block does the processing of the data using AIML algorithms for predicting diseases precisely. Its responsibility is to find the insight and detect patterns in medical big data. With the proper data analysis using various ML tools, doctors can cure many diseases even before the occurrence. For early detection, it will use various data mining algorithms. DL can further supplement AIML algorithms for preventing errors in diagnosis to generate more refined results.

iii. The next block as per the threshold value set for parameters under consideration does the disease detection.

iv.   As per the precise prediction, AI-assistant will suggest precautionary "Lifestyle Management and Monitoring" and nutrition. AI assistants can give useful recommendations based on a patient's habits and preferences. Thus, AI can trigger a new class of diagnosis and cure.

v.   The next block can analyze the changes as per the new advised treatment and decide the medication and its impact on patients and connect to experts in case of problems [20].

Demonstration of the AIoMT system is done in the next section.

1.4.5   SIMULATION RESULTS OF AIOMT SYSTEM

The system starts by collecting sensor data and uploading it to the cloud. As we had already demonstrated sense and send operation for the IoMT in Section 1.3. So, in this section for demonstration, we will be directly using the dataset for chronic kidney disease [21]. The dataset has many parameters for the detection of disease as per the standard requirements.

We will use the X-G boost ML algorithm for detecting chronic kidney disease [21]. X-G boost is a ML algorithm based on a decision tree approach that uses a gradient boosting technique. The area under the curve (AUC) and receiver operating characteristics (ROC) curves are used in ML to quantify performance for classification issues (AUC-ROC Curve). The AUC-ROC is one of the most significant assessment measures for assessing the effectiveness of any classification model. This tells us about the capability of the model in differentiating between the classes. Greater the AUC, the more accurate will be the prediction of model 0 classes like 0 and 1 classes as

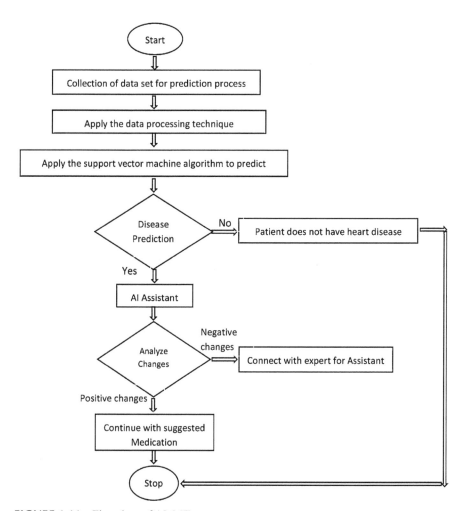

FIGURE 1.11 Flowchart of AIoMT system.

1. Therefore, we can say that the higher the AUC, the better the model of differentiation between patients suffering from the disease or no disease.

The XGB classifier AUC-ROC curve for the kidney disease detection for the data set under consideration is shown in Figure 1.12. It shows that the model can achieve the expected results with a high AUC of 1.00 and it is best suited for the processing of data for kidney disease detection.

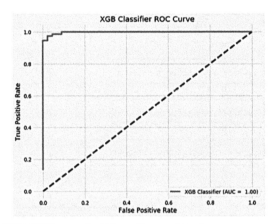

FIGURE 1.12   XGB ROC curve for kidney disease detection.

Figure 1.13 shows the importance of each feature in the prediction model as per their contribution to disease detection. To increase the system's performance in terms of processing time, features that are less important can be removed from the table.

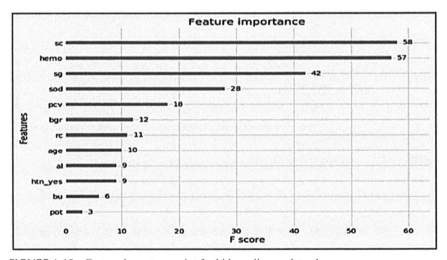

FIGURE 1.13   Feature importance plot for kidney disease detection.

Using the AUC-ROC we can predict the accuracy from the algorithm, and it comes out to be 99.76%.

To further test the performance of the system for other disease detection we applied it to the Parkinson's disease data set [22] and heart disease data set [23]. We got the accuracy to be 91.80% and 94.87% respectively.

So, this experiment demonstrates that disease detection using X-G boost is possible. Further, if the system is integrated with the AI Assistant, which could be an app or a chatbot, it can help the patients in getting timely assistance and prevent worsening of the situation. So, we could demonstrate the potential of AIoMT to:

   i.   Provide diversity to IoMT;
   ii.   Analyze complex medical conditions;
   iii.   Make the right decision for the patient's well-being.

But we all know that the AIoMT system is collecting data from multiple sensors, including the personal and financial details of the patient. Therefore, it becomes very critical to make the system reliable by considering the security challenges while designing the AIoMT system. The security challenges and probable solutions are discussed briefly in the next section.

1.5 IOMT SYSTEM: CHALLENGES AND SOLUTION

Each layer of IoT frameworks is likely to be intruded on by various cyber-attacks and threats. These attacks can be various types like active-passive attack, passive attack, internal or external attack. Threats at the physical layer, network layer, application layer, and transport layer, as well as services supported at each layer, can be divided into four categories. Now we will consider the challenges related to each layer and the related solution in detail in this section [24].

1.5.1 *PHYSICAL SENSING LAYER SECURITY THREATS*

1.5.1.1 *CHALLENGES RELATED TO PHYSICAL LAYER*

1. **Eavesdropping:** In this, there is theft of information transmitted over a network by IoT devices.

2. **Cyber-Physical Attack:** In this, the intruder takes the physical control of the computing device or communicating component.

3. **RFID Tracking Attack:** In this the RFID tags are disabled, or their content is modified or imitated.

1.5.1.2   SECURITY COUNTERMEASURES AT PHYSICAL LAYER

1. Some effective solutions against eavesdropping RFID tracking attacks, are tag-blocking, re-encryption, tag-killing, and faraday cage.
2. To identify faulty nodes in the IoMT network localized fault-detection algorithms are efficient. It is based on a decentralized intrusion-detection model with an estimated probability of intrusion-detection in IoMT networks [25].

1.5.2   NETWORK LAYER SECURITY THREATS

1.5.2.1   CHALLENGES RELATED TO NETWORK LAYER

1. **Breaching:** A middleman in any system can breach the secrecy and integrity of data.

2. **Distributed Denial-of-Service (DDoS) Attack:** In this network resources are unavailable for the user due to congestion generated at the server because of false requests flooding from hackers or users hacked by the intruder.

3. **Replay Attack:** In this, the data transmitted is maliciously repeated or delayed creating confusion for the server [25].

1.5.2.2   SECURITY COUNTERMEASURES AT NETWORK LAYER

1. All these attacks can be controlled by using an Intrusion detection system that can monitor a network for malicious activity or policy violations and the use of a VPN, which is an encrypted connection over the Internet.
2. We can remove the denial-of-service attack by using various filtering techniques like Ingress Filtering, Egress Filtering, Hop Count Filtering for defense against spoofed IP Traffic like SYN Cookies which is a technical attack mitigation technique, and D-WARD which is a defense technique at the source end against flooding and denial of service attack, etc.
3. By using timeliness in a message, the congestion in the network can be reduced as the packets will self-destroy after the timeline [26].

1.5.3 TRANSPORT LAYER SECURITY THREATS

1.5.3.1 CHALLENGES RELATED TO TRANSPORT LAYER

1. **TCP Flooding:** In this, the attacker transmits too many packets to the target server through TCP (transmission control protocol) to affect the ability to respond.

2. **UDP Flooding:** A huge quantity of UDP (user datagram protocol) packets are sent to a target server in this attack to disrupt its capacity to reply.

3. **TCP Desynchronization Attack:** In this, the attacker breaks the packet sequence by injecting a packet with the wrong sequence number.

1.5.3.2 SECURITY COUNTERMEASURES AT TRANSPORT LAYER

1. SVM (support vector machine) based on DDoS (Detection for Distributed Denial of Service) to prevent TCP flooding attacks.
2. SYN cookie is a defense technique for eliminating the effects of TCP flooding.
3. Authenticating all the packets in the TCP session is also effective against Flooding attacks [27].

1.5.4 APPLICATION LAYER SECURITY THREATS

1.5.4.1 CHALLENGES RELATED TO APPLICATION LAYER

1. **Mirai Malware Attack:** In this, the attacker gains access to IoT through a default Telnet or SSH.

2. **IRC Telnet Attack:** In this, the attacker gains access to the Telnet port of the IoT device by infecting the Linux operating system.

3. **Injection Attack:** In this, the intruder supplies untrusted inputs to the executing program. This untrusted input is processed as a part of command which results in abnormal functioning of the program.

1.5.4.2   SECURITY COUNTERMEASURES AT APPLICATION LAYER

1. Application layer attacks can be minimized by disabling or changing the default account of Telnet and SSH.
2. Disabling the port number of Telnet is also useful in some cases to minimize Application layer attacks.
3. Input validation control in which is proper filtering of input is done for any unwanted malicious packets before supplying the input to the application for processing.

1.5.5   SECURITY THREATS BASED ON CLOUD SERVICES AND DATA

1.5.5.1   CHALLENGES RELATED TO CLOUD SERVICES AND DATA

1. **Data Poisoning:** In this attack, the attacker pollutes the ML model's training data. When the processing is performed on this incorrect data using ML algorithms the predictions obtained in the output are incorrect.

2. **Evasion:** In this, the attacker bypasses the information security device to attack a targeted IoT network without being detected.

3. **Impersonate:** In this attack, an email is sent to the victim that seems to come from a trusted source. Sometimes the email may start with greetings from the CEO, CFO, Chairman, or another high-ranking official, these are also known as whaling attacks.

4. **Inversion:** In this attack, the intruder gathers information about the ML model and tries to recreate the training data from model parameters on the ML model [27].

1.5.5.2   SECURITY COUNTERMEASURES AT DATA AND CLOUD SERVICES

1. **Data Sanitization:** It is a process of permanently deleting or destroying the data from the storage device to make sure that deleted data cannot be recovered.

2. **Adversarial Machine Learning:** It is an ML technique in which that attempts to fool the implemented models by supplying misleading input. This technique is used to make the ML model more robust.

3. **Defensive Distillation:** It's a training strategy that makes an algorithm's classification process more flexible, making the model less sensitive to attacks.

4. **Differential Privacy (DP):** This technique in which the observer who is seeing the output cannot tell if particular information was used in the computation.

5. **Data Encryption:** It is a technique of protecting confidential data by encoding it and transmitting end and decoding it at receiving end.

If these security challenges at various layers are considered while designing the AIoMT system, it will gain acceptability and the designs will be robust against cyber-physical attacks.

1.6 CONCLUSION

IoMT is an emerging technology that continues to ensure a promising future and is truly transformational in the field of healthcare. In this chapter, an IoMT and AIoMT-based health monitoring system was studied and designs for the same were proposed and demonstrated. The study shows that the strength of AI integrated with IoMT is making AIoMT popular nowadays as it has resulted in improved customer satisfaction.

It allows for the safe storing of individual personal data in the cloud, the reduction of patient stays in hospitals for routine tests, and, most crucially, the remote monitoring of health and illness diagnoses by any doctor. AIoMT which is an extension of IoMT helps to obtain relevant and meaningful insights from the medical data by analyzing it, ensure accurate forecasts, maintain the confidentiality of data, get easy personalized medical recommendations, and ensure utmost security against cyber-attacks.

1.7 FUTURE SCOPE

Advancement to the proposed system could be personalized medicine which will be most suitable to the patient based on his DNA. This will make the system proactive to make healthy decisions. The research and Manufacturing sector are finding new ways to benefit from this trend by making it economical and available for day-to-day use. There are other more open concerns and challenges that must be addressed in order to provide better secure IoMT networks, including lack of standardized lightweight encryption techniques for IoMT, usage of ML to improve IoMT security, blockchain in Smart IoMT, and protecting 4G/5G and beyond applications are all issues that need to be addressed. So, the next-generation device will be using tools in AIML and DL techniques to address various AIoMT challenges.

KEYWORDS

- **AI-Enabled IoMT**
- **Critical Parameter Detection**
- **Doctor Assistance**
- **Internet of Medical Things**
- **Internet of Things**
- **Parameter Analysis**
- **Patient Assistant**
- **Preventive Tool**
- **Secured System**
- **Smart System**

REFERENCES

1. Wu, Z., Chitkushev, L., & Zhang, G., (2020). A review of telemedicine in time of COVID-19. In: *2020 IEEE International Conference on Bioinformatics and Biomedicine (BIBM)* (pp. 3005–3007). doi: 10.1109/BIBM49941.2020.9313088.

2. Gelogo, Y. E., Oh, J., Park, J. W., & Kim, H., (2015). Internet of things (IoT) driven U-healthcare system architecture. In: *2015 8th International Conference on Bioscience and Biotechnology (BSBT)* (pp. 24–26). doi: 10.1109/BSBT.2015.17.

3. Shah, J., Jain, R., Jolly, V., & Godbole, A., (2021). Stock market prediction using bi-directional LSTM. In: *2021 International Conference on Communication Information and Computing Technology (ICCICT)* (pp. 1–5). doi: 10.1109/ICCICT50803.2021.9510147.

4. Raj, C., Jain, C., & Arif, W., (2017). HEMAN: Health monitoring and nous: An IoT based e-health care system for remote telemedicine. In: *2017 International Conference on Wireless Communications, Signal Processing and Networking (WiSPNET)* (pp. 2115–2119). doi: 10.1109/WiSPNET.2017.8300134.

5. Yadav, E. P., Mittal, E. A., & Yadav, H., (2018). IoT: Challenges and issues in Indian perspective. In: *2018 3rd International Conference on Internet of Things: Smart Innovation and Usages (IoT-SIU)* (pp. 1–5). doi: 10.1109/IoT-SIU.2018.8519869.

6. Bansal, M., & Gandhi, B., (2018). IoT based development boards for smart healthcare applications. In: *2018 4th International Conference on Computing Communication and Automation (ICCCA)* (pp. 1–7). doi: 10.1109/CCAA.2018.8777572.

7. Balakrishnan, L., & Krishnaveni, (2021). An internet of things (IoT) based intelligent framework for healthcare – a survey. In: *2021 3rd International Conference on Signal Processing and Communication (ICPSC)* (pp. 243–251). doi: 10.1109/ICSPC51351.2021.9451739.

8. Shafaque, N. S., & Lochan, J., (2017). Improved medical healthcare system based on IoT. *International Journal of Innovative Research in Science, Engineering and Technology (IJIRSET), 6*(8), 15920–15926. ISSN: 2319-8753.

9. Antonio J. Jara (2014). Wearable Internet: Powering Personal Devices with the Internet of Things Capabilities. In *Proceedings of the 2014 International Conference on Identification, Information and Knowledge in the Internet of Things (IIKI '14).* IEEE Computer Society, USA, 7. https://doi.org/10.1109/IIKI.2014.9.

10. Sharma, Vineeta, Som, S., & Khatri, S. K., (2019). Future of wearable devices using IoT synergy in AI. In: *2019 3rd International Conference on Electronics, Communication and Aerospace Technology (ICECA)* (pp. 138–142). doi: 10.1109/ICECA.2019.8821915.

11. Wangoo, D. P., & Reddy, S. R. N., (2020). Smart learning environments framework for educational applications in IoT enabled educational ecosystems: A review on AI based GUI tools for IoT wearables. In: *2020 IEEE 17th India Council International Conference (INDICON)* (pp. 1–8). doi: 10.1109/INDICON49873.2020.9342150.

12. Zhang, C., (2021). Intelligent internet of things service based on artificial intelligence technology. In: *2021 IEEE 2nd International Conference on Big Data, Artificial Intelligence and Internet of Things Engineering (ICBAIE)* (pp. 731–734). doi: 10.1109/ICBAIE52039.2021.9390061.

13. Arumugam, S. S., et al., (2019). Accelerating industrial IoT application deployment through reusable AI components. In: *2019 Global IoT Summit (GIoTS)* (pp. 1–4). doi: 10.1109/GIOTS.2019.8766398.

14. Song, M., et al., (2018). In-situ AI: Towards autonomous and incremental deep learning for IoT systems. In: *2018 IEEE International Symposium on High Performance Computer Architecture (HPCA)* (pp. 92–103). doi: 10.1109/HPCA.2018.00018.

15. Ip, K., Asok, A., Xu, Y., Le, D., Mionis, N., & Batoukov, R., (2020). ML-assisted monitoring and characterization of IoT sensor networks. In: *2020 IEEE Conference on Evolving and Adaptive Intelligent Systems (EAIS)* (pp. 1–8). doi: 10.1109/EAIS48028.2020.9122775.

16. Ahmed, B., (2018). Secure and smart internet of things (IoT) using blockchain and AI. In: *Secure and Smart Internet of Things (IoT): Using Blockchain and AI* (pp. i–xx). River Publishers.

17. D'Aloia, M., et al., (2020). IoT indoor localization with AI technique. In: *2020 IEEE International Workshop on Metrology for Industry 4.0 & IoT* (pp. 654–658). doi: 10.1109/MetroInd4.0IoT48571.2020.9138275.

18. Liu, F., Lv, Y., Yang, P., Liu, Y., Xu, Z., & Luo, J., (2020). Innovation of business model for electrical household appliance enterprises to deploy IoT+AI and IoT+5G. In: *2020 International Conference on E-Commerce and Internet Technology (ECIT)* (pp. 245–247). doi: 10.1109/ECIT50008.2020.00063.

19. Knickerbocker, J. U., et al., (2018). Heterogeneous integration technology demonstrations for future healthcare, IoT, and AI computing solutions. In: *2018 IEEE*

68th Electronic Components and Technology Conference (ECTC) (pp. 1519–1528). doi: 10.1109/ECTC.2018.00231.

20. López, P. M. A., & Muñoz, F. I., (2019). SAT-IoT: An architectural model for a high-performance fog/edge/cloud IoT platform. In: *2019 IEEE 5th World Forum on Internet of Things (WF-IoT)* (pp. 633–638). doi: 10.1109/WF-IoT.2019.8767282.

21. https://archive.ics.uci.edu/ml/datasets/chronic_kidney_disease (accessed on 24 January 2023).

22. https://archive.ics.uci.edu/ml/datasets/parkinsons (accessed on 24 January 2023).

23. https://archive.ics.uci.edu/ml/datasets/heart+disease (accessed on 24 January 2023).

24. Roukounaki, A., Efremidis, S., Soldatos, J., Neises, J., Walloschke, T., & Kefalakis, N., (2019). Scalable and configurable end-to-end collection and analysis of IoT security data: Towards end-to-end security in IoT systems. In: *2019 Global IoT Summit (GIoTS)* (pp. 1–6). doi: 10.1109/GIOTS.2019.8766407.

25. Hasan, M. K., et al., (2021). Lightweight encryption technique to enhance medical image security on internet of medical things applications. In: *IEEE Access* (Vol. 9, pp. 47731–47742). doi: 10.1109/ACCESS.2021.3061710.

26. Uma, N. D., & Shaik, R., (2019). IoT evolution and security challenges in cyberspace: IoT security. *Countering Cyber Attacks and Preserving the Integrity and Availability of Critical Systems*. IGI Global.

27. Shin, S., & Seto, Y., (2020). Development of IoT security exercise contents for cyber security exercise system. In: *2020 13th International Conference on Human System Interaction (HSI)* (pp. 1–6). doi: 10.1109/HSI49210.2020.9142678.11.

CHAPTER 2

ADVANCEMENT IN HEALTHCARE BY CLOUD AND EDGE COMPUTING

SUNIL GAUTAM,[1] MRUDUL BHATT,[2] and KAUSHAL SINGH[3]

[1]Department of Computer Science and Engineering, Institute of Technology, Nirma University, Ahmedabad, Gujarat, India

[2]Department of Engineering and Physical Science, Institute of Advanced Research, Gandhinagar, Gujarat, India

[3]School of Engineering, P.P. Savani University, Surat, India

ABSTRACT

The real-time healthcare monitoring system is a challenging area in biomedical. Due to the rapid growth of the Internet of biomedical things with emerging cloud and edge computing, healthcare industries play an important role to identify diseases with high accuracy. In this context, dealing with huge amount of which should be processed in a timely manner therefore a novel computing model is seen that merging the cloud and edge computing approach in Healthcare Solution. A typical Internet of biomedical things model merged these two technologies and solve several problems in the healthcare area. Though, Cloud computing isn't an excellent desire for programs that require actual time responses because of excessive community latency.

2.1 INTRODUCTION

As far as figuring force and response time, current, and recently versatile medical care give countless administrations that have made one more game

---

Handbook of Research on Artificial Intelligence and Soft Computing Techniques in Personalized Healthcare Services, Uma N. Dulhare, A. V. Senthil Kumar, Amit Datta, Seddik Bri, Ibrahiem M. M. El Emary, (Eds.)

plan of essentials. To work to the apex of their propensity, these fresher gadgets need fast likewise, energy proficient registering, more conspicuous stockpiling cutoff, and region care that traditional distributed computing can't adjust with. Perhaps the most reassuring innovation is haze registering, which is a portion of the time named "edge processing" in light of haze suggesting the improvement of figuring to the organization. The beginning of edge handling, compact circulated figuring is depicted by means of high data transmission costs, long reaction times, and bound consolidation. Two identical enlisting techniques, cloudlet, and close by cloud, offer shoddy nature of organization for impending contraptions [1]. In spite of the fact that cloudlet-based game plans have lower inactivity than MCC, they really disregard the necessary versatility for gadgets on account of limited Wi-Fi incorporation. Many works have contemplated the showcase of cloud-based and edge-based enrolling and discoveries show that from a certain point of view edge-based can satisfy current basics for torpidity, convey ability, and energy adequacy. In one event, the usage of cloud-simply registering in video assessment achieved a duplicated response time diverged from client simply processing. The further developed execution of edge registering appeared differently in relation to ordinary distributed computing and can be utilized conspicuously through the medical services region as proof of certain applications. Edge-based game plans give the substructure to diminished inactivity as proof of time-subordinate courses of action, for instance, central sign checking or fall acknowledgment for the older. They can in like manner give customers added security that stood out from ordinary registering, which thinks about beat, heartbeat, glucose, and wellbeing history information to be shipped off parental figures through a related system. Due to advancements in after and portability that goes with edge processing systems, wellbeing providers can truly zero in on people with steady afflictions in homes using encompassing sensing elements put in homes in blend with wearable critical sign sensing elements. These sensing elements can accumulate region subordinate information from inside and outside, which grants medical workers to choose if a patient is genuinely critical. Medical care would have the option to transform into an altered help, specially designed expressly to each individual and their necessities. To fitfully offer steady quality help to patients, the edge gadgets what's more, centers need information assignments to perform with low idleness, energy proficiency, region care, and an irrefutable level of wellbeing [2]. The distinctive proof of express information movement strategies that consider quality execution of an edge-based medical services structure is the main target of this survey. Consequently, this data can be taken to give ideal grouping, validation, encryption, also, information decline methodologies for the association of an edge device.

2.2   ADVANCEMENT OF COMPUTING IN HEALTHCARE

This part looks at starters of medical care figuring and aims to progress from incorporated distributed computing to a more dispersed engineering, which is the reason for edge and haze registering. Moreover, inspected are the specific qualifiers of edge medical services similar to cost, energy productivity, and nature of involvement.

2.2.1   TYPES OF IMPLEMENTATIONS IN HEALTHCARE

There are a couple of various methods of organizing medical services utilities. They can be collected via gadgets, information, or by unequivocal use cases.

Presently these terms are the significant things we need in medical care, and it very well may be done without a hitch or proficiently by the force of processing [3].

Progressively wellbeing checking can utilize various stages meanwhile. For example, wellbeing checking of fundamental signs ought to be conceivable on a mobile phone device, wearable sensing elements or both, which is visible in Figure 2.1. In the event of crisis, observing frameworks resemble steady wellbeing checking beside that they produce a warning when a patient's vitals plunge under particular edge. With the incident to current splendid PDAs, patients are furnished with trademark resources in the palm of their hand. Clinical consideration data is quickly open on different regions, and at this point, through cells, changed applications further provide prosperity data and guidance to patients, particularly as for unequivocal steady difficulties. Current clinical thought in like manner goes with different plans of the customer like habiliment Sensors, Smart Devices Sensors, encompassing Sensors, habiliment Sensors can see beat characteristics, circulatory strain, inner warmth level, or sucrose levels speedier than league enhancements, for instance, bones pierce sucrose analyzers. The data from a control figuring submission is overall referred far away to the trained professional. Cell phones are ready for tackling essential sensors, like the beneficiary or gyrator, for clinical purposes. Perhaps than habiliment and remote based parts, it is really nearer to the persistent, merging parts are set everywhere an apartment or quantity of housings to aggregate statistics on consumer activity without the persevering tiring them [4]. They have to consider a more specific level of straight weight in much the same way as the plan is now and again utilized in submissions including drop ID or, in dementia circumstances, at the areas following the more settled. Enveloping devices can have independent interior, or free external locale limits, or both in a few unequivocal sensors.

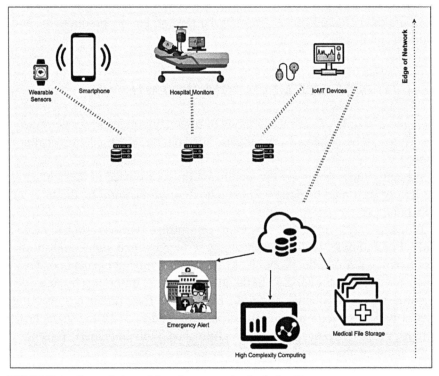

FIGURE 2.1   General view of the edge computing in the healthcare.

2.2.2   SOLUTIONS BASED ON CLOUD COMPUTING

Cloud-based clinical designs contain a wireless, cloud workers, and an association. These parts might have enormous intervals between parts, which further disturbs the issue of high inertness (shown in Figure 2.1). Lately, various clinical checking game plans have consolidated a connection between regular cloud structures and a scattered, or haze, approach. When using cloud just courses of action, the information recuperation times are unreasonably high for a continuous edge emergency circumstance, for instance, fall recognition or stroke relief, the two of which require fast response times from clinical specialists. Continually sending data to the workers for calculation tends to have higher force use and expenses related, fundamentally extra so nowadays, precisely when the extent of facts made by devices is remarkably enormous. A characteristic spot Cloud organization showed to have an extreme inertness and short upheld execution diverged from scattered enrolling design with a couple of handling center points at different geographical regions. Cloud-based plans likewise don't offer the client an immaterial expense helpful climate, which is needed for a huge package of the patient actually looking at circumstances.

2.2.3   SOLUTION BASED ON EDGE OR FOG COMPUTING

Potentially than ceaselessly moving information to the cloud for enlisting tasks, which watches out for the liveliness charges, information can be excavated and managed anxious gadgets and workers nearby the customer [5]. For cases including prosperity noticing, less idleness oversaw by edge and fog strategies considers crisis clinical assistance to show up in a fortunate way. By ethicalness of the beast level of data by and large moved off cloud affiliations, assurance, and security stay a focal matter of interest, particularly in conditions where an affected role clinical figure could be hewed. By streaming info all around a fog rather than social affair immense information in a solitary piece of the association, further created security can be refined. Straightforwardness in solace in the contraptions is comparatively enormous, since these sensors should be easy to use enough for lacking work ability to utilize effectively for careful data transmission. Coming up next are paying special attention to the central marks of cloud-based plans that proficient the requirements for the amazing time of clinical contraptions. Current works that underline all of the fundamentals are feast out in Figure 2.2. The most required things in this are cost, usability, low dormancy, region care, insurance, Energy capability. Could we see all of the fundamental parts.

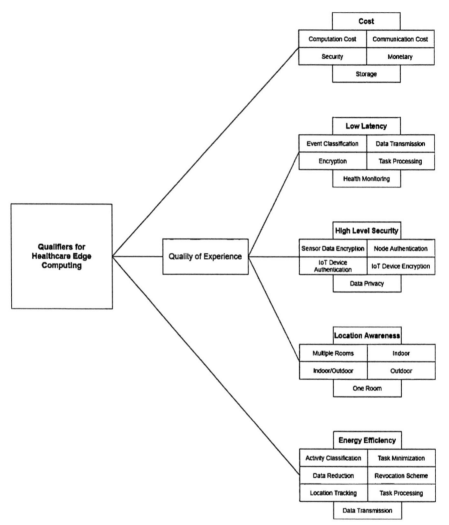

FIGURE 2.2   Healthcare edge computing qualifiers.

2.2.3.1   COST

Of the huge number of troubles related with execution of flexible edge taking care of in clinical thought applications, the functioning expense for the provider equivalently as the client is crucial. There are a few game plans of cost, for example, high storage use (limit of encryption block size, key length), use of the power of sensor, storage use and computational costs. As guaranteeing customer data is of most senseless significance in clinical benefits applications, assessment of various secure models the degree that key age time, memory essentials, move speed need and encryption/disentangling time have been investigated in persistent making [6]. While remaining mindful of safety and insurance of discrete persevering statistics is basic, it should be completed inside sensible goals, both as confirmed by the standpoint of customers' unscrambling cargo in basically the same manner as the supplier's edge handling materials. Another component to think about all through development of tele-achievement and tele-maintenance affiliations is the customs for a machine-care affiliation supplier. The Single audit completed showed the cash related authenticity of a robot-based assist with caring sending plan in a clinical consideration office. The advantage from experience (RoI) is shown to be negative for no under five years after the sending reliant upon current measures.

2.2.3.2 PRIVACY

In light of the ordered thought of wellbeing and area data, guarantee customers an unquestionable level of safety. Wellbeing data at the edge of the organization, habitually on cell phones, ought to be scrambled before transmission to various hubs. As a result of the energy necessities, this ought to be done in a capable yet feasible manner [7]. Incalculably possible figuring hubs achieves better methodologies for obtaining a patient's data, but then, could consider a more raised degree of security as a result of transport of basic data. To ease the shot at interference, approval shows, and trust assessments are taken in edge figuring applications. A more thorough and thorough review of safety instruments is associated with a later portion of this section. Patient data interference has legitimate consequences in various countries.

2.2.3.3 TRACKABLE LOCATION

Region care is additionally a crucial requirement for prosperity-related edge enrolling since it ponders the patient to be found in the event of a prosperity-related crisis. By utilizing limitation methodology unequivocally utilized for edge applications rather than every one of the more over the top GPS region systems, a more recognizable degree of exactness can be developed. Utilizing basically a cloud laborer and fundamental infrared sensor, a solitary situation inside or outside, can be aggregated utilizing calculations. There may be numerous levels of amalgamation for area of claims. For occurrence, some have agendas that acknowledge a specific space to be checked, while others give area care for different (three to four) rooms in a home.

2.2.3.4   LATENCY

For some purposes, medical services related use cases, constant preparation is a key essential. Haze and edge arrangements provide a lower inertness than standard cloud arrangements, and some particular parts of the system design consider this. In existing haze associations, an extended number of haze hubs adds to a lower inertness in information move Various edge mining procedures can moreover add to bringing down the proportion of time spent moving information to cloud or haze/edge hubs for estimation or limit [8]. In the present composition, the most notable case needed for low idleness is more established in homes. In specific courses of action, sensors accumulate patients' information on current body status and convey to an individual progressed partner, which does close by dealing with and cautions family or crisis associations if a fall is perceived or an avoidance from solid heartbeat or circulatory strain is noticed.

2.2.3.5   FUNCTIONALITY

PDAs, for example, mobile phones, have adequate enrolling capacities to run edge handling clinical benefits applications. Regardless, these applications ought to in like way, be on a very basic level satisfactory for affected role with refusal of clinical or unambiguous arrangement to use. For illustration, in one scrutiny, a cell fall region structure plan thinks about the changing situation of a phone in a specific pocket. The calculations that unexpected spikes famous for the phone are most likely going to course and space of the handset on the physique. Other old seeing constructions use merging devices set nearby an apartment or many housings with the true in minute man mediation is required. Fundamentally, habiliment instruments in fruitful claims should be shallow in their game plan and not unquestionably enormous for a persevering to attire in traditional standard presence [9]. As a rule, success edge enlisting contraptions ought to be not hard to use, solid to changes ready, and consider ordinary body degrees of progress.

2.2.3.6   EFFICIENT ENERGY

Edge registering continues to beat distributed computing similar to energy proficiency. Two or three works show that an appropriated configuration eats up less force than customary conveyed figuring. Nevertheless, with the appropriate processing being performed on more unassuming gadgets, a fundamental disquiet is registering applications that will save the confined battery life. Lower energy edges can be refined through attentively making or picking encryption plans and portrayal strategies for the clinical consideration applications. Edge Computing, which reduces the extent of gatherings conferred to cloudiness or cloud centers, can comparatively without a doubt rot the extent of energy devoured [10]. Genuine assets the executives can moreover be a benefactor of high energy productivity. In this particular situation, a couple of papers proposed an arrangement for inert asset the board that hopes to utilize free computation openings on PDAs in edge groups.

2.2.4 EDGE COMPUTING COMPACT IN HEALTHCARE

Edge enlisting contributes as well as cultivating the clinical consideration norms by giving quicker and more wide treatment unavoidably. Through a giant level of relationship of flourishing devices, enduring calls to emergency work environments and centers can moderate, particularly through sending plans that can give choosing capacities to confirmation of infection and patient checking. These edge sensor gadgets can be agreeably stayed aware of by patient role and principal to new bits of information on clinical advantages over their indefatigable seeing of urgent signs. Enlisting on the advantage can in a manner cut down data communication expenses by wandering huge information from the professionals to the authority. Having statistics in a nearby district besides reduces torpidity issues in the Cloud stages. Notwithstanding the way that edge figuring offers different benefits, there are different compromises and inconveniences while utilizing a decentralized system. Using various kinds of stages, workers present countless hardships that fuse network, scaling, asset, and information the board, and relentless nature of hubs [11]. The coordination of these assorted devices and focuses would necessitate supplementary assets and information the board methods restless focuses, while cloud-based enlisting basically requires one concentrated organization and managing the workplace. Probable wellsprings of bottlenecks and limits in this extraordinary structure ought to be recognized and directed progressively [12]. Additionally, these IoT gadgets have lower estimation and limit assets, which jumbles appropriation. Another work presents the possibility of EdgeMesh, which passes on the dynamic for asset what's more, computation the board among edge gadgets inside the organization. EdgeMesh also has an inborn breaking point concerning asset exposure, which is key since IoT gadgets have limited information on other close-by working stages. In any case, supplementary exertion on improvement of the administration plans is crucial. Safekeeping of individual information is an alternative trial that IoT for medical services should discourse earlier tremendous extension movement. The Steady nature of new correspondence shows for IoT use isn't incredibly high, which causes frustrations in the organization. The explanation is that some clinical solicitations require earnest idea before others. This requires a pre-depicted show for penniless associations inside the dissipated edge association.

2.3   SOLUTIONS IN HEALTHCARE USING EDGE COMPUTING

This fragment follows existing answers for medical services edge figuring. The fundamental subject talked about is proposed plans, where inside the constructions are the particular parts, including edge contraption, dimness or edge focus focuses, and the cloud, as displayed in Figure 2.3. This image additionally focuses on the regions where the assessments vary inside an edge-or mist-based affiliation happen. Such tasks performed anxious, and haze based, or gadgets are the subject of Section 2.3.1. We talk about all the recovery, encryption, grouping, and pressure procedures and separate their presentation to the extent of energy effectiveness, inactivity, and exactness.

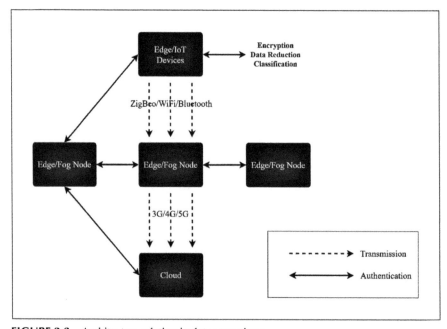

FIGURE 2.3   Architecture relation in data operations.

2.3.1 FRAMEWORK

General plan of an edge figuring strategy expectedly incorporates a customer expedient, device, or IoT maneuver, a radiocommunication with enlisting limits, and a superiority, fog, or carried registering center point. The handling is regularly appropriated concerning the client maneuver and the fog center. The relationship among edge and cloud is a huge portion of the development [13]. The superiority bases on fast arbitration, while the edge benefits are perceived in much the same way as significant length data. This relationship achieves difficulties in load changing and controlling tense and cloud workers. The general plan and the standard kinds of contraptions utilized. A really proposed arrangement wires assessments for an IoT film paying little mind to a fog and cloud layer, which is an ordinary strategy recorded as a printed copy for a cloudiness or edge clinical idea structure. In this IoT deposit, all clinical devices are functioned over an IoT web with every contraption partaking a sharp identifier. The objective of this clinical statistics is a data place coating or edge for more attracted coordinating undertakings. This conventional game plan considers enrolling to be finished with lower idleness when separated from a fundamentally joined strategy. The pieces of an all-around common fog enrolling climate are fanned out in after subsections.

2.3.1.1 DEVICES OF USERS

At the genuine edge of the association is the client gadget. Routinely the client contraptions can deal with some handling before more power concentrated errands are acted in an alternate edge or fog center point. These contraptions can be mentioned in three basic get-togethers: shrewd devices, heritage clinical instruments, and IoT-based sensor units. Prior kinds of edge handling used unimportant expense contraptions, as Nokia cells or PDAs [14]. As associations began conveying splendid gadgets in mass, cell phones like the Samsung gadgets ended up being more sensible for medical care applications. Cells can use work in sensors or intensifiers to make prosperity data, for example, beat or to gauge clear heart resonances. Anyway the remote based instruments proposal usability to patient role, confined in the social event of sensors that can be introduced in its hardware. Of course, committed clinical sensors have the ability to create and manage greater sensor information which prompts more precise analyzes. Typical vocations of sensors fuse heart and breath rate, heartbeat, and glucose levels for well-being noticing. Additional recognizing limits join choosing development states, for instance, type of activities, steps count, or rest. The most state-of-the-art design for wellbeing edge registering is the use of internet of things (IoT) gadgets. These gadgets meander from the standard sensor class as a result of their normal between availability, which is absent in legacy medical services sensors [15]. Different devices, occasionally put across the body, are connected with a course of action and can also talk with one another utilizing distinctive machine-to-machine (M2M) shows. Regardless, a perspective that has been examined is actually the best course of action of these distinguishing gadgets [16]. Novel customer gadgets, similar to the remote case endoscope (WCE), or then again express model contraption, could also be utilized as an edge client gadget. Another piece of making a simple-to-utilize clinical consideration framework is to furnish clients with an honorable degree of understanding on their contraption.

2.3.1.2   CONNECTION AND NETWORK

Whenever info is amassed at the specialized advantage of the association where the instruments exist, it goes concerning the nearby termination and far-finish of the alliance to be made due, or a part of the time, furthermore managed. Utilizing a fog place point can give a clinical consideration framework more basic figuring power that seriously unassuming hand-held devices probably won't have the decision to accomplish [17]. In an edge-taking care of plan, information works out, similar to depiction or strain, are done at the edge of the affiliation. These edge centers are reliably little laborers that consider the quick preparation of data that phones can't accomplish. Edge or shadowiness focus can be an epic number of contraptions, passed on at dissimilar expanses between the system of Clouds customer stratagem, reliant upon the working reach. In past creation, fiscally accessible things like Raspberry Pi, Arduino, and field-programmable entryway bunch (FPGA) stages filled in as edge doorways. These are eminent plans because of irrelevant expense and fundamental programming. Other evaluation utilizes a diagram dealing with the unit in conditions where pictures are the data obligation to be enlisted.

2.4   RESEARCH CHALLENGES IN FUTURE

To grant the future 5G organization perspective for helping the edge processing contained medical facilities systems and really recognize benefits to the neighborhood, not many exploration challenges which fill in as a block ought to be endured.

2.4.1   ON A LARGE SCALE

Most of the edge processing answers for medical services are attempted in limited scope conditions [20]. For instance, the proposed framework has a normal deferral of about a large portion of a second and around 0.003 KWH power utilization for 1,50,000 clients using 50 cloudlets. This records for countless clients and considers a powerful model that could assist with generating wellbeing workers notice designs in infection spread. Comparable model frameworks reproduce a clinical help that can deal with incalculable haze hubs. The framework showed by Borthakur, Dubey's contains up to 25 haze hubs and 1,000 clients in every one of the 10 local area organization hubs, while Kafhali and Sahah's framework can deal with up to 25 haze hubs [21]. Nevertheless, in spite of the way that both of these assessments use endless clients, they really don't come close to the real necessities of a huge clinical local area. A clinical thought design ought to oblige colossal quantities of patient role being preserved in an emergency place. The proportion of operated beds in chosen clinical focuses in the USA and Europe was 8,43,982 out of 2007. The medical clinic affirmation for the same year stayed at 37,368,897 [22]. These numbers do bar more modest, particular emergency clinics like gynecology, ENT, and restoration emergency clinics. Edge-empowered medical services frameworks will help with decreasing the glaring difference between the current foundation and emergency clinic necessities for synchronous record stockpiling and patient checking.

2.4.2   MANAGEMENT OF BIG DATA

An enormous scope of medical services framework got together with ongoing information getting guarantees that a huge proportion of information ought to be researched and gotten. This issue is to some degree tied to edge mining strategies, which essentially diminishes the proportion of information transported off cloud administrations, in any case, further decline is needed for long stretch and constant information combination from clinical sensors [23]. Much of the time this information doesn't definitely should be reduced, but inspected in mass sums, now, and then as extensive as exabytes. This infers that new examination methods that rely upon information features ought to be made.

2.4.3   PRIVACY OF THE PATIENTS DATA

While edge-engaged clinical consideration contraptions empower better near and dear satisfaction for patients also as open compensation roads for clinical benefits suppliers and 5G association chairmen, there are astonishing worries related to patient information security that will twist with enormous increase sending. Now, present HIPAA rules are non-agreeably settled to be suitable tense permitted clinical consideration checking frameworks [24]. As a few accomplices, for example, research affiliations and security affiliations believe patients to be a basic resource, any data break will be joined by real ramifications for both the prosperity supplier comparably as the association administrator. To confuse materials, these commandments and deterrents on understanding data conglomerating shift on nation and area. For sample, Italians and Germans have no such terminations [25]. Existing persevering data assurance shows rely upon safeguarding individual nuances, similar to name, address, and government-maintained retirement number. In their work on ensuring clinical thought attestation, a couple of papers reveal that "any information, whenever related with a prominent distinct, can developed person in landscape, be it individual, ordinary, ancestral, evident, respect based, locational, social, computational, skilled, or reputational" [26]. Pondering the imparted genuine variables, refined security and anonymization structures are basics for enormous expansion clinical consideration frameworks [27]. Computational complex cryptographic strategies hazard assessment proficiency, yet anonymization may correspondingly have danger of break or burglary [28]. The dissipating of the commitment between sensor center points and edge handling stages with no consider affirmation and security additionally stays an investigable test.

2.5 CONCLUSION

Edge figuring is an enthralling space of things to come cell networks that means to help huge quantities of IoT campaigns complete short lethargy managing. Since the monstrous number of utilization circumstances, our obsession in this chapter was its submission in clinical idea structures. Over this work, we endeavored to fill the opening in existing clinical thought audits, which will overall attention in on arranging and submission types rather than the most obvious nature of relationship for information tasks. Similarly, we have introduced the associated planning, data exercises, and the customer viewpoint as organized in the explored breaks down. We have in like way fanned out the assessments according to the point of view of contestants of superiority discovering that intersection charge, slowness, safekeeping, region care, and liveliness reasonableness. Considering our wide making study, we endorse further assessment to address the hardships related to colossal information volume, data security, equivalence with very much trustworthy low-latency correspondence, and AI intricacy accuracy tradeoffs. It is hard to plainly consider a tremendous piece of the examination since tests are done on an assortment of stages and with various enlightening files. Regardless, even with these limitations, no-nonsense close to evaluation of each datum advancement obtainable in the fragment can benefit researchers/ flourishing specialists pick the unsurpassed confirmation, information rot, encryption, portrayal, or surmise methodology for a precise edge figuring blueprint use situation in a clinical thought scenery.

KEYWORDS

- **Bio-Medical Things**
- **Cloud Computing**
- **Edge Computing**
- **Field-Programmable Entryway Bunch**
- **Fog Computing**
- **Healthcare**
- **Internet of Things**

REFERENCES

1. Liu, K. L., Yangchi, K., & Zhaoxi, S., (2017). *Remote Medicine Monitoring System,* 29(2), 214–224.
2. Abhijeet, K., & Luxi, H. Y., (2019). *Cloud Computing for Mobile Users: Can Offloading Computation Save Energy?* 3(2), 193–201
3. Chi, L., Ching Xi, R., & Zhuhsi, R., (2016). *Fog Computing and Its Role on the Internet of IoT.* 5(11).
4. Kumar, K., & Kunta, D., (2014). *Computer Science and its Applications: A Novel Mobile Application for Health Workers in Rural India.*
5. Yi Xhi, S., Hao, K., & Li, R. Chi., (2017). *LAVEA: Cloud Computing: Latency-aware video analytics on edge computing platform. Vol. 3.*
6. Jack, R. K., Ching, L. L., Murli, K., et al., (2013). *Computing Advancement: Performance Analysis of High-Performance Computing Applications on the AWS Cloud.*
7. Li, C., Yuoi, R., & Bhunia, S. S., (2014). *Sensor-Cloud: Enabling Remote Healthcare Services.*

8. Thiyagaraja, S. R., Dantu, R., & Shrestha, P. L., (2019). *Optimized and Secured Transmission and Retrieval of Vital Signs from Devices. 11*(2), 28–33

9. Althebyan, Q., Li, C., Jararweh, Y., & Al-Ayyoub, M., (2012). *Cloud Support for Large Scale e-Healthcare System*s, pp. 128–130.

10. Mietnen, A. P., Smith, J., & Nurmien, J. K., (2015). *Energy Efficiency of Mobile Clients in Cloud Computing, 1,* 45–54.

11. Cao, Y., Brown, C. D., Wang, Y. J., & Chen, S., (2017). *Distributed Analytics and Edge Intelligence,* Vol. 3.

12. Bhargava, K., Anderson, K., & Ivanov, S., (2012). *A Fog Computing Approach for Localization in WSN.* No 2, pp. 13–19.

13. Yu, Y., & Ching, L., (2014). Vision, recent progress, and open challenges. *China Communications,* Vol. 11.

14. Smith, W., Wadley, G., & Ameily, K., (2019). *Designing an App for Pregnancy Care for a Culturally and Linguistically Community*, pp. 128–133.

15. Jacobs, M., Singh, K., & Rehna, S., (2017). *Designing Personalized Technology to Augment Patient-Centered Care*, Vol. 4, No. 5.

16. Thiyagaraja, S. R., Vempati, J., Sarma, T., & Dantu, S., (2010). *Smart Phone Monitoring of Second Heart Sound Split,* Vol. 2.

17. Chandrasekaran, V., Dantu, R., & Lias, K., (2019). *Cuffless Differential Blood Pressure Estimation Using Smart Phones,* Vol. 4, pp. 28–33.

18. Al Hamid, H. A., Kashti, K., & Alamri, A., (2017). *Fog Computing Facility with Pairing-Based Cryptography.* Springer.

19. Giri, D., Anderson, P., & Liu, K., (2015). *Transmission of Healthcare Sensors for e-Medical System,* Vol. 6.

20. Tang, W., Xen, R., KuangX, O., & Shen, X., (2015). *Lightweight and Privacy-Preserving Fog-Assisted Information Sharing for Big Data*, Vol. 23, pp 34–45.

21. Lin, H., Shao, J., Zhang, C., & Fang, Y., (2016). *Cloud Computing: Cloud-Assisted Privacy Preserving Mobile Health Monitoring.*

22. Soldani, D., Fadini, F., Anderson, K., & Amy, C. K., (2018). *5G Mobile Systems for Healthcare*, Vol. 3, pp. 344–349.

23. You, C., & Ching, L., (2016). *Artificial Intelligence and Robotics.* Financial Times.

24. Muhammed, T., Ander, K., & Rehman, S., (2018). A personalized ubiquitous cloud and edge-enabled networked healthcare system for smart cities. *IEEE Access.*

25. Mekala, S., Ashish, L., & Uma, N. D., (2018). A review: Map reduce framework for cloud computing. *International Journal of Engineering & Technology.*

26. Garibaldi-B, J. A., & Vazquez, B. M., (2016). *Personal Mobile Health Systems for Supporting Patients with Chronic Diseases,* Vol. 8.

27. Wu, W., Cao, J., & Li, K., (2009). *WAITER: A Personal Healthcare and Emergency Aid System,* No 2, pp. 13–19.

28. HHS.gov. (2019). *Software Optimization HIPAA for Individuals,* https://www.hhs.gov/ (accessed on 1 March 2023).

CHAPTER 3

DISEASE IDENTIFICATION AND DIAGNOSIS USING ARTIFICIAL INTELLIGENCE

SHAIK RASOOL,[1] UMA N. DULHARE,[2] and A. V. SENTHIL KUMAR[3]

[1]Methodist College of Engineering and Technology, Hyderabad, Telangana, India

[2]Muffakham Jah College of Engineering and Technology, Hyderabad, Telangana, India

[3]Hindusthan College of Arts and Science, Coimbatore, Tamil Nadu, India

ABSTRACT

The rapid growth in technology over the last few years contributed to enormous data generation needed for changing face of healthcare services. Enhanced and sophisticated models have been built leveraging data in machine learning (ML) and artificial intelligence (AI) algorithms leading to delivering the best healthcare. Healthcare system have started embedding AI and ML technologies into every service. Healthcare sector is being transformed and modernized with evolving technologies. The natural ability of humans to recall information over a period is limited due to which it becomes difficult to perform apt diagnosis of diseases. A plethora of research in healthcare in the form of books, papers, and reports is available but no doctor can grasp all and utilize them in diagnosis efficiently. This can be conquered by employing AI and ML into healthcare to feed them with the data and utilize their true potential in making good use of available knowledge for

Handbook of Research on Artificial Intelligence and Soft Computing Techniques in Personalized Healthcare Services, Uma N. Dulhare, A. V. Senthil Kumar, Amit Datta, Seddik Bri, Ibrahiem M. M. El Emary, (Eds.)
© 2024 Apple Academic Press, Inc. Co-published with CRC Press (Taylor & Francis)

making accurate decisions. Thus, disease identification and diagnosis using AI and ML is the right choice in today's unpredictable conditions of the world environment.

3.1 INTRODUCTION

The success of life and happiness of every individual depends on health. As of 21 October 2021, 4.9 million people died due to COVID-19 only [1]. Cardiovascular, respiratory, and neonatal diseases are the main reason behind most of deaths around the world [2]. Life expectancy is still unpredictable even after the tremendous technological revolution. Adopting artificial intelligence (AI) into research and development has proven to be an efficient option to combat with the diseases. By reuse of enormous amount of big data, the medical data training process has become easier with the utilization of deep learning (DL) technology. Efficient disease identification and prediction with accurate symptoms are possible through AI and ML on the patient record history, test reports, and scan results. Past data analysis has shown that there are about 1.8 doctors available globally for 1,000 people. This poses a great challenge to doctors in providing proper treatment and facilities to patients. Strenuous efforts are required in training the medical professional to facilitate the huge population. Quick diagnosis of diseases is made possible with the application of AI. This led to accurate diagnosis using a lot of time and brain work. This challenging environment in the world needs the application of AI.

Computers can think like humans and are very intelligent by leveraging AI. ML is part of AI. Learning is vital for developing intelligence whether its human or computers. ML has different learning techniques as discussed below:

1. **Supervised Learning:** It involves classification or accurate prediction of outcomes by training the algorithms, utilizing the labeled datasets. Types of supervised learning involve classification and regression Classification techniques give the output results as YES or NO. For example, to find whether a patient is suffering from heart disease, the classification output would be yes or no. In case of regression, the output would be in terms HOW MANY or HOW MUCH.

2. **Unsupervised Learning:** It involves classification or prediction of outcomes by training the algorithms, utilizing unlabeled or

unclassified datasets. Classification is done based on similarities between input and output data. Clustering is part of unsupervised learning which involves clusters based on similarity.

3. **Semi-Supervised Learning:** It belongs to supervised learning class. It utilizes labeled and unlabeled datasets as part of its training. A high portion of the data set is unlabeled and very less labeled data is available. It can be said as an intermediary between supervised and unsupervised learning algorithms.

4. **Reinforcement Learning (RL):** It explores learning by testing all possible values till desired outcome is attained. Using the actions, the model's agent reaches maximum rewards. Maximum rewards are gained by the model beginning with trials and taking decisions.

5. **Evolutionary Learning:** For enhancing designing and building the DL model, the evolutionary algorithms were built. This learning model is based on evolution that maps like a human brain rather than mapping like neurons in human brain.

6. **Deep Learning (DL):** It is like a replica of the human brain. It is based on ANN. It doesn't require to program to program everything explicitly. To obtain high level features from the raw input DL utilizes multiple layers for extracting high level features progressively.

The classification and pattern recognition process were cherished processes from long time. Humans possess very strong skills that assist in sensing the environment. They observe the environment and act accordingly. Big data is being put to use owing to the collective efforts of ML, databases, and analytics. A disease diagnostic test is very crucial in medical science that can be used to study the true nature of disease and can be of great assistance for quick and effective diagnosis of patients. Computer decision support systems play a vital role in cost management and apt diagnosis. Data organization is crucial in healthcare as a huge amount of data is generated from the patients test reports, medication slips, diet, etc.

Inefficient management of data led to low quality in analysis. An efficient way of data extraction and processing is needed. Data attributes can be utilized by the machine learning (ML) to build efficient classifier for partitioning data. Such partitioned datasets are used in healthcare disease identification and diagnosis.

Originally, ML techniques were devised and utilized to examine health data sets. To achieve effective assessment of data, ML proposed a variety of tools. Notably, in previous years, digital transformation provided relatively low cost and accessible methods intended for gathering and storing of data. Modern hospitals have adopted new technologies and installed smart devices capable of data collection and utilizing collected data for efficient analysis. ML tools are extremely capable for assessment of medical data, and tremendous effort is done regarding symptomatic challenges. Precise analytical records are shown as a health data or statements in modern-day hospitals or their data division. To execute an algorithm, precise analytical patient data is registered in a pc as input. Outcomes can be autonomously attained from prior decoded incidents. Surgeons need support through the developed classifier at the same time when analyzing new patient at a rapid pace and with better accuracy. These classifiers may be utilized in training of non-experts or scholars for analyzing the problem [3].

3.2   CHALLENGES OF USING AI AND ML IN HEALTHCARE

3.2.1   CHALLENGES TO ADOPTION IN HEALTHCARE ACCORDING TO EXPERTS

A general question for embracing ML and AI into healthcare is that would be it feasible to apply these technologies if they lead to less cost and save time? For providing a response to this problem we require to realize the challenges being faced in current time [4]. Several prominent experts have given their views on these challenges as stated below:

1. **Randy Hamlin (SL and VP for Point-of-Care Ultrasound at Philips):** Continuous development is among major challenges in the implementation of AI. AI in other fields remains easy to implement due to high data availability whereas in healthcare there are several regulatory approvals needed to access the healthcare data. As AI needs more and more images from the reports to be able to predict the outcome accurately, it clearly needs to address privacy concerns of users and make data available for analysis, training, and validation. This will lead to the development of many AI enable devices.

2. **Laura Marble (Vice President, Information Technology at BCBS, Michigan):** Data Integrity is very essential in AI, ML, and DL. The data generated in healthcare organizations is very huge, but the data managed is not digitized which is required for processing

in AI techniques. Privacy of patient data becomes a hurdle for the organizations when they want to adopt modern technologies as strict regulations have been in place by various nations in regard to privacy. The process involved in mining the data for obtaining the insights is very complex when compared to non-health organizations. Auspiciously, transitioning to AI and ML technologies has been accepted by organizations and are in the process of building the environment necessary for such adoption. The outcome of adoption of AI in other industries should be closely studied by healthcare organization for successful implementation of AI.

3. **Dr. Anuj Shah MD (Apex Heart and Vascular Care Founder):** A biggest hurdle in transition to AI is regulatory standards in place. The risks associated in adoption of AI in healthcare is much higher than other domains. The decisions made by AI and ML technologies in healthcare may have severe consequences if the models are not trained with quality data. Thus, before implementation and integration of AI into healthcare it is extremely crucial to do enormous testing and validation using real-time datasets. The entire process would require an investment of money and time for the benefit of society. The world needs a truly working concept model with proof of accuracy demonstrating the amount of research done and required to convince all nations to effortlessly work together.

4. **Russell Glass (CEO, Ginger):** The performance of AI systems is dependent on training using the data provided, especially the quality and reliability is biggest challenge forward. The amount of data generated is rapidly increasing with digitization of patient records involving images, test reports, data generated from the chat bots and adoption of advanced technology equipment. But without the required quality in data it would be very difficult to integrate AI technology in medical environment as it may lead to deadly consequences. Obtaining the recommendations from the data provided by the patients might not be apt due to insufficient or incompleteness or inaccurate thus raising obstacles in building health profile for the patients. Privacy policies from regulatory standards also pose difficulties in AI adoption.

5. **David Maman (CTO, CEO, and Co-founder of Binah.ai):** The equipment possessed by most healthcare organizations in developing countries are not capable of adopting the modern technology

solutions as they are human driven and require continuous monitoring for functioning. They also possess challenges in investment
and difficulties due to regulatory standards such as HIPAA, which
make difficult for AI adoption quickly. As the governments for
different nations have started to recognize immense benefits offered
by implementing AI, their support for organization through project
funding and easing of standards might help healthcare organization
for quick adoption and organizations will start seeing saving and that
these technologies bring along.

3.2.2   ENCAPSULATION AND DIGITIZATION OF DATA

To acquire better results in healthcare from AI we require high quality of
input data. Also, the data is required in huge volumes to get accurate results.
Unstructured and fragmented health data spread across the organization
is the root cause of concern. As patients change their heath advisors and
insurance companies, it becomes even more difficult to acquire the data.
Digitization of health data is challenging in countries where the quality of
data is low and often due to isolated systems. However, many countries have
started to digitize and facilitate the health data for wider implementation of
AI and quick diagnosis. It is worth to spend amount and time for building
high quality digitized system.

3.2.3   ETHICAL CHALLENGES

For transforming the healthcare sector into the modern era, integration of AI
technology plays a vital role. In regards, it is also essential to address issues
related to ethics [5].

3.2.3.1   DATA ETHICS

One of the core elements of AI are data ethics that constitute different aspects
like privacy, Information security, Authentication, fairness, and transparency
[6]. AI smart apps developed for healthcare like imagery, diagnostics, and
surgical treatment will power the patient and clinician association. The question lies in Does utilizing AI techniques for taking care of patients adhere to
privacy? It might be concerning issue which is not put forward during the

ethical discussion, Considering privacy as direct challenges in embedding AI into medical procedures. A study needs to be done to understand all the constraints and places where privacy is essential and needs to be employed in the medical field. How much are the medical experts responsible in educating the patients to know their rights? What kind of algorithms and systems are used to process the data in AI? Which approaches will be employed for utilizing the data? What are the constraints under which medical experts should inform the users about the use of AI?

Providing answers to these questions is challenging in case where AI may effect from non-understandable ML practices which stands extremely challenging for medical experts to comprehend completely. Apps developed using AI for healthcare are progressively now employed at almost every situation, varying through nutritional regime assistance to wellbeing assessments for boosting treatment observance and evaluation of records accumulated from wearable smart inventions. In distinction to the conventional privacy practice, Individuals must always agree to an agreement without any interaction with the manufacturer or developer of applications. Agreements are not read by most users. Furthermore, regular revision in software leads to extremely challenging for people to adhere to whatever conditions of service they are obliged to comply. Which data ought to be provided to people utilizing developed software and voice assistants? Are customers adequately aware about potential utilization of the AI-enabled software for healthcare may be restricted on acknowledging modifications to the conditions of application? How carefully should consumer contracts be like privacy certificates? How morally accountable consumer contract is represented in this framework? Dealing with above concerns is complicated, and it turn out to be much more challenging to resolve when documents acquired through utilization of AI enabled software by patients is embedded again inside medical choices.

3.2.3.2   TRANSPARENCY AND PROTECTION

Security pose as major tasks for utilizing AI technologies in healthcare. To understand the ability of AI, patrons, especially AI designers should be assured of two key elements: consistency and authenticity of datasets, transparency of datasets. Initially utilized datasets should remain consistent and authentic. AI would work much better if the data provided is of high quality. Accurate outcomes can be achieved from AI techniques as they are tuned and improved using adequate training. One more huge concern is records sharing: Situations that AI requires to be exceptionally secure, enormous volumes of data may be needed. Nevertheless, it has also been observed in cases where fewer records are shared. The amount of data that needs to be shared is always dependent on the type of algorithm being used in AI and the place where it is deployed.

Next, Transparency should be guaranteed to the patient by making them understand the process adopted for maintain security. Although in an idyllic domain all information and processes are made amenably available for the public to inspect, few genuine problems concerning to shielding asset and non-increasing online threat, mediators or administrative assessing could signify a potential resolution. Furthermore, designers of AI ought to be passably transparent for issues involving nature of information utilized along with the flaws that exist in software.

3.2.3.3   PRIVACY OF DATA

If patients and medical experts do not have faith in each other, AI and their effective incorporation into medical practice will eventually fail. It is profoundly critical to sufficiently advise patients regarding handling of collected data and adopt a free dialog for maintaining confidence. Further than the issue relating to accumulated, it's crucial in safeguarding counter to utilization beyond the clinic expert and patient association which could severely impact patients and cause effects on wellbeing or additional assurance expenses, employment prospects, or personal associations [7]. Few of which will demand robust anti-discrimination act like policies in amendment for genomic confidentiality [8].

3.2.4   LEGAL CHALLENGES

Hiring of employees in healthcare organizations undergo with strict assessments before they are considered to work, and they are required to oblige the rules and standards set for everyday schedule to comply with local regulations. Specific International laws for medical experts conduct in the organization or neither any laws are set for utilizing the AI in medical field [9]. If the criminals have used AI for the purpose of crime, then it is considered to be a special crime in AI [10]. Consequently interpretation of comprehensive and comprehensive AI regulations is immediately required. Nevertheless, numerous concerns ought to be deemed. To begin, it is not just the responsibility of official authorities to build laws. We require the involvement of investors those concerned in the building or advancement of AI-centered medical ecosystem. Later, during confronting AI concerned violation, we are required to explain either responsibility is of AI firm, consumer, or maintainer. What is the scope of boundary for every investor? During the handling of complex cases, how much amount of accountability has to be dispersed rather than anticipating medical experts to be blamed for all risks of AI medical medication? In the end, it is necessary to constantly improve the policies that have been conceived. Investigations demonstrated that information related to health have greatly surpassed the initial privacy protection laws. Providentially, several new laws have been presented to standardize AI data protection, accountability, and supervision.

Yet if a legitimate organization is created, no transparent AI monitoring organization or accountability way is at present offered to legalize AI. As in case, the NHS 111 operated by Babylon, a children's smart investigation app, was accepted as a medical apparatus by the Medicines and Healthcare products Regulatory Agency irrespective of the inadequacy, thorough medical authentication and adequate testimony [11].

3.2.5 SECURITY

Security is an extremely crucial concern in leveraging of AI in medical production, and it entails the extremely meticulous review [15].

3.2.5.1 HARDWARE SECURITY

Every part of AI invention presently needs a sequence of electrical manufactured devices to accomplish tasks belonging to them, such as laptops, cellular handsets, and rings [13]. Three major interests concerning the security of such hardware ought to be mentioned. To begin with, yet the best manually replicable events are impacted by aspects like electromagnetic intervention, humidity variations and cost [14]. Next complication and expertise of medicinal expertise and data expertise proves to be challenging for doctors or researchers to use AI which incorporates various Techniques. At one side, researchers ought to be reeducated to retrieve and control medical records, which may interrupt the medical roadmap and lead to information leak. On the other side, doctors could be possessing weak comprehension of the procedures and management methods of AI products in real practice, triggering challenges like decreased effectiveness and expanded inaccuracies. Lastly, the concern of AI network security must be tackled. An international flowing reaction may arise if major nodes are confronted or break in the complicated network broadcast means.

3.2.5.2   SOFTWARE SECURITY

Yet system programs together with effective functions are extremely susceptible to design attacks [15]. The implementation of AI approach is repeatedly inadequate in directed strategy disagreement regardless of how performance has been outstanding as part of preliminary model assessment. Entire phases of the AI system development method long to be vulnerable, presuming that intruder has complete information of all associated to trained model of neural network. A false-positive incident can be utilized to generate a negative test or a false-negative incident can be utilized to generate a positive test, activating ambiguity in approach categorization. Incidents can even be cause without any information of configuration and constraints of the focused model or the training data set. Errors may also be awakened in the system deprived of external interference. The preliminary process would progressively diverge from the correct path due to the disparities in infection samples, unavailability of information and independent update errors.

3.3   PROBABLE RISKS OF AI AND ML IN THE HEALTHCARE SYSTEM

3.3.1   THREATS DUE TO INACCURACIES IN AI AND ML

Patients may face severe problems when an AI system provides inaccurate result. As AI is driven by data and unavailability of data leading to defective AI-based system may suggest wrong medicines or may not be able to identify the tumors in the low-quality health image. It may also recommend and schedule appointments to the patients who may not need it and eventually leading to loss of time and cost [16]. A small defect may also lead to several deaths in the healthcare domain.

3.3.2   PRIVACY CONCERNS

Another biggest and important challenge in AI and ML systems is privacy concerns of the patients, which delays and causes problem in acquiring the needed data. Several mechanisms have been employed to safeguard and protect the privacy of patients, but recent malicious attacks by hackers have worsened the situation raising more concern over security. Many software giants like Apple, Google, and Twitter were targets of such attacks endorsing the great risk to privacy online. Also, since AI and ML systems are more powerful for predictions, they may predict information based on past learning about patients even when their available data is insufficient, leading to privacy risk.

3.3.3   INEQUALITY AND DISCRIMINATION

AI systems are not free from unfair and biased handling of data from the experts. As AI and ML systems require high quality and huge amount of data, the data sourced only from specific regions or medical centers may not be proved viable to build strong, accurate predictive models. As data differs region to region and results vary based on the reports of individual patients residing in heterogeneous geographical locations.

3.3.4   PROFESSIONAL RELOCATION

The need for medical experts to migrate may arise with the complete implementation of AI at health organization. The increasing power of AI and reduced use of human brain is becoming widespread across the nations. There may be a sustainable point for AI where it may have no defects and accuracy of prediction triumphs. The dependency on human power may be reduced and echo for AI and ML adoption would increase.

3.4   IDENTIFICATION AND DIAGNOSIS OF DISEASES USING AI AND ML

Feature extraction from the data obtained is done through the application of analytical algorithms offered in ML. The characteristic features of a patient and features that may be reason for concern are taken as the input for these algorithms [17]. The features may include all the essential data of the patient that describes the condition of the patient and medical background details. Age, gender, height, and weight constitute the basic parameters for any patient and specific features that differ from patient to patient may include symptoms, history of disease diagnosis, test reports, medications prescribed and family history as well. The medical research also collects such information from the patients as per routine procedures. The data collected for research may differ like critical symptoms over a period, variation in occurrence of disease, complexities in treatment, various levels of disease such as variation in size of tumors, blood glucose, heart beats, body temperatures, etc.

The algorithms based on ML can be classified into supervised and unsupervised depending on whether these algorithms utilized the above data for analysis. For feature extraction from the data, unsupervised learning technique are employed in as the best model. When prediction of output is needed for an input data by establishing a relationship between available and expected outcome, supervised learning is the best case for this model of prediction. Supervised learning results in accurate outcomes when compared to unsupervised learning. The solutions built using the application of AI thus use supervised learning algorithms. Unsupervised learning may also be employed in the process of supervised as an intermediary to refine the process or building subsections or to improve the effectiveness of steps in supervised learning. Neural networks, linear regression, support sector machines, random forest (RF), naïve bayes, logistic regression, decision trees, nearest neighbor, KNN, discriminant analysis are most used ML techniques over years [18]. Figure 3.1 demonstrates the status of employability of a variety of supervised learning methods in health applications, which undoubtedly indicates that NN and SVM are the extremely popular techniques.

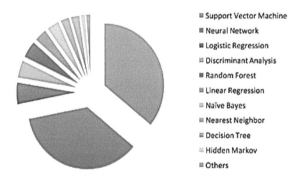

FIGURE 3.1   Adoption and application of ML algorithms as per PubMed data.

Disease diagnosis was carried out by several medical researchers by employing ML techniques. It was observed that ML algorithms perform well on heterogeneous diseases. Various diseases that were diagnosed by utilizing ML algorithms are illustrated in Figure 3.2.

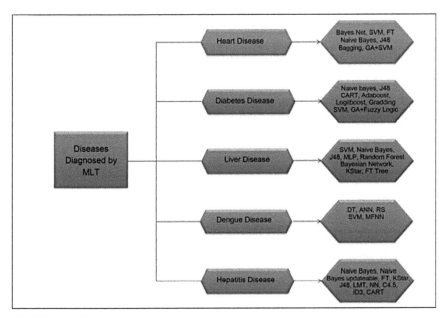

FIGURE 3.2   Diseases diagnosed by ML.

3.4.1   NEED OF AI IN DISEASE DIAGNOSIS

The top application of AI includes employing NLP and Image processing. As healthcare involves huge datasets of images, image processing assists in analyzing and classifying the images using image processing algorithms often termed as computer vision. The technique is equipped with a huge dataset of images which are utilized in the diagnosis of diseases. The succeeding section discusses diagnosis of several diseases by application of AI and ML technologies.

3.4.2   ARTIFICIAL INTELLIGENCE (AI) FOR CANCER DETECTION

3.4.2.1   LUNG CANCER DIAGNOSIS

The world observes the loss of millions of lives every year due to cancer which is considered the second most life-threatening diseases. Lung cancer was the cause of several deaths in Hungary. The digitized reports of the patients are being sourced as input for training algorithm by the researchers for early detection and successfully diagnosing the disease. There was a steep decrease in mortality rate by 25–50% due to early diagnosis of lung cancer. US has integrated this diagnosis into its guidelines. Nature Medicine Journals published research on use DL for medical diagnosis. The study employed tomography scans of patients for training the algorithm preceded by manual diagnosis. The dataset contained reports from 6,716 patients that included 1,139 patients' data confirmed as lung cancer. When the algorithm was compared with the results produced by 6 radiologists, it outperformed them with 94% accuracy. This study emphasized the new prospects and possibilities that DL possess.

3.4.2.2   SKIN CANCER DIAGNOSIS

New Zealand and Australia are the most affected nation with patients suffering from skin cancer. A dark circumference around the brown spots on the skin, i.e., a hemorrhage mole or tiny abnormal abrasions are the symptoms of skin cancer. Non-cancerous and cancerous abrasions could be differentiated by ML by utilizing pigmented mole as a target. Training set can be constituted with recording of presence of abrasions. A successful training with accurate predictions may lead to an apt diagnosis of skin cancer. Mela Sciences developed AI cancer detection system named MelaFind for diagnosis of skin cancer. It was capable of scanning abrasions utilizing infrared up to a few millimeters below the skin. Later images were passed to an AI algorithm built with a huge amount of trained data. It was approved by FDA for assisting the dermatologists, but the system was not cent percent accurate in diagnosing all varieties of cancer abrasions.

An important milestone was reached in AI with development of mobile SkinVision application. It is based on the cloud and uploads the image taken by the patient to cloud for diagnosis by analyzing it against thousands of trained images. All the risks associated with abnormal abrasions are given within 30 seconds to the patient. SkinVision successfully identified more than 6,000 skin cancer cases in the UK utilizing the power of AI and ML. The application is supported with 4 million images provided by 2 million users. Quick detection of skin leads to early diagnosis and recovery of patients.

3.4.2.3 CANCER DETECTION EMPLOYING GENE EXPRESSION DATA

Over the decades research was carried out to find the presence of cancer utilizing the gene expression data. There are 3.2 billion nucleotides in the human genome that constitute millions of proteins. The challenge lies in finding the gene responsible for cancer from such huge amount of data. Normal cells could be separated from cancerous using DL by detecting the signals in gene expression. An algorithm was proposed by Oregon State University researchers that employed Stacked Denoising Autoencoder for the above task. Input is directly linked to the output by autoencoders and are part of pretraining.

To directly link the input and output autoencoders are required. The pretraining phase constitutes this process. A team of researchers were intelligent to discover protein sequence accountable for breast cancer by employing the above autoencoders. Therapeutic biomarkers were efficiently discovered using the same. This algorithm can perform more accurately with training using more datasets.

3.4.2.4 BRAIN TUMORS DIAGNOSIS

Brain tumors end the life of human gradually. The survival window for a patient is five years that depends on the age. Proper diagnosis is needed for successful treatment of brain tumors. Distinguishing between brain cancer and radiation necrosis is the foremost difficulty encountered by the medical professionals. Both are identical to be differentiated using MRI image. Diagnosis of both requires separate treatment plans. To detect the vital differences between the two using radiomics, Case Western Reserve University researchers developed a program. It works by detecting deep features of images that are not possible to observe using the naked eye. The SVM classifier of ML successfully diagnosed 12 results out of 15 when compared against two expert neuropathologists. Experts were able to identify 7 and 9 out of 15.

3.4.2.5 HEART DISEASE DIAGNOSIS

The heart rhythm and activity are measured using the Electrocardiogram. When a patient who is suffering from heart disease feels any abnormal activities like pain in the chest, fast beats, abnormal heart beats, and shortness of breath, then for such symptoms the doctors recommend taking ECG test. The results of ECG test are presented in the form of waves that can be viewed in the display of the connected computer. ML have the advantage of huge amount of data for diagnosis of heart diseases as most developing nations started to maintain these health records. With the help of these data, the ML algorithm will be powerful to identify the normal and abnormal activities using trained data set leading to efficient diagnosis and prevention of disease to occur at the first place.

3.4.3 APPLYING AI FOR RECOGNITION OF DIABETIC RETINOPATHY (DR)

Diabetes disease leads to abnormal condition of the eye retina of the patient. It may also lead to visual loss as diabetes damages the light sensing tissues of eye blood vessels. Corresponding to Diabetes Atlas, 500 million diabetic people existed in 2020 worldwide. Only around 5% of total diabetes cases are not type 2 diabetes. Among all these 90 to 95% of type 2 diabetic patients, 21% of patients are identified with diabetic retinopathy (DR) at some stage in diabetes identification. DR is analyzed with Fluorescein angiography. Retina images are captured, and dilated pupils are observed by the physician in both the tests. A fluid injected by the physician drifts through the retinal blood veins that assists them to identify if the vessels are deflated or blocked.

The objective in applying AI is to diagnose by predicting the outcome by utilizing and comparing the trained data over new data. The images captured after examinations are of remarkable significance for scientists. Through the application of the huge data available, new algorithms can be designed by the researchers for accurate diagnosis of DR. Few of the examples are discussed in subsections.

3.4.3.1 IDX-DR

The FDA approved AI based IDx-DR is used for DR diagnosis that is developed by IDr Technologies. This system is constituted with a microscopic camera that is used to capture two images of each eye. The images are analyzed by comparing it against the trained set and produce the result within a minute of time. Patients with mild DR are advised to meet the expert and patients with negative result are advised to take the test a year after again. Around 900 mild DR patients were successfully diagnosed using IDx-DR with 87% sensitivity and 90% specificity.

3.4.3.2   EYEART EYE SCREENING SYSTEM

Another AI based technique for diagnosis of DR is EyeArt developed by the EyeNuk. The functionality of the system is like that of IDx-DR except not involving any professional expert and pupil dilation. The feeds of the fundus camera are utilized by the algorithm for analyzing DR and determine the amount of abrasion through international medical standard protocols. A report for the patient can be generated in less than a minute.

3.4.4   NLP FOR PROBABILITY OF DISEASE IDENTIFICATION

NLP works by manipulating, understanding, and interpreting the words for gaining perceptions. Diagnosis of any disease is through identification of the symptoms of patients. Patients explain their symptoms to the physicians using natural languages. A system could be trained to foresee the infection based on new warning sign if it is trained using phrases of symptoms and related diagnosis approaches.

AI based medical chatbots are an application of such system and have been deployed by most healthcare centers for diagnosis of most diseases through symptoms identified from patient interaction. The medical chatbots provide an interactive interface to the patient that performs detailed conversation to acquire all possible symptoms. Once the symptoms are acquired and compared with the trained dataset an appropriate advice is given to the patient. The condition of the patient is determined, and severity is calculated through analysis. The patient may be advised to meet the expert in hospital or basic medication may be recommended based on the situation. In an emergency the chatbots may direct the ambulance operators to attend the patients immediately and bring them to hospitals. This AI-based NLP chatbots may also recommend diet plans for the patients based on their disease identification. All the data is stored for future use and learning purpose.

3.5.1   ACCESSIBILITY REACH

Although we have technological revolution most countries are not equipped with the facilities to keep up with the trends. These nations have limited accessibility to data and standards. The life expectancy in such countries is very less. These nations can however benefit with adoption of AI technologies to achieve efficient and reliable healthcare system. They can offer quick

3.5   ADVANTAGES OF AI AND ML IN HEALTHCARE (FIGURE 3.3)

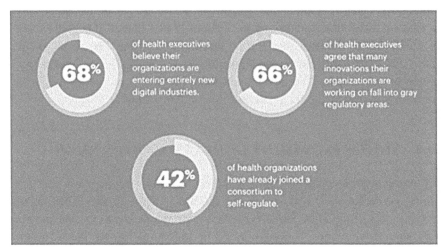

FIGURE 3.3   Adoption of AI.

diagnosis and recovery from diseases to their patients with support from AI technology. AI have been extensively employed by many developed nations and put forward to help international organizations to leverage the potential of AI together for better of society.

3.5.2   RAPID DETECTION AND DIAGNOSIS

Assessing the patient's health based on their present and past data have become a vital part of AI tools. AI provides the healthcare professionals with much needed data analysis of patients to accurately diagnose the disease. With outreach of AI-based mobile applications, the amount of health data collected constitutes millions of symptoms that could assist in rapid diagnosis. The system can provide future insights to an individual to help him take preventive measures from spreading of disease at first place. A proper diet plan and medication can be provided at the right time. The world can also prepare for the future and be ready for any pandemic situation or take measures to avoid such situations from occurring. Health experts are now equipped with powerful predictive analytics system for better analysis of disease and strengthening of future research.

3.5.3 FASTER PROCESSES AND DECREASED EXPENDITURES

The amount of cost needed to be spent by healthcare organizations has decreased by huge percentage and healthcare processes have become faster with the adoption of AI and ML in the healthcare sector. The complete view has been changed by AI whether its examination of patient or disease diagnosis, the overall speed has increased. Biomarkers for identifying the diseases in the body are provided through AI implementation. The manual work needed to specify these biomarkers has been reduced due to AI algorithms. Enormous lives could be saved, and overall lifestyle could be improved through automation provided by AI and ML technologies. The traditional methods have proven costlier compared to modern techniques proposed by AI. Results are provided faster and at the place of the user by employing AI, saving time and efforts of patients visiting laboratories (Figure 3.4).

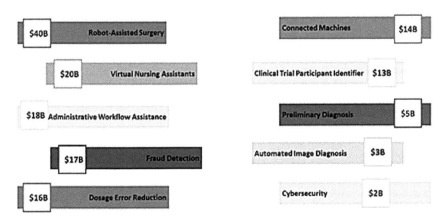

FIGURE 3.4   Potential cost savings.

3.5.4 EFFECTIVE ASSISTANCE IN SURGICAL TREATMENT

The revolution of AI has led to immense development of solutions through robotics. Surgical procedures have also been eased with the implementation of ML. Around 100% accurate surgical instruments have been developed that are capable of performing surgeries involving complex movements. The traditional risks that were involved in operations and side effects like blood loss, pain can be greatly reduced through efficient procedures. Thus the recovery process for the patient post-operation is also reduced and they can recover faster and easier. Antibacterial nano-robots are utilized to remove the infections in blood of patients before they are sent to surgery. The surgeons have access to AI built reports and present data of patients in real-time that could be of great assistance and overcomes the fear of patients who fear operation under anesthesia.

3.5.5 IMPROVED HUMAN CAPABILITIES AND PSYCHOLOGICAL HEALTHCARE

AI based robots are now capable of assisting the medical experts as well as patients. Paralyzed patients are now relieved with development of exoskeleton that assist them in walking independently avoiding the need of a helper. Traditional limb fitted into the patients are now replaced with AI-based smart prosthetic parts equipped with sensors for quick response and analysis. Patient monitoring has become much easier through the deployment of service robots. The robots assist the patients by giving them pills, performing basic tests like blood pressure, checking body temperature and maintaining diabetic levels by guiding proper diet. Patients suffering from psychological disorders can be supported through smart analysis capabilities of robots. They can assist the patients to be more positive by changing their mood through interaction.

3.5.6 PREDICTION OF EPIDEMICS

In the unpredicted COVID-19 era, it has become very essential to use AI and ML technologies to get the insights of future required to monitor and overcome the occurrence of future epidemics across the world. There are challenges ahead for the researchers to mine the big data available from enormous devices deployed across the globe like satellites, social networks, surveillance systems, etc. AI can play a vital role in analyzing the mined data from big data and can provide insights to predict the outbreaks like malaria or chronic infections that pose life risk to people. As most developing countries lack the infrastructure and facilities in handling such outbreaks, the AI model could save enormous lives.

3.5.7 MEDICAL RESEARCH AND TESTS

AI can be of great potential for exploring opportunities in medical field through research and in conducting the tests to understand working of application or drugs. Traditionally drugs and devices were tested using human as sample for analyzing the performance and usefulness. They led to severe side effects in most cases posing a threat to life. The trials also require huge investment and time. It may take years to evaluate a drug. On the positive side Ai and ML integration may provide platform necessary for quick analysis and diagnosis of diseases. The mined data from big data generated through multiple sources could be harnessed and made good use for getting insights required for accurate diagnosis. Errors in recording the results of tests from devices and drugs could be greatly minimized with powerful analytics available from AI and ML. The overall cost is reduced, and the time taken for the test is shortened by a huge margin.

3.5.8   ELECTRONIC HEALTH RECORDS (EHRS)

Maintaining the health records is a tedious process. Traditionally records were stored manually at the organizations requiring human efforts and time. Even with modern tools considerable amount of time is needed in managing the records. The focus of using AI and ML in managing health records is to ease the process by saving efforts and most importantly time. The OCR techniques of ML can be utilized to convert handwritten reports to digital text for storage. All the test report data, prescriptions, and medical images can be stored in cloud services for easy share and access. The Intelligent cloud equipped with AI and ML algorithms will assist in analyzing the data online and getting the reports in no time. Smart electronic health records (EHRs) are developed by MIT that leverages cutting edge technologies like AI and ML at initial level to assist effectively in diagnosis and provide personalized medical care to the patients.

3.6   FUTURE SCOPE

After several studies and research health experts can harness the true potential of AI and ML in healthcare. They have regarded these technologies as critical aspects of the medical field that would be proven to provide insights that could be lifesaving. We believe that assistance provided by AI and ML is not limited to technological workflow or cost reducing. The examples discussed below shows the scope of future for these technologies:

1. **Avoid Multiple Hospital Visits:** AI and ML could be used to assist doctors in making decisions about the patients who may require more visits or none. Using predictive analytics they could accurately

determine the amount of time needed for diagnosis. The insights could be used to reduce and monitor the patients online.

2. **Effective Appointment Scheduling:** As more and more patients visit hospital for intensive care or for taking care of their loved ones, it is essential to effectively manage the in- and out-flow of patients to avoid disease spread when in proximity with infected patients. AI face recognition and human tracking can be used to monitor the movement of patients and visitors in the hospital.

3. **Leveraging Intelligent Cloud for Quick Diagnosis:** Cloud technologies are now equipped with AI and ML algorithms. Medical organization may adopt intelligent cloud and harness their power and avoid spending amount on upgrading infrastructure or services. Since the cloud has already been proven to be a very cost-effective solution in multiple industries, with AI and ML embedded in the cloud could be a viable solution for healthcare organizations as well.

4. **Minimizing Recuperation Phase of Patients in Hospital:** Availability of beds in hospital is also a concern during a pandemic. The effectiveness of hospital may also depend on the amount of time a patient recovers in hospital. AI and ML algorithms insights could be used in predicting the accurate time required for diagnosis to decrease the recovery period of patients. Patients could also be monitored through powerful tools on mobile and diagnosed online as well.

KEYWORDS

- **Artificial Intelligence**
- **COVID-19**
- **Deep Learning**
- **Diagnosis**
- **Healthcare**
- **Machine Learning**
- **Natural Language Processing**

REFERENCES

1. *WHO Coronavirus (COVID-19) Dashboard.* World Health Organization. https://covid19.who.int/table (accessed on 24 January 2023).
2. *The Top 10 Causes of Death.* World Health Organization. https://www.who.int/news-room/fact-sheets/detail/the-top-10-causes-of-death (accessed on 24 January 2023).
3. Fatima, M., & Pasha, M., (2017). Survey of machine learning algorithms for disease diagnostic. *Journal of Intelligent Learning Systems and Applications, 9,* 1–16.
4. Sam, M., (2019). *What Are the Challenges to AI Adoption in Healthcare? 26 Experts Share Their Insights.* Disruptor Daily. https://www.disruptordaily.com/ai-challenges-healthcare/ (accessed on 24 January 2023).
5. Gerke, S., Minssen, T., & Cohen, G., (2020). Ethical and legal challenges of artificial intelligence-driven healthcare. *Artificial Intelligence in Healthcare,* 295–336. doi: 10.1016/B978-0-12-818438-7.00012-5.
6. Jiang, L., Wu, Z., Xu, X., et al., (2021). Opportunities and challenges of artificial intelligence in the medical field: Current application, emerging problems, and problem-solving strategies. *Journal of International Medical Research.* doi: 10.1177/03000605211000157.
7. Gerke, S., Minssen, T., Yu, H., & Cohen, I. G., (2019). Ethical and legal issues of ingestible electronic sensors. *Nat. Electron., 2,* 329–334. doi: 10.1038/s41928-019-0290-6.
8. Roberts, J. L., Cohen, I. G., Deubert, C. R., & Lynch, H. F., (2017). Evaluating NFL player health and performance: Legal and ethical issues. *Univ. Pa. Law Rev., 165,* 227–314.
9. Mitchell, C., & Ploem, C., (2018). Legal challenges for the implementation of advanced medical digital decision support systems in Europe. *J. Clin. Transl. Res., 3,* 424–430.
10. King, T. C., Aggarwal, N., Taddeo, M., et al., (2020). Artificial intelligence crime: An interdisciplinary analysis of foreseeable threats and solutions. *Sci. Eng. Ethics, 26,* 89–120.
11. McCartney, M., (2018). Margaret McCartney: AI in medicine must be rigorously tested. *BMJ, 361,* k1752.
12. Uma, N. D., & Shaik, R., (2019). IoT evolution and security challenges in cyber space: IoT security. *Countering Cyber Attacks and Preserving the Integrity and Availability of Critical Systems.* IGI Global.
13. Uma, N. D., & Shaik, R., (2016). Digital evidence in practice: Procedure and tools. *Combating Security Breaches and Criminal Activity in the Digital Sphere.* IGI Global.
14. Pu, Y. F., Yi, Z., & Zhou, J. L., (2017). Defense against chip cloning attacks based on fractional Hopfield neural networks. *Int. J. Neural Syst., 27,* 1750003.
15. Shaik, R., & Shaik, R., (2021). Data center security. *Green Computing in Network Security: Energy Efficient Solutions for Business and Home* (p. 53). CRC Press.
16. Upendra, P., (2020). *Artificial Intelligence in Healthcare: Top Benefits, Risks and Challenges.* Tristate Technology. https://www.tristatetechnology.com/blog/artificial-intelligence-in-healthcare-top-benefits-risks-and-challenges/ (accessed on 24 January 2023).
17. Jiang, F., Jiang, Y., Zhi, H., et al., (2017). Artificial intelligence in healthcare: Past, present and future. *Stroke and Vascular Neurology, 2.* doi: 10.1136/svn-2017-000101.
18. Goodfellow, I., Bengio, Y., & Courville, A., (2016). *Deep Learning* (1st edn.). The MIT Press.

19. Otoom, A. F., Abdallah, E. E., Kilani, Y., Kefaye, A., & Ashour, M., (2015). Effective diagnosis and monitoring of heart disease. *International Journal of Software Engineering and Its Applications, 9*, 143–156.

CHAPTER 4

AN APPROACH FOR ACCESSING PATIENTS RECORDS USING MEDICAL SUITE BLOCKCHAIN

J. S. SHYAM MOHAN[1] and N. KUMARAN[2]

[1]*Assistant Professor, Department of CSE, GITAM University, Bangalore, Karnataka, India*

[2]*Assistant Professor, DCSE, Sri Chandrasekharendra Saraswathi Viswa Mahavidyalaya (SCSVMV), Enathur, Tamil Nadu, India*

ABSTRACT

In the present world, the patient's data or health reports in the form of electronic medical record (EMR) and electronic health report (EHR) are being stored in the hospitals for global access. This creates problems for the healthcare industry or sectors as they lack data integrity and security. We tried to avoid these major issues by adopting blockchain technology to our proposed technique called Medical Suite that is used for creating a unique collection of records that consists of all the information regarding the one's medical health history since his/her birth. For providing effective interaction between the hospitals and interoperability between the various organizations, the information in the distributed peer-peer network is stored as encrypted data using statistical methods and algorithms for ensuring reliability, integrity, and security of the data as blockchain provides highly general data protection regulation (GDPR). This chapter deals with ways to enhance the data-sharing application of the health sector and pharmacy built on concepts of hyper ledger fabric and Practical Byzantine Fault Tolerance consensus using hyper ledger fabric. The validation technique of the blocks

Handbook of Research on Artificial Intelligence and Soft Computing Techniques in Personalized Healthcare Services, Uma N. Dulhare, A. V. Senthil Kumar, Amit Datta, Seddik Bri, Ibrahiem M. M. El Emary, (Eds.)
© 2024 Apple Academic Press, Inc. Co-published with CRC Press (Taylor & Francis)

is done using the path-based fund transfer (PBT) algorithm and security is achieved with the determined permissions to the distributed ledger.

4.1   INTRODUCTION

One of the major problems today is the storage of patient medical records and accessing the records. In order to ensure security and tamper-proof of data, Blockchain tries to solve this problem by creating a secure and efficient smart healthcare system. A smart healthcare system provides cost effective and easy access to patients' electronic health records (EHRs). The concept of Blockchain technology was introduced by Satoshi Nakamoto that uses blocks, with cryptography to ensure a secure and reliable system. Blockchain emerged to solve big problems like the elimination of central organization and the problem of double spending. The architecture of the blockchain is designed using consensus algorithms [2]. This works on the concept of digital signature and is a collection of the ledger. As the current health sector (3.0) is being carried with electronic copies, EMRs, EHRs. Developments in digitization and cloud storage has brought made the process of migrating the data from one location to another in an easier and more convenient way. The most common problem affecting the health sector is the location where medical records are kept. For instance, let us ignore non-electronic records for a moment, and focus on EHR for this project. Every corporate hospital we visit can have its database management system to store and manage records. Others use a cloud service provider or a third party. Some store data in a format that matches the insurance companies, others do not care. Majority of the patient data is stored on a third-party database server or a hospital server. The data made into blockchain is immutable, that means that data cannot be altered, deleted or modified.

Digital storage is getting popular these days. Blockchain version 3.0 includes features like traceability, enhanced security, faster settlement, decentralized network. In future, blockchain technology will be in all the aspects of healthcare sector for managing and monitoring of EHRs. Developed by Linux foundation, Hyperledger fabric provides permissioned and private blockchain and hence, making it ideal for developers to adopt easily. Hyperledger Fabric is implemented through chain code, can connect to peer nodes and receive block events [3]. The doctor gives prescriptions, etc., that at sometimes consists of tests to be done including scanning, X-ray, etc. The results or the reports obtained are stored for future use and are stored in a

Medical blockchain. The same data can be used by the insurance companies for claim settlement by verifying the treatment details [4–15]. The weekly change of the drug will restore the EHR and value transfer in the blockchain data of the wearable fitness device. Innovations in healthcare systems provide a platform for healthcare researchers, practitioners, etc., to build, test, and deploy applications for healthcare monitoring and analysis. Challenges faced in the blockchain-based healthcare system are [16]:

1. Traditional blockchain-based smart healthcare systems fail to provide: an effective and proper format for storing data, lack of providing high-quality data exchange methods, and system interoperability [17–25].
2. In any situation, especially if no one can provide it, an emergency data collection procedure must be connected to a government-approved public database to retrieve data for all patients [26, 27]. Once blockchain-based medical methods are adopted, biometric technology can be used to collect this data. This is useful in multiple subsystems such as patient databases, insurance, medical monitoring, smart contract design, clinical trials, surgery, and more.
3. In the current scenario, lack of knowledge in adopting blockchain technology to smart healthcare system lead to several healthcare-related frauds. When the blockchain technology is correctly adopted, it is very helpful to maintain the health of patients within a reasonable budget. Adopting blockchain technology in healthcare would bring transparent, safe, and ethical procedures that are useful for the ecosystem.
4. There is a huge gap for active participation from government sectors, private sectors in the promotion of policies, practices, legal design and health programs, development, monitoring, and analysis of the blockchain-based health system. Large numbers of people hope that their government will derive fair healthcare practices from the personal experiences of 4,444 people. However, such measures lacked the correct authorities.
5. Adopting blockchain technology along with the Industry 4.0 will make the processing of data easier. It avoids data leakage and provides tamper-proof and transparent data to the healthcare providers.
6. At present, it is not feasible to replace doctors with robotic surgery on a large scale. Therefore, the fully automated surgical system does not have possibilities. Human intervention (medical and healthcare

professionals) is mandatory at this time. In summary, smart health systems offer more benefits to all stakeholders than alternative perceptions.

Figure 4.1 shows communication between patient, doctor, and pharmacy. Once patients' details are entered in the ledger, a unique id is generated for each patient. Now patients are identified through unique id. Through this unique id patients' diagnostics details are updated by the doctor for future references.

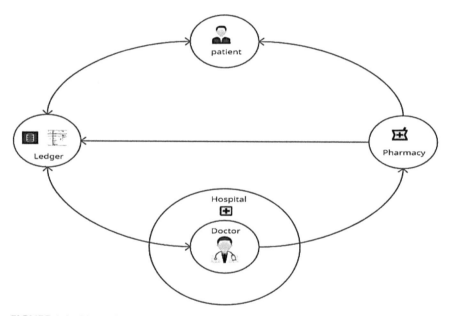

FIGURE 4.1   Network community.

This chapter is organized into the following sections: Sections 4.2 and 4.3 discuss motivation and problem statement. Section 4.4 highlights about the existing works related to the problem statement. Sections 4.5 and 4.6 state the method and experimental setup of the proposed work followed by conclusion.

4.2   MOTIVATION

Blockchain refers to a set or chain of blocks that are used for data transfer. Ex: Bitcoin, Ripple, etc. Some of the key features of Blockchain are decentralization, tamper-proof, distributed ledgers, etc. Blockchain plays a vital role in healthcare sectors. In healthcare sectors, patients' data is needed by various stakeholders in such a way that no details are misused or tampered. For example, the Gem Health Network project provides an insight into patients' data access to all the healthcare stakeholders without any tampering of data and therefore, saves time to retrieve data from old databases, etc.

In this chapter, we propose a system that can be effectively used in the local hospitals. This system is capable of providing secure and reliable health record storage system. The participants should be members of this permissioned blockchain to access and use their health records. All the stakeholders on this network can collaborate and discuss medical issues without any central intervention. The proposed work is best suited for a network of hospitals connected within a same group, possibly using a permissioned blockchain.

4.3 PROBLEM STATEMENT

The health records of the patients like EMRs and electronic copies are being stored with the different hospitals. It is causing a big trouble of maintaining a single collective record of a particular patient, where all the data of patients are stored and authorized. When he/she visits a doctor for a severe treatment, they are finding it difficult to provide information of past health track, which in turn makes the doctor's job tough and time-consuming. Even the data maintained by the hospitals lack integrity and standard data management. More importantly, the patient is lacking data authority.

4.4 RELATED WORKS

Medical Blockchain (MedBlock) also effectively solves big data management issues that share EMR systems. Patients can easily access EMRs in various hospitals using previous medical data. Here, without submitting the data to a trusted third party, some institutions ensure that the patient's original medical information is inaccessible. Proper and encrypted designs that use blocks can improve the efficiency of the system, provide effective data sharing in collaboration with blockchain, hospitals can better understand patient medical records before consulting. MedChain is designed to connect to existing EMR data and improve current EMR management systems that provide easy, safe, and secure access to healthcare providers, patients, and third-party EMRs. On the other hand, it uses timed smart contracts for managing and controlling MedChain transactions. Access to electronic medical records (EMRs) proposed a new incentive scheme to increase the quality of healthcare providers in their efforts to embrace advanced encryption technology by providing continuous security and build new blocks that maintain medical records and maintain patient privacy.

Statistical and simulated optimization techniques and algorithms are well discussed in healthcare 4.0 and blockchain 3.0. Researchers have proposed optimization techniques of the system by combination of analysis and simulation modeling built on Ethereum and Smart contracts developed using solidity, Athena, and web3.js. Ethereum virtual machine (EVM), Remix, Metamask provide the comparative analysis of smart healthcare systems.

Jobs related to IoT, Industrial IoT (IIoT), AI, in-system cognitive computing have suggested that they are well suited for large-scale commercial systems with many participants and operations on network. The PRISMA (preferred reporting items for systems analysis and meta-analyzes) framework is used to study and analyze the various models implemented. The functional and bibliographic distribution of 143 articles were shown. Global health information exchange (HIE) statistics report in Google Trends Analytics explores health systems, factors for archival patterns, blockchain types, consensus mechanisms, analysis standards analysis, different platforms, security, cost, performance analysis.

Ahmed et al. [28] Researched blockchain technology and its importance in today's medical environment. As mentioned earlier, blockchain technology has many advantages in medical databases. Thanks to the advanced digital framework, it provides immutability and transparency. The blockchain network has been proven to be secure, creating new challenges each second and presenting them in the form of hashes. There are many organizations responsible for processing patient data. Patients are interested to know their information, however, it is difficult for them to access their data due to many. Adopting blockchain makes the process of data sharing, storing and access, easier, and delivering it immediately when needed. This chapter highlighted a few applications of blockchain in the healthcare sector that solves the problems, faced in healthcare sectors. However, some work needs to be validated the framework and test it in a real environment.

Blockchain technology has a coordinated and self-learning feature that allows patients to share the security of their information and hence, establishing trust in the framework [29]. This is fundamental since it takes care of different issues like information security, information security, and advancement. Changes in understanding or information preparing commitments, and so on improve on the learning system of the clinical information preparing framework and effectively share it in a climate with legitimate security angles. The main point of this work is information security and protection, support, responsibility, and building patient confidence in the framework. Presently notice that the patient is exceptionally certain about the framework, realizing that the framework is protected and can show himself, this will just help him. This examination shows that the current form of the blockchain-based medical services framework has numerous deficiencies. For instance, patients don't have the foggiest idea how blockchain-based medical services are unique in relation to a one-stop advanced record-based medical services framework. How to give treatment information to different spots? Is the framework incorporated? Non-clinical necessities during oneself investigation (like protection, transportation, offices, and so forth).

Tripatti et al., discussed the technical, social, and safety barriers to the adoption of smart healthcare systems based on digital technology in the United States. The author follows the guidelines of the digital health system and prioritizes the user experience. These guidelines analyze from the perspective of user perception and try to solve them by providing a safe and intelligent healthcare system based on blockchain technology. When considering the integrity and security features inherent in the proposed framework, more attention is paid to data security. Other challenges include: (i) the mechanisms for data exchange; (ii) the design of smart contracts when the data expires; (iii) how the existing data in medical or health records will be used on the blockchain network; (iv) patients' lack of understanding of the benefits of using blockchain in health; (v) lack of Government initiatives to promote blockchain-based solutions on application development and use; and (vi) the healthcare industry in determining the blockchain-based solutions. Apart from this, a sensor framework was integrated into the human body in 4,444 different ways and used as a data source for 4,444 healthcare solutions. The framework design initiative is substantial, but now we must take steps to start using the same framework in experiments and test the applicability and integration of each subsystem.

4.5 METHOD

We tried working on managing authorization, access rights, and data sharing among the participants on the Hyperledger network. We can make appointments with the doctors by checking their availability status. We can even choose among the doctors concerning their specializations among the list and in various hospitals. We encrypt data which are EMR's in our case and store them with the access permissions. The summary in block made up of diagnostic information from the health organizations contains disease description, examination results (contains illness portrayal, assessment results), fee, and treatment plan. Openness of the ledger may enable the browsing information by anyone, but one must satisfy the access control protocol to read the data. The consensus of the blockchain is achieved by using the practical Byzantine Fault Tolerance. The Proposed architecture consists of mainly three participants: Doctor, Patient, and the Pharmacist. Assets are Appointment, Medical Prescription, Profile, and Examination Report.

As shown in Figure 4.2, circles represent the nodes; arrows depict transactions within the ledger. There are a total of three transactions that take place in this working model. They are making appointments, consultation, and medication. Discussing them in detail, confirm appointment-transaction to get appointment of the doctor of a particular hospital.

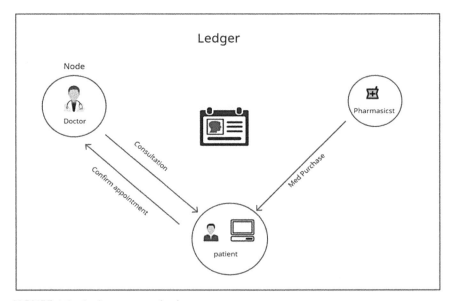

FIGURE 4.2   Ledger communication.

The patient queries the doctor list and checks the appointment availability. Consultation-transaction for recording the interaction between doctor and patient during appointment. On invoking this function, we get prescriptions, examination reports by the doctor. Medical purchase-transaction to record purchase of medicines by patient from the pharmacist in the pharmacy. The patient buys medicine; the chemist makes a receipt including the cost which is stored on the ledger.

4.5.1 ALGORITHM: PRACTICAL BYZANTINE FAULT-TOLERANCE (PBFT)

We rely on PBFT (practical byzantine fault-tolerance) to provide agreement. PBFT was introduced by Liskov and Castro in the late 90s. Widely used in blockchain and distributed computing systems. PBFT seeks to minimize risk and provide a working replica of the Byzantine national system that can operate even if a malicious node operates from the device. Nodes in a distributed system that employ PBFT are sorted in the order that one node is the primary node, and the other nodes are backup nodes. All eligible nodes in the system may appear as leader nodes by switching to the first node on the secondary node (typically if one node fails). All the trusted nodes help to reach an agreement on success in the final state of transaction validation. This concept reduces the effects of rogue nodes in the system and provides a healthy environment (Figure 4.3).

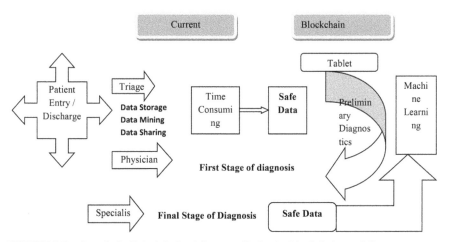

FIGURE 4.3 A typical clinical derived from medical suite blockchain workflow.

The interesting feature of a practical Byzantine fault-tolerant system consensus protocol is that it can characterize a situation where the maximum number of faulty nodes should be at least one-third of all nodes in the system. As the nodes are increased, the security of the device will increase (Figure 4.4).

Figure 4.5 shows PBFT operation in normal case where consensus rounds are highlighted into four levels as given below:

➢ **Level 1:** The client sends a request to the leader node.

➢ **Level 2:** The primary node sends a request to all the secondary nodes.

➢ **Level 3:** Both primary and secondary nodes perform provider tasks upon request, and then send the response back to the client.

➢ **Level 4:** When the client receives 'k + 1' responses from exclusive nodes in the community with the same result, the request is successfully serviced, where k is the maximum number of failed nodes allowed in the system.

Event no: 0005

Patient id: 3005

Doctor id: 7005

Appointment: Successful

Transaction id: MD5SUMS000145

Transaction info: Appointment made and examined by the Doctor

Transaction Timestamp: 2021-05-24 00:00:08

FIGURE 4.4   Sample block structure.

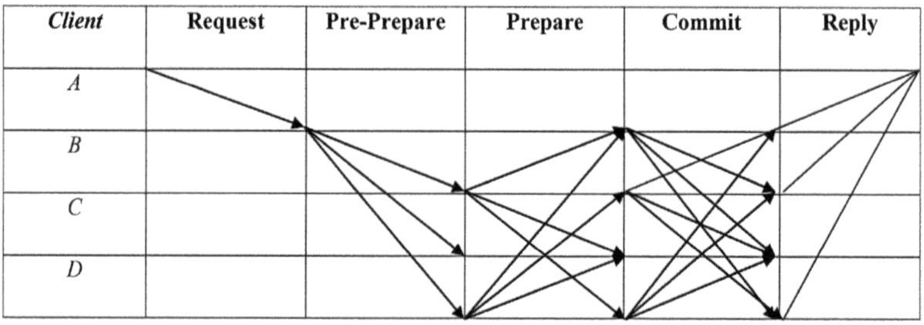

FIGURE 4.5   PBFT operation in normal case where.

Note: (A) Leading node; (B), (C), (D) Back-up nodes; and (C) being faulty node.

4.5.2   IMPLEMENTATION OF MEDICAL SUITE BLOCKCHAIN SOLUTION

To implement a Medical Suite Blockchain Solution, all the Electronic Healthcare Records and other files are encrypted and decrypted and stored in a public healthcare blockchain like Med. Suite. The transactions consist of a digital signature that can be tracked by using patient's blockchain ID. All the data after storing can be accessed on a web UI or via a smartphone.

Medical suite blockchain has number of advantages compared with existing record keeping techniques:

   i.   Patients can easily access the platform with a self-controlled UI for healthcare data. Transferring the files to any other healthcare provider is easy.
   ii. All the data is stored in a decentralized network, and hence there is no data leakage or data theft.
   iii. Data is encrypted and stored in the blockchain and can be accessed with the patient's private key and hence, the data remain tamper-proof.
   iv. Medical suite blockchain provides the entire required infrastructure for auditing and non-repudiation related tasks. Further, it also provides methods for adding data including timestamp, account IDs, and techniques to check or monitor that no data is altered during the transactions.

Medical Suite's blockchain-based medical data storage method covers all criteria expected of a medical record keeping system and can be implemented by existing centralized type systems to improve access to patient records and increase security against data breaches.

4.5.3   STEPS INVOLVED IN MEDICAL SUITE BLOCKCHAIN SOLUTION

It is naive to think that the healthcare industry will abandon current solutions and redeploy a record keeping system on top of a blockchain architecture. Healthcare is a risk-averse industry, and it is unlikely to be willing to accept the time and expense to switch to new, unproven technologies. In addition, the current situation is still a lot of inertia and investment. The Centers for Medicare and Medicaid Services (CMS) has spent more than $30 billion since 2011 to achieve high adoption rates of the EHR. It is very difficult for organizations that manage medical data in a centralized system to recognize patient data as a valuable asset and to change their mind. While current blockchain solutions may be an option for some time in the future, proximity requires a bridge solution. The proposed Medical Suite Blockchain solution includes the creation of a new system for storing clinical data based on blockchain technology, while EHR systems continue to use the system that provides many benefits of blockchain solutions. In the current scenario, there are many standards and guidelines for copying data across sources or across systems that provide a holistic solution for blockchain-based personal health record (PHR).

Blockchain Medical Suite solution starts with today's healthcare IT systems, primarily EHR, but can include Exam Information System, Radiology System, Payers Database, Economics calculation of medical devices and consumer devices. The system stores the data in its own database and continues to operate as it is today. In addition to storing its own copy of the data, each system sends a copy to the blockchain-based PHR. All EHR systems used for mission-critical applications must allow patients to view, download, and transmit their health information in a machine-readable, human-readable format 15. The document format is CDA, a format Machine readable XML. Applying a style sheet to a CDA document produces an HTML file that is readable in a web browser.

Many healthcare systems make CDA documents available to patients on the patient portal, meeting the view/download/upload criteria. From there, the patient can download the document or send it to a location of their choice. Some HER systems offer alternative delivery methods that do not require a patient portal. There are three options for linking EHR viewing/downloading/uploading functionality to a blockchain-based PHR:

i.   EHR providers implement blockchain clients in their EHR software. This client sends the healthcare data automatically to the blockchain-based PHR. While this is a desirable option, it requires the effort and cooperation of EHR providers and cannot be achieved without regulation and incentives.

ii. DSE providers that use REST, SOAP direct messaging, etc., to send status information to a blockchain-based PHR can receive data based on this standard. In other words, a blockchain-based PHR must be configured to receive documents from a variety of sources that will handle these communication protocols. These features are messy for a blockchain-based system designed for simple electronic transaction managers.

iii. Patients receive information through the existing patient portal and upload files to the blockchain-based PHR. This "lowest common denominator" approach works in all situations, but relies on additional manual procedures for mid-stage patients. In the worst case, records are incomplete unless the patient completes the procedure manually.

Step 3 is the easiest option to do. The other two possibilities depend on the EHR provider's wishes. For non-HCE systems, the situation is less clear. Conceptually, these systems have a way to isolate the data stream and send a copy to the blockchain-based PHR. However, the implementation of these efforts can be complicated and delayed due to the financial and regulatory issues involved.

The steps involved in Figure 4.6 are given below:

i. When the module or counter data is complete, it stores the EHR data locally and prepares the CDA version of the counter data. Later, this counter data is sent to the embedded blockchain client.

ii. The native blockchain client uses the patient's public key to link the document to the cryptographic blockchain to send the document.

iii. CDA documents are transactionally committed to the blockchain along with metadata about the source and topic of the document. Nodes in the blockchain network use a consensus algorithm to determine the validity of the transaction and are permanently committed to the public board when the node's quorum agrees to the change.

iv. The blockchain stores all documents for all patients.

v. PHR clients can connect to the blockchain and download all patient documents. The document is decrypted using the patient's private key.

vi. Patient can display documents and share them with others.

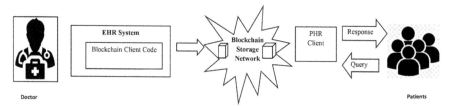

FIGURE 4.6   Architecture and data flow for the HER with medical suite blockchain solution of medical suite as stated in Step 1.

4.6   EXPERIMENTAL SETUP

The proposed work is deployed on Hyperledger ledger developed by the Linux Foundation. We require four types of files for the execution of the business logic. They are .cto, .acl, .js, .qry files. The .cto file is a model file that defines the data schema and consists of assets, a list of participants, and transactions. All the access permissions in the chain are listed in the .acl file. The .js, .qry files contain programming scripts for the transaction's logic and the data querying, respectively. To deploy our chain code on the network we need a .bna file which we can produce by packaging all the above files. One of the main compelling features of the fabric is network capacity enabled. Ubuntu 18.04, Hyperledger Fabric v1.4 + and other related files were used for implementation.

4.6.1   DISCUSSION

For making this project medical suite, we need Hyperledger Fabric v1.4+, Visual Studio Code, Git, and Docker on our machine. We need to install and configure the fabric samples and binaries as required. We need to deploy our chain code on the test network provided by fabric and in the form of containers using docker image. A fabric channel for transactions between doctor and patient is created from the script files from the peer and the orderer nodes. Channels act as a layer between members and are visible only to the invited organizations. After creating a channel, a chaincode is started and using commands, the chaincode is started and stopped after the task is completed. The command will stop and delete the node and chaincode containers, remove the key material, and remove the stringcode images from our Docker registry. The commands also delete channels, artifact, and docker episode of the previous run if is present.

Figure 4.7 shows the outcomes of the proposed Medical suite blockchain solution for healthcare sectors. The top layer shows the stakeholders who can access the medical records, however, they cannot alter the data as it is stored in a secure environment using blockchain technology. Various machine learning (ML) techniques are used for analyzing the results of the healthcare or medical records. In Figure 4.7, the left side shows the techniques used for analysis. The right side shows the outcomes of using or adopting blockchain technology to the same. The outcomes provide researchers and medical practitioners suggestions to overcome the difficulties faced by existing methods. Access time and performance is also high and easy when compared with existing methods. Medical suite blockchain provides an effective and easier way to access the patients records to patients via web version or smartphones. Transferring files from one healthcare provider is also easy which can be done by the patients using their smartphones. All the data transferred is safe and secure and is tamper-proof while keeping the identity of the patient details confidential.

4.7 CONCLUSION

The implementation of Blockchain in the medical field solves the problem of managing and sharing data in the EMR system. By using Textured Hyperledger, the system is made reliable and secure against any third party attack. Patients can easily access EMRs from different hospitals using the blockchain offered by the Ministry of Health.

We have developed the recommended approach to provide an efficient solution for the secure exchange of data between healthcare professionals for the processing of medical records, offering auditability, interactivity, and accessibility. Data sharing and blockchain collaboration can help understand a patient's medical history in advance before consulting. Adding new blocks can be supported by healthcare providers while also allowing patients to securely control access to their EMR with the help of a key. Other third party users or stakeholders cannot access patients health data or information. This may include working with local health organizations and simulating aspects of the system's effectiveness in the wild. This chapter has proposed a solution to some of the weaknesses illustrated in the existing system. The blockchain medical toolkit can establish better communication between hospitals and healthy societies around the world.

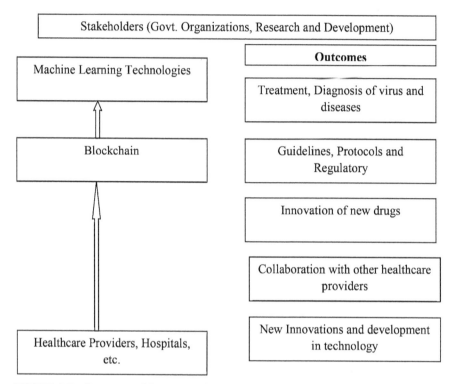

FIGURE 4.7   Outcomes of the proposed medical suite blockchain.

KEYWORDS

- **Byzantine Fault Tolerance**
- **Data Protection Regulation**
- **Distributed Ledger**
- **Electronic Health Report**
- **Electronic Medical Record**
- **Hyperledger Fabric**
- **Path-Based Fund Transfer**

REFERENCES

1. Fan, K., Wang, S., Ren, Y., et al., (2018). MedBlock: Efficient and secure medical data sharing via blockchain. *J. Med. Syst., 42*, 136. https://doi.org/10.1007/s10916-018-0993-7

2. Daraghmi, E., Daraghmi, Y., & Yuan, S., (2019). MedChain: A design of blockchain-based system for medical records access and permissions management. In: *IEEE Access* (Vol. 7, pp. 164595–164613). doi: 10.1109/ACCESS.2019.2952942.

3. Pongnumkul, S., Siripanpornchana, C., & Thajchayapong, S., (2017). Performance analysis of private blockchain platforms in varying workloads. In: *2017 26th International Conference on Computer Communication and Networks (ICCCN)* (pp. 1–6). doi: 10.1109/ICCCN.2017.8038517.

4. Manukyan, N., Eppstein, M. J., & Horbar, J. D., (2013). Team learning for healthcare quality improvement. In: *IEEE Access* (Vol. 1, pp. 545–557). doi: 10.1109/ACCESS.2013.2280086.

5. Rajput, A. R., Li, Q., Taleby, A. M., & Masood, I., (2019). EACMS: Emergency access control management system for personal health record based on blockchain. In: *IEEE Access* (Vol. 7, pp. 84304–84317). doi: 10.1109/ACCESS.2019.2917976.

6. Zarour, M., et al., (2020). Evaluating the impact of blockchain models for secure and trustworthy electronic healthcare records. In: *IEEE Access* (Vol. 8, pp. 157959–157973). doi: 10.1109/ACCESS.2020.3019829.

7. Kish, L., & Topol, E., (2015). Unpatients—Why patients should own their medical data. *Nat. Biotechnol., 33*, 921–924. https://doi.org/10.1038/nbt.3340.

8. Coelho, I. M., Coelho, V. N., Araujo, R. P., Yong, Q. W., & Rhodes, B. D., (2020). Challenges of PBFT-inspired consensus for blockchain and enhancements over neo dBFT. *Future Internet, 12*(8), 129. https://doi.org/10.3390/fi12080129.

9. Yuan, P., Xiong, X., Lei, L., & Zheng, K., (2019). Design and implementation on Hyperledger-based emission trading system. In: *IEEE Access* (Vol. 7, pp. 6109–6116). doi: 10.1109/ACCESS.2018.2888929.

10. Chukwu, E., & Garg, L., (2020). A systematic review of blockchain in healthcare: Frameworks, prototypes, and implementations. In: *IEEE Access* (Vol. 8, pp. 21196–21214). doi: 10.1109/ACCESS.2020.2969881.

11. Singh, S., Hosen, A. S. M. S., & Yoon, B., (2021). Blockchain security attacks, challenges, and solutions for the future distributed IoT network. In: *IEEE Access* (Vol. 9, pp. 13938–13959). doi: 10.1109/ACCESS.2021.3051602.

12. Kumar, A., Krishnamurthi, R., Nayyar, A., Sharma, K., Grover, V., & Hossain, E., (2020). A novel smart healthcare design, simulation, and implementation using healthcare 4.0 processes. In: *IEEE Access* (Vol. 8, pp. 118433–118471). doi: 10.1109/ACCESS.2020.3004790.

13. Sun, Y., Zhang, R., Wang, X., Gao, K., & Liu, L., (2018). A decentralizing attribute-based signature for healthcare blockchain. In: *2018 27th International Conference on Computer Communication and Networks (ICCCN)* (pp. 1–9). doi: 10.1109/ICCCN.2018.8487349.

14. Alhadhrami, Z., Alghfeli, S., Alghfeli, M., Abedlla, J. A., & Shuaib, K., (2017). Introducing blockchains for healthcare. In: *2017 International Conference on Electrical and Computing Technologies and Applications (ICECTA)* (pp. 1–4). doi: 10.1109/ICECTA.2017.8252043.

15. Mamoshina, P., Ojomoko, L., Yanovich, Y., Ostrovski, A., Botezatu, A., Prikhodko, P., Izumchenko, E., et al., (2017). Converging blockchain and next-generation artificial

intelligence technologies to decentralize and accelerate biomedical research and healthcare. *Oncotarget, 9*(5), 5665–5690. https://doi.org/10.18632/oncotarget.22345.

16. Xia, Q., Sifah, E. B., Smahi, A., Amofa, S., & Zhang, X., (2017). BBDS: Blockchain-based data sharing for electronic medical records in cloud environments. *Information, 8*(2), 44. https://doi.org/10.3390/info8020044.

17. Gordon, W. J., & Catalini, C., (2018). Blockchain technology for healthcare: Facilitating the transition to patient-driven interoperability. *Comput. Struct. Biotechnol. J., 16*, 224–230.

18. Zheng, X., Mukkamala, R. R., Vatrapu, R., & Ordieres-Mere, J., (2018). Blockchain-based personal health data sharing system using cloud storage. In: *2018 IEEE 20th International Conference on e-Health Networking, Applications and Services (Healthcom)* (pp. 1–6). doi: 10.1109/HealthCom.2018.8531125.

19. Hölbl, M., Kompara, M., Kamišalić, A., & Nemec, Z. L., (2018). A systematic review of the use of blockchain in healthcare. *Symmetry, 10*(10), 470. https://doi.org/10.3390/sym10100470

20. Funk, E., Riddell, J., Ankel, F., & Cabrera, D., (2018). Blockchain technology: A data framework to improve validity, trust, and accountability of information exchange in health professions education. *Academic Medicine, 93*(12), 1791–1794. doi: 10.1097/ACM.0000000000002326.

21. Nicholas, J. W., (2015). *Healthcare Transaction Validation Via Blockchain Proof of Work, Systems and Methods.* U.S. Patent 14 711 740.

22. Bodkhe, U., Bhattacharya, P., Tanwar, S., Tyagi, S., Kumar, N., & Obaidat, M. S., (2019). BloHosT: Blockchain enabled smart tourism and hospitality management. In: *2019 International Conference on Computer, Information and Telecommunication Systems (CITS)* (pp. 1–5). doi: 10.1109/CITS.2019.8862001.

23. Gupta, R., Tanwar, S., Tyagi, S., Kumar, N., Obaidat, M. S., & Sadoun, B., (2019). HaBiTs: Blockchain-based telesurgery framework for healthcare 4.0. In: *2019 International Conference on Computer, Information and Telecommunication Systems (CITS)* (pp. 1–5). doi: 10.1109/CITS.2019.8862127.

24. Vora, J., et al., (2018). BHEEM: A blockchain-based framework for securing electronic health records. In: *2018 IEEE Globecom Workshops (GC Wkshps)* (pp. 1–6). doi: 10.1109/GLOCOMW.2018.8644088.

25. Shen, B., Guo, J., & Yang, Y., (2019). MedChain: Efficient healthcare data sharing via blockchain. *Applied Sciences, 9*(6), 1207. https://doi.org/10.3390/app9061207.

26. Nichol, P. B., & Brandt, J., (2016). Co-creation of trust for healthcare: The cryptocitizen framework for interoperability with blockchain. *Res. Proposal., 3*, 1–12. ResearchGate.

27. Ahmad, S. S., Khan, S., & Kamal, M. A., (2019). What is blockchain technology and its significance in the current healthcare system? A brief insight. *Current Pharmaceutical Des., 25*(12), 1402–1408.

28. Gross, M. S., & Miller, Jr. R., (2019). Ethical implementation of the learning healthcare system with blockchain technology. *Blockchain in Healthcare Today.* http://dx.doi.org/10.2139/ssrn.3391034.

29. Gautami, T., Mohd, A. A., & Sara, P., (2020). S2HS – A blockchain based approach for smart healthcare system. *Healthcare, 8*(1), 100391. ISSN 2213-0764. https://doi.org/10.1016/j.hjdsi.2019.100391.

CHAPTER 5

SECURITY ISSUES AND INTELLIGENT SOLUTIONS FOR IOMT-ENABLED HEALTHCARE SYSTEMS

B. SATEESH KUMAR[1] and MOHAMMAD SIRAJUDDIN[2]

[1]*Professor, Department of Computer Science & Engineering, JNTUH-College of Engineering, Jagitial, Telangana, India. ORCID: 0000-0002-8560-4991*

[2]*Research Scholar, Department of Computer Science & Engineering, JNTU, Hyderabad, Telangana, India*

ABSTRACT

Advancements in soft computing techniques have changed the entire paradigm of personal healthcare. In IoMT-enabled healthcare systems, various smart devices are connected to outfits or even attached to the body of the patient for sensing the actions of various body parameters. The data collected from the patient is sent to the sink node. The aggregated healthcare data is forwarded to BS by the central coordinator via intermediate devices and reaches the doctors. As a result, the doctor can prescribe suitable medications to the patient. When this IoMT device is not protected, it puts patients at risk and disrupts a healthcare organization's entire system. This chapter covers a variety of security, privacy issues, and various attacks on smart devices. Intrusion detection systems, intelligent solutions such as malware identification, AI and ML-based security frameworks and machine learning (ML) applications in personalized healthcare systems are some of the methods that are explored and summarized in this chapter. The reader will gain an understanding of the numerous types of attacks that can occur on smart healthcare

Handbook of Research on Artificial Intelligence and Soft Computing Techniques in Personalized Healthcare Services, Uma N. Dulhare, A. V. Senthil Kumar, Amit Datta, Seddik Bri, Ibrahiem M. M. El Emary, (Eds.)
© 2024 Apple Academic Press, Inc. Co-published with CRC Press (Taylor & Francis)

devices and their effect on medical equipment. Readers may learn about various technologies that are used to safeguard healthcare data.

5.1   INTRODUCTION

The internet of things (IoT) is a platform of networked equipment, mechanical and digital machines, and things with unique IDs that can exchange data without the need for human interaction [1]. The IoMT is about enhancing the power of IoT and internet connectivity beyond computers to a complete range of other medical devices which consist of smart devices; these sensors are utilized to assess the state of many parameters of a patient's body, including blood pressure, ECG, temperature, heartbeat, movement, etc. The WBN is a subgroup of WSNs that may be used to evaluate the status of the patient. Experts utilize the internet to find information from the BS to check the health of the patient continually. To perceive the activities of various sections in healthcare applications, multiple medical devices are linked to clothes or fixed into the body of the human body. The WBAN (wireless body area network) architecture consists of three phases: inter WBAN, Intra WBAN, and even beyond WBAN. In the third phase, the medical data can be accessed by doctors remotely and provide emergency treatment. Figure 5.1 depicts WBAN technology.

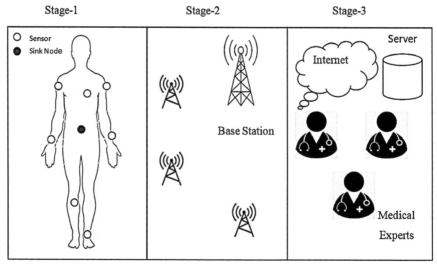

FIGURE 5.1   IoMT environment for E-healthcare.

The WBAN is derived from WSN, the implanted medical devices of WBN, like WSN, require prolonging battery energy for appropriate operation and dealing with medical data. WBAN must meet several main requirements, including low latency, low power consumption, QoS communication, secure data aggregation, and patient's sensitive data is sent through an unsecured Internet, and an unauthorized user can tamper with healthcare measurements; therefore, data security and integrity are crucial.

5.2   SECURITY REQUIREMENTS

The introduction of IoMT has resulted in numerous advancements in the health and medical fields. IoMT security vulnerabilities, on the other hand, can result in life-threatening situations. It is critical to ensure protection in the IoMT environment [3]. This section discusses several security needs in the IoMT environment.

5.2.1   AUTHENTICATION

Authentication is the process of validating the communicating party's identity during transmission. Both the source and the destination of IoMT environment mutually confirm their identities before initiating secure communication [2].

5.2.2   INTEGRITY

Integrity is a mechanism for assuring that medical information is true and accurate. It ensures that during communication, the message received did not have any fraudulent insertions, unauthorized deletions, or modifications [1]. We have to protect the data from unauthorized modifications. Medical data Integrity is also an important factor for its transmission in WBSNs.

5.2.3   CONFIDENTIALITY

Confidentiality ensures that unauthorized individuals do not access health information. It is also known as privacy, which ensures that exchanged communications are safeguarded from any information disclosure attack.

IoMT devices must protect the original medical data from dissemination. An attacker can sneak the medical conversations and use the gathered medical data for various illegal purposes; this eavesdropping procedure can pose serious risks to patients.

5.2.4 NON-REPUDIATION

It means two communicating entities cannot reject one another. Non-repudiation ensures that somebody cannot reject the legitimacy of something. It is a commonly used safety check that verifies the source of the message and the Integrity of the heal the information it contains.

5.2.5 AUTHORIZATION

It is a security method used to find a user's or device's privileges or at what level system resources are available. Medical data authorization is also an important aspect of its transmission in the IoMT context.

5.2.6 AVAILABILITY

The Availability property ensures that only authorized parties (doctors) have access to the information. If an attacker cannot breach the Integrity and Confidentiality of current interaction, they may try alternative methods. In the context of IoMT, medical data and network resources must be available to authenticated users.

5.2.7 FORWARD SECRECY

If smart equipment leaves an IoMT environment, it is no longer permitted to access future data.

5.2.8 BACKWARD SECRECY

In the IoMT communication environment, when a new smart device is installed, it should not access before previously exchanged messages.

5.3 MALWARE ATTACKS

Malware (sometimes called "malicious software") is a type of software that is transmitted through the internet into IoMT environment. It infects, steals, or does other suspicious actions as directed by the attacker [7–9]. Malware may be classified into several groups based on its functional characteristics. They usually work to achieve the following goals.

- It allows the attacker to operate an infected system through remote control;
- It spreads additional malware from the afflicted computer to other computers;
- It looks into the infected user's local network in order to conduct more malware attacks;
- It's used to steal sensitive information (like a patient's medical records) from an infected computer.

5.3.1 SPYWARE

It's a form of malware that monitors patients' behavior without their permission. In the network, malicious activities such as collecting keystrokes, monitoring, and harvesting data, such as account passwords and financial data, such as credit card numbers, are feasible. It may potentially change the software's security settings. It takes advantage of software flaws and attaches itself to a regular program [1].

5.3.2 KEYLOGGER

It's a suspicious part of the software that a hacker employs to track patients' keystrokes. Everything a user types of information like username password on their keyboard is saved [10]. This dangerous application tries to infiltrate equipment by convincing them to download it by clicking on an e-mail link. It is the deadliest malware since even a powerful password isn't enough to protect you from it. As a result, multiple-factor authentication is recommended.

5.3.3 VIRUS

This malicious application has the ability to replicate itself and propagate to other devices in IoMT environment. It infects other computers by connecting itself to various applications and next running the program when a user runs an infected app. It may also be used to obtain data, damage the host system, and create botnets [1].

5.3.4 WORM

It replicates on a network by exploiting flaws in the OS. It harms their host networks by using excessive bandwidth. It might have of code to harm a host computer. Attackers frequently use this to steal important information, destroy data, or build a botnet [1]. Normally worms self-replicate and spread on their own, whereas viruses require human intervention to propagate (for example, the opening of an infected file. Malicious attachments distribute worms in e-mails.

5.3.5 ADWARE

It is also known as an ad-supported code (software). As part of its functioning, it automatically distributes advertising. A pop-up advertisement on a website is a frequent example of Adware. Ransomware is malware that encrypts a machine (such as an IoMT device) and demands payment from its owner. It limits user access to the computer by encrypting the data on a hard disk or locking it.

5.3.6 ROOTKIT

It is a type of malicious code that is very destructive. The Rootkit used by intruders for remotely controlling the equipment remotely. Once installed successfully in a IoMT device, the attacker can execute the files remotely, steal critical data, change computer settings, and change the functioning of the security application. Because of its covert nature, identification and prevention are extremely challenging. A rootkit will constantly try to disguise its presence, making security appliances ineffective in detecting and removing it. As a result, manual approaches are used to identify it. We should always try to patch possible threats in the machines' operating systems (i.e., IoMT devices) [2] (Figure 5.2).

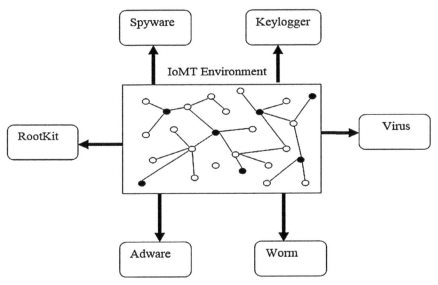

FIGURE 5.2   Different types of malware attacks in IoMT.

5.4   THE SCENARIO OF A MEDICAL SENSOR ATTACK IN IOMT

The IoMT environment is made up of a variety of IoMT devices. Healthcare practitioners utilize these sensors to keep track of the condition of the patient. Anyhow, during data communication from the sensor to the base station and then to the cloud, the hacker can interrupt this communication because of design errors and insufficient authentication actions [15, 16]. As a result, cyber-attacks such as black hole attacks, Denial-of-Service attacks, jammer attacks, spoofing, and ransomware attacks are all possible. Additionally, The biosensor authentication method and lack of security might be exploited by an attacker. Figure 5.3 depicts the scenario of a medical sensor attack in the IoMT environment [19].

5.5   THE SECURITY PROTOCOLS TAXONOMY IN IOMT ENVIRONMENT

This section goes over the security protocols utilized in the IoMT communication environment to protect both the shared and stored data. Diagram in Figure 5.4 depicts the security protocols taxonomy in the environment of IoMT [7].

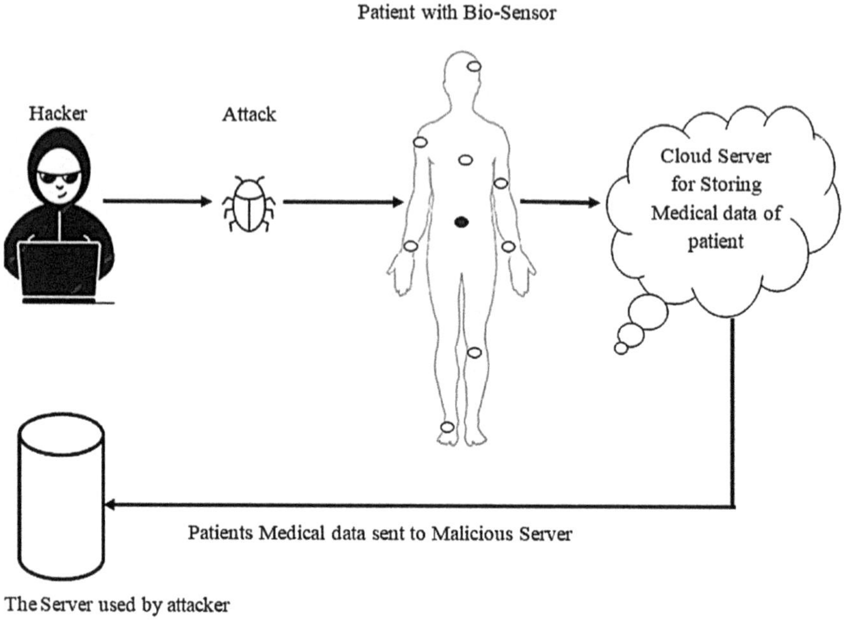

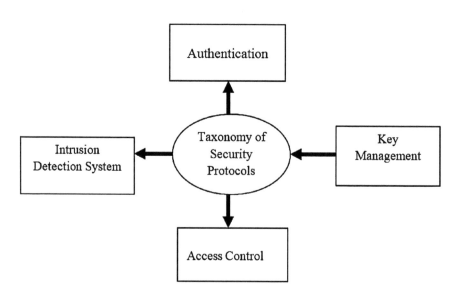

Patient with Bio-Sensor

Hacker   Attack

Cloud Server for Storing Medical data of patient

Patients Medical data sent to Malicious Server

The Server used by attacker

FIGURE 5.3   The scenario of medical sensor attack in IoMT environment.

Authentication

Taxonomy of Security Protocols

Intrusion Detection System

Key Management

Access Control

FIGURE 5.4   Taxonomy of security protocols in IoMT.

5.5.1 AUTHENTICATION

Authentication is the process of validating the During the communication of IoMT devices, the contacting parties' identities are revealed. Both the sender and the receiver mutually confirm their identities before initiating secure communication.

5.5.2 KEY MANAGEMENT

Key Distribution, Management, and establishment of keys among biosensor nodes of the Environment for IoMT is the responsibility of Key Management Protocol. The entire process is divided into different parts as per the requirements, including key generation, key exchange, key usage, and key revocation [18]. To perform secure communication, A solid key management method should be in place. In most cases, a key management process includes the phases which are discussed in subsections.

5.5.2.1 DEFINITION PHASE

A trusted authority defines numerous parameters for various network entities registration of various biosensor nodes and devices happen at this phase. After completing the registration, the registered data is saved in memory.

5.5.2.2 KEY GENERATION AND SHARING PHASE

At this stage, the trusted authority produces a variety of cryptographic keys for various network entities, and the produced keys are disseminated utilizing symmetric and asymmetric key cryptography principles.

5.5.2.3 KEY ESTABLISHMENT PHASE

The key establishment procedure can commence when the different network entities have been successfully registered and deployed. The equipment calculates some elements first, then communicates these values with other entities via message exchange.

5.5.2.4   *KEY ABROGATION AND DYNAMIC DEVICE ADDITION PHASE*

The adversary can obtain the secrets after any malicious event. In this situation, a trusted authority must deploy new devices in the deployment region. The trusted authority creates a new set of keys and saves the appropriate settings in the device's memory before installing it in the network. A reliable source also announces the information.

5.5.3   ACCESS CONTROL

User access control techniques are critical in the IoMT context to ensure that only genuine users access various services, information, and resources. Access control is a method that restricts a user's or device's access to a system or network. The user has been given privileges and access to various available resources using this approach. However, it is necessary to include new devices to the network to extend the life of the IoMT communication environment. It occurs when devices cease to function due to battery depletion or physical capture of that equipment. Therefore, we need to provide safe access control systems to prevent malicious devices from entering the IoMT environment. The Access control mechanism is divided into the following two types:

1. **Access Control Based on Certificate:** The Trusted Authority may store a digital certificate in each deployed device in a certificate-based access control system. The pre-loaded certificate is then used to prove the identification of a node to its neighbors.

2. **Access Control Without Certificate:** The hash-chain-based technique is used most of the time in a "certificate-less access control mechanism."

5.5.4   INTRUSION DETECTION SYSTEM

A technique that observes and analyzes harmful activity within a network or computer is normally known as IDS. It identifies and protects many types of equipment against potential attacks. In the environment of IoMT, an IDS verifies and monitors all traffic, then looks for harmful indications.

The corresponding component takes the appropriate action if it detects any harmful behavior. An attacker may physically catch some equipment in an IoMT scenario. After that, the adversary may attempt to steal sensitive data from the device or install malicious equipment in the environment of the IoMT. These malicious devices may have characteristics that allow them to launch more destructive assaults. The transferred data might be discarded, revealed, altered, or delayed before being sent to their destination under various attacks. As a consequence, the continuing communication performance suffers significantly. The IDS performs the following functionalities:

- It recognizes the signs of an attacker;
- It gives the intruder's location's information;
- It keeps track of activities in the IoMT environment;
- If harmful actions are identified, it attempts to halt them;
- It then informs the administrator of harmful actions;
- It also contains information on the different types of intrusions.

Intrusion detection systems in IoMT context are classified into the following categories:

- Behavior-based IDS for IoMT;
- Knowledge-based IDS for IoMT;
- Agent-based IDS for IoMT;
- Network-based IDS for IoMT.

5.5.4.1   BEHAVIOR-BASED IDS FOR IOMT

This model of IDS monitors the actions linked with attack behavior, increasing the possibility of a malicious activity being detected and mitigated before the IoMT network is compromised.

5.5.4.2   KNOWLEDGE-BASED IDS FOR IOMT

It utilizes well-known attack signatures, a database of former attack profiles, and device vulnerabilities in IoMT context to recognize active intrusion attempts.

5.5.4.3   *AGENT-BASED IDS FOR IOMT*

It requires tiny computer programs called agents installed on each IoMT system. The agents examine the computer operating system and network write data to log files.

5.5.4.4   *NETWORK-BASED IDS FOR IOMT*

It typically includes a bio-sensor node running in promiscuous mode and a separate managing interface with a network interface card (NIC). The IDS is positioned along the section or border of the network and tracks all traffic in it.

5.6   SECURITY MEASURES OF IOMT USING MACHINE AND DEEP LEARNING (DL) TECHNIQUES

Machine learning (ML) is a form of AI that learns without explicitly programming from information and experiences. For constant data analysis and the creation of relevant data. In IoMT, ML can play a critical role, particularly at biosensors. Recently, ML has been used in a variety of IoMT applications. However, classical security mechanisms may not defend the computer against intensive attacks for the environment of IoMT systems. ML can be utilized in a variety of ways to address the security challenges of the IoMT [4].

Three types of ML algorithms are utilized to solve IoMT security problems: supervised, semi-supervised, and unsupervised. The Supervised method is for labeled data with established classifications or labels. Classification and regression are the two types of supervised learning. Decision Trees, Neural Networks and SVM are examples of supervised learning. These approaches, used in signature-based Intrusion Detection Systems to identify attacks and malware in IDS. Unsupervised methods are used to categorize the data based on its comparable features because human labeling is not always possible. These approaches are efficient in detecting new attacks and anomalies. However, not all unlabeled data can be used to make predictions. As a result, adding some labeled data can help to solve this problem. Semi-Supervised learning is a part of ML in which certain data are labeled from a large set of learning data [5].

Deep learning (DL), an enhanced form of Neural Network, has just emerged as a new discipline. It contains many layers of ANN that replicate the working process of the human brain. In contrast to standard ML approaches requiring an additional feature selection, DL makes feature selection based on its learning process without using any other method.

5.6.1 MACHINE LEARNING (ML)-BASED IOMT SECURITY AND PRIVACY SOLUTIONS

The IoMT system's modular design, which includes tiny devices, a heterogeneous network, and a variety of protocols, has made standard security frameworks challenging to deploy for medical firms. As a result, the IoMT system is vulnerable to various assaults. Recent advances in ML techniques and technology have resulted in effective ways to address IoMT security concerns. The IoMT system, on the other hand, has greater problems than traditional network systems [6]. Devices that are part of the IoMT create many data in the form of streaming data. The variety of this info, with the restricted energy and resources of IoMT devices, particularly implanted medical devices, places a significant computational load on standard ML algorithms, limiting their usefulness in IoMT devices. As a result, new techniques are necessary to deploy ML approaches effectively [10, 14].

5.7 MACHINE LEARNING (ML) APPLICATIONS IN HEALTHCARE SYSTEMS

Healthcare is a data-driven industry. Even if a model is designed to provide insight, it must have the ability to influence patient treatment. The first step in developing a ML solution is identifying the good problem to tackle using ML [16].

5.7.1 MEDICAL IMAGERY

Medical imagery refers to the procedures and techniques used to produce pictures of body components for therapeutic and diagnostic reasons, and ML has applications in this field. Magnetic resonance imaging (MRI) and X-ray radiography are two examples of imaging methods used today. Currently, these pictures are taken and manually examined by a health expert to detect any anomalies. This procedure is not only error-prone but also time-consuming. The use of ML algorithms increases disease prediction, detection, diagnostic accuracy, and timeliness. Artificial neural networks (ANN) and other ML techniques can be linked to medical imagery to allow illness detection, diagnosis, and prediction, diagnosis, and detection. DL techniques are powerful tools for image and video processing, crucial in medical imaging. CT scanners and X-ray equipment, commonly present in healthcare systems, are examples of IoMT devices employed in a ML configuration. The supervised learning technique is extensively used in medical imagery.

5.7.2 DIAGNOSIS OF DISEASE

Disease diagnosis is an important part of treatment. ML is useful in disease diagnosis since it allows for analyzing environmental and physiological variables to diagnose disorders properly. In addition, it enables the development of models for linking factors to diseases. ML may be used to detect risk factors and indications and symptoms linked with a disease, improving diagnostic efficiency and accuracy. Glaucoma, age-related macular degeneration, and other diseases are presently being identified using ML. SVM, DL systems, convolutional neural networks, backpropagation networks and convolutional neural networks are ML approaches utilized in disease diagnosis. Depending on the condition being diagnosed, the input data type varies. Image data is regularly utilized in most imaging diagnosis ML research. To discover patterns from data and allow illness detection, ML can use either supervised or unsupervised learning techniques. The IoT devices and sensors used are determined by the data input necessary. Scanning equipment is the primary IoT device for imaging-based diagnostics. IoT devices may also be used to collect data like weight, heart rate, and blood pressure to diagnose diseases.

5.7.3 BEHAVIORAL MODIFICATION OR TREATMENT

As the name implies, behavioral modification is assisting a patient in changing undesired behavior. Behavioral modification is an example of a treatment that is frequently recommended to patients whose poor habits are contributing to their health problems. ML for behavioral change is made feasible by the IoT, which allows for the collecting of massive volumes of data on individuals. As a result, ML algorithms may be used to analyze individual behavior and suggest appropriate modifications. ML may also be used to assess behavioral change therapies in order to identify which is the most successful for a particular patient. The Bayes network classifier, decision trees, and SVM are some of the ML methods used in behavioral modification. Feature extraction, which provides tabular data, is used to get the input data for these methods. As a result, the IoT devices that are relevant are those that gather data that may be used to describe human behavior, such as videos, pictures, and recordings.

5.7.4 CLINICAL RESEARCH

Clinical research are investigations that are conducted to ascertain the efficacy and safety of pharmaceutical treatments. ML can help improve the clinical trial process by enabling researchers to learn about the efficacy of therapies through the analysis of publicly available clinical and biological datasets, health record data, and practical evidence from sensors. Healthcare practitioners may use ML algorithms to sift through massive quantities of data to find insights about the efficacy and safety of a specific intervention. For instance, ML may be used in clinical trials to develop COVID-19 medicines. Extracting characteristics from datasets is the first step in using ML algorithms in clinical trial research. As a result, pictures and tables from the clinical study are included in the input data. The IoMT devices in place should be able to collect data on the clinical trial's variables. Blood pressure, weight, heart rate, and blood glucose are examples of sensor data.

5.7.5 SMART ELECTRONIC HEALTH RECORDS (EHRS)

Patient charts have been replaced with electronic health records (EHRs), which enable quick access to patient information, allowing physicians to provide high-quality treatment. ML may be used to integrate intelligence into electronic medical records (EMRs). Rather than serving as a repository for patient data, EHRs may be supplemented with smart features thanks to ML. Smart EHRs, for example, may evaluate patient data, propose the best therapy, and assist in clinical decision-making. Indeed, it has been demonstrated that combining ML with electronic health data may enhance ophthalmology. Smart electronic records can also analyze large quantities of data to assess the quality and safety of care delivered in a facility and indicate areas that need improvement. Linear and ANN, and SVM are examples of ML models incorporated into EHRs. Text, pictures, tables, and time series can all be used as input data. When incorporated into electronic records, recurrent DL architectures have been demonstrated to predict illnesses accurately. Blood glucose, heart rate, weight, blood pressure, and temperature are among the IoMT sensor data used in ML models.

5.7.6   EPIDEMIC OUTBREAK PREDICTION

Emerging and spreading diseases in a community may be catastrophic and difficult to control. As a result, players in the healthcare industry realize the need to develop tools and methods to forecast and prepare for epidemic outbreaks. Regulators, administrators, and healthcare professionals may use ML algorithms to forecast epidemics thanks to the Availability of big data. ML methods for illness prediction. Overall, disease monitoring is critical since it aids in the prevention of epidemics and allows stakeholders to plan for potential outbreaks.

5.7.7   HEART DISEASE PREDICTION

In most areas of the world, heart disease is the leading cause of mortality. Heart disease is becoming more common throughout the world. Globally, cardiovascular illnesses claimed the lives of 17.6 million people in 2016, up 14.5% from 2006. Being able to foresee the disease and execute the appropriate preventive and treatment methods is an important part of controlling heart disease. This skill is provided by ML, which allows healthcare practitioners to examine patient data and anticipate cardiac disease. Patients who are found to be at an increased risk of developing heart disease may be encouraged to take preventative measures. Images, time series, text, and tabular data are all examples of input data types for ML algorithms for heart disease prediction.

5.7.8   COVID-19 PROGNOSTIC AND DIAGNOSTIC MODELS

ML can also help in COVID-19 diagnosis and prognosis. The goal is to create an algorithm that considers prognosis and diagnostic predictions and produces precise results. ML methods are useful because they can evaluate many lung pictures from COVID-19 patients and distinguish between those who are and are not impacted. The research found that utilizing eight binary characteristics such as age, gender, contact with an infected individual, and five first clinical symptoms, and it was possible to predict COVID-19 with good accuracy. As a result, IoT sensor devices used in this ML configuration should capture temperature readings and pictures of the lungs. ML methods are quick and efficient, and they improve the accuracy of COVID-19 diagnosis and prognosis.

5.7.9 PERSONALIZED CARE

Patients deserve treatment that is tailored to their specific requirements, expectations, and beliefs. Personalized care promotes patient happiness and usage of formal health services in addition to enhancing clinical results. By allowing healthcare personnel to evaluate each patient's data and build tailored treatment plans, ML algorithms can help provide personalized care. ML systems use the potential of health records to uncover person-specific patterns of illness development by combining diverse data sources. The data gathered aids clinical decision-making by allowing healthcare providers to deliver tailored treatment. Text, time series, and tabular data may all be used as input data for ML customized care. ML algorithms may be used to identify the optimal course of therapy utilizing tabular data from the patient's medical record.

5.8 ENERGY-EFFICIENT AND SECURE FRAMEWORK FOR IOMT-ENABLED HEALTHCARE SYSTEMS

The proposed secured and energy efficient IoMT architecture for digital healthcare applications lowers the energy consumption of biosensor nodes while sharing information rapidly. Proposed strategy to cut down on communication costs and overheads, the suggested data collection and routing methodology is based on artificial intelligence (AI) technologies [3]. The framework suggested is appropriate for digital healthcare apps that employ For detecting patients' pre-primary maintenance data. The suggested framework enables intelligently evaluating patient data, allowing medical specialists to provide the best treatment possible on time [7]. The suggested framework combines AI techniques with body sensor nodes to automate the observation of patient data and achieve the best results with the least amount of processing and transmission. As a result, digital healthcare-related applications have a huge potential to improve medical findings through treatment analysis and suggestions [3, 18, 19]. Furthermore, the suggested framework includes safe and authentic techniques for preventing data breaches and maintaining data integrity in digital healthcare systems.

The proposed framework for healthcare utilizing IoMT are divided into two phases, as shown below:

i. The intelligent channel aware routing strategy qualifies low-power biosensors for communication and determines a secure and efficient routing channel for IoMT sensors data packets with the least network overhead and energy consumption.

ii. Patients' essential and sensitive medical information is protected from harmful and prospective attacks via the internet using light-weight encryption techniques. The suggested framework uses the Modified Rijndael Algorithm, an authentic and secure mechanism, to route the patient's healthcare information and maintain its Integrity.

The experimental analyzes revealed increased outcomes for e-healthcare and IoMT systems in comparison to previous work.

5.8.1   RELATED WORK

Routing protocols that are cognizant of QoS, temperature, clustering, and cross-layering are described in WBAN [20–22]. A variety of network parameters are taken into consideration for data transfer in the QoS-aware routing system. The network is subdivided into groups, each with one CH, and communication to B Scan. Sensor node temperature rises while also balancing energy consumption and making efficient routing decisions.

The authors suggested an energy-efficient and cost-effective routing strategy for WBAN in [23], with the goal of increasing energy efficiency and dependability. The suggested method employs a depends on remaining power, connection dependability, and route loss factors, a genetic algorithm (GA), and an optimized cost function were used. Furthermore, the suggested approach employs more than one hope routing to shorten node distances. In comparison to previous studies, the simulation trials show increased performance.

In Ref. [24], the authors presented routing protocol with an energy harvested-aware and clustering (EH-RCB) method for WBAN that was both resilient and efficient. For the election of the optimal next nodes, the suggested approach stabilized WBAN operations. Depends on the remaining power, connection depend on ability, and route loss factors, a GA and an optimized cost function were used. In comparison to previous research, the simulated findings show enhanced network throughput in terms of several performance indicators.

The authors developed an effective forwarding node election method for multi-hop WBANs (ENSA-BAN) in Ref. [25], with the goal of improving network performance over existing routing systems. For data forwarding, the proposed method tries to choose the best next-hop from among the neighbors. The suggested method balances energy usage and reduces the end-to-end delay ratio by using the cost function.

The authors of Ref. [17] suggested enhancing healthcare-related applications of energy-oriented network metrics using an energy-aware link efficient routing approach for WBAN. For the process of network startup, the suggested method initially uses beaconing information. Second, the route cost value determines the next-hop for data routing based on energy and link-aware efficiency. Finally, hop count, residual energy, connection efficiency, distance, and connection efficiency to the body node coordinator go into the route cost function. The simulation-based study shows that the alternative options perform better in terms of network throughput and energy usage.

In Ref. [27], to enhance the network's energy level and longevity. The suggested approach eliminates unnecessary data packets by only sending important health data to the sink node. The smart devices observed the packets and calculated their threshold levels, dividing data packets into critical and non-critical categories. Compared to alternative methods, the simulated tests show that the suggested approach enhances network performance in terms of throughput, packet loss rate, collision ratio, and network stability.

WBAN is a subclass of WSN, and resource scarcity limits biosensors, as demonstrated by similar studies. Energy, computation, processing, transmission, and storage resources are all important bottlenecks. Various authors have offered ways to increase WBAN network performance. However, the most critical research concerns in WBAN healthcare applications are reliable and energy-efficient data forwarding. Some methods depend on the tree methods that have been developed, but these systems augment the latency ratio; in the event of a bottleneck, many route rediscoveries are triggered. Although various cost-function-based strategies for improving network performance have been presented, such solutions involve an excessive amount of control message exchange and fail to account for the biosensors' limited constraints, resulting in the use of extra energy resources and packet overheads. Furthermore, several methods based on clustering strategies have been presented;

these approaches enhanced network connection, but they quickly perform the re-clustering phase without analyzing the node state [17].

Most solutions based on WBAN additionally include path assessment in the computation of cost function, resulting in consistent path selection and data delivery performance. However, due to the flooding of multiple control messages, such systems incur extra overheads when computing the cost function. Furthermore, such systems neglected node integrity and data security, both of which are critical components of stable and reliable e-healthcare applications. Patients' sensitive data is sent through the internet, which is unsecure and vulnerable to malicious and prospective assaults, from local body coordinators to remotely located medical facilities.

5.8.2 *INTELLIGENT ROUTING-BASED ENERGY-EFFICIENT AND SECURE FRAMEWORK FOR IOMT*

The proposed framework, built for medical applications, is discussed in depth here. From a biosensor device to servers, the proposed mechanism improves energy efficiency between biosensors while also increasing the security level of patient data using WBN. The framework provides effective, reliable, and secure ways for monitoring patients' physical health in an emergency.

After gathering patient data the sink node sends healthcare data to medical specialists via intermediary devices. Malicious nodes have the ability to assault network infrastructure in order to destroy security.

The biosensor device sends a Route Request to the device closest to it. The nearby node checks the request within a reasonable time interval and delivers the Route Response back to the source biosensor Node. The neighbor node's appropriate and relevant answer marks it as a proper node, and the neighbor node sequence number is increased by one. If the node is valid, just the count will be increased; otherwise, it will contain attack content. This type of biosensor node is appropriately inhibited in the current circumstance, and the source looks for alternate or other neighbor nodes to communicate with. The sensor node selection or path selection procedure depends entirely on the Shortest Path Routing technique in standard network strategies. These operations have been changed to provide some secure and efficient standards using the suggested routing logic to improve security. Rather than choosing another path for the energy deficient nodes, the sink node in the WBAN behaves as an evaluator node, checking the energy level of the deficient node and providing enough power to restore the deficient node's status as a normal node and qualify it for the next transmission.

5.8.3   SECURE DATA TRANSMISSION

This section describes an efficient method designed for the proposed architecture that uses the Rijndael algorithm to send sensitive patient data from a sink node to remote servers. The proposed technique also uses the Rijndael algorithm to encrypt the data at senders and decrypt at the receiver (Figure 5.5).

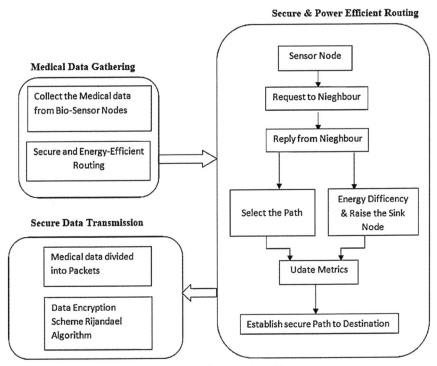

FIGURE 5.5   Secure and energy-efficient framework architecture.

5.8.4   SECURE AND ENERGY EFFICIENT ROUTING ALGORITHM

- The initialization of the biosensor and sink nodes;
- Transit RREQ from sender to neighboring equipment;
- Reply from the neighbor will be checked to evaluate the forwarding node;
- If the node is not proper then elevator node will be raised;
- Metrics of the route will be updated;
- Secure route between sender and receiver will be selected.

5.8.5   SIMULATION SETUP

This section explains how to set up a simulation using the NS2. The sensor nodes are spread out over a 50-meter radius. The number of sensor nodes implanted on the patient's body has been fixed at 20. The sink node is a local coordinator that is placed in the middle of the patient's body. In terms of resources, a sink node is considered to be more powerful than a sensor node. A constant bitrate is used to transmit data between sensors and the sink node (CBR). Table 5.1 shows the simulation parameters.

TABLE 5.1   Simulation Parameters

Sl. No.	Simulation Parameter	Range
1.	Simulation area	20×20 m
2.	Number of nodes	20
3.	Transmission range	50 m
4.	Sink node presence	Yes
5.	Packet transmission rate	8 to 320 kbps
6.	Channel type	Wireless communication channel
7.	Packet size	1,000 to 1,200 kb
8.	Packets transmission speed	30–70 bps
9.	Packet transmission frequency	2.5 to 5 GHz

5.8.6   EXPERIMENTAL RESULTS

Figure 5.6 depicts the proposed framework's behavior in contrast to existing solutions for packet delivery rate. The simulation output shows that the designed technique improved the packet delivery rate when compared to other solutions at different time intervals. Secure routing decisions and link-aware and the inclusion of data security mechanisms The Rijndael algorithm further improves the security of each data packet by making it difficult for malicious nodes to change or drop them. Malicious nodes can create traffic on the communication media since existing solutions lack device recovery and data security (Figure 5.7).

In terms of energy efficiency, the proposed scheme's outcomes are compared to previous studies, the numerical analysis shows that the suggested technique enhances energy efficiency over time intervals. The proposed strategy is designed with energy-efficient and secure routing methods in mind, balancing energy utilization of sensor nodes. The node

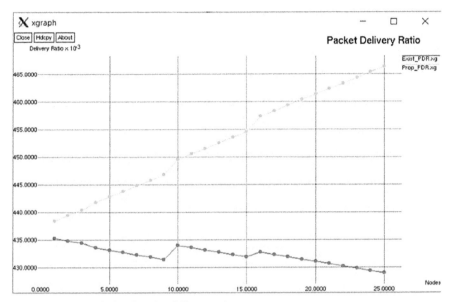

FIGURE 5.6   Analysis of packet delivery ratio.

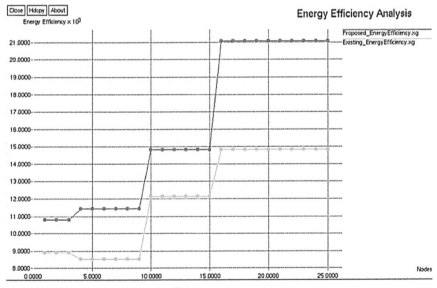

FIGURE 5.7   Analysis of energy efficiency.

selection technique lowers the ratio of power utilization of the nodes in creating unneeded route request packets by reducing additional over-heads caused by the selection of recovered bio-sensor nodes.

Figure 5.8 presents a comparison of the proposed framework with existing work's delay. In comparison to alternative methods, the suggested framework reduces the ratio of delay throughout varied time intervals, according to the experimental results. The proposed framework selects more energy-efficient, secure routes for medical data transmission and reduces the likelihood of data delay by reducing the number of wireless retransmissions.

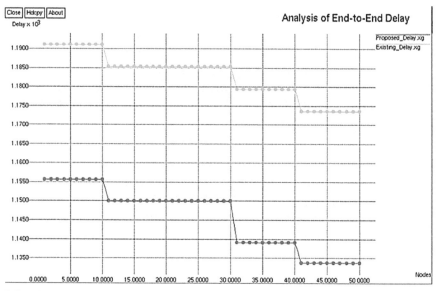

FIGURE 5.8   Analysis of delay.

5.9   CONCLUSION

The internet of medical things (IoMT) is focused on small healthcare devices communication. WBANs are a subclass of Wireless Sensor Network that can track human body characteristics. Medical experts used the internet to gather information from the BS to track the patient's health. However, wireless transmission of sensitive medical data to remote computers increases the risk of data breaches and exploitation without addressing security concerns. When this IoMT equipment is not protected, patients are put at risk, and the entire healthcare system is disrupted. The proposed IoMT-based secure and energy-efficient strategy for IoMT aims to lower energy usage and increase security by sending medical data on time. Furthermore, critical medical data can be encrypted using a cryptographic algorithm, ensuring data security. Simulation experiments were conducted, and statistical analysis revealed that the suggested framework is more energy-efficient and secure than previous work, with a smaller network delay.

KEYWORDS

- **Artificial Neural Networks**
- **Deep Learning**
- **Healthcare Systems**
- **Internet of Medical Things**
- **Magnetic Resonance Imaging**
- **Routing**
- **Security**
- **Wireless Body Area Network**

REFERENCES

1. Wazid, M., Das, A. K., Rodrigues, J. J. P. C., Shetty, S., & Park, Y., (2019). IoMT malware detection approaches: Analysis and research challenges. In: *IEEE Access* (Vol. 7, pp. 182459–182476). doi: 10.1109/ACCESS.2019.2960412.
2. Sun, Y., Lo, F. P., & Lo, B., (2019). Security and privacy for the internet of medical things enabled healthcare systems: A survey. In: *IEEE Access (*Vol. 7, pp. 183339–183355). doi: 10.1109/ACCESS.2019.2960617.
3. Aldahiri, A., Bashair, A., & Walayat, H., (2021). Trends in using IoT with machine learning in health prediction system. *Forecasting, 3*(1), 181–206.
4. Lin, K., Li, C., Tian, D., Ghoneim, A., Hossain, M. S., & Amin, S. U., (2019). Artificial-intelligence-based data analytics for cognitive communication in heterogeneous wireless networks. In: *IEEE Wireless Communications* (Vol. 26, No. 3, pp. 83–89). doi: 10.1109/ MWC.2019.1800351.
5. Newaz, I., Sikder, A. K., Rahman, M. A., & Uluagac, A. S., (2019). HealthGuard: A machine learning-based security framework for smart healthcare systems. In: *2019 6ᵗʰ International Conference on Social Networks Analysis, Management and Security (SNAMS)* (pp. 389–396). doi: 10.1109/SNAMS.2019.8931716.
6. Alshehri, F., & Muhammad, G., (2021). A comprehensive survey of the internet of things (IoT) and AI-based smart healthcare. In: *IEEE Access* (Vol. 9, pp. 3660–3678). doi: 10.1109/ACCESS.2020.3047960.

7. Uma, N. D., & Shaik, R., (2019). IoT evolution and security challenges in cyber space: IoT security. *Countering Cyber Attacks and Preserving the Integrity and Availability of Critical Systems.* IGI Global, February.

8. Faisal, A., Abdullah, A., Vivek, S., & Sajjan, S., (2019). IoMT-SAF: Internet of medical things security assessment framework. *Internet of Things, 8,* 100123. ISSN 2542-6605. https://doi.org/10.1016/j.iot.2019.100123.

9. Gatouillat, Badr, Y., Massot, B., & Sejdić, E., (2018). Internet of medical things: A review of recent contributions dealing with cyber-physical systems in medicine. In: *IEEE Internet of Things Journal* (Vol. 5, No. 5, pp. 3810–3822). doi: 10.1109/JIOT.2018.2849014.

10. Hatzivasilis, Soultatos, O., Ioannidis, S., Verikoukis, C., Demetriou, G., & Tsatsoulis, C., (2019). Review of security and privacy for the internet of medical things (IoMT). In: *2019 15th International Conference on Distributed Computing in Sensor Systems (DCOSS)* (pp. 457–464). doi: 10.1109/DCOSS.2019.00091.

11. Sagar, A. K., Singh, S., & Kumar, A., (2020). Energy-aware WBAN for health monitoring using critical data routing (CDR). *Wirel. Pers. Commun.,* 1–30.

12. Luca, G., Gennaro, P., Pierluigi, R., Francesco, T., & Mario, V., (2020). Trends in IoT based solutions for health care: Moving AI to the edge. *Pattern Recognition Letters, 135,* 346–353. ISSN 0167-8655. https://doi.org/10.1016/j.patrec.2020.05.016.

13. Irfan, M., & Ahmad, N., (2018). Internet of medical things: Architectural model, motivational factors and impediments. In: *2018 15th Learning and Technology Conference (L&T)* (pp. 6–13). doi: 10.1109/LT.2018.8368495.

14. Karmakar, K. K., Varadharajan, V., Tupakula, U., Nepal, S., & Thapa, C., (2020). Towards a security enhanced virtualized network infrastructure for the internet of medical things (IoMT). In: *2020 6th IEEE Conference on Network Softwarization (NetSoft)* (pp. 257–261). doi: 10.1109/NetSoft48620.2020.9165387.

15. Prabhat, K., Govind, P. G., & Rakesh, T., (2021). An ensemble learning a fog-cloud architecture-driven cyber-attack detection framework for IoMT networks. *Computer Communications, 166,* 110–124. ISSN 0140-3664. https://doi.org/10.1016/j.comcom.2020.12.003.

16. Hameed, S., Hassan, W., ALatiff, L., & Ghabban, D., (2021). A systematic review of security and privacy issues on the internet of medical things; the role of machine learning approaches. *PeerJ Computer Science, 7,* e414. 10.7717/peerj-cs.414.

17. Anwar, M., Abdullah, A. H., Altameem, A., Qureshi, K. N., Masud, F., Faheem, M., et al., (2018). Green communication for wireless body area networks: Energy aware link efficient routing approach. *Sensors, 18*(10), 3237.

18. Nomikos, K., Papadimitriou, A., Stergiopoulos, G., Koutras, D., Psarakis, M., & Kotzanikolaou, P., (2020). On a security-oriented design framework for medical IoT devices: The hardware security perspective. In: *2020 23rd Euromicro Conference on Digital System Design (DSD)* (pp. 301–308). doi: 10.1109/DSD51259.2020.00056.

19. Sandeep, P., Oluwarotimi, W. S., Wanqing, W., Arun, K. S., & Guanglin, L., (2019). A joint resource-aware and medical data security framework for wearable healthcare systems. *Future Generation Computer Systems, 95,* 382–391. ISSN 0167-739X. https://doi.org/10.1016/j.future.2019.01.008.

20. Zuhra, F. T., Bakar, K. A., Ahmed, A., & Tunio, M. A., (2017). Routing protocols in wireless body sensor networks: A comprehensive survey. *J. Netw. Comput. Appl., 99,* 73–97.

21. Yessad, N., Omar, M., Tari, A., & Bouabdallah, A., (2018). QoS-based routing in wireless body area networks: A survey and taxonomy. *Computing, 100*(3), 245–275.

22. Ahmed, G., Mahmood, D., & Islam, S., (2019). Thermal and energy aware routing in wireless body area networks. *Int. J. Distrib. Sens. Netw., 15*(6), 1550147719854974.

23. Kaur, N., & Singh, S., (2017). Optimized cost effective and energy efficient routing protocol for wireless body area networks. *Ad. Hoc. Netw., 61*, 65–84.

24. Ullah, Z., Ahmed, I., Ali, T., Ahmad, N., Niaz, F., & Cao, Y., (2019). Robust and efficient energy harvested-aware routing protocol with clustering approach in body area networks. *IEEE Access, 7*, 33906–33921.

25. Ayatollahitafti, V., Ngadi, M. A., Bin Mohamad, S. J., & Abdullahi, M., (2016). An efficient next hop selection algorithm for multi-hop body area networks. *PLoS One, 11*(1), e0146464.

PART II
Artificial Intelligence and Techniques in Healthcare Services

AN AI-DRIVEN MULTI-MANAGEMENT SYSTEM FOR MEDICAL RESOURCE ALLOCATION PROVIDING PERSONALIZED HEALTHCARE SERVICES

S. GEETHA[1] and TVISHA TRIVEDI[2]

[1]Faculty, School of Computer Science and Engineering, Vellore Institute of Technology, Chennai, Tamil Nadu, India

[2]Student, School of Computer Science and Engineering, Vellore Institute of Technology, Chennai, Tamil Nadu, India

ABSTRACT

Allocation can become a challenge when resources become restricted, and demand exceeds availability. Whether healthcare is provided in a public or private environment, there are always constraints, whether they are restricted by limited personnel or lack of medical facilities or medicinal products. The wellbeing of medical experts is also a priority, since they may get ill while treating the patients and need care. Recent pandemics have proved that effective healthcare services require a suitable management structure. Artificial intelligence (AI) has been employed for effective action to boost for the systems utilized in healthcare management with the emergence of automated models and systems. In the areas of disease detection, patient monitoring, and medical advancement, AI has been widely employed. Virtual aids that are incorporated with AI can assist in all emergencies by guiding both the patient and their caretaker. It could also be used to monitor patients electronically

Handbook of Research on Artificial Intelligence and Soft Computing Techniques in Personalized Healthcare Services, Uma N. Dulhare, A. V. Senthil Kumar, Amit Datta, Seddik Bri, Ibrahiem M. M. El Emary, (Eds.)
© 2024 Apple Academic Press, Inc. Co-published with CRC Press (Taylor & Francis)

or foresee clinical setting objectives while offering patients with individualized healthcare coverage. This study suggests a paradigm that integrates an AI-driven distribution of resources with a personalized healthcare system, offering medical services to both the hospital and the patient. The strategy for optimizing the error rates, expenditure, processing period and patient wellbeing and productivity is a multi-response methodology.

6.1   INTRODUCTION

Storing medical data can be a challenge, especially since all patients are going to have differences in their body structure regardless of the problems they face. In order to maintain any semblance of a uniformity in the medical sector regarding data management, health records as a tool have been deployed to help hospitals to understand and provide better care to their patients while patients get ample medical support. Electronic health records (EHRs) have been generated by digitizing this health record. In health information technology, EHRs emerged as a "constructive application" to enhance healthcare performance and reliability and health inequalities [1].

Although EHRs currently have a lot of longitudinal patient data that can get us closer to establishing individualized healthcare solutions for patients, they're still scattered and disproportionately available. Some patients may be willing to share their information, while others might not feel that comfortable in doing so. Some hospitals may have the facility to store and utilize these records while there may be places, especially in remote rural areas, where getting hold of a doctor is a major task, having EHRs goes out of the question. Even if the data is stored from a patient, it can vary from hospital to hospital and cause a misunderstanding of one patient's data when compared with the other. And like most of the other times, these types of data are usually stored in a tabular format, which can be long and lengthy to study. In other words, data from the EHR could be quite chaotic and scarce. However, if EHR data is effectively utilized, they can offer real-world data on patient travels, treatment patterns, forecasting a future code for diagnosis, or chance of recovery, mortality, and so on [2].

Effective treatment methods for an illness must be developed at different phases as per distinct symptoms. In proper categorization of a disease that has the features of many stages of study, diverse symptoms and multi-pathogenesis, most techniques of identification may not be efficient. In addition, there's little interchange and collaboration across multiple agencies and hospitals in disease diagnostics and therapy. Thus, novice clinicians may have difficulties diagnosing them efficiently and precisely when infectious threats develop with unique symptoms [3]. Health experts generally identify ailments and choose medication regimens mainly dependent on first-hand skill and understanding. The incapacity to acquire and to draw advice from the experiences, prognosis, and potential treatments of appropriately qualified doctors leads to false or incorrect, sharing of experiences and coordination among young and older doctors. While copious health records relating to individual patients, illnesses, diagnostic procedures, and outcomes are generated and available, such data cannot be properly examined and therefore is not effectively distributed among healthcare providers. The consequences of this information are not really properly assessed.

During the previous decade, the Massive Data Concept has put strain on traditional relational databases. In order to represent the acquired data more effectively, the academies and the industry have proposed numerous different database plans. The most promising applicant for supplemental relational schemes among those techniques, appears to be the graphical databases [3]. Because of a lack of diagnostic expertise, it may be difficult for young physicians to appropriately diagnose the illness of a patient with an unusual illness; therefore, the prescription of successful treatment strategies is uncertain. Therefore, discussing and advising clinical expertise can contribute to improved diagnostic and therapeutic experience for emerging physicians. To harmonize the health assistance of developing and advanced institutions as well as the medical know-how of seasoned physicians and novice doctors, a disease diagnostic and therapeutic recommendation system is designed [4].

Due to the huge number, diversity, and continual refreshing of patient records, a critical task has been the effective utilization of health data as well as the responsiveness to the recommendation in the real time. Big data and artificial intelligence (AI) are fortuitous enough to not only deliver powerful skills to handle and analyze enormous data, but also provide personalized services related to it. Different hospitals have built advanced medication guidance systems and have taken numerous health service enhancement steps [4]. This study studies the issue of resource allocation with extra antecedent limitations, deadlines, and inventory restrictions in order to meet the necessary scheduling of complicated built objects. Neo4j has been creatively designed to address this issue as a highly powerful graph database that deals with linked data and integrates interconnections into customizable graphs. A framework was also developed based on Neo4j, which integrates graphic databases. The semanticization of the table header ensures a seamless transition between tabular csv format and Neo4j graph data [4]. It focuses on the pooling of healthcare resources and the understanding of medication in big data, providing a paradigm that blends an AI-driven allocation with a personalized medical system by providing both a hospital and a patient with hospital facilities. Multiple data records of observation were evaluated for groups of illness symptoms. Past medical data have shown linkage patterns between diseases, diagnosis, and therapies. On this basis, effective illness diagnosis and management strategies in line with the present disease phases are proposed for patients and physicians [5].

6.2   EXPERIMENTAL METHODS AND MATERIALS

Significant scientific progress in the healthcare sector has notably increased to fulfill the needs of patients and provide better medical judgment. Machine learning (ML) and data techniques can alter the data accessible to important insights which can be used to prescribe adequate treatments through the analysis of clinical manifestations. A deep learning (DL) approach to multi-disease can be suggested to supply patients with multiple conditions with appropriate medicine recommendations. This technique gives cardiac, common cold, fever, obese, optical, and ortho patients adequate advice. DL supervised algorithms can be used to make suggestions for patients, for example, support vector machine (SVM), random forestry (RF), decision tree, and K-nearest neighbors (KNN). Researchers are investigating SVM medication recommendation algorithms, neuro-fuzzy algorithms and diagnostic data-driven decision tree algorithms of DL [6, 11]. The key components of some of the DL approaches are multilayer perceptron (MLP), auto-encoder (AE), convolutional neural network (CNN), recurrent neural network (RNN), restricted Boltzmann machine (RBM) and adversarial neural networks (ANN) [7]. Furthermore, for the great precision, good efficiency and robustness of the medical recommender system, four different methodologies were chosen, namely, KNN, RBM, CNN, and SVM.

6.2.1   USER INTERFACES

A real-life system was established for this service. The user experience is basic and user-friendly. The user is required to enter the ailments they are seeking for so that the prescription is anticipated based on the ailments in the response field and the outcome of the enquiry can be seen.

6.2.2 HARDWARE INTERFACES

There are minimum hardware interfaces in the design. The setup is good for running an ordinary personal computer or laptop. In order to calculate and anticipate faster, it's suggested that the device has greater memory and faster processors.

6.2.3 SOFTWARE INTERFACES

To use DL, often known as neural network models, a library called Tensor Flow must be imported into Python. In addition, Keras, a comparable library, has been imported to facilitate computational methods. Pandas, NumPy, SKlearn, and other supporting libraries are included. Matplotlib is a library that's used to map data into graph format. The algorithms are run using Pycharm or Jupyter Notebooks. Also, the allocation of medical data was tracked using Neo4j. Cypher script was mainly utilized to form graphical relations in the dataset [7].

6.2.4 STAGES OF THE SYSTEM (FIGURE 6.1)

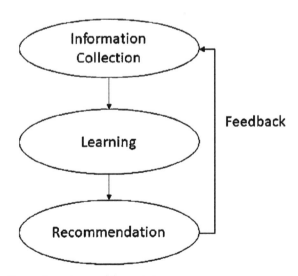

FIGURE 6.1 The various stages of the system.

6.2.4.1   INFORMATION COLLECTION STAGE

This stage gathers crucial clinical information and creates a patient history based on the patient's characteristics, habits, or tools utilized. A recommendation systems engine cannot function correctly sans a well-defined patient assessment. A recommendation systems framework is structured on data gathered through many methods, such as formative assessments, implicit responses, and multimodal feedback. Clear and unambiguous honest feedback is offered by patients based on their involvement in an object, whereas implicit appraisal is done indirectly by monitoring patient behavior.

6.2.4.2   LEARNING STAGE

This whole step takes an appraisal of the situation acquired in the previous phase as inputs and strategies it as outputs by applying a pre-trained model to utilize the patient's traits.

6.2.4.3   RECOMMENDATION STAGE

Patients at this stage should be given optimal pharmaceuticals. The system can make a forecast depending on the model, memory-based, or observable actions of patients by assessing review and evaluation during the data collection stage.

6.2.4.4   FEEDBACK STAGE

At this stage, feedback is taken from the patient, collected as data, and relayed back to the information stage [8].

6.2.5   SYSTEM ANALYSIS AND DESIGN

The data for medicines is massive and includes a variety of criteria. The data set is divided into diseases, and the data indicated drugs as well as feedback from patients who have used it. This data was utilized to train the model and forecast the medicine using AI techniques.

6.2.5.1   GRAPHICAL USER INTERFACE

The prescription system collects information from the patient regarding the ailments that the patient is experiencing, and then recommends various drugs which could be used to treat the illnesses.

6.2.5.2   RELIABILITY AND AVAILABILITY

Because it would not rely on the internet or cloud computing, this system would be readily scalable. This solution relies on pre-stored information and therefore doesn't require a connection to a third-party provider for resource management.

6.2.5.3   PERFORMANCE

This method outperforms other approaches in terms of productivity. It has a root mean square error (RMSE) between 2.5 and 2.9, which really is higher than just about any other technique currently used [8].

The personalized recommendation framework is structured on predictive modeling, which anticipates and suggests suitable things to patients. This mechanism can be used for a variety of purposes. Healthcare analytics is a significant field of big data analytics that can be included in recommendation systems. The proposed health-based framework is a decision-making solution that gives appropriate health-related information to both patients and caregivers as end users. Patients are recommended the right diagnosis and management to minimize a potential hazard by using this approach, and medical practitioners' profit from the extraction of features of crucial data for clinical practice guidelines and the distribution of high-quality health treatments to patients. This Module should be dependable so that potential users can stand to gain from it.

Medical institutions may leverage the relationships underlying their current data to achieve new possibilities and advantages. That summary of the graph database inside the healthcare area is currently among the most quantifiable features of the medical field in the linked genomic, or managed services platform and/or therapy. Among some of the healthcare software accessible, Neo4j technology can give a simpler and more efficient relevance to huge databases that would otherwise ravage this field, based upon the diagram data model that connects millions of free-text keywords utilized in the public healthcare group [9].

6.3   RESULTS AND DISCUSSION

As a multidimensional array, TensorFlow takes input, also called tensors. Users can create a kind of flow chart that they wish to conduct on this entry (called a graph). The input enters at one endpoint and then runs through this multiple operating system and exits at the other point. That is because the tensor passes through the operation list and then arrives at the other end. It's called TensorFlow. It's designed to become accessible to anybody. TensorFlow is the finest library of all. The TensorFlow library includes many APIs to build DL architectures such as CNN or RNN. TensorFlow is built on a schematic analysis, allowing the programmer to view the creation using the Tensor board of the neural net. It's useful for debugging the software. TensorFlow has now been designed to be used on a scale where CPU and GPU are operated on a mass level.

Keras is a Python-based high-level neural network API that can operate on TensorFlow, CNTK, or Theano. It was created with the emphasis on quick experiments. This is important to make a deep dive from concept to concept with the minimal possible delay. NumPy is a Python library open source used mostly for scientific computing and has certain characteristics that enable the usage of high-efficiency arrays and matrices by a Python coder. Furthermore, Pandas is a data handling tool that leverages R-Data Frame objects as well as different R packages.

Cosine similarity is a technique used to assess how equivalent two things are regardless of their size or type. It estimates the cosine of an angle in multi-dimensional distance between two vectors. In this way we can estimate the similarity of any sort of material. Because of a multidimensional array, it's possible to utilize a certain set of possibilities or dimensions, supporting huge texts in turn. The cosine of the angle of two vectors is calculated theoretically from the point-product of the two vectors divided by the product of the magnitude of the two vectors. The similarity equation used to calculate theoretical point-product of two vectors is shown in Eqn. (1):

$$Similarity\ (p,q) = \cos\theta = \frac{p \cdot q}{\|p\|\|q\|} = \frac{\sum\limits_{i=1}^{n} p_i q_i}{\sqrt{\sum\limits_{i=1}^{n} p_i^2}\ \sqrt{\sum\limits_{i=1}^{n} p_i^2}} \qquad (1)$$

This graph depicts that there are more female patients registered in the database rather than male patients (Figures 6.2 and 6.3).

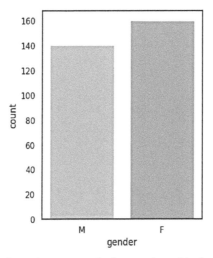

FIGURE 6.2 Gender wise patients count who have registered in the database.

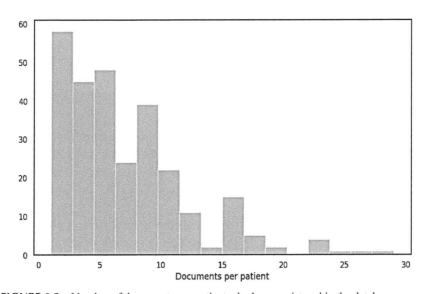

FIGURE 6.3 Number of documents per patient who have registered in the database.

This bar graph shows the number of documents that are registered per patient. A higher number of patients have documents less than 5. The number of patients having more documents decreases with the number of documents, with less than 10 patients having documents more than 20 (Figure 6.4).

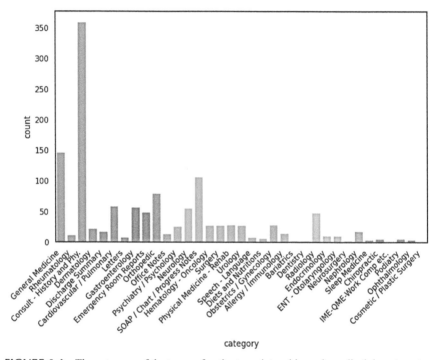

FIGURE 6.4   The category of the types of patients registered in each medical department.

The chart depicts the types of patients that are registered in the medical department. More patients are registered as consult-history and physiology than general medicine. Other prominent departments to have a sizable number of patients include SOAP/chart/progress notes, orthopedic, cardiovascular/pulmonary, and gastroenterology (Figure 6.5).

The graph describes the age of the patients that are registered in the database. Patients aged 50 to 60 are the highest in number, followed by patients aged 40 to 50 (Figure 6.6).

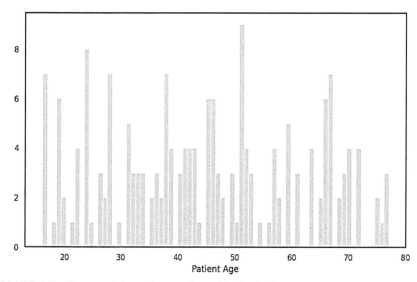

FIGURE 6.5   The age of the patients registered in the database.

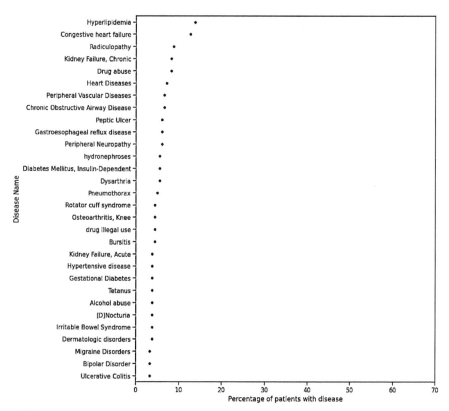

FIGURE 6.6   The percentage of patients with disease.

The scatter plot shows the spread of the percentage of patients with disease. Hyperlipidemia has the highest percentage of patients per disease while Ulcerative Colitis has the lowest percentage per disease (Figure 6.7).

FIGURE 6.7   Word cloud of the top 10 diseases affecting the patients.

Most repeated words in the database are featured in the word cloud. Some of the words include supplement (Figure 6.8).

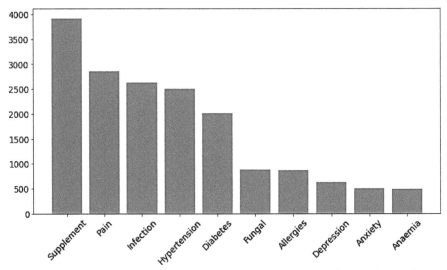

FIGURE 6.8   Top 10 diseases affecting the highest number of patients registered in the system.

Common diseases have a higher number of patients compared to rarer diseases (Figure 6.9).

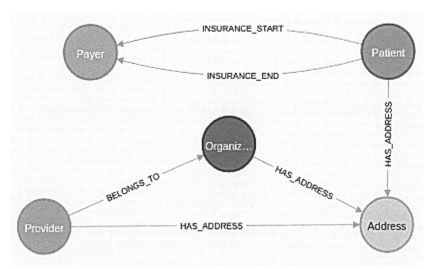

FIGURE 6.9 Relationship indicating the time at which medical coverage had started or ended generated using neo4j.

The patient and the provider are connected through a common address in the Neo4j while the provider belongs to the organizer who has access to the address along with the patient (Tables 6.1 and 6.2).

TABLE 6.1 Drugs Available in the Inventory – Query Response in neo4j

Drug Name	Count
Gefer Capsule 10'S	2
M Cold Plus CZ Tablet 10'S	2
Berirab P 300 IU Injection 2 ml Berirab P 750 mg Injection 5 ml	1
Cepy 1,000 mg Injection 1'SCepy 250 mg Injection 1'S	1
C One SB 1,000/500 mg Injection 1'SC One SB 375 mg Injection 1'S	1
Fortagesic Tablet 10'S	1
Caldikind Suspension 200 ml Caldikind 60 K Sachet 1 gm	1
DOZEE M Tablet 10's	1
BG Prot Syrup 200 ml BG PROT Syrup 450 ml	1
Human Monotard 40IU Injection 10 ml	1
Human Monotard 100IU Injection 10 ml	

TABLE 6.2   Comparison of RMSE (Root Mean Square Error) of Different Classifiers

Number of Epoch	KNN	RBM	CNN	SVM
2	2.64777	2.69252	2.70322	2.85532
4	2.68838	2.67733	2.68529	2.82468
6	2.76137	2.66228	2.67414	2.78478
8	2.74317	2.62367	2.63333	2.74989
10	2.73245	2.58211	2.58477	2.74155

The comparison analysis is based on RMSE which is calculated and checked for:

$$RMSE = \sqrt{\frac{\sum_{i=1}^{n}(y_i - \hat{y})^2}{n}} \tag{2}$$

where *RMSE* is the root-mean-square error; i is the data point number; n is the number of non-missing data points; y_i is the actual observations time series, $\hat{y} = $ estimated time series.

6.4   CONCLUSION

This chapter develops a conceptual model for the recommendation of common healthcare that includes a database management method, data pre-processing layer, concept recommendation subsystem, measurement, and evaluation subsystem and system data visualization, using big data technology for diagnostic purposes. But every component is specifically implemented on the basis of an open database. The studies are conducted for evaluating these models for its better performance in these public datasets for the medicine recommendation system. This chapter has also suggested a graphical visualization of allocation of medical resources using Neo4j, which guarantees variety as well as quality of services, with respect to medical viewpoint.

6.4.1   FUTURE ENHANCEMENTS

A cluster-algorithm could be otherwise proposed for something like the grouping of patients' illness and disability relying on the manifestations retrieved from huge history examination information to track the more precise signs of disease, particularly in illnesses with many phases of therapy and multi-pathogenesis which can also be used and distributed so that the useful know-how of skilled healthcare practitioners in diagnosing and treating diseases is available with ease. For providers and nurses, dynamic suggestion displays could be created and deployed. These recordkeeping requirements as well as the appropriate therapeutic suggestions may be accessed at numerous therapy phases by healthcare providers and clients. Anyone can amend the findings of the assessment to get suggestions. Throughout the data repository, significant amounts of clinical information could be kept for achievement of improved performance and reduced delay-sensitive responsiveness requirements and a concurrent productive capacity on the software system can be used.

KEYWORDS

- **Artificial Intelligence**
- **Auto-Encoder**
- **Convolutional Neural Network**
- **Healthcare**
- **Multilayer Perceptron**
- **Personalized System**
- **Resource Allocation**

REFERENCES

1. Kruse, C. S., Anna, S., Heather, T., & Harmander, K., (2018). The use of electronic health records to support population health: A systematic review of the literature. *Journal of Medical Systems, 42*(11), 1–16.
2. Choi, E., Mohammad, T. B., Andy, S., Walter, F. S., & Jimeng, S., (2016). Doctor AI: Predicting clinical events via recurrent neural networks. In: *Machine Learning for Healthcare Conference* (pp. 301–318). PMLR.
3. Chen, J., Kenli, L., Huigui, R., Kashif, B., Nan, Y., & Keqin, L., (2018). A disease diagnosis and treatment recommendation system based on big data mining and cloud computing. *Information Sciences, 435*, 124–149.
4. Zhu, Z., Xionghui, Z., & Kang, S., (2019). A novel approach based on Neo4j for multi-constrained flexible job shop scheduling problem. *Computers & Industrial Engineering, 130*, 671–686.

5. Ballas, I., Vassilios, T., Evaggelos, P., & Vassilios, T., (2020). Assessing the computational limits of GraphDBs' engines-a comparison study between Neo4j and Apache spark. In: *24th Pan-Hellenic Conference on Informatics* (pp. 428–433).

6. Kraljevic, Z., Thomas, S., Anthony, S., Lukasz, R., Kawsar, N., Daniel, B., Aurelie, M., et al., (2021). Multi-domain clinical natural language processing with medCAT: The medical concept annotation toolkit. *Artificial Intelligence in Medicine, 117*, 102083.

7. Goyal, V. A., Dilip, J. P., Namaskar, I. J., & Komal, C., (2020). Medicine recommendation system. *Medicine, 7*(03).

8. Sahoo, A. K., Chittaranjan, P., Rabindra, K. B., & Harishchandra, D., (2019). DeepReco: Deep learning-based health recommender system using collaborative filtering. *Computation, 7*(2), 25.

9. Isinkaye, F., Folajimi, Y., & Ojokoh, B., (2015). Recommendation systems: Principles, methods and evaluation. *Egyptian Informatics Journal, 16*. 10.1016/j.eij.2015.06.005.

10. Gil, M., Reem El, S., Manon, P., Benjamin, C. M. F., Roland, G., & Pierre, P., (2019). Towards a knowledge-based recommender system for linking electronic patient records with continuing medical education information at the point of care. *IEEE Access, 7*, 15955–15966.

PREDICTION OF AUTISTIC SPECTRAL DISORDER INFLICTIONS AMONG CHILDREN USING REINFORCEMENT-BASED LEARNING APPROACH

KIRAN L. N. ERANKI

Associate Professor, School of Computer Science and AI, SR University, Warangal, Telangana, India

ABSTRACT

Development of skills for social, communication, and behavior is delayed among some children due to autism spectral disorders (ASD). We attempt to address learning disorders among autistic learners through user profile characterization. Reinforcement learning (RL) facilitates measures to identify metrics based on standardized test results of each learner. Autism challenge dataset was used for the analysis and compared using fMRI (functional magnetic resonance imagery) data to determine the level of autism among the learners. Theoretical model of exploration – exploitation traits would be applied to predict the progress of the learner. Parameterized RL approach is also applied to characterize the learner's profile and generate a knowledge graph to assess the learner on numerical, communication, and comprehension skills. Research studies have shown that during the learning process, four main characteristics related to prior knowledge, learning style, intelligence, and motivation are important factors for any learning process. We applied a deep learning (DL) neural network with auto-encoder (AE), CNN model to determine the autistic characteristics. Our proposed model outperforms by more than 86% accuracy and can be extended to other spectral disorders

Handbook of Research on Artificial Intelligence and Soft Computing Techniques in Personalized Healthcare Services, Uma N. Dulhare, A. V. Senthil Kumar, Amit Datta, Seddik Bri, Ibrahiem M. M. El Emary, (Eds.)
© 2024 Apple Academic Press, Inc. Co-published with CRC Press (Taylor & Francis)

depending on the knowledge-repository and hyper-parameter fine tuning of machine learning (ML) applied to address the infliction disorders.

7.1   INTRODUCTION

Recent studies related to child mental health disorders reveals that almost 56.3% of urban middle-class children (1–10 years of age) suffer from Autism [1]. ASD is a disability which restricts children on communication, thought process and sociability [2]. However, the effect of disorder in some of these children is inevident, as they exhibit extraordinary performance in studies, artistic skills, questioning the potential capabilities of such children is a research curiosity for scientists to provide answers. Studies conducted by Elveva et al. using Latent Dirchlet Analysis (LDA) to reduce speech issues and prediction of conversational coherence, phonetic consistency and content disparities among the participants showed better accuracy.

Research studies have shown increased communication coherence could be associated with children having psychotic disorders with clinical risk of 70–80% accuracy [3]. Other approaches applied in NLP to predict autistic disorders include graph analysis [4], weighted measure of lexical and logical density [5] and figurative expression detection [6].

Natural language processing (NLP) based methods contributed to 10% of improvement in language disorders compared to traditional approaches. Automated expression synthesis also contributed to some improved scores in communication among some subjects. Using a corpus of word dictionaries, sentences, and phonemes to reiterate the language pronunciation, sentence structure among the subjects showed more than 70% accuracy.

Furthermore, harnessing the benefits of NLP semantic analysis also accounted for a variance of performance between clinical ratings and tests conducted through automated speech recognition systems based on word per sentence pronunciations, word identification, word phonetic and n-gram features to discriminate between autistic disorder and control speech children showing 80% accuracy [7].

However, studies with negative or conflicting results were also noticed pertaining to usage of NLP in speech recognition and its disorders in children. Usage of emotion words has also shown a progressive effect on speech infliction disorders. Existing NLP methods in speech disorder use GloVe and Word2Vec [8] to analyze non-coherent word pronunciations, identification, and recognition. However, these methods are unable to implement contextual clues such as for word *bank – Ajay plans to visit bank; Walking along the banks*, these two sentences are completely different in context but referred with same word.

Current research work attempts to address some of these challenges and provides possible solutions through the application of cognitive science and machine learning (ML) methods. To address mental disability issues such as poor conversational skills, low numerical recognition issues characterized as ASD. ML techniques such as SVM, reinforcement learning (RL), HMM, forward and backward chaining and others have been applied to perform prediction. ML methods help to identify the pattern of learning behaviors inputs, which could help clinicians and trainers, provide robust diagnoses and prognoses for disorders. Followed by we present the research methodology used in the study, analysis of our findings and conclude with future scope of the work.

7.2 LITERATURE REVIEW

Neuroimaging data serves as ASD biomarker using autism brain imaging data exchange (ABIDE) providing large collection of gathered from multiple subjects related to structural and function magnetic resonance imaging (fMRI) along with dimensionality quality metrics provided in public domain [9]. ABIDE data provides the necessary features to perform statistical analysis and apply ML algorithms. Studies conducted by Ghiassian et al. [10] applied feature extraction from fMRI, sMRI using ABIDE dataset and obtained 65% accuracy. Another study by Sen et al. [11] using sMRI and rs-fMRI data using support vector machine (SVM) classifier improved the accuracy by 0.042%. In addition to existing features of ABIDE dataset Katuwal et al. [12] added verbal IQ and age features by evaluating them to random forest (RF) classifier which gave them improved AUC of 0.68. Based on standard assessment tests conducted on thought, language, and communication (TLC) evaluating on features between healthy control (HC) subjects and autistic spectral disorder (ASD) subjects as shown in Table 7.1. A sample of 22 subjects were evaluated using TLC assessment and the sample is distributed by gender, ethnicity, educational level, recording characteristics of the subjects based on duration of recording (min) an average timeframe of 11–13 min. has been chosen for the study. Mean sentence length and word count was recorded and compared with language metrics as well. And the processed TLC data is also evaluated using the bidirectional representations from transformer (BERT) model score comparing with the subject scores. Most of the studies showed subject specific scores on communication as listed in Table 7.1. Results show clinically significant language disorder among five ASD participants (5.0±9.0) which doesn't exist among HC participants. Two ASD participants with overall scores ≤2 is removed as outliers in this sample. However, these outliers do not contribute to any significant change in global scores as shown in Table 7.1. We have taken the TLC datasets and its findings to compare it with the Autistic dataset obtained from ABIDE open-source repository. In the current study, Q-learning approach has been applied to study the effect of ASD infliction among the subjects. RL applies the learning by maximizing the reward for a given action *at* to reach a goal or reward state *st*. Q-learning implements off-policy RL where in *[action, state]* parameters can choose a random policy rather than opting for policy with max reward. As a result, this approach allows the learning to happen with either *exploration or exploitation* within the environment. The Q-learning state, action can be described as shown in Eqn. (1) [14].

$$Q\pi(st,at) = \alpha[Rt + 1 + \gamma Rt + 2 + \gamma 2Rt + 3 \ldots -Q(st,at)]$$ (1)

$Q\pi(st,at)$ is the expected cumulative action to be performed for a given action *a* to reach a goal state *s*. While $E[Rt+1 + \gamma\ Rt+2$ provides the temporal difference between expected discounted reward for the given *[st,at]* action and goal states of the episode. Learning rate (α) would be $0 < \alpha \geq 1$ and discounted factor (γ) would be $0 \leq \gamma \geq 1$, making it off-policy to choose the reward in near future (1) or immediate (0), making it greedy. By considering exploitation rather than exploration by utilizing the existing data points to consider for reward, the trade-off between exploration and exploitation can be identified using ϵ factor which determines the learning policy to be implemented for the reward-penalty episodes.

Intelligent tutoring systems (ITS) are a promising means of teaching children with ASD [15]. However, most existing ITS are not directly applicable for children with ASD for several reasons. First, most ITS lack support for children with neurological disorders. Fail to account for the working memory deficits common among ASD [16]. Similarly, children with ASD also show higher overwhelmed behavior as they progress from one zone of proximal development to another which is not effectively captured by ITS [17]. By not considering the Zone of Proximal Development of these students, an ITS may pose questions that cause the student to either become bored or discouraged. Second, most existing ITS put static tutoring strategies, where

TABLE 7.1 Descriptive Analysis of TLC Assessment Test between ASD and HC Subjects

Sample	HC	ASD	p	d
N	10	12	–	–
Cohort 1	5	6	–	–
Cohort 2	5	6	–	–
Age	36.8±5.8	37.5±5.5	–	0.12
Gender (n, %)				
Female	4(40%)	5(50%)	0.32	–
Male	6(60%)	7(70%)	–	–
Race (n, %)				
African, American	7(70%)	6(60%)	–	–
Asian	3(30%)	6(60%)	–	–
Education level	16±2.5	15.5±2.5	0.01	–1.00
Recording Attributes				
Record (min)	10.8±5.5	11.8±6.5	0.52	0.33
Average count	16.8±2.5	15.5±2.5	0.03	0.88
Word count	1,660±480	1,720±360	0.84	0.04
Language Metrics				
Global TLC scores	0.0	0.51.0	0.11	0.66
Obtained scores – TLC	0.91.8	5.0±9.0	0.10	0.4
Sentence prediction – BERT score	0.94±0.02	0.93±0.02	0.18	0.45

Note: Assessment scale for TLC provided by Andreasen et al. [5] has been used for analysis.

each child is presented with the same sequence of lessons and examples irrespective of their performance on previous lessons. Customized tutoring strategies are especially desirable for students with ASD, as the challenges each individual faces differ widely; thus, teaching policies must be tailored accordingly. RL offers one way of customizing these tutoring strategies;

7.2.1 IMAGE-BASED PREDICTION APPROACH

Recent studies have shown increased usage of neural network-based models on brain tumors, autism, and ASD image datasets. Datasets for study were taken from public access autism challenge [18] to identify autism disorders among individuals from the controlled sample. In another study, CNN model was used to perform classification of placebo subjects and control group with autistic characteristics on their neural network using resting state functional MRI data. The sample used for the study had 500 ASD participants and 550 placebo control group subjects data obtained from 15 different image challenge portals. CNN architecture used auto-encoder (AE) to extract low dimensionality features. These models gave 71% accuracy and 61% specificity which authors believe model performed better than support vector kernels (SVM) and ensemble classifiers. Studies have also show noise as important factor caused due to varying intensity resolutions of the scanned images and also computing power necessary to perform the required number of epochs to run the model. So depending upon the GPU and memory requirements fine tuning of hyper-parameters was done to improve model performance.

Studies related to attention deficit disorders (ADHD) and ASD carried using 3D functional MRI (fMRI) datasets [11], showed the multi-model features of the learner brain morphology to predict the differences and similarities among the two disorders. Authors obtained 69% accuracy with ADHD-200 datasets and 66% accuracy with ABIDE datasets. Although these results were not clinically proven as several other factors vary to conclude the relationship between both. However, similar studies conducted by Parikh et al. [19] using profile characteristic data gathered from 800 subjects comprising 450 ASD and rest non-ASD recorded in ABIDE data-sets to predict autistic disorders gave better performance metrics compared to earlier models discussed. Learner characteristic data has contributed to improved performance of the model compared to other models. Most of the existing models used multiple sources of clinical datasets which mostly lacked uniform structure and were provided with a lot of noise or outlier data which requires a lot of pre-processing procedures to data augmentation, storage size as well. As most of the datasets are either in MRI scanned data or textual metadata provided along with image to re-structure the original MRI image mappings. Studies have also used synthetic sampling technique (SMOTE) [20] which allows the data augmentation of fmRI datasets gave 73% accuracy. In the remaining section, we will also present questionnaire based and behavioral based prediction methods popular in the ASD and ADHD research.

7.2.2 QUESTIONNAIRE-BASED PREDICTION APPROACH

Research studies conducted using crowd-sourced short home videos by the parents of the children aged between 2 and 17 yrs. with prior consent of approval procedures was analyzed using a standardized questionnaire [21]. The survey questionnaire was collected from 250 ASD and 150 ADHD subjects which was correlated with a survey conducted earlier comprising of 2550 ASD and 150 ADHD subjects. Both the datasets were subjected to five different types of classifiers was used namely – Elastic Net, L1 and L2 regularization, SVM, discriminate classifier to analyze the responses recorded from the subjects. When new survey and old survey datasets were trained on these five models, results showed an accuracy of 90% for both Elastic net and LDA models while using a combined randomized dataset gave an accuracy of 88% which is still promising considering the performance of the model is well tuned. One limitation with datasets obtained through crowd gathering is the quality of the observations recorded as most of them were biased as subject responses were recorded by parents themselves which could have overfit or underfit the model performance. So due care has to be taken in terms of validity and reliability of sample collected from such studies, as authors claim to have taken care of validity of samples confirming the results to be legitimate.

In another study conducted by researchers in a controlled environment by bringing the subjects to the research facility who have agreed to share their responses with due consent of approvals to study ASD and ADHD subjects [22]. The study used standard Questionnaire repository validated on Autistic Diagnostic Interview formats gathered from 2,300 samples split across 1,580 ASD, 360 ADHD and rest with other speech ailments. Responses from the questionnaire are subjected to ridge regression (L2 regularization). Results of the study show improved accuracy using questionnaire approach. Compared to earlier crowd sourced datasets, as data was collected without the intervention of parents and researchers had better control on the validity and reliability of the model design.

7.2.3 BEHAVIORAL-BASED PREDICTION APPROACH

We now look at behavioral measures applied to predict ASD and ADHD characteristics among the subjects [23]. These studies were conducted using the social responsiveness scale (SRS) based questionnaire to collect the response of the subjects. Datasets were obtained from autism genetic resource exchange (AGRE) [24] which had 2350 ASD and 150 ADHD subjects. Datasets were evaluated using ML models – SVM, RF, LDA, regression models, Decision tree to minimize error, redundancy besides fine tuning the model fit issues. Results of the study gave 96.5% accuracy considering only 5 out of 65 behaviors indicators identified from the datasets. However, one drawback of the study was related to the imbalance data obtained from ASD and ADHD subjects. Authors have used TensorFlow architecture with ReLU activation function to support both high sparse and large search space through normalization. The study was performed using ResNets, MobileNets, and EfficientNets which can be applied to both Batch dependent architecture as well as sample dependent by accepting only certain set of batches and rejecting the other based on a penalty (λ) function applied to the normalization. Results show that combination of architecture lead to improved model performance and also well generalized to support different kinds of classification, prediction tasks efficiently. Followed by the remaining sections of the chapter discuss on improved ML models build on hybrid AE classifier used in the prediction.

7.3   IMPROVED MACHINE LEARNING (ML) MODELS

In this section, we will discuss about the improved ML models used in the implementation of AE based classifier. We have combined the features of AE with other well know classifiers in deep learning (DL) architectures for dimensionality reduction and improved model performance. We have considered K-nearest neighbor (KNN), RF, and SVMs from ML models. And from DL models we have considered convolutional neural network (CNN) architecture. We will discuss about each of these models and their role in the implementation of hybrid architecture.

7.3.1   AUTO-ENCODER (AE)

In any ML models where information encoding and decoding is required to retain the essential information without much loss is performed using AE. It takes the input and creates a similar number of output nodes as it does required labeled data so it works with unsupervised datasets. Mathematically, the two essential components of AE consist of encoder which takes y input and creates a same number of nodes for y' which is referred as decoder. AE performs a dimensionality reduction using non-linear optimization function as shown in Eqns. (2) and (3). From Eqn. (2), where h is the hidden layer, and its function value is obtained by multiplying the vector x with weights W, bias b and activation function (σ). The decoder x' would be Eqn. (3).

$$h = \sigma(W_y + b) \tag{2}$$

$$y' = W_h + b \tag{3}$$

AEs occur in multiple variants to the need within the architecture such as adversarial, sparse, and de-noising AEs where each variant has been designed to perform specific task. One of the challenges in medical imaging classification is to reduce re-construction error while generating the input image from the output image. As the typical medical imagery obtained from raw scanning device provides datasets in large dimensions and require more storage, GPU, and memory. AEs help to overcome the dimensionality issue by reducing the input data without losing any essential detail while re-constructing the output. Studies have also shown the usage of principal component analysis (PCA), Feature selection algorithms such as Fourier Transformation, Wavelets are applied in dimensionality reduction methods. Studies have shown the usage of AEs for handwriting recognition using MNIST datasets where the performance was better than PCA. Results also show that AE not only helped in dimensionality reduction but also in projecting the digit representation correctly signifying the role of building recurrent structures [25]. As the essential details of the input data are retained even in the output generated from the encoder segment which can directly be sent to the other neural networks to improve the performance of the model.

7.3.2 SUPPORT VECTOR MACHINES (SVMS)

Support vector machine (SVM) Kernels are applied to handle non-linear data using linear regression and classification tasks. As shown in Figure 7.1 when given data set has multiple class which have to be classified as labeled in N-dimensional vector space. Consider two classes as shown in the figure, in order to segregate the classes into two different clusters SVM implements hyperplane. Using which the margin of the hyperplane determines the amount of penalty and weight (W) to estimate the accuracy of the model. From the figure, we can see class A data points are close to hyperplane Y1 and similarly class B data points are close to Y3 and in between the two hyperplanes we find a marginal difference represented using another hyperplane Y2. While performing binary classification of data based on the distribution of data points across the vector space determines the penalty (ε) considering the slack variable gives marginal difference for a given bias (b) using Eqn. (4):

$$yi(Wxi + b) \geq 1 - \varepsilon \qquad (4)$$

SVM uses different types of kernels to perform dot product of transformed input vectors allowing to apply non-linear boundaries as well. As a result, SVM kernels can be applied to different forms of data even if the data is sparsely spread across the vector space or densely populated with multiple classes. By selecting the appropriate kernel functions we will be able to analyze the data points into appropriate classes. Which also means we still be using linear classifier for non-linear datasets. However, one drawback with this approach is model overfitting as we tend to increase the number of epochs and reduce learning of the model. So optimal fine tuning of the hyper-parameters is required to improve the performance and fine tune the model.

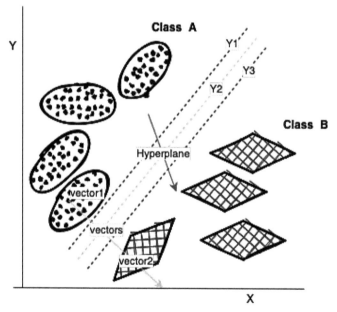

FIGURE 7.1   Support vector machine with two class classification model and hyperplane to segregate the data points in N-dimensional vector space.

7.3.3   RANDOM FOREST (RF)

This is an ensemble approach to perform classification using decision trees. Each forest comprises of selective set of decision trees which determines the number of classes formed and their classification criteria. One disadvantage with decision trees is the formation of split and convergence criteria which fails to generate a correct number of branches leaving sometimes with unbalanced tree structure. RF model improves the decision tree disadvantage by using bootstrapping and boosting methods as shown in Figure 7.2.

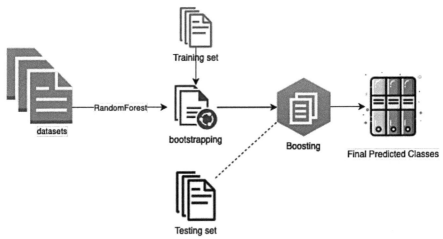

FIGURE 7.2   Random forest implementation showing data flow and prediction approach to classify the data points within the datasets.

Selection process of RF involves the following phases:

1. **Phase 1:** Selection of decision trees from the datasets using the bootstrap method. After the pre-processing datasets are distributed as training, test sets. While the set selected for train would generate decision trees by selecting only certain set of columns or features within the dataset and leaving the rest. Same procedure is carried till entire dataset get exhausted.

2. **Phase 2:** Random subset of variables are considered at each iteration of bootstrap and chosen as eligible candidate trees for selection.

3. **Phase 3:** Selected decision trees become eligible for voting which contest among all the other trees formed from the datasets.

4. **Phase 4:** Decision trees chosen with the highest votes will be tested with the testing datasets to make the final prediction out which also computes the entropy, loss function to determine the accuracy of the classifier.

7.3.4   K-NEAREST NEIGHBORS (KNNS) CLASSIFIER

K-nearest model applies using unsupervised learning approach by computing the median of a centroid formed by the closest data points located in the vicinity of the centroid. By considering the k for the given neighborhood of x data points. As no label or class are provided in the datasets. Based on the characteristics or features extracted from the datasets cluster of proximity will be formed. Size of the cluster is determined by the ε values of the cluster and the number of data points to be considered. Performance of the algorithm degrades as the size of the data points considered for clustering increase, eventually, this also leads to over-fitting of the model considering the outliers are also part of the datasets classified as clusters.

7.4   CONVOLUTION NEURAL NETWORK (CNN)

Convolution neural network (CNN) is used for image applications. Neural network model uses image datasets as the input and classifies them into binary or multi-class representations depending upon the number of features and classes considered for training the model. In the rest of the section, we will discuss some of the essential operations performed in CNN to improve the performance of the model.

7.4.1   STRIDE

CNN architecture takes the input images of larger dimensions and processes it to smaller image segments performed using convoluted layers run with kernels or filters to reduce the dimensionality of the datasets. As shown in the example, stride process implements a filter by shifting two units at a time. For example, as shown in Figure 7.3, when filter or kernel is convoluted on the image matrix, the dimension of the image would be transformed from 5×5 to 2×2. Stride is implemented by multiplying corresponding pixel with the filter pixel, when stride = 2, we get $(1\times2) + (0\times0) + (3\times2) + (2\times1) = 10$; Similarly when stride=1 it gives $(1\times0) + (2\times2) + (2\times2) + (1\times1) = 9$; The reduced size of the image is computed using Eqn. (11).

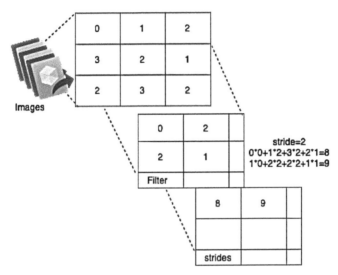

FIGURE 7.3 Stride operation convolutes the image size to reduced size by running the kernel.

Given the input image (*imageinput*) and provided with padding size of $p=0$. While kernel or filter size applied is 2 along with the stride s factor of 2 to generate the required number of output features as (*imageout*). Using Eqn. (5), we can compute the required number of features output from the given input features.

$$Image_{out} = \frac{Image_{in} + 2p - k}{s} + 1 \qquad (5)$$

7.4.2 PADDING

Through padding we pad the non-existing image pixels is required with zero to the edges of the image which helps in detecting feature from extreme corners of matrix which otherwise could be lost if not padded. Considering we provide an image of $5\times5\times1$ dimensions and pad it with zeros considering $p=2$ leads to $7\times7\times1$ image size. In the remaining section, we will focus on max-pooling feature which helps in dimensionality reduction and increases the computation power of the model.

7.4.3   MAX-POOLING

Max-pooling improves model performance through dimensionality reduction and retaining the essential information. Two different type of pooling is usually implemented in CNN architectures using either average or maximum pooling. Max-pooling selects the largest values among the members of the kernel. Whereas the average pooling takes the mid value of image matrix as the kernel. Given a 4×4 image as input with a stride =2 when subjected to max pooling would pick the top or highest value returned from the matrix is considered. On the other hand, if the same input image is considered for average polling the median or mid value returned from the image matrix of the kernel is taken.

All the methods and classifiers explained in this section have been applied to the proposed hybrid model implemented. Subsequently, discussion on research methodology, datasets, and preprocessing methods applied. Followed by we will present the model implementation, evaluation with analysis and discussion. Finally, we will conclude the study with our findings and future scope of the work, its extensibility for another researcher to improve the existing model performance.

7.4.4   HYBRID ARCHITECTURE ENVIRONMENT

Hybrid AE based CNN architecture was built using Pytourch, Keras, and TensorFlow. Improved ML model using Scikit package. We also run the CNN architecture by using rectified linear unit (ReLU) and Sigmoid functions (σ). Given a function derivative to predict the likelihood of a features can be explained using Eqn. (6):

$$\sigma(y) = \frac{1}{1+e^{-z}} \tag{6}$$

Similarly, when we provide the functional derivative to predict the likelihood using ReLU can be explained in Eqn. (7):

$$R(x) = \left\{ \begin{smallmatrix} 1 \, if \, x \geq 0 \\ 0 \, if \, x \leq 0 \end{smallmatrix} \right\} \tag{7}$$

7.5   CONTEXTUAL REINFORCEMENT LEARNING (RL) MODEL

Our proposed model uses contextual RL model which broadly comprises of three main segments – contextual infliction analysis and processing from the ABIDE datasets. Implementing Q-learning sequence model to regularize the stimulus-response chain in context dependent features and finally we will automate the RL feedback-response loop through classical conditioning approach. Q-learning algorithm in RL model establishes relationship between stimulus and response states based on the input and conditional action sequence performed by the algorithm [26]. Based on the classical RL model when a stimulus is generated in the context of learning situation, initial learning may be context insensitive which later after a few iterations of training relearning makes context specific. As a result, learning in one context could be generalized for several other contexts as well. However, learning extinct during training need not appear in the subsequent contexts. In our model we have applied the contextual inflictions or features recorded as responses in the ABIDE datasets were used for analysis. This also indicates that RL is controlled by the state-action-response sequence chain contextual flow illustrated in Figure 7.4.

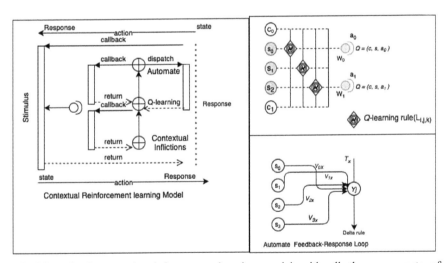

FIGURE 7.4 Contextual reinforcement learning model with all three segments of implementation which contribute to prediction within CNN architecture.

Through this approach, the contextual model acts as working memory capturing the target reactions of the system. This also helps Q-learning to shift the state and action sequences according to the current contextual state. Instead of using a single policy, our approach will have gradual development of state-transition sequences in the RL model pipeline.

7.5.1   CONTEXTUAL INFLICTION PROCESSING

In this segment, we focus on the contextual inflections or features related to autism tasks on attention characteristics obtained from the ABIDE datasets which provide the attention fixations while contextual system starts with $s_i(a) = (s_0, \ldots, s_n)$ state of each stimulus at a_0 and $L_t(a)$ for a given attention spot a_t. Given a set of all fixations points we determine the relationship code $d(X)$, which computes the sum by taking the outer product of two vectors $s_i(a)$ and $L_t(a)$ given in Eqn. (8):

$$d(X) = \sum_{x \in X}^{n} S_t(a) \oplus L_t(a) \tag{8}$$

Each relationship code represents a context or semi-contextual state, where output integrated for each state can be given as $b(t) = (b_0, b_1, \ldots, b_n)$ and output vector for code can be generated using Eqn. (9):

$$b(t+1) = \frac{b_i(t) + \delta d_i + E_i}{\sum_{j=0}^{n} (b_j(t) + \delta d_j + E_j)} \tag{9}$$

While b_i values are used for normalized output; and E_i is additional input added to control the sequence flow as $E_i = \varphi y i(t)$. We determine the learning rate $\varepsilon = 0.001$ and $\varphi = 50$ epochs of iterations are performed.

7.5.2   Q-LEARNING SEQUENCE MODEL

To determine the relationship between stimulus-response sequence is carried using Q-learning algorithm which is used to generalize from one context to another context in a streamlined manner. Given state can be represented using a state vector $s_t = (s_0, \ldots, s_n)$ for action set $a_t = (a_0, a_1, \ldots, a_n)$. By computing the value function $Q(s,ai\ j)$ using which we assign a value for each action produced at each state. We define the context using a context vector $c_t = (c_0, c_1, \ldots, c_n)$ obtained from context system. Followed by we add the context to estimator with weights $uijk$ which binds the weight $wi\ j$ to the context state ck. The sequence flow of the state-action space has been shown in Figure 7.4.

7.5.3   AUTOMATED FEEDBACK-RESPONSE LOOP

Finally, we combine all the RL sequence states obtained through the pipeline to determine the state-action-response feedback loop. This is implemented through classical conditioning approach similar to the traditional eye-blink response mechanism. Apart from conditioning, our model also automates the flow sequence states in the pipeline. First this segment attempts to bind the state-to-state change as it occurs based on an action triggered at that state. And the automated feedback-response loop model has been shown in Figure 7.4.

7.6 DATASETS AND METHODOLOGY APPLIED

In this section, we present the research methodology and datasets applied to conduct the study. We have explained the procedure followed to cleanse the datasets and apply them to the proposed model using parameterized RL algorithm [14].

7.6.1 DATA PRE-PROCESSING

For the current study, we have used the challenging datasets provided by autism challenge community (ABIDE) which provides data related to the functional resonance imagery (fMRI) comprised of 17 different facets of brain facilities. Most classifiers require more computational time for automatic diagnosis and better classification accuracy. The dataset contains details of 125 subjects with ASD and 100 placebo's from the controlled group. ABIDE-II datasets [18] are pre-processed using four different pipelines as provided in by the Autism Spectrum Disorder Research and Clinical Program. These pipelines include – connectome computation system (CCS), Neuro-imaging analysis kit (NIAK), Configurable Connectomes (CPAC) and lastly, data pertaining to state fMRI (DPARSF).

Firstly, all the fMRI images have to extracted using the CPAC pipelines which gathers the details pertaining to slice time, motion correction of the scan device calibration, noise attenuation, frequency swift and voxel rectifications are performed. Using a hybrid CNN architecture with AE along with supervised learning classifiers are integrated to analysis the autism characteristics.

Apart from the CPAC pipeline, other pipelines are also used to gather further information related to variations in heartbeats, head movements and frequency shifts, voxel intensity of the brain as recorded by fMRI device. Bandpass filter and nuisance variable regression was performed to control the variance in signal and frequency output of the datasets. Both functional and anatomical images have to be normalized as they caries varying signal and intensity proportions which is one of the major drawback for several researchers to normalize the data as no standard platforms exist to complete the procedure. We have created a PyTorch and TensorFlow, Keras architecture to disseminate the data from the challenging datasets.

Other parameters such as oxygen levels of the blood, along with metadata provided by atlases namely Harvard-Oxford (HO), Craddock, Anatomical labeling atlas are used for computation. We have provided all the three atlases of three dimensions namely 90×90 fully connected AAL, 110×110 symmetric for HO and 200×200 symmetric fully connected for CC200 atlas. In addition to the fMRI datasets, demographic details are provided in the earlier study conducted by researchers was also applied [27].

7.6.2   MULTI-CHANNEL ATTENUATED DEEP NEURAL NETWORK

Multichannel attenuated neural network architecture consists of inputs blocks from AAL, HO, and CC200 datasets. Neural network comprises of self-attenuated improved perceptron to perform aggregation of voxel intensity, variable regression and resolve model fit issues. We will discuss each of these components and their role in the prediction of ASD characteristics. The architecture uses four densely connected layers with one drop-out layer as illustrated in Figure 7.4. And hybrid neural network architecture is shown in Figure 7.5.

Hybrid CNN architecture aggregates data sets from multi-layer perceptron to process the data and regularize using drop out method. In the figure, white circles denote the layers which are dropped out leaving the rest dense layer. Although neural network is only shown to scale which does comprise of hidden units of four dense layer nodes having 1,024, 512, 128, 32 supported with activation functions namely Sigmoid (σ), tanh (τ), ReLU in the architecture.

Self-attention has gained importance in recent studies considering its usage to predict the alignment score between any two given data sources. As our proposed architecture uses multi-channel data source attention approach works well. Through this approach adjacency matrix with series of sequence $x_i[x_1, x_2, \ldots]$ can be represented as query set $q \in Rd$. Using which we compute the alignment fit between q and subsequent element xi using a fitness function $f(xi,q)$. From the computed alignment score, distribution of best fit is taken by subjecting to SoftMax function as $p(z|x,q)$, where z would be used to determine the element from q. Attention carried in CNN architecture is shown in Eqn. (11):

$$f(xi) = wT\sigma(WdR) \qquad (10)$$

$$p(z = i|x,q) = softmax(\alpha) \tag{11}$$

In addition to self-attention, we also have applied fusion gate to combine the outputs of the two dense layers used in the CNN architecture. As shown in Figure 7.4. Fusion gate can be implemented using Eqn. (12):

$$f = \sigma(Wf1 + Wf2 + bf) \tag{12}$$

where; $Wf1$, $Wf2 \in Rd0$ represent output dimension; and $b\,f$, R represent inputs for fusion gate. Followed by we perform aggregation to data processed. During aggregation, we combine the outputs of both dense layers followed by sigmoid activation functions to classify the data generated.

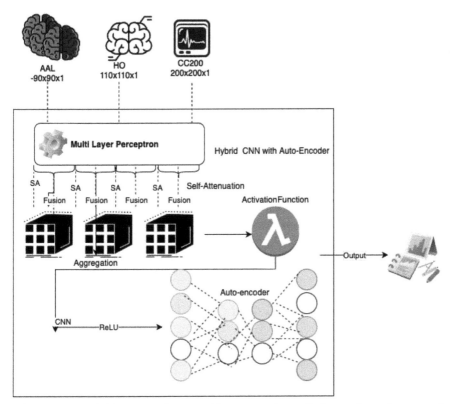

FIGURE 7.5 Hybrid CNN architecture with auto-encoder applied to predict autism spectral disorders.

7.7 HYBRID AUTO-ENCODER (AE) CNN MODEL

We have implemented using AE with self-attention, fusion methods added to the CNN architecture as shown in Figure 7.3. Role of AE is to reduce the reconstruction error caused due to coding-encoding of data as it passes through the AE. Through this addition, the CNN model is able to improve and control performance metric, model fit issues by providing higher accuracy as compared to other classical ML models.

7.7.1 MODEL IMPLEMENTATION AND EVALUATION

Hybrid model was implemented as shown in Figure 7.5. Our implementation has already been done by other researchers with selective ML models [9, 28]. Our approach implements classification using different ML classifiers to improve the prediction of autism characteristics. We also adapted two measure to ensure the randomization of sample and control the model fit issues which is quite common among the classical ML classifiers. ABIDE datasets are subjected to k-fold and skip-one-off validation to ensure that outliers are cleansed and data is available as processed sample which will be put forth to training and testing datasets. Sample for training would be distributed till testing has been evaluated at least once. Similarly leave-one site has also been executed for 40 times to understand the variability of test results to indicate the difference between training and test datasets. Based on the analysis of datasets, we have presented the visualization of results obtained through k-fold and skip-one-off validation of the ABIDE datasets. From the seaborn graphs depicted to visualize the analysis of dataset based on Class/ASD, Jaundice, and Autism were considered as features as shown in Figures 7.6 and 7.7.

7.7.2 MACHINE LEARNING (ML) CLASSIFIERS

Our improved model includes other ML classifiers within the hybrid architecture. Classical classifiers – ensemble forests, KNN, SVM kernels, are used to support multi-channel data acquisition:

- Ensemble forests are used to predict the decision trees formed from the hierarchical classification. Model overfitting needs to be controlled as decision tress classifier suffer from overfit issues which can be controlled in RF using cross-entropy, Gini Index and

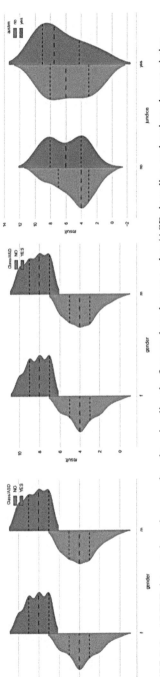

FIGURE 7.6   ABIDE datasets have been analyzed to visualize the features based on age, class/ASD, jaundice, and autism characteristics.

Note: (a) Number of people with jaundice; (b) autism sample; and (c) sample with gender and autism together has been shown in collated data.

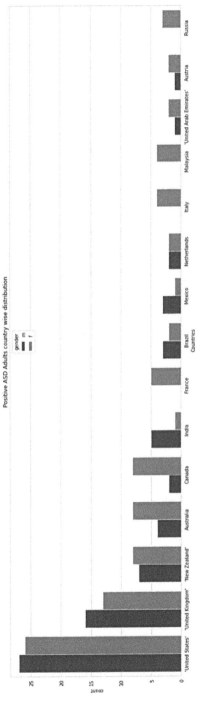

FIGURE 7.7   Graph of country-wise distribution of autism among the subjects.

Information Gain will be computed to analyze the performance of the model.

- SVM Kernels help to fine-tune the binary classification of data using the hyperplane and the margins of the hyperplane would determine the penalty to be applied to control hinge fit error and regularization of the model.

- K-nearest neighbors (KNN) model was applied to perform binary classification of datasets features to predict the feature selection process and improve the model performance. Multi-features are obtained from the ABIDE datasets. However, we ran the correlation matrix after k-fold and skip-one-off validation to predict the correction among the features of the dataset.

- Deep neural net-based hybrid CNN model was built previously for ASD classification [29]. Existing deep neural network model comprises of multiple layers organized as convolution layers which perform stride, padding, and max-pooling operations to process the data as it passes through specified number epochs which determine the model loss function, accuracy performance metrics. Our model is fine-tuned with hyperparameters of 100 epochs and learning rate of 0.00001 (1E4).

We also found KNN algorithm performance on ABIDE dataset which gave an ROC value of 0.68, sensitivity of 0.62 and specificity 0.35 While AUC also gave 0.68 indicating the performance of KNN with AE as well as classical ML model performs better than other models as shown in Figure 7.8. However, the performance of hybrid CNN model was much higher than the KNN and other ML models.

Followed by, we will present the results and discuss about the performance of the model using ABIDE datasets and its metric applied to predict the autism characteristics.

7.8 RESULTS AND DISCUSSION

Results of the study are drawn from comparative analysis of autism prediction using the proposed hybrid CNN model and classical ML models. Evaluation of dataset was performance at 10-fold cross-validation run for 50 epochs to validate the entire ABIDE dataset. The proposed hybrid CNN showed higher accuracy than SVM (16%), and RF (9%). Similarly, hybrid CNN also gave better F1-score compared to SVM (3%), and RF (2%).

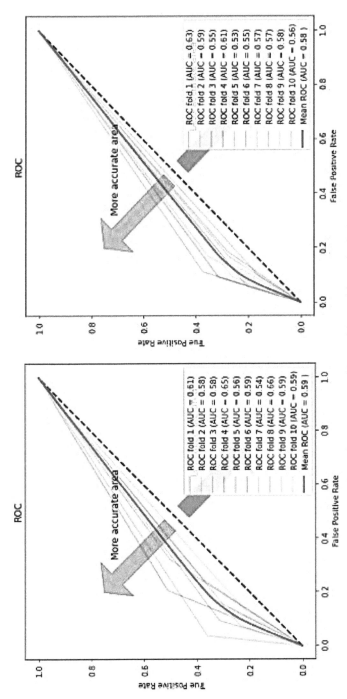

FIGURE 7.8 Graph showing the region under and above true positive to false positive ratios indicating the performance of KNN algorithm.

From the graph we can interpret the relationship between Class/ASD subjects with Jaundice who also claimed to be the relatives of the toddlers with Autism and Jaundice. We found some subject to show this behavior (Figure 7.9).

However, these results also need to be clinically proved to determine, if genetically inherited such characteristics from the parental/maternal relatives is not clear. But result show that the white European community shows such characteristics. Although it is not that prominent for other country origins.

Graphs showing the features between Class/ASD, Parents with ASD, Toddlers with ASD. We have found no specific relation between Toddlers born with ASD and their relative having ASD which indicates that ASD can be hereditary but not necessary that all toddlers born would inherit their paternal/maternal relative ASD characteristics has been shown in Figure 7.6–7.10.

We found the accuracy of AE based CNN significantly better giving 86% as compared to other ML methods. We also found the specificity of CNN (0.0088) was higher as compared to SVM (0.0053), RF (0.002). However, CNN model gave lower sensitivity (0.0068) which has contributed to its precision score. In terms of precision, we found CNN model to be higher as compared to SVM (0.004), RF (0.002). While KNN (0.007) was better as compared to the other two ML models. Overall, the proposed hybrid AE CNN showed improved accuracy and performance metrics when compared with classical ML models. CNN models out perform in all the performance metrics as well as controlling model fit issues.

Interestingly, our model performed well on accuracy by 86%, sensitivity by $p \leq 0.076$, F-score by $p \leq 0.014$, and specificity by $p \leq 0.013$. Attention mechanism in the model will help in identifying which features to select and consider for further processing by calibrating the weights added to features. Model can predict features which contribute to ASD and autism. The performance of the model is also improved and also contributes to the validity of the attention mechanism. We also found the model performance to be significantly better than SVM and RF. Improvement in performance of the model is contributed by attention mechanism carried using self-attention, fusion tasks discussed in earlier sections (Figure 7.11).

7.8.1 LEAVE ONE VALIDATION

Model performance and generalizability requires leave one validation approach to train the datasets repetitively by leaving tuning the hyper-parameter which sets number of each subsets to be given opportunity as test

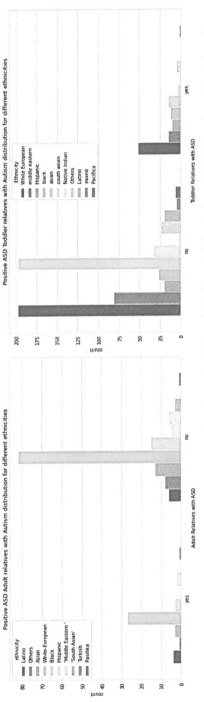

FIGURE 7.9 Graph showing the features of parents with ASD and toddlers with ASD and their relatives with ASD to determine if there is any correlation among the features.

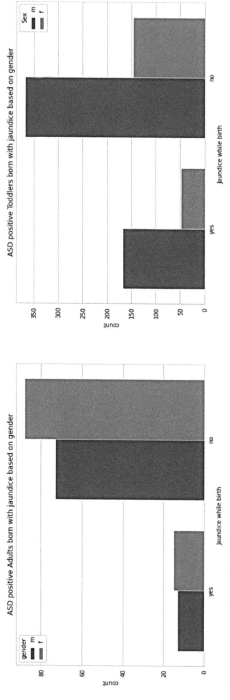

FIGURE 7.10   Graph showing the relation of class/ASD based on ethnicity and gender of the subjects.

set while considering other subsets for training. We found the proportion of true negative identified precisely through our approach. Results are in line with the accuracy of the model computed based on the AE output combined with CNN which led to improved model performance metrics. We also found the receiver operating characteristics (ROC) curve of the AE based CNN better than the classical ML models.

7.8.2 ROBUSTNESS OF MULTI-CHANNEL HYBRID CNN

When we analyzed the impact of data modality on classification, we found the hybrid CNN performance better for ASD classification as compared to other models. All the results were obtained by performing 10-fold-validation for 40 epochs using hybrid CNN model. We also found the combined datasets accuracy was higher ($p \leq 0.014$) as compared to individual AAL, CC200, HO [30]. This could also be accounted for metadata provided by each of these datasets contribute to complete information formed by all brain atlases assisting in ASD and Autism classifications.

7.9 CONCLUSIONS

In summary, we developed a hybrid AE based CNN model by using self-attention mechanism and fusion based automated diagnosis using improved ML on ASD and Autism features. Results as shown in graphs indicate that subjects with Class/ASD characteristics with Jaundice and its relationship with Autism gave no statistically significant score. As results, establishing the subjects with/without Jaundice could be associated with Autism or ASD is not clear. However, we found a better correlation between Parents with ASD and Autism either maternal/paternal relatives could contribute to toddlers with ASD and Autism features could be established as statistical significance of ($p = 0.0013$) was noticed. This indicates the either hereditary or genetic reasons for acquaintance of ASD or Autism in toddlers could be possible. We also found the country-wise split-up of subjects with ASD and Autism where white Europeans nations seems to be higher than compared to other nations. So as the dataset is a mixture of data acquired from various nations, this gives an indication of autism and ASD related disorders are more noticed in Europe than other emerging nations.

The k-fold validation results indicate our Hybrid CNN gave an accuracy of 0.863, better other ML methods. The results of leaving one validation to clinical data helps in the generalization of the model. From our results, we also found adding multiple data sources contributed to different data modalities which improve the performance of the ML usage in clinical measures of ASD and Autism related automated diagnosis tools. Sample for the current study includes a cohort chosen mostly of adolescents and toddlers which hinders the generalizability. ASD and Autism have few common and varying characteristics which cannot be analyzed and more over which could also vary across demographics which is also limited in the datasets. Future studies should focus more on wider age groups of the population to capture a complete profile of ASD and Autism characteristics.

In addition to the survey data, we also found the video recorded clip of the participant to analyze the ASD and Autism behavior. Video sample can be further analyzed to label the specific features commonly noticed among ASD and Autism subjects. Complex models like ResNet, VGG, E-net improve fMRI data as it allows you to select a greater number of features. Most of these models have found their usage in neural transfer and vision applications. We also found the usage of feature selection methods such as component analysis, transformations, wavelets are efficient to reduce dimension and enhance performance.

Results of KNN, SVM, and RF have been analyzed to compare with DL AE based CNN model. As it helps to define and restructure the predefined hyper-parameters and fine-tune the model classifiers. As the tuning parameters vary across the ML models, we also have applied Grid Search cross-validation to ensure the selection of feature is randomized and no model over-fitting is reported. So finally, we could obtain the best features from the predefined hyper-parameters provided for training set. To conclude, we have also compared the performance of AE added with self-attention approach in CNN to evaluate classical ML models. Resulting hybrid CNN gave the best score as compared to other models. Adding other models to hybrid CNN model was to emphasize the need to identify as many distinct features as possible to classify ASD and Autism subjects using multi-channel datasets provided in the form of fMRI images. We were able to predict the Autism infliction's and draw a few conclusions based on the dataset analysis. However, clinically these results need to be verified as most of the evaluation in the real world is carried through expert analysis which to an extent can be improved if ground truth metadata is also provided along with the datasets.

KEYWORDS

- **Autism Spectral Disorders**
- **Functional Magnetic Resonance Imagery**
- **Latent Dirchlet Analysis**
- **Learning Analytics**
- **Natural Language Processing**
- **Neural Network**
- **Parameterized Reinforcement Learning**

REFERENCES

1. Satabdi, C., Pramod, T., Triptish, B., Vishwajit, L. N., & Smita, N. D., (2015). Assessment of severity of autism using the Indian scale for assessment of autism. *Indian Journal of Psychological Medicine, 37*(2), 169–174.
2. Alokananda, R., Saoni, B., Nidhi, S., Merry, B., Shaneel, M., & Bhismadev, C., (2014). Translation and usability of autism screening and diagnostic tools for autism spectrum conditions in India. *Autism Research, 7*(5), 598–607.
3. Cheryl, M. C., Facundo, C., Ferna'ndez-Slezak, D., Gillinder, B., Casimir, K., Daniel, C. J., Carrie, E. B., & Guillermo, A. C., (2018). Prediction of psychosis across protocols and risk cohorts using automated language analysis. World Psychiatry, 17(1), 67–75.
4. Natalia, B. M., Nivaldo, A. P. V., Nathalia, L., Ana, C. P., Osame, K., Guillermo, A. C., Mauro, C., & Sidarta, R., (2012). Speech graphs provide a quantitative measure of thought disorder in psychosis. *PloS One, 7*(4), e34928.
5. Neguine, R., Elaine, W., & Phillip, W., (2019). A machine learning approach to predicting psychosis using semantic density and latent content analysis. *NPJ Schizophrenia, 5*(1), 1–12.
6. Dario, G. E., Guillermo, A. C., Cheryl, C., & Philip, C., (2017). Using automated metaphor identification to aid in detection and prediction of first-episode schizophrenia. In: *Proceedings of the 2017 Conference on Empirical Methods in Natural Language Processing* (pp. 2923–2930).
7. Tomas, M., Ilya, S., Kai, C., Greg, S. C., & Jeff, D., (2013). Distributed representations of words and phrases and their compositionality. In: *Advances in Neural Information Processing Systems* (pp. 3111–3119).
8. Dominique, F., & Irina, I., (2021). Bert-based semantic model for rescoring n-best speech recognition list. In: *INTERSPEECH 2021*.
9. Adriana Di, M., O'connor, D., Bosi, C., Kaat, A., Jeffrey, S. A., Michal, A., Joshua, H. B., Leslie, B., Anita, B., Sylvie, B., et al., (2017). Enhancing studies of the connectome in autism using the autism brain imaging data exchange II. *Scientific Data, 4*(1), 1–15.

10. Sina, G., Russell, G., Ping, J., & Matthew, R. G. B., (2016). Using functional or structural magnetic resonance images and personal characteristic data to identify ADHD and autism. *PloS One, 11*(12), e0166934.

11. Bhaskar, S., Neil, C. B., Russell, G., & Matthew, R. G. B., (2018). A general prediction model for the detection of ADHD and autism using structural and functional MRI. *PloS One, 13*(4), e0194856.

12. Gajendra, J. K., Stefi, A. B., Nathan, D. C., & Andrew, M. M., (2016). Divide and conquer: Sub-grouping of ASD improves ASD detection based on brain morphometry. *PloS One, 11*(4), e0153331.

13. Nancy, C. A., (1986). Scale for the assessment of thought, language, and communication (TLC). *Schizophrenia Bulletin, 12*(3), 473.

14. Richard, S. S., & Andrew, G. B., (2018). *Reinforcement Learning: An Introduction.* MIT press.

15. Al Mondragon, Dufresne, A., Nkambou, R., & Poirier, P., (2017). An effective intelligent tutoring system in the special education of individuals with autism. *EDULEARN17 Proceedings, 1*, 4114–4122.

16. Zoe, E. R., Liam, M., Abigail, J., George, D. S., Penton-Voak, I., Angela, S. A., & Marcus, R. M., (2021). Examining the bidirectional association between emotion recognition and social autistic traits using observational and genetic analyses. *Journal of Child Psychology and Psychiatry.*

17. Benjamin, B., Lucy, B., & Bronwyn, H., (2021). Virtual reality and augmented reality for children, adolescents, and adults with communication disability and neuro developmental disorders: A systematic review. *Review Journal of Autism and Developmental Disorders, 1–24.*

18. Michael, P. M., & Adriana Di, M., (2019). *Autism Brain Image Data Exchange.* http://fcon_1000.projects.nitrc.org/indi/abide/abide_II.html (accessed on 12 February 2023).

19. Milan, N. P., Hailong, L., & Lili, H., (2019). Enhancing diagnosis of autism with optimized machine learning models and personal characteristic data. *Frontiers in Computational Neuroscience, 13*, 9.

20. Taban, E., & Fahad, S., (2019). Auto-ASD-network: A technique based on deep learning and support vector machines for diagnosing autism spectrum disorder using fMRI data. In: *Proceedings of the 10ᵗʰ ACM International Conference on Bioinformatics, Computational Biology and Health Informatics* (pp. 646–651).

21. Peter, W., Qandeel, T., Emilie, L., Brianna, C., Kaitlyn, D., Aaron, K., Haik, K., Yordan, P., Kelley, P., Catalin, V., et al., (2021). Crowdsourced privacy-preserved feature tagging of short home videos for machine learning ASD detection. *Scientific Reports, 11*(1), 1–11.

22. Duda, M., Haber, N., Daniels, J., & Wall, D. P., (2017). Crowdsourced validation of a machine-learning classification system for autism and ADHD. *Translational Psychiatry, 7*(5), e1133–e1140.

23. Greg, P., (2018). The value of early intervention for children with autism. *Paediatrics and Child Health, 28*(8), 364–367.

24. AGRE, (2021). *Autism Genetic Resource Exchange(agre).* boston. https://www.autismspeaks.org/agre (accessed on 24 January 2023).

25. Jasem, A., Khaled, E., & Abde, L. E., (2017). Comparison of autoencoder and principal component analysis followed by neural network for e-learning using handwritten

recognition. In: *2017 IEEE Long Island Systems, Applications and Technology Conference (LISAT)* (pp. 1–5). IEEE.

26. Mae'l, L., Karin, B., Stefano, P., & Jan, B. E., (2019). Contextual influence on confidence judgments in human reinforcement learning. *PLoS Computational Biology, 15*(4), e1006973.

27. Ramos-Sa'nchez, C. P., Dianne, K., Debbie, V. B., Davy, V., & Tine, V. D., (2021). The relationship between motor skills and intelligence in children with autism spectrum disorder. Journal of Autism and Developmental Disorders, 1–11.

28. Pablo, L., Daniel, O., Anja, P., Yuichi, Y., Yukie, N., & Gordon, C., (2020). A review on neural network models of schizophrenia and autism spectrum disorder. *Neural Networks, 122*, 338–363.

29. Mindi, R., Paula, J. W., Xin, L., & Shuo, W., (2021). Deep neural network reveals the world of autism from a first-person perspective. *Autism Research, 14*(2), 333–342.

30. Yaya, L., Lingyu, X., Jie, Y., Jun, L., & Xuan, Y., (2021). Identification of autism spectrum disorder using multi-regional resting-state data through an attention learning approach. *Biomedical Signal Processing and Control, 69*, 102833.

CHAPTER 8

REINFORCEMENT LEARNING FOR AUTOMATED MEDICAL DIAGNOSIS AND DYNAMIC CLINICAL REGIMES

PAWAN WHIG,[1] ARUN VELU,[2] RAHUL REDDY NADIKATTU,[3] and PAVIKA SHARMA[4]

[1]Dean Research, Vivekananda Institute of Professional Studies, New Delhi, India

[2]Director Equifax, Atlanta, USA

[3]Research Scholar, University of Cumberland, USA

[4]Assistant Professor, Bhagwan Parshuram Institute of Technology (BPIT), Rohini, Delhi, India

ABSTRACT

In reinforcement learning (RL), various machine learning (ML) models are taught how to variety a categorization of conclusions based on a set of inputs. A machine learns how to accomplish a goal in an unexpected, maybe complex environment. RL places artificial intelligence (AI) in a play environment. It solves the issue by experimentation. Depending on what it does, AI is rewarded or penalized. Its goal is to maximize the total amount of money paid out. In addition to defining the game's rules, the designer does not provide the model with any feedback or ideas on how to win. In order to maximize payment, the model must figure out how to best perform a task, starting with completely random trials and working up to sophisticated tactics and superhuman powers. With the strength of search and a variety of trials, RL is perhaps the most effective technique to hint to a system's

Handbook of Research on Artificial Intelligence and Soft Computing Techniques in Personalized Healthcare Services, Uma N. Dulhare, A. V. Senthil Kumar, Amit Datta, Seddik Bri, Ibrahiem M. M. El Emary, (Eds.)

creativity. Unlike humans, AI can learn from thousands of concurrent gaming industry if a reinforced classification technique is run on a suitably powerful computer architecture. The chapter RL for automatic diagnostic testing will be covered in full in this book chapter.

8.1 INTRODUCTION

Machine learning (ML) includes reinforcement learning (RL). It's really about engaging in suitable action to maximize profit in a given situation. Various apps and computers utilize it to evaluate the finest possible course of action to have in a particular event.

Developers design a way of rewarding desired actions and punishing bad ones in RL [1]. To motivate the agent, this technique provides positive values to desired activities and negative values to undesirable behaviors. To reach an ideal solution, the agent is programmed to seek long-term and greatest overall benefit [2].

To avoid the agent from stagnating on smaller targets, these long-term goals are essential. He or she learns to avoid the bad and focus on finding the good through time and experience [3]. Through incentives and punishments, this learning approach has been implemented in artificial intelligence (AI) in order to drive unsupervised ML. The basic of RL is shown in Figure 8.1 and is working is shown in Figure 8.2.

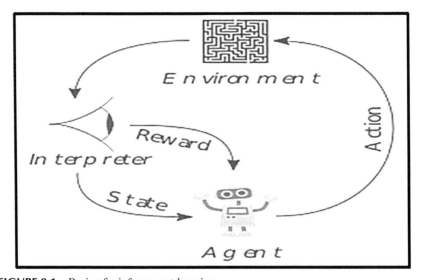

FIGURE 8.1   Basic of reinforcement learning.

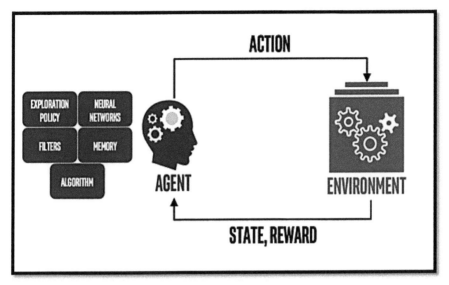

FIGURE 8.2 Working of reinforcement learning.

8.1.1 REINFORCEMENT LEARNING (RL)

The main components required for RL is described as following:

1. **Initial Stage:** Input can be considered an initial state and model starts its initial move from this point;

2. **O/P:** Output can be existing for a variety of solution to a given problem;

3. **Learning:** It can be done on the feedback of user it. The model is still learning.

The optimal answer is determined by the highest possible payment.

8.1.2 TYPES OF MACHINE LEARNING (ML)

Different types of ML are described as in Figure 8.3:

i. Supervised;
ii. Unsupervised; and
iii. Reinforcement learning.

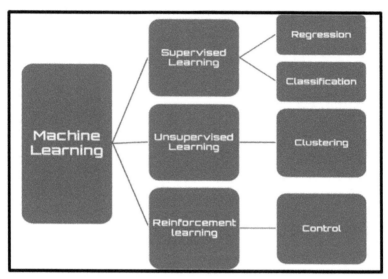

FIGURE 8.3   Types of machine learning.

8.1.3   SUPERVISED

Supervised learning is the first form of shallow ML. And it's precisely what the name implies [4–6]. This form of learning occurs when the developer names the variables with which the machine will interact. There are two types of learning in this domain: regression and classification.

Numbers may be recognized and grouped by the machine to produce predictions. As an example, the overall square footage of a home, the number of bathrooms, and the number of bedrooms can all be considered. It can forecast the cost of a house using linear regression by grouping different samples of houses and learning from their distinct factors.

8.1.4   UNSUPERVISED

Unsupervised learning may be understood by using the preceding example of playing flashcards with a machine [7–9]. The machine is playing a game of flashcards with itself instead of other people, a cat or dog appears on one side of the image on the reverse of the card, there is a blank space. So, for example, the computer may detect that the cats have pointed ears and the dogs have floppy ears, which is a difference between the two. Cats and dogs are placed in separate piles. Clustering is the term used to describe the process of grouping objects together [10].

The system is also capable of noticing many objects at the same time, which is quite useful. That the cats had four legs, emerald eyes and pointed ears may have been noticed by the computer program. Dogs with brown eyes and floppy ears with four legs are also noted. To differentiate between cats and dogs, it uses fewer characteristics and reduces variables connected to the pictures such as the number of legs. Dimension reduction is the term for this.

8.1.5 PROCESS OF REINFORCEMENT LEARNING (RL)

Reinforcement learning (RL) is the process of training a computer by rewarding it for good behavior. A mouse attempting to find its way out of a maze will help us comprehend this one. Around 1,000 points are provided to the mouse before he starts. The goal is to keep and improve his points [11]. It loses points when it strikes a dead wall or a mousetrap, or when it takes the incorrect direction. Points are awarded for completing the maze or taking the proper turn, which leads to the cheese. As a result, the computer is compelled to produce correct predictions and take the appropriate actions in response.

RL occurs when a mouse is able to mentally model a labyrinth and plan out a set of routes and steps to take. Model-free learning occurs when the mouse develops a habit of traveling through the labyrinth many times.

They each have their own advantages and disadvantages. For voice and visual data prediction, supervised learning through regression and classification is most effective. There are a number of applications of unsupervised learning, including the generation of advertising ideas [12]. Physical robots employ RL, which involves learning through incentives. The difference between different ML is shown in Figure 8.4.

8.1.5.1 TYPES OF REINFORCEMENT

There are two types of reinforcement:

1. **Positive Reinforcement:** As a result of an event that occurs as a result of certain behavior, positive-positive reinforcement enhances the strength as well as the occurrence of the performance [13].

2. **Negative Reinforcement:** It refers to behavior that is reinforced because an undesirable state is prevented or avoided. Difference between the two types and their characteristics are revealed in Figures 8.5 and 8.6.

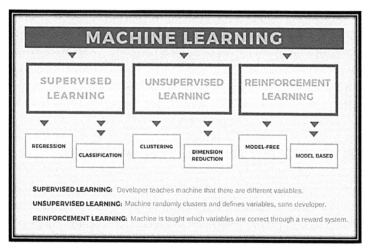

FIGURE 8.4   Difference between different machine learning algorithm.

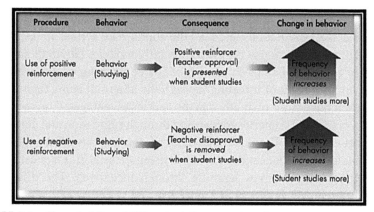

FIGURE 8.5   Characteristics of different reinforcement learning.

8.1.5.2   VARIOUS PRACTICAL APPLICATIONS OF REINFORCEMENT LEARNING (RL)

The various RL applications are shown in Figure 8.7:

- Reinforcement learning may be used in industrial robotics to automate processes.
- Machine learning and data processing can benefit from reinforcement learning.
- Students' needs can be met using reinforcement learning-based training methods.

Positive Reinforcement	Negative Reinforcement
• Adding a desirable stimulus to increase the likelihood of a behaviour to reoccur	• Removing an undesirable stimulus to increase the likelihood of a behaviour to reoccur
• Stimuli here work as a reward, given for doing something appropriate	• Stimuli here work as a penalty, for not doing something
• It strenghtens the probability of a behaviour to occur again.	• It teaches us to behave in a manner that help us get rid of a nasty respones.
• It works a motivation.	• It works as a lesson.
• Example: Going out with friends to watch a movie if you finish your assignment. Thus, increasing the likelihood of you completing assignment.	• Example: Taking umbrella with you even and using it when it starts to rain. Thus, preventing you from getting wet and teaching you to carry umbrella more often.

FIGURE 8.6   Differences between PRL and NRL.

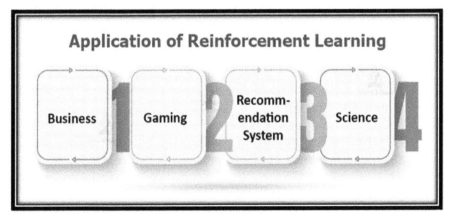

FIGURE 8.7   Application of reinforcement learning.

8.2   COMMON REINFORCEMENT LEARNING (RL) ALGORITHMS

RL does not relate to a single method, but rather to a collection of algorithms that adopt diverse approaches [14–16]. Most of the distinctions can be attributed to the way in which they explore their surroundings. Although there are many RL algorithms but as shown in Figure 8.8, but some very important algorithms are discussed below:

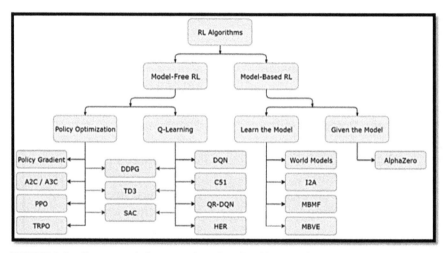

FIGURE 8.8   Common reinforcement learning algorithms used.

1. **State-Action-Reward-State-Action:** As a first step, a policy is given to the agent. In essence, the policy is a probability, which informs it how likely it is that particular behaviors will result in rewards or positive states for the policy.

2. **Q-Learning:** When it comes to RL, this method takes a completely different approach. Due to this, the agent's exploration of the world is more self-directed.

3. **Q-Networks in Depth:** In addition to RL approaches, these algorithms make use of neural networks [17]. RL is based on self-directed world exploration. In the neural network, a random sample of beneficial acts from the past is used to predict future actions.

8.3   REINFORCEMENT LEARNING (RL) IN HEALTHCARE

Early adopters and big beneficiaries of technology advancements have always been healthcare. RL has repeatedly produced improved results in the healthcare system. In addition to being a branch of ML, RL's goal is to improve an individual's ability to make decisions based on their interactions with the environment around them and provide them with feedback [18].

Reward indicators were traditionally used in supervised learning techniques, but the RL approach involves a progressive decision-making process that is concurrently sampling, evaluative, and delayed. RL's unique characteristics make it a viable option for generating cutting-edge solutions in a wide range of healthcare fields. So, diagnostic judgments or treatment regimens are typically marked by a long and chronological process.

Today, ML plays a critical role in a number of healthcare organizations. As a result, ML has spawned a plethora of applications in the healthcare system. It has also considerably aided in improving administrative operations in health institutions, personalizing health treatments, and mapping and medicating communicable illnesses, among many other things [19].

General practitioners and healthcare systems are also affected by the use of ML, since it is crucial for clinical resolution sustainability, allowing for early detection of illnesses and customized treatment methods to ensure optimal outcomes. Using ML, doctors and patients may see and learn about potential illness courses and outcomes, as well as dissimilar treatment options [20]. As a result of this, healthcare structures will become more competent while expenses are reduced. It will take generations of wisdom to improve the development of novel medicines and ensure the delivery of existing ones.

ML algorithms have been developed in healthcare systems to assist both patients and employees, with the most prevalent areas of use being.

8.3.1   THE SMART RECEIVER

8.3.1.1 HEALTH QUOTIENT

With this software, produced by Quotient Health, the company hopes to reduce the costs of supporting electronic medical records (EMRs) by improving and standardizing the procedures by which these systems are developed. To enhance the healthcare system and reduce expenses is a clear goal [21].

8.3.1.2   KENSCI

RL is used by KenSci to predict illnesses and treatments, allowing medical practitioners and patients to intervene earlier in the process. As a bonus, it aids in the forecast of public health concerns by detecting trends, increasing dangerous signs, and predicting illness progression, among other features.

8.3.1.3   CIOX HEALTH

When it comes to health data control and alteration, Ciox Health uses ML. It helps to expand and enhance patient access and increases the accuracy of health data.

This makes RL ideal for systems with inherent delays, such as autonomous cars, robots, video games, and financial and business management, as well as – yes – healthcare. Yu et al. claim that RL's unique type of progressive decision-making is ideal for healthcare applications because it "addresses sequential decision-making difficulties with sampling, evaluative, and delayed input concurrently." To make somewhat well-informed judgments, RL is also flexible enough to take into account the delayed effects of therapies and doesn't require as much contextual information [22–25].

According to the researchers, "RL is able to identify optimum policies using just past experiences, without requiring any prior information of the mathematical model of biological systems." Because of nonlinear, variable, and delayed interactions between therapies and human bodies, RL is more attractive than many existing control-based methods in healthcare domains.

8.4   REINFORCEMENT LEARNING (RL) IN HEALTHCARE APPLICATIONS

RL is being used in a variety of healthcare settings, but it has been most successful in the implementation of dynamic treatment regimens (DTRs) for patients with chronic diseases or disorders. Additionally, it has reached a certain degree of capability in automated medical diagnosis (AMD), health resources scheduling and resource allocation, medication research and development, and health management [26].

8.4.1   DTR

The development and continuous setup of DTRs for patients with long-term illnesses is RL's most prevalent real-world healthcare application. As a patient's medical history and circumstances change over time, DTRs become more and more specific in terms of treatment options – such as therapy type, drug dose, and appointment schedule. As a result of clinical observations and patient assessments as input data, the algorithm generates therapy choices that will give the patient with the best desired environment state possible. These treatment regimens employ RL to automate decision-making [27]. A number of chronic illnesses, such as cancer and HIV, have already benefited from the use of DTRs. Example of DTR is shown in Figure 8.9.

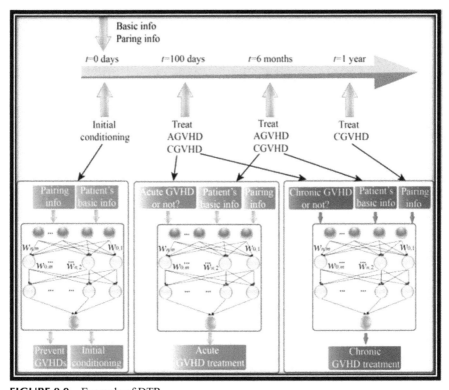

FIGURE 8.9   Example of DTR.

8.4.2   AMD (AUTOMATED MEDICAL DIAGNOSIS)

Patient information (such as history and present symptoms) is used to match the proper illness profile. Even while it may appear easy, it may be an immensely complicated process for busy physicians, both in terms of time and cognitive resources required [28].

Misdiagnosis expenses have been detailed in a previous blog post: Misdiagnosed patients have been compensated for more than $40 billion over the previous 25 years. Healthcare professionals and patients alike depend on ML algorithms to enhance diagnosis. It's just that ML diagnostic solutions require enormous volumes of labeled data in order to learn. RL agents, on the other hand, require less labeled data [29, 30]. Example of AMD is shown in Figure 8.10.

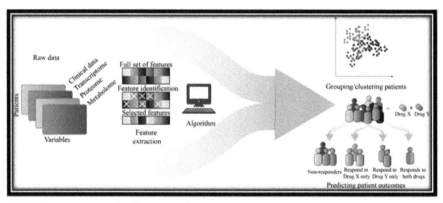

FIGURE 8.10   Example of automated medical diagnosis (AMD).

8.4.3   SCHEDULING AND DISTRIBUTION OF HEALTHCARE RESOURCES

Patients are the consumers, while healthcare resources are the service providers in the healthcare industry [32]. Business process management (BPM) can benefit from RL because of its well-documented appropriateness for it. RL can assist hospitals and clinics manage their daily operations by evaluating seasonal trends, current inpatient and staffing levels, as well as other data points.

8.4.4   DISCOVERY, DESIGN, AND DEVELOPMENT OF PHARMACEUTICALS

The human-driven, trial-and-error approach of traditional drug development has several faults, the most severe of which is that it is time and cost prohibitive. Using contemporary approaches such as computer models and simulations (M&S) to study the behavior of molecules and atoms, this is still true today [33]. But despite all of that effort and money, success rates are still low, with less than 10% of molecules making it to the first round of clinical trials. In order to automate and enhance drug design hypotheses and compound selection, RL techniques are increasingly being applied to de novo drug discovery. Flowchart of design and development of pharmaceuticals is shown in Figure 8.11.

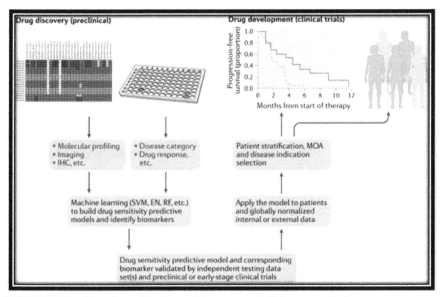

FIGURE 8.11   Flowchart of design and development of pharmaceuticals.

8.4.5   *MANAGEMENT OF THE HEALTH OF THE POPULATION*

Researchers have also utilized RL as a tool to develop adaptive and customized interventions for continuous health management, such as exercise and weight control regimens for obese or diabetic patients [34]. Patient engagement and compliance with health management programmers have already been improved with the use of AI. Management in the healthcare sector is shown in Figure 8.12.

8.5   CHALLENGES OF REINFORCEMENT LEARNING (RL) IN HEALTHCARE

As promising as RL in healthcare is, there are numerous obstacles to overcome before it can be used on a wide basis in clinical practice. It can be

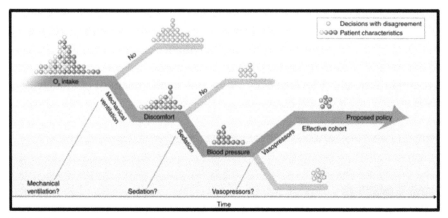

FIGURE 8.12   Management in healthcare sector.

difficult to transfer a real-time agent from a training or simulated environment to the actual world, and because the agent can only understand rewards and punishments, upgrading or adjusting the algorithm can be challenging [35–38]. This video from OpenAI shows an RL agent figuring out how to receive prizes without finishing the race.

8.5.1   SHORTAGE OF DATA

Isaac Godfried, a deep learning (DL) researcher, points out that utilizing actual patients to train RL algorithms isn't always the most ethical method, despite the fact that RL agents learn best on the job. In order to do so, they must train in simulated environments using historical observational data on specific therapies, which is sometimes challenging for numerous reasons, including HIPPA compliance and personal health information (PHI) [31, 39–42].

8.5.2   PARTIAL OBSERVABILITY

Even while real-time agents can frequently account for the complete state of simulated settings, the human body is considerably more complicated and dynamic than even the most thorough simulations or historical data sets can capture. It's fairly uncommon for RL agents in healthcare settings to have a partial awareness of their surroundings because of the partial observability of blood pressure, temperature, and other data.

8.5.3 FORMULATION AND DESIGN OF THE REWARD

Achieving long-term success with real-time agents in healthcare is easier said than done when trying to balance long-term advantages with short-term gains. According to Godfried, "periodic improvements in blood pressure, for example, may not lead to better outcomes in sepsis." When there is only one reward at the end.

The application of RL in healthcare is still far from ideal, but significant progress has been made on numerous fronts, including the more efficient and precise construction of DTRs for chronic diseases and other conditions, among other things. It is certain that as reward policies are adjusted and more data is made available to construct settings for RL agents, we will witness additional gains – and in the end, better health outcomes for patients and more efficient operations for health organizations.

8.6 SUMMARY

However, this technique is not always appropriate because ML relies on increases in performance over predicted statistical approaches as the basis for claims of improvement. A ML algorithm's influence must be evaluated.

RL, with its capacity to govern final behaviors within a given context, is a fascinating prospect in the realm of healthcare. A more thorough and precise treatment is provided at a lower cost with its implementation.

RL techniques can be supplied with key to identifying that can guide knowledge in its initial stages more toward valuable and secure areas of the state vector, or with protests and instructor guidance from an experienced professional that can disturb exploration as well as provide expertise when the agent confronts unpredictable circumstances to enable effective transfer.

It is expected that RL, if well-implemented, would have a significant impact on the management and control of chronic illnesses by linking patient centered health information with external variables such as weather and economic dynamics or pollution exposure in the next years. Through the use of accessible genetic information, it will efficiently produce exact pharmaceutical solutions that are tailored to each individual's unique characteristics.

The scenario is fast changing, driven by both significant advances in RL theories and methodologies, as well as practical needs from healthcare practitioners and management. The concept of using RL in healthcare has experienced a spike of interest in recent years, which may be substantiated by a spike in the number of publications on this issue for a long time.

This book chapter seeks to provide the scientific public with a methodical knowledge of the basics, an extensive pallet of methodologies, approaches accessible, current difficulties, and fresh visions of this developing pattern as the first complete assessment of RL applications in healthcare. We believe that by doing so, more scholars from diverse disciplines would be able to use their expertise in their respective fields and collaborate to create more applicable solutions to optimum healthcare decision making.

Different sectors seem to be taking notice of RL and other ML techniques. This Book Chapter is very useful for the researchers working in the same field.

The use of RL in healthcare is at the intersection of computer science and medicine. Such multidisciplinary research necessitates the participation of ML. Researchers and doctors who interact directly with people to provide medical treatment and make decisions Despite its significant success, RL has received significantly less attention of researchers in either computer science and medicine, when tried to compare to certain other research philosophies inside the health sector, such as traditional computer vision, DL, and numerical ML techniques learning-based and regulate.

KEYWORDS

- **Artificial Intelligence**
- **Automated Medical Diagnosis**
- **Business Process Management**
- **Diagnosis**
- **Dynamic Treatment Regimens**
- **Healthcare**
- **Machine Learning**
- **Reinforcement Learning**

REFERENCES

1. Steeve, H., (2018). *Introduction to Various Reinforcement Learning Algorithms. Part I (Q-Learning SARSA DQN DDPG).* Towards Data Science.

2. Madhu, S., (2018). *Model Free Reinforcement Learning Algorithms (Monte Carlo SARSA Q-Learning)*. Medium.

3. Rajat, H., (2018). *Choosing the Right Machine Learning Algorithm*. HackerNoon.

4. Abolfazl, R., (2018). *How to Choose Machine Learning Algorithms?* Medium.

5. Daniil, K., (2017). *Machine Learning Algorithms: Which One to Choose for Your Problem*. Stats and Bots.

6. Madhu, S., (2018). *CH12.1: Model Free Reinforcement Learning Algorithms (Monte Carlo SARSA Q-Learning)*. Medium.

7. Matthias, P., Rein, H., Prafulla, D., Szymon, S., Pieter, A., Marcin, A., et al., (2017). *Better Exploration with Parameter Noise*. OpenAI.

8. Rosiene, J. A., & Pe Rosiene, C., (2020). SPAM: Simplifying python for approaching machine learning. In: *2020 IEEE Frontiers in Education Conference (FIE)* (pp. 1–3).

9. Khalaf, M., et al., (2018). A data science methodology based on machine learning algorithms for flood severity prediction. In: *2018 IEEE Congress on Evolutionary Computation (CEC)* (pp. 1–8).

10. Ray, S., (2019). A quick review of machine learning algorithms. In: *2019 International Conference on Machine Learning Big Data Cloud and Parallel Computing (COMITCon)* (pp. 35–39).

11. Simeone, O., (2018). A very brief introduction to machine learning with applications to communication systems. *IEEE Transactions on Cognitive Communications and Networking, 4*(4), 648–664.

12. Ding, W., Luo, F., Gu, C., Lu, H., & Zhou, Q., (2020). Performance-to-power ratio aware resource consolidation framework based on reinforcement learning in cloud data centers. *IEEE Access, 8*, 15472–15483.

13. Chen, P., Han, D., Tan, F., & Wang, J., (2020). Reinforcement-based robust variable pitch control of wind turbines. *IEEE Access, 8*, 20493–20502.

14. Latifi, K., Kopitca, A., & Zhou, Q., (2020). Model-free control for dynamic-field acoustic manipulation using reinforcement learning. *IEEE Access, 8*, 20597–20606.

15. Bouhamed, O., Ghazzai, H., Besbes, H., & Massoud, Y., (2020). A generic spatiotemporal scheduling for autonomous UAVs: A reinforcement learning-based approach. *IEEE Open Journal of Vehicular Technology, 1*, 93–106.

16. Shin, Y., Kim, J., Jin, K., & Kim, Y. B., (2020). Playtesting in match 3 game using strategic plays via reinforcement learning. *IEEE Access, 8*, 51593–51600.

17. Du, H., & Zhang, S., (2020). Hawkeye: Adaptive straggler identification on heterogeneous spark cluster with reinforcement learning. *IEEE Access, 8*, 57822–57832.

18. Silva, S. H., Alaeddini, A., & Najafirad, P., (2020). Temporal graph traversals using reinforcement learning with proximal policy optimization. *IEEE Access, 8*, 63910–63922.

19. Lee, H., Song, C., Kim, N., & Cha, S. W., (2020). Comparative analysis of energy management strategies for HEV: Dynamic programming and reinforcement learning. *IEEE Access, 8*, 67112–67123.

20. Ashiquzzaman, A., Lee, H., Um, T., & Kim, J., (2020). Energy-efficient IoT sensor calibration with deep reinforcement learning. *IEEE Access, 8*, 97045–97055.

21. Masinelli, G., Le-Quang, T., Zanoli, S., Wasmer, K., & Shevchik, S. A., (2020). Adaptive laser welding control: A reinforcement learning approach. *IEEE Access, 8*, 103803–103814.

22. Zhou, Z., Oguz, O. S., Leibold, M., & Buss, M., (2020). A general framework to increase the safety of learning algorithms for dynamical systems based on region of attraction estimation. *IEEE Transactions on Robotics, 36*(5), 1472–1490.

23. Zhang, D., (2020). Research on AGC performance during wind power ramping based on deep reinforcement learning. *IEEE Access, 8*, 107409–107418.

24. Yang, D., Qin, X., Xu, X., Li, C., & Wei, G., (2020). Sample efficient reinforcement learning method via highly efficient episodic memory. *IEEE Access, 8*, 129274–129284.

25. Fu, Q., (2019). Incorporating category taxonomy in deep reinforcement learning based image hashing. In: *2019 IEEE International Conference on Multimedia and Expo (ICME)* (pp. 127–132).

26. Chathurangi, S., Silva, & Asoka, K., (2020). Reinforcement learning in dynamic task scheduling: A review. *SN Computer Science, 1*, 306.

27. Zhang, J., Zhan, Z. H., Lin, Y., Chen, N., Gong, Y. J., Zhong, J. H., et al. (2019). Evolutionary computation meets machine learning: A survey. *IEEE Computational Intelligence Magazine, 6*(4), 68–75.

28. Mahmud, M., Kaiser, M. S., Hussain, A., & Vassanelli, S., (2018). Applications of deep learning and reinforcement learning to biological data. *IEEE Transactions on Neural Networks and Learning Systems, 29*(6), 2063–2079.

29. Nguyen, T. T., Nguyen, N. D., & Nahavandi, S., (2020). Deep reinforcement learning for multiagent systems: A review of challenges solutions and applications. *IEEE Transactions on Cybernetics, 50*(9), 3826–3839.

30. Sun, X., & Bischl, B., (2019). Tutorial and survey on probabilistic graphical model and variational inference in deep reinforcement learning. In: *2019 IEEE Symposium Series on Computational Intelligence (SSCI)* (pp. 110–119).

31. Velu, A., & Whig, P., (2021). Impact of COVID vaccination on the globe using data analytics. *International Journal of Sustainable Development in Computing Science, 3*(2), 1–10. Retrieved from: https://ijsdcs.com/index.php/ijsdcs/article/view/11 (accessed on 24 January 2023).

32. Saravanan, R., & Sujatha, P., (2018). A state of art techniques on machine learning algorithms: A perspective of supervised learning approaches in data classification. In: *2018 Second International Conference on Intelligent Computing and Control Systems (ICICCS)* (pp. 945–949).

33. Huang, H., & Li, S., (2019). The application of reinforcement learning in amazons. In: *2019 International Conference on Machine Learning Big Data and Business Intelligence (MLBDBI)* (pp. 369–372).

34. Pawan, W., & Ahmad, S. N., (2017). Controlling the output error for photo catalytic sensor (PCS) using fuzzy logic. *Journal of Earth Science and Climate Change, 8*(4), 1–6.

35. Rahul, R. N., Sikender, M. M., & Pawan, W., (2020). Novel economical social distancing smart device for COVID-19. *International Journal of Electrical Engineering and Technology* (IJEET) (Vol. 11, No. 4, pp. 204–217). Scopus Indexed.

36. Velu, A., (2019). The spread of big data science throughout the globe. *International Journal of Sustainable Development in Computing Science, 1*(1), 11–20. Retrieved from: https://ijsdcs.com/index.php/ijsdcs/article/view/6 (accessed on 24 January 2023).

37. Velu, A., (2019). A stable pre-processing method for the handwritten recognition system. *International Journal of Machine Learning for Sustainable Development, 1*(1), 21–30.

Retrieved from: https://ijsdcs.com/index.php/IJMLSD/article/view/60 (accessed on 24 January 2023).

38. Whig, P., (2019). Exploration of viral diseases mortality risk using machine learning. *International Journal of Machine Learning for Sustainable Development, 1*(1), 11–20. Retrieved from: https://ijsdcs.com/index.php/IJMLSD/article/view/53 (accessed on 24 January 2023).

39. Whig, P., (2019). A novel multi-center and threshold ternary pattern. *International Journal of Machine Learning for Sustainable Development, 1*(2), 1–10. Retrieved from https://ijsdcs.com/index.php/IJMLSD/article/view/54 (accessed on 24 January 2023).

40. Velu, A., & Whig, P., (2021). Protect personal privacy and wasting time using NLP: A comparative approach using AI. *Vivekananda Journal of Research, 10*, 42–52.

41. Velu, A., (2021). Influence of business intelligence and analytics on business value. *International Engineering Journal for Research & Development, 6*(1), 9–19.

42. Khera, Y., Whig, P., & Velu, A., (2021). efficient effective and secured electronic billing system using AI. *Vivekananda Journal of Research, 10*, 53–60.

CHAPTER 9

SURGICAL PHASE RECOGNITION USING VIDEOS: DEEP NEURAL NETWORK APPROACH

VISHAKHA BANSOD[1] and ASHA AMBHAIKAR[2]

[1]*PhD Scholar, Kalinga University, Naya Raipur, Chhattisgarh, India*

[2]*Professor and Dean Student Welfare, Kalinga University, Naya Raipur, Chhattisgarh, India*

ABSTRACT

Phase recognition has been studied in several surgical contexts, including cataracts, neurological, laparoscopic surgery, and using endoscopic video. In surgical phase recognition, adopt deep learning (DL) techniques CNN and RNN, to find surgical instruments in cataract, laparoscopic, and endoscopic surgery videos, which can be used to identify real-time phase and can be used to clarify the scale and action of automated surgical phase using visual information. DL techniques are applied to new sets of endoscopic videos. It helps to identify the automatic development of the procedure. It evaluates the probability of methods concerning practical consideration, performance, and scalability. This chapter discusses the possibility to recognize information that holds in surgical videos automatically using DL. This chapter also focused on visions into the use of this type of technology to support operating room (OR) planning.

9.1 INTRODUCTION

Surgery is a branch of medicine that deals with manual and instrumental media on injuries, diseases, and other disorders. We first discuss the signal

Handbook of Research on Artificial Intelligence and Soft Computing Techniques in Personalized Healthcare Services, Uma N. Dulhare, A. V. Senthil Kumar, Amit Datta, Seddik Bri, Ibrahiem M. M. EI Emary, (Eds.)
© 2024 Apple Academic Press, Inc. Co-published with CRC Press (Taylor & Francis)

available in the operating room (OR) for which it is used introduction to the surgical activity. We then focus the discussion on the arrival of visual information from the cameras used during the surgical procedure. We also describe the benefits as challenges in using visual information to identify surgical operations work. Finally, we present the types of videos we use for work.

Getting an indication of the tool used in the OR is not easy. They are usually collected through a non-trivial process: either via manual commentary or using additional equipment like a camera-equipped to collect trocar signals. In addition to the above digital tools, there are advances in technology that also introduced the use of imaging equipment to better provide surgeons visualization of the anatomy. For example, in cataract surgery, microscopy is used to provide a better view of the eye lens. In laparoscopic surgery, a fiberoptic instrument (i.e., an endoscope) is inserted through the abdominal wall organs inside the abdominal cavity. An endoscopic camera generates video signals in an endoscopic procedure. The surgical team takes the action with the help of these observable signals.

This naturally ready (to be used) motion viewing record sign put out is selected before for made automatic what is in observations to help science, medical experts. As an outcome of that, a great number of operations of making observations communities have offered methods for processing and getting at details it, either in now or for post-process use [17].

We discuss techniques that recognize phases. This recognition technique uses convolution neural networks (CNN). The features in different surgery videos are learned automatically by these techniques. This is the first survey to discuss CNN for numerous identification tasks on different surgery videos [1]. The surgery involves several steps, if we go through the whole process, it will offer AI guidance to the surgeons. It reduces the burden and load, uncertainty, and improves accuracy. A deep learning (DL) model is developing which will help to provide transparency and better communication with patients with the help of post-procedure surgery video commentary.

9.1.1 SUBFIELD OF MACHINE LEARNING (ML): DEEP LEARNING (DL)

Deep learning is a new technology that is a discipline of ML. It is a new technology on teaching representation of study from data that emphasizes learning continuous levels of meaningful representations from data. Deep learning is not a reference obtained from the point of view of any kind of perfection, instead, it is the way of consecutive layers of representation. Multiple levels devoted to a data model are the depth of the model. Other suitable names for this area might be layered representation and hierarchical representation learning. Modern DL often consists of tens or hundreds of consecutive layers of representation – and they have all learned automatically from the display of training data. Meanwhile, other methods of ML focus on representing only one or two levels; Hereafter, they are occasionally called superficial education. In DL, neural networks layer is organized in a sequence of one on top of other layers. A neural network is based on neurons and some terms are extended in DL as per our understanding of the brain. DL is not at all model which represents the human brain but is a mathematical model which represents data.

9.1.2   DEEP-LEARNING MODEL (CNN)

CNN also called convnet, is the deep-learning model used almost everywhere in computer vision applications. You'll apply convnet for image-classification issues – especially with small training datasets, the most common thing in use if you're not a big company. The five most popular CNNs are LeNet, AlexNet, VGGNet, Inception, and Reset. LeNet was developed in 1998 whose function is to better recognize handwritten letters. More advanced and ultra-deep networks have been developed by Incept and Resnet in 2014 and 2015, respectively.

The feature extraction and the classification part are the two sections of the convolutional network. In the last few years, ConvNets derived from AlexNet and LeNet. Recently Inception and ResNet have come out from CNN.

The depth of the image increases and the dimension decreases. An image is a result of the input data of each layer. A new convolutional layer is applied to each layer of the new image. In this way, we can think generically about the image. The height, depth, and width are three dimensions of each image. The depth of the 3D object represents the channel where its numeric value 1 as is signed to grayscale images and 3 is assigned to color images.

In the next layers, images have no color per second but still, have depth. Features extracted from earlier layers are represented by feature maps. The depth of the images, therefore, increases as we go deeper.

The next layer is fully connected. The pattern of this layer is different than the two previous layers. All fully connected layers may have reduced layers or the same hidden units. The neural network does not have trouble if the constant number of units is present in layers. The next step is the selection of several units of the layer. Now, these selected units can apply to all fully connected layers.

9.1.3 DEEP-LEARNING MODEL (RNN)

Sequential information is handled by recurrent neural networks (RNNs) and spatial information is efficiently processed by CNN. RNN introduces state variables for past archiving aggregate information according to current input, to determine the current output. RNN sequences can handle data better. There may be such techniques when experienced professionals face the problem of learning a wide sequence, they are not enough now. The mathematical uncertainty of RNN is a prominent issue in practice. Implementation tricks like gradient clipping have been adapted to add to this issue. Gated RNNs is a more common practice. In this practice, two models have existed. These models are the short-term input latent variable and the long-term information protection model.

9.2 TYPES OF CONVOLUTIONAL NEURAL NETWORK

Some of the CNN architectures used to achieve more accuracy and reduce computer costs are discussed in subsections.

9.2.1 LENET

LeNet-5 was first introduced in 1998 by Lekun et al. The architecture of this LeNet-5 is simple and has five weight layers. Therefore, this is referred to as LeNet-5. In this architecture, fully connected layers are two in numbers whereas convolutional layers are three.

Researchers now use the activation function tanh in place of the ReLu. In DL, ReLu was not referred at that time. Tanh or sigmoid were generally used in hidden layers as an activation function [13]. The architectural feature of the LeNet consists of the following:

- Kernels of size 5×5 for a convolutional layer;
- Pooling layers with an activation function such as tanh;

- Three fully connected layers with 120, 84, and 10 neurons, respectively.

LeNet-5 is a small neural network having 61,706 parameters as compared to the other modern Neural network.

9.2.2 ALEXNET

On the MNIST dataset, LeNet-5 performs admirably. However, the MNIST dataset turns out to be relatively simple because it just comprises grayscale pictures (1 channel) and only separates them into 10 categories, making it a straightforward challenge. AlexNet's major goal is to create a deep network capable of learning increasingly difficult jobs.

AlexNet took first place in the ILSVRC image categorization competition in 2012. The ImageNet dataset was used to train Krichevsky et al.'s neural network design. Because it was the first real "deep" network to open the door, AlexNet was considered cutting-edge at the time. The convolution network should be seriously considered by the CV community in their applications. AlexNet is similar to LeNet in many ways, however, it contains more hidden layers and filters per layer. They're made up of the same components: convolution and pooling piled on top of each other, then fully linked levels and softmax. LeNet contains around 61,000 parameters, but AlexNet has over 1 million parameters and 6,50,000 neurons, allowing it to learn a great lot to comprehend more complicated aspects. AlexNet was able to win the ILSVRC Image Classification Competition in 2012 as a result of this.

AlexNet has eight weight layers, five of which are convolutional and three of which are completely linked. The output is supplied to a 1,000-neuron softmax from two of the 4,096 neurons. Instead of the conventional tanh and sigmoid functions for classic neural networks, AlexNet employs reels for nonlinear sections (like LeNet). Because Relu learns quicker, it was employed in the hidden layers of the LexNet architecture. This is because the sigmoid function's derivatives are very tiny in the saturated zone, and so the weight updates nearly vanish. The vanishing gradient issue is the name given to this event.

9.2.3 VGGNETERS

VGGNet was developed by Oxford University's Visual Geometry Group (named VGG). No new elements are introduced here other than the dense layer. VGGNet has 16 weight layers and therefore it is also referred to as VGG16. These 16 layers are consisting of convolution layers-13 and fully connected layers-3. Its uniform architecture makes it attractive to the DL community as it is very easy to understand [15].

The concept of VGGNet is that it has a simple architecture with uniform elements (convolution and pooling layers). Kernel-shaped filters that are 11 and five in the first and second convolution layers on AlexNet were modified by replacing 3×3 pool-sized filters one after another. VGGNet architecture is developed by stacking a three-by-three convolution layer with a two-by-two pooling layer inserted after several convolution layers. This is followed by the traditional classifier, which is made up of fully connected layers and Softmax [22].

9.2.4   INCEPTION NETWORK

When a group of Google researchers released their paper "Going Deeper with Convolution" in 2014, it gave birth to Inception Network. GoogLeNet is a particular iteration of the Network Inception network that was utilized in the team's ILSVRC201 entry. It employs a 22-level network (deeper than VGGNet), reduces the number of parameters by 12 times, and produces substantially more accurate results. The network employed CNN, which was influenced by traditional networks like AlexNet and VGGNet, but included a new component called the installation module.

The design of the Inception starts with a convolutional layer and a pooling layer, then stacks inception modules and pooling layers to form the feature extractors, before adding the standard dense classifier layers. GoogLeNet had a top-5 error rate of 6.67%, which was very similar to human performance and far better than earlier CNNs such as AlexNet and VGGNet.

9.2.5   RESNET

The residual neural network (ResNet) was developed by a team of Microsoft research team in 2014. They presented the novel's residual module architecture with a skip connection. There is also a generalization of heavy batches for layers hidden in the network. This technology led to the training of ultra-deep neural networks (DNNs) with 50, 101, and 152 weight layers, with less complexity than smaller networks such as VGGNet (19 layers). In the ILSVRC 201 competition, ResNet was able to achieve a top-error error rate of – 77%, which outperformed all previous ConvNets.

ResNet-152 took first place in the 2015 Classification Competition, with the first model scoring 49.49% and a combination of models scoring 7.77%. This was far better than any other network, such as GoogLeNet, which had a top-five error rate of 6.67%. ResNet also came out on top in several object identification and picture localization competitions.

9.3 TYPES OF RNN

With sequential data, RNN is commonly employed. Vanilla RNN, LSTM, and GRU are the three most prevalent forms of RNNs.

9.3.1 GATED RECURRENT UNITS (GRU)

GRU has two features: reset gates and update gates. Reset gates capture short-term dependencies, but update gates collect long-term requirements based on the sequence completed [19]. Large time interval sequence dependencies can capture more accurately by Gated RNNs. The GRU contains the default RNN when the reset gate is turned on, that sub-components can also be skipped by turning on the updated gate.

9.3.2 LSTM NETWORKS

GRU is simpler in design than LSTM. GRU come into existence 20 years [19]. The flow of information is controlled by the three gates of LSTM. These three gates are input gates, forget gates, and output gates. The LSTM has a hidden layer that consists of the memory cell and a hidden state. The hidden state of the LSTM only goes into the output layer and the memory cell does not go to output. It is an internal state.

9.4 SURGICAL ACTIVITY RECOGNITION ON LAPAROSCOPIC VIDEOS

9.4.1 DATASET

1. **Cholec 80:** The Cholec 80 dataset contains a laparoscopic video with the recording rate of the video being 1 frame per second. While

recording it takes the first frame from the set of each 25 frame. This complete dataset is categorized into phase and tool presence comments. Videos are recorded at different resolutions, but the aspect ratio is similar. Surgical instruments are divided into seven categories.

2. **Endovis:** This dataset is divided into 45-s video sequences of training data and the remaining video for testing data. The 720×576 resolution of video sequences are exist with one or two types of surgical instruments.

3. **m2cai16:** The first 10 videos in the m2cai16-tool dataset contain local tool annotations for 2,532 frames, including a total of 15 videos. The dataset contains 3,141 interpretations of 7 surgical instrument classes, with an average of 1.2 labels per frame and 7 video classes per video.

9.4.2 *METHOD ESTABLISHED ON CNN WITH STOCHASTIC GRADIENT DESCENT (SGD)*

In this method, develop and train simple neural networks for the detection of surgical instruments in laparoscopic images. With the advent of advanced DL software libraries such as TensorFlow in Google Collaboratory, many steps of working with the neural network have been taken out, allowing for a much simpler process. CNN takes the input image containing surgical tools and classifies the image. For this purpose, used the Cholec80 dataset.

> **Step 1:** Download and extract the dataset.
> **Step 2:** Store the dataset in some variable.
> **Step 3:** Define the dataset characteristics.
> **Step 4:** Preprocess the image in the dataset.
> **Step 5:** To visualize the different appearances of the four types of tooltips in the dataset.
> **Step 6:** Apply convolution for horizontal edge detection and vertical edge detection.
> **Step 7:** Combine horizontal and vertical edges to identify all edges in the image.
> **Step 8:** Random convolution operation and normalized output value.
> **Step 9:** Apply max pooling and average pooling.

- ➤ **Step 10:** To build a neural network for surgical tool classification.
- ➤ **Step 11:** Defining the optimization method, a loss function and a metric (method is stochastic gradient descent (SGD).
- ➤ **Step 12:** Train the neural network.
- ➤ **Step 13:** Visualize the results on the test set.

9.4.3   METHOD BASED ON RNN

The information obtained temporarily is very useful and has a prime role in tracking and detecting the instruments used in surgery as shown in Figure 9.1. This information is used to train relationships with adjacent frames. So, the implementation of RNN is adopted by many researchers recently in tracking and detecting the instruments used in laparoscopy videos.

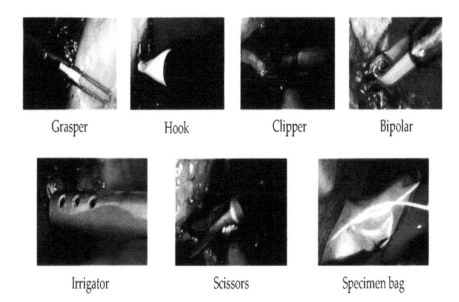

Grasper   Hook   Clipper   Bipolar

Irrigator   Scissors   Specimen bag

FIGURE 9.1   The tools used in surgery in the Cholec80 dataset.

To get temporary information, some researchers like Mishra suggested a method that depends on LSTM [16]. In this method, ResNet-50 is used to extract high-level features from surgical video. The Block diagram of this method to detect the surgical tools using ResNet-50 and three layers of LSTM is shown in Figure 9.2.

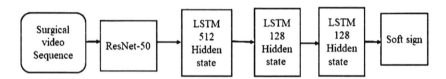

FIGURE 9.2   A method based on ResNet-50 with 3-layers LSTM.

The 3D convolutional networks can be used to draw out special temporal details. This 3D fully CNN as shown in Figure 9.3 is efficient in detecting actions, objects, and assessment of surgical skills [9, 10, 20]. In place of single-frame processing 3D fully CNN performed better.

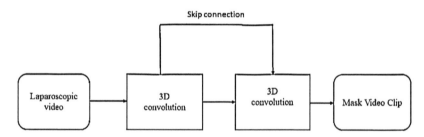

FIGURE 9.3   3D fully CNN.

To track surgical tools in the laparoscopic video [18] introduced a weak maintenance method using convLSTM to combine its spatiotemporal capabilities. This method is presented in Figure 9.4. This method applies to the Cholec80 dataset and has shown 92.9% accuracy.

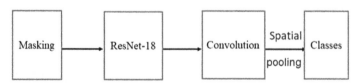

FIGURE 9.4   ResNet-18 with convolution.

DL tracking model for surgical instruments in laparoscopic videos using a convolution LSTM approach as shown in Figure 9.5 under weak supervision for tool detection, localization, and tracking from image-level. This approach consists of CNN and Convolutional LSTM neural networks that are monitoring tool binary presence labels. Using ConvLSTM, this model learns spatial-temporal information in the time-space domain only from the binary presence label [19].

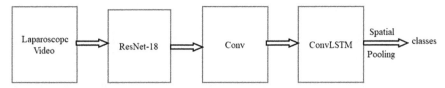

FIGURE 9.5   Deep learning model for object tracking in laparoscopic videos.

This approach uses a ResNet-18 to extract high-level features from the video frame [2, 5]. Based on a feature drawn by CNN, a ConvLSTM is trained to correctly detect the presence of a device by including temporary dimensions of information. The ResNet-18 architecture is used for its outstanding performance when it comes to object detection. In this method, ResNet-18 extracts the spatial feature map and the 7-channel convolution layer extract the temporal feature map. A configuration with three different configurations can be made with the same architecture [6]:

- ResNet + Convolution + ConvLSTM;
- ResNet + ConvLSTM + Convolution; and
- ResNet + ConvLSTM.

9.4.3.1   *RESNET + CONVOLUTION + CONVLSTM*

ConvLSTM refines spatial input features collected from the convolution layer with temporal information to produce spatiotemporal LH-maps in this setup. ConvLSTM was added immediately after the ResNet + Convolution unit to refine the spatial Lh-map with spatiotemporal data [22]. The size and design of the tools segmentation mask also aid to streamline class peak activation. It's worth noting that the localization procedure is carried out on spatiotemporal Lh-maps.

9.4.3.2   RESNET + CONVLSTM + CONVOLUTION

It refines R local features with spatiotemporal information before localization by C by adding the ConvLSTM unit before the baseline FCN convolution layer. Based on transient information throughout the video frame, this model selects relevant characteristics [22]. C becomes the receptive field awareness of worldly information as a result of this. The C layer is where the key localization occurs [20]. The spatial LH-map is generated from the spatiotemporal feature map. This type is expected to be more resistant to noise and vibration.

9.4.3.3   RESNET + CONVLSTM

The ConvLSTM layer is responsible for localization and feature map refining. The localization process on the ConvLSTM layer results in the spatiotemporal creation of Lh-maps, resulting in a less complicated architecture.

9.5   SURGICAL ACTIVITY RECOGNITION ON ENDOSCOPIC VIDEOS

CV applications in surgery have mostly focused on recognizing the operative phase in laparoscopic films. The CV approach for identifying steps in an endoscopic treatment, peroral endoscopic myotomy (POEM), was explained in this section [25].

9.5.1   DATASET

Various hospitals in Massachusetts and Japan provided peroral endoscopic films of myotomy surgeries. Surgical videos tagged with the following truth phases: (i) submucosal injection; (ii) mucosotomy; (iii) submucosal tunnel; and (iv) myotomy are the four procedures used to treat submucosal injection.

To train and develop POEMNet, the deep-learning CV model uses a convolutional neural network and long short-term memory (LSTM). In the subsequent films, POEMNet was used to identify operating stages.

9.5.2   METHOD BASED ON RESNET WITH LSTM

In this method, Convolutional Neural Network ResNet is combined with LSTM. Here CNN is used as a visual model and LSTM is used as a temporal model as shown in Figure 9.6. The visual model attempts to identify each frame of video only based on visual characteristics, whereas the sequential model is based on the temporary order in which frames occur.

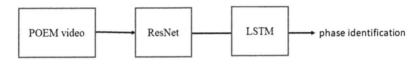

FIGURE 9.6   Method based on ResNet with LSTM.

POEMNet's total automatic phase detection accuracy was 87.6%. Straightforward cases almost perfect phase identification, while more difficult in cases where frequent tunneling inspections, the scope is required due to the cleaning and repair of mucous membranes machine for incorrect classification of phases.

9.6   SURGICAL ACTIVITY RECOGNITION ON CATARACT VIDEOS

9.6.1   DATASET

The data set includes videos of over 100 cataract surgery procedures that were performed at the Wilmer Eye Institute in Maryland from 2011 to 2017. The procedure featured various stages, including a side incision, the main incision, hydro section, cataract removal, and corneal hydration.

Each phase is marked by a trained commentator using various tools, such as the paracentesis blade, the crescent blade, the handpiece, and the intraocular lens. For each example, we took samples from different frames and created a cross-section for each tool used.

9.6.2   METHOD BASED ON RNN WITH MULTIPLE LSTM NODES

RNN using instruments in this method labeled as time series data with multiple LSTM nodes as shown in Figure 9.7. A RNN is used to analyze the data. It utilizes multiple time series nodes to control how much information is maintained on each individual.

There is a temporary encoding of the video for the phase using a single LSTM layer and a fully connected layer that yields a feature vector of 128. A softmax layer with 10 dimensions (corresponding to 10 phase labels) was employed for this encoding. The projected label had the greatest phase label Softmax probability.

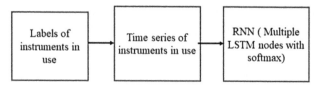

FIGURE 9.7   Method based with multiple LSTM nodes.

9.6.3   METHOD BASED ON SQEEZENET

This approach exploited local information in images to train a CNN, squeeze (University of California, Berkeley; and Stanford University) are used in this technique to represent local characteristics in pictures discriminating in one phase. By convolution, which incorporates data changes in patches of input characteristics to encode particular parts of data. Local patterns in data are learned using CNNs (in this example, the reference in the surgical field).

SqueezeNet as shown in Figure 9.8 is made up of many fire modules, each of which has a set of 1×1 convective filters that squeeze the data, followed by a set of 1×1 and 3×3 convective filters. CNN was trained for 100 years of data in 128 pictures using cross-entropy loss, with an initial learning rate of 0.001, decay of 0.0004, and speed of 0.9. For each picture frame video, 512-dimensional encoding is retrieved from the last convoluted layer. A Softmax estimate level of 10 dimensions guesses label was used for this encoding.

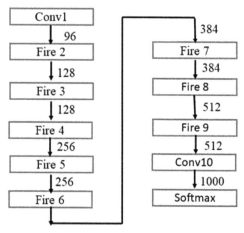

FIGURE 9.8   SqueezeNet architecture.

9.6.4 METHOD BASED ON CNN-RNN

As illustrated in Figure 9.9, this method employed the CNN-RNN pipeline to model spatiotemporal characteristics across pictures. For each picture instrument label remark, 512-dimensional encoding was acquired from the matching third algorithm to learn temporal encoding for the complete phase. The trained feature was utilized to learn the Spatiotemporal patterns that eventually differentiated in the LSTM network. As the encoding for the phase, LSTM set up 512 hidden units that produce a 512-dimensional, temporary average pooled vector. Softmax was used to encode the expected label at the forecast level of 10 dimensions.

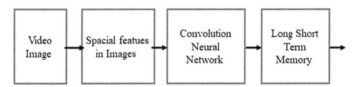

FIGURE 9.9   Method-based CNN-RNN.

9.6.5 METHOD BASED ON CNN-RNN INPUT WITH THE TIME SEQUENCE OF IMAGES AND TOOL LABELS

As illustrated in Figure 9.10, the CNN-RNN pipeline was introduced to the picture as time-series data with instrument labels for modeling spatiotemporal characteristics. This approach employed the same CNN-RNN pipeline as the previous method, but before conducting temporal modeling with LSTM, it added instrument labels for 512-dimensional encoding from CNN.

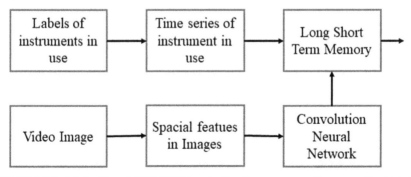

FIGURE 9.10   Method-based CNN-RNN input with a time sequence of images and tool labels.

9.7   EXPERIMENTAL RESULTS

For endoscopic video, a method based on ResNet and LSTM worked well. There were some memories for the "submucosal" "injection" and "urostomy," which account for 5% of total video frames, for the smaller phases. For each phase, total metrics were derived as weightless and prevalent-weighted averages. Overall, the accuracy was 87.6% (frames properly detected/total frames) (Tables 9.1 and 9.2; Figure 9.11).

TABLE 9.1   Four Surgical Tools Detection Using CNN with SGD Method Summary

Layer (Type)	Output Shape	Parameters
Conv2D layer 1	None, 82, 124, 16	1216
MaxPooling	None, 16, 24, 16	0
Conv2D layer 2	None, 14, 22, 32	4640
Flatten	None, 9856	0
Dense	None, 4096	40374272
Dense	None, 2048	8390656
Dense	None, 4	8196

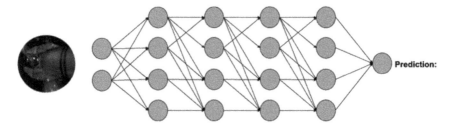

FIGURE 9.11   Four surgical tools detection using CNN with SGD.

TABLE 9.2   Summary Surgical Activity Recognition on Laparoscopic Video

Dataset	Type	Detection Accuracy (%)	References
Cholec80	CNN with SGD	82.14	[3]
M2CAI16	ResNet-50 with 3-layers	88.75	[16]
Cholec80	CNN or RNN with temporal sequence augmentation strategy	97.87	[2]
Endovis	3D CNN	85.1	[7]
Cholec80	Partial CNN	81	[1]
Cholec80	Full CNN	92.9	[18]

For cataract video, the SqeezeNet method worked wonderfully. Surgical phase recognition using a DL approach can be done with great accuracy according to the model, data type, and procedure complexity. Various intra-operative data sources have proven to be effective in training DL models. However, for most models, manual expertise is still required. DL models have the potential to move surgical workflows toward uniformity, efficiency, and objectivity in the future, resulting in better patient outcomes (Tables 9.3 and 9.4).

TABLE 9.3 POEMNet's Performance Throughout Time

Phases	Precision
Submucosal injection	0.667
Mucosotomy	0.837
The tunnel beneath the mucosa	0.955
Myotomy	0.791
Closure of the mucosotomy	0.848

TABLE 9.4 Performance for Phase Classification on Cataract Video

Metric	RNN with Multiple LSTM Nodes	A Method Based on SqeezeNet	A Method Based on CNN-RNN	With the Time Sequence of Images and Instrument Labels, the Method is Based on CNN-RNN Input
Unweighted accuracy	0.959	0.956	0.921	0.915
Frequency-weighted accuracy	0.957	0.955	0.919	0.913
Inverse variance-weighted accuracy	0.976	0.958	0.928	0.920

9.8 CONCLUSION

The users through a basic neural network implementation pipeline, from basic programming concepts in the python programming language to data handling and DL operations. Finally, the user will be able to design, train, and test a simple neural network for surgical tool classification.

Despite the number of algorithms that have been proposed for CNN-based algorithms, there are still many technical difficulties that need to be addressed to minimize them.

Researchers are still trying to improve the accuracy of tracking and identifying laparoscopic devices. Currently, the methods used for this task are not ideal.

Data are critical for the training of neural networks. Aside from being able to identify and apprehend surgical tools, the availability of publicly-available datasets can also allow the study of temporal information.

In 3D FCNN architecture, spatial-temporal features can be utilized to improve the performance of 2D models based on a single-frame surgical information tool.

For end-to-end tracking, there is one completely Convolution spatiotemporal model that is suited for training with less supervision. It relies on a ConvLSTM, which uses current provisional information to streamline class peak activation in video and improve device detection, localization, and operation over time.

ML and DL algorithms may employ instrument labels to recognize distinct phases in cataract video phase identification. DL methods for spatiotemporal modeling video pictures may be more accurate than local image modeling features of video images in identifying pre-segmented phases.

This chapter exhibits the capacity of DL can now recognize details in videos generated by surgery videos. This capability could be used to aid in planning operations.

KEYWORDS

- **Cataracts Video**
- **Convolution Neural Networks**
- **Deep-Learning Model**
- **Endoscopic Video**
- **Gated Recurrent Units**
- **Laparoscopic Video**
- **Operating Room**
- **Phase Recognition**
- **Recurrent Neural Networks**
- **Surgical Instruments**

REFERENCES

1. Twinanda, A. P., & Sherif, S., (2017). EndoNet: A deep architecture for recognition tasks on laparoscopic videos. *IEEE Transactions on Medical Imaging, 36*(1), 86–97. doi: 10.1109/TMI.20.

2. Al Hajj, H., & Lamard, M., (2018). Monitoring tool usage in surgery videos using boosted convolutional and recurrent neural networks. *Medical Image Analysis, 47*, 203–218.

3. Alapatt, D., & Pietro, M. (2020). *Artificial Intelligence in Surgery: Neural Networks and Deep Learning*. Retrieved from arXiv:2009.13411.

4. Armine, V., & Mutter, D., (2018). *Weakly-Supervised Learning for Tool Localization in Laparoscopic Videos*. Retrieved from arXiv:1806.05573.

5. Choi, B., & Jo, K., (2017). Surgical-tools detection based on convolutional neural network in laparoscopic robot-assisted surgery. *Proceedings of Annual International Conference of the IEEE Engineering in Medicine and Biology Society* (pp. 1756–1759). New York (NY): IEEE.

6. Chung, J., & Gulcehre, C., (2014). Empirical evaluation of gated recurrent neural networks on sequence modeling. *NIPS 2014 Workshop on Deep Learning.*

7. Colleoni, E., & Moccia, S., (2019). Deep learning-based robotic tool detection and articulation estimation with spatio-temporal layers. *IEEE Robotics and Automation, 4*(3), 2714–2721.

8. Congmin, Y., & Zhao, Z., (2020). Image-based laparoscopic tool detection and tracking using convolutional neural networks: A review of the literature. *Computer Assisted Surgery, 25*(1), 15–28. doi: 10.1080/24699322.2020.1801842.

9. Daniel, M., & Sebastian, S., (2015). VoxNet: A 3D convolutional neural network for real-time object recognition. *Proceedings of (IROS) IEEE/RSJ International Conference on Intelligent Robots and Systems* (pp. 922–928).

10. Funke, I., & Mees, S., (2019). Video-based surgical skill assessment using 3D convolutional neural networks. *International Journal Comput. Assist Radio Surg., 14*(7), 1217–1225. doi: 10.1007/s11548-019-01995-1.

11. Guedon, A. C. P., & Meij, S., (2020). Deep learning for surgical phase recognition using endoscopic videos. *Surgical Endoscopic*. Retrieved from https://doi.org/10.1007/s00464-020-08110-5.

12. Guédon, S. E. P. M., & Osman, N. M. M. H., (2020). Deep learning for surgical phase recognition using endoscopic videos. *Surg Endosc*. Retrieved from: Https://doi.org/10.1007/s00464-020-08110-5.

13. Krizhevsky, A., & Sutskever, I., (2012). ImageNet classification with deep convolution neural network. *Advances in Neural Information Processing Systems, 25.*

14. LeCun, Y., & Bottou, L., (1998). Gradient-based learning applied to document recognition. *Proceeding of IEEE Transaction.*

15. Loukas, C., (2019). Surgical phase recognition of short video shots based on temporal modeling of deep features. *Proceedings of the 12ᵗʰ International Joint Conference on Biomedical Engineering Systems and Technologies (BIOSTEC 2019)* (pp. 21–29).

16. Mishra, K. A., (2018). Learning latent temporal connectionism of deep residual visual abstractions for identifying surgical tools in laparoscopy procedures. *Proceedings of the IEEE Conference on Computer Vision and Pattern Recognition (CVPR).*

17. Münzer, B., Schoeffmann, K., & Böszörmenyi, L., (2018). Content-based processing and analysis of endoscopic images and videos: A survey. *Multimed. Tools Appl., 77,* 1323–1362.

18. Nwoye, C. I., & Gonzalez, C., (2020). Recognition of instrument-tissue interactions in endoscopic videos via action triplets. *MICCAI.*

19. Nwoye, C. I., & Mutter, D., (2019). Weakly supervised convolutional LSTM approach for tool tracking in laparoscopic videos. *International Journal Comput. Assist Radio Surgery, 14*(6), 1059–1067. doi: 10.1007/s11548-019-01958-6.

20. Rui, H., & Chen, C., (2017). *An End-to-end 3D Convolutional Neural Network for Action Detection and Segmentation in Videos.* Retrieved from arXiv:1712.01111v1.

21. Sahu, M., & Mukhopadhyay, A., (2017). Addressing multi-label imbalance problem of surgical tool detection using CNN. *Int. J. CARS, 12,* 1013–1020.

22. Sahu, M., & Szengel, A., (2020). Surgical phase recognition by learning phase transitions. *Current Directions in Biomedical Engineering, 6*(1). Retrieved from https://doi.org/10.1515/cdbme-2020-0037.

23. Simonyan, K., & Zisserman, A., (2015). Very deep convolutional networks for large-scale image recognition. *International Conference on Learning Representations.*

24. Szegedy, C., & Liu, W., (2015). Going deeper with convolutions. *IEEE Conference on Computer Vision and Pattern Recognition (CVPR).*

25. Ward, T. M., & Hashimoto, D., (2021). Automated operative phase identification in peroral endoscopic myotomy. *Surgical Endoscopic, 35*(7), 4008–4015. doi: 10.1007/s00464-020-07833-9.

26. Yu, F., & Silva, C., (2019). Assessment of automated identification of phases in videos of cataract surgery using machine learning and deep learning techniques. *JAMA Netw. Open,* 1860. doi: 10.1001/jamanetworkopen.

27. Zisimopoulos, O., Flouty, E., Luengo, I., Giataganas, P., Nehme, J., Andre, C., & Stoyanov, D., (2018). *DeepPhase: Surgical Phase Recognition in CATARACTS Videos.* ArXiv.

28. Zhang, X., & Zou, J., (2016). Accelerating very deep convolutional networks for classification and detection. *IEEE Transactions on Pattern Analysis & Machine Intelligence, 38*(10), 1943–1955.

CHAPTER 10

WEARABLE SENSOR-BASED MONITORING AND CLASSIFICATION USING DEEP LEARNING FOR PERSONALIZED HEALTHCARE

MURUGAN SUBRAMANIAN,[1] S. KANAGA SUBA RAJA,[2]
A. SAMPATH KUMAR,[3] MANIKANDAN RAMACHANDRAN,[4] and
AMBESHWAR KUMAR[4]

[1]*Assistant Professor, Department of Computer Science and Engineering, Sri Aravindar Engineering College, Tamil Nadu, India*

[2]*Professor, Department of Computer Science and Engineering, Easwari Engineering College, Tamil Nadu, India*

[3]*Assistant Professor, Department of Computer Science and Engineering, Dambi Dollo University, Ethiopia*

[4]*School of Computing, SASTRA Deemed University, Tamil Nadu, India*

ABSTRACT

Wearable sensors are important in the medical field because they allow doctors to monitor patients' health. Wearable sensors are being developed to diagnose continuous key biomarkers, as well as to evaluate and monitor physical health. So, employing deep learning (DL) and IoT through wearable sensors, our suggested system delivers a health monitoring system based on personalized healthcare. Both features were extracted using a pre-trained RCNN, and treatment was started for patients with anomalous numerical data range. The imaging data of the patients can be gathered and has been

Handbook of Research on Artificial Intelligence and Soft Computing Techniques in Personalized Healthcare Services, Uma N. Dulhare, A. V. Senthil Kumar, Amit Datta, Seddik Bri, Ibrahiem M. M. El Emary, (Eds.)

graded for disease prognosis and stage. The data was categorized using VGG-16 and inception V3 algorithm hybrid CNN architectures. Examine for diabetes, heart disease, and a rapid rate of breathing. When compared to existing machine learning (ML) algorithms, the simulation results produced the greatest results, overall testing accuracy of 96.2%. The readers gain the knowledge about healthcare monitoring devices. The wearable sensor device enables the physician relatives and friends to keep track of the patient's health. They are indeed influenced by the concepts of real-time monitoring and faster disease diagnosis.

10.1 INTRODUCTION

Different patients with various disease and predicted with various risk are treated by medicine also known as precision medicine. As Hippocrates stated, "It is far more important to know what sort of person the disease has then what sort of disease the person has" [1], This gives core of personalized medicine, focused towards gene, living style and inheritance of patients, etc., rather than the phenotype of disease, which treats an "average patient" having "one-size-fits-all" medical process. Due to development of medical database in size in characterizing the responses and genes of patient, personalized medicine is more and more feasible substitute to conventional medicine system depends on the data of omics. The diseases which are highly complex and predicted on the basis of genes, history of medicine and environment are treated by personalized medicine because of its various applications. Cancer, diabetes, cancer, and psychological disorder are treated by this personalized medicine. Patient's clinical response for drugs prescribed having huge diverse profile is difficult to predict and considered as a major difficulty in this personalized medicine. In CVD treatment, there occurs the dramatic variation in the response of the patient towards VioxxTM and Coumad in TM [2]. The differences among the individual are perfectly provided by studying the medical record of a patient and the patient's characteristics are contrasted with records and produce consistent drug response prediction. In 1st two decades of the 21st century produced several algorithms of machine learning (ML) necessary for the behavior of "learning." By increasing the experience, the algorithm performance is also increased, which attracted the attention of medical industry towards the personalized medicine realm. This personalized medicine is focused on the root for the causes of disease. Identification of pathogens problems caused by the data problems are treated by

ML, whereas the correlation is unscrambled among the profile and disease phenotype of patients by utilizing the statistical power. Recent development in the ML algorithm is a promising tool for discovering the pattern of data, which is a challenging task. These data pattern is used for disease prediction with deep inferences [3].

The details of patients having weight, age, BP, data of medical history and genomics are also dealt by this personalized medicine. Based on these data generated by the personalized medicine, doctors will start the treatment. The data obtained are unstructured and inhomogeneous with huge size and dimensions, which is very useful for the system of computation [4]. The "learning system" is adopted due to its consistency towards the information update. So, the solution for the treating the patients are continuously produced, which depends on various laboratory tests and the electronic medical records (EMRs). The patient's current status and their medical reports are fed into the system. If there are any advances in the medical system, this system also has the flexibility to change. Accuracy and prediction of discovering disease, treatment, and administration of drug are built or set up based on the techniques of artificial intelligence (AI). In some people, opposing reactions of drugs and metabolism of enzymes are controlled, and the problems of removing those drugs from their body, when it is overdosed, it is removed before its action [1]. Nowadays, electronic health records (EHR) or computerized clinical medical records will provide the patient's details by the data present in it and improves the delivery of medical service.

Deep neural networks (DNNs) are recent ML algorithms [6]. Automatic feature identification of data and huge dataset is trained by DNNs advancement. In the biomedical field of drug discovery, repositioning the drug, ADMET (absorption, distribution, metabolism, excretion, and toxicity) property prediction, retro synthesis, and protein folding is some of the applications of DNN. Because of these applications, synthesis of 'generalized' medicine to struggle the diseases are enabled. Adopting the personalized medicine is a new challenge. DNNs are capable of handling highly complex and multi-dimensional data whereas the conventional ML techniques are not. DNNs are used in the personalized medicine due to its high potentiality to efficiently relate the medical history, data from laboratory, genotype, and family inheritance [7].

Organization of this research is as follows: Section 10.2 discuss related works. Section 10.3 system model proposed personalized medicine. Section 10.4 discusses performance analysis. Finally, Section 10.5 concludes the chapter with further research directions.

10.2   RELATED WORKS

Numerous ML algorithms and AI algorithms are utilized in the biomedical field and particular personalized medicine. Few of these algorithms are described in this section. The fall types are classified and detected by SVM in a study by Suwinski [8]. To prevent the elder members of the society in falling accidents, this study is used, and it is classified and detected. SVM resulted the accuracy of 99% among the five various classifiers are used in this method. The cardiac monitoring device's accuracy is detected by using SVM in Ref. [9]. The differences between the artifacts and the real events of cardiac arrests among the patients are not monitored correctly by the generic systems. Highly accurate results of patients are obtained by using SVM's refining process. This study proved that there is a specificity improvement of patients in the detection of Atrial Fibrillation (AF) whereas the generic detector produces low specificity. Fuzzy cognitive maps are extended to produce case based fuzzy cognitive map (CBFCM) used to classify and predict the data. The pattern of inference and the fundamental connection among various perceptions are represented by CBFCM. Personalized medicine uses this technique to analyze the connection among various diseases and information of particular patient like BP, type of blood, gene which is the basis for pattern inference method to detect disease in patient. Genomic and Personalized Medicine research by Ahmed [10]. They developed a decision support system for detection of disease through classification. They considered three parameters (C1, C2, and C3) for every patient, which is the input value, they are genetic information, age, clinical signs or biological results. Later applying the concepts of fuzzy perfect similarity is obtained between the cases known and patient and the results are drawn from it. In this diagnosis and decision of therapy are provided by FCM. Heart disease detection is performed by fuzzy logic in Ref. [11] utilizing six fields of input (chest pain, BP, blood sugar, cholesterol, maximum heart rate, old peak) and two fields of output (result, and precautions) with 22 rules comprised as rule base. According to the output the heart disease is detected, and precautions are taken. The results observed have the accuracy of 92%. Neural networks and decision tree are used in the work [12] for developing a patient specific real time alarm algorithm. They experienced that alarms are constructed in retrospect with a dataset that incorporates thousands of patients for detecting contrary clinical and medical environments. This study produced worse performance on considering one and two patients as a population. Further, patient-specific alarming models from a specific individual models' data are explored by employing neural network and decision tree. This result in higher accuracy rate (96%, 99%, 79%, and 99%) for NN and (84%, 98%, 72%, and 98%) for Decision Tree. NN achieved the best results. Around 11 patients at various ages were gathered in 196 hours. And single output layer in a neural network having one hidden layer was utilized having 2 various training times (2 and 8 hours). Even though the network performance was poor, several studies show the ability of ANN to accurately diagnose some diseases, e.g., malignant melanoma, eye issues, and various forms of cancer are accurately diagnosed by ANN with the criteria of diagnosis and spectral data. Various disease diagnoses use ANN application; ANN application in the medical field is studied in Ref. [13]. Stones present in the kidney are diagnosed by ANN in Ref. [14]. Dataset with the records of 1,000 patients in that 7 attributes consists of kidney stone symptoms. Learning vector quantization (LVQ), MLP (multilayer perceptron) and RBF (radial basis function), with back propagation are three NN algorithm used in this research. Also, testing of 15%, validation of 15% and training of 70% is performed by WEKA tool. Around 92% of accuracy with 922 instances with perfect classification was achieved by MLP and this algorithm performs well as compared to another algorithm. In Ref. [15], a rule based expert system was proposed which generates the data relevant to information of results, consultation, and probable diagnosis. Chicken pox, Malaria, diabetics, diarrhea, asthma, cholera, hepatitis, jaundice, thyroid, typhoid, sciatica, migraine, Alzheimer's disease and bronchitis are the main scope of this research. Another rule based expert method was developed in Ref. [16] in which the symbols are inferenced, by transforming the particular knowledge to form of standard symbols. Symptoms/signs and diseases of the patients were collected as data. Groups were formed by symptoms, suspicion, or suspension or suggestion categorizes the outcome and provides idea to the doctor. SVM and RBF type of ANN forms the basis for the intelligent system implemented in Ref. [5]. This system of ANN is used for heart disease diagnosis. SVM also proposed in this system and it achieved 86.42% of accuracy when compared with RDF. ML algorithms are widely used in the development of personalized medicine are described in this section. This system is in the beginning stage and still faces a few challenges when linked to ML algorithm in this report.

10.3   SYSTEM MODEL

This section discusses about the proposed personalized healthcare model using wearable device-based monitoring system using IoT and ML techniques. Patients can wear smart bands that monitor their condition and transmit regular information to a database that doctors and medical practitioners can access thanks to the internet of things (IoT) and ML AI. The gadgets can track a patient's vital signs and organs, as well as provide a progress report to a database. Pathogen presence and symptoms are also collected and reported by the system. This is a significant development that will aid the healthcare sector in delivering optimal practices. Initially, data has been collected as numerical data through wearable sensor. Then the data has been collected from hospital database for particular patient through IoT module, by combining both the dataset has been created. The data has been processed for cleaning the data with respect to get good outcomes. This will be achieved by steps of pre-processing on data training. It has to filter and remove the noise of the data using a median filter. Any text piece and image which is irrelevant to the data context and output at end will be quantified as noise. E.g., language stop words (words of a language that are used often – am, is, of, in, the, etc.), links or URLs, entities of social media (hash tags and mentions), punctuations and words specific to industry. Entities of noise present in the text are eliminated in the next step. Entities of noise dictionary are prepared to remove noise in a general approach, and by using tokens, the text objects are iterated, and finally, these tokens are eliminated. The architecture of the proposed model is given in Figure 10.1.

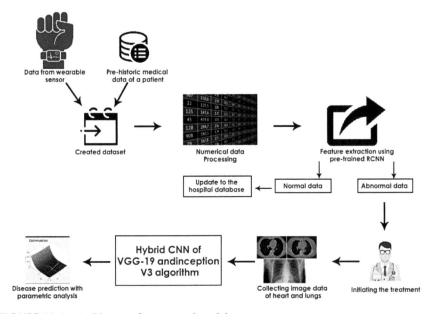

FIGURE 10.1   Architecture for proposed model.

Then the data has to be segmented for dividing a string of written language into its component text. Here the text segmentation has been carried out using N-grams segmentation. Multiple words combined together to create N-grams. When the value of N=1, it is called unigram, if the value of N is 2 it is called bigrams, and if it is 3 means then it is known as trigrams, etc. So many information's are not present in unigram as like bigram and trigram. The structure of language was captured by N-grams. Working of context is more when the value of N is high. Application decides the optimal length of N, when N-grams are so small, significant variations in the image will not be captured, if the N-grams are big means "general knowledge" was not captured and it will work only for specific cases.

10.3.1 PRE-TRAINED RCNN-BASED FEATURE EXTRACTION

The neural network of pre-trained RCNN comprises of 5 convolution layers, 1 recurrent layer and 2 layers of fully connected. In relation with initial five stages frequently used seven-layer Alex-Net, the central stage has been studied using CNN layers and obtains visual patterns. To evaluation of spatial requirements among the visual patterns of the central stage that is deployed using RNN layer. To collect the RNN results two fully connected layer has been used finally along with studying broad illustration of image. Subsequently softmax layer of N-way has been employed for image classification. The detail discussion of pre-trained RCNN has been given in Figure 10.2.

As shown on the left part of Figure 10.2, we initially use layers of five convolutions in evaluating the depiction of feature from the central layer of pixels from raw images. On the basis of the output in visualization, maximum abstract and feasible patterns have been extracted when there are numerous convolution layers. When image net train the image, the fifth layer of convolution has been probably localizing segments as well as the image objects. Hence these features of CNN have become highly appropriate in depicting the features of the central stage, on the basis of which they are similarly study the spatial requirements of highly suitable for using RNN, along with attaining optimal broad depiction of image through linking with the two layers which are fully connected. By back propagation, the broad depiction might be transformed in reverse for RNN which could enhance encoding due to requirements spatially also CNN get assistance from RNN for optimal learning of features at middle-level and low-level.

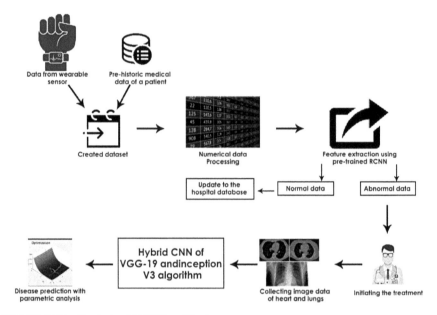

FIGURE 10.2   Pre-trained RCNN architecture.

The image training requires image which is resized initially by 256×256 pixels, where these are minimized through their mean value of pixel, on the basis of where the 10 subcrops with 227×227 size (one center, four corners, with its horizontal flips) has been obtained for training the data. The similar settings of filter in Alex-net have been required by CNN as shown in Figure 10.6. The sizes (numbers) of filters were: 11×11 (96), 5×5 (256), 3×3 (384), 3×3 (384), and 3×3 (256). The stride is 2 and remaining is 1 in the layer initially. For the 1st, 2nd, and 5th layer, they also have three layers of pooling correspondingly, and each one of them has kernel size of 3×3 with max pooling as well as their strides will be 2. Hence the feature size for their response maps of layer five in CNN is given as 256×6×6 (channel number × width × height), and this will be input for RNN layer. But the output region in layer five of CNN is 6×6 regions; hence the RNN sequence length must be 36. The scanning window size has been fixed as 6 (1×6 for one row or 6×1 for one column of regions) for RNN layer, as well as 6 RNN windows are present for every four sequences. Each region has been depicted as a vector feature of 256 dimensions (5th layer CNN's channel number). Therefore, RNN matrix for weight and their size is given as Whh→, Wih→; Whh←, Wih← Whh↓, Wih↓; Whh↑, Wih↑ 256×256 were set. The transformation which is non-linear are fh, fg, and fo were all set to functions of ReLU (Figure 10.3).

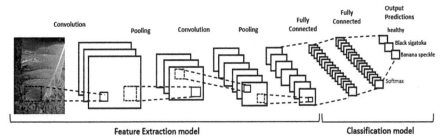

FIGURE 10.3 Pre-trained RCNN architecture for banana leaf.

10.3.2 PRE-TRAINED RCNN ALGORITHM

10.3.2.1 PROCESS OF TRAINING

➤ **Input:** Labeled data trained as $X' = \{X^{(1)}, X^{(2)}, ..., X^{(K)}\}, K$ is the sum of all classes.

$CNN \leftarrow X'$; % Feature vectors are extracted by sending the raw training data are into CNN.

$F' = \{F^{(1)}, F^{(2)}, ..., F^{(K)}\}$; high-dimensional space is mapped with the extracted feature vectors to be enclosed by class-by-class CGC.

for i 1 to K do

$D^{(i)} \leftarrow F^{(i)}$; % Distance between any of ith class two points is calculated.
$\{T_{i1}, T_{i2}\} \leftarrow$ arg min $(D^{(i)})$; % Invent the closest two points from $D^{(i)}$, note it T_{i1} and T_{i2}.

$F^{(i)} = F^{(i)} - T_{i1}, T_{i2}$; Marked points are deleted.

$T_{i3} \leftarrow$ Calculate P to N $(F^{(i)}, \{T_{i1}, T_{i2}\})$; The minimum distance from $F^{(i)}$ to T_{i1} and T_{i2} is calculated.

$\theta_1 \leftarrow \{T_{i1}, T_{i2}, T_{i3}\}$; % T_{i1}, T_{i2} and T_{i3} constitutes the first plane triangle θ_1

$P_1 = \{X \mid d_{X\theta_1} < Th_1, X \in R^n\}$ % P_1 is θ_1 coverage having Th_1 as covering radius known as $\psi3$ neuron, and the distance between X and θ_1 is indicated by $d_{X\theta_1}$.

$F^{(i)} = F^{(i)} - \{T_{i1}, T_{i2}, T_{i3}\}$;

$F^{(i)} \leftarrow$ *exclude P* $(F^{(i)}, P_1)$; % Exclude P is a function used to exclude points from $F^{(i)}$ covered by P_1 from which the points are excluded and *exclude P* is the function for that.

$j = 1$;

While F(i) $\neq \emptyset$% repeat the steps above until $F^{(i)}$ is empty.

$\theta_{j+1} \leftarrow$ Find P to N $(F^{(i)}, \theta_j)$;

$$P_{j+1} = \{X \mid d_{X\theta_{j+1}} < Th_i, X \in R^n\};$$
$$F^{(i)} \leftarrow exclude\ P(F^{(i)}, P_{j+1});$$

$j = j + 1$;

End

$T_i = \cup_{j=1}^m P_j$; % the class i's final CGC with $\psi 3$ neuron

End

➢ **Output:** T = $\{T_1, T_2 \dots \dots T_K\}$; % the set CGC of all classes.

Feature extraction method

➢ **Input:** an image x' and text to be extracted.

$f' \leftarrow CNN \leftarrow x'$;

$\rho_i = min_{j=1}^{M_j} \rho_{ij}, i = 1, 2, ..., K$; % ρ_{ij} is the f' and class i with neuron j coverage distance.

➢ **Output:** class $- argmin\ K_{i=1}\ \rho_i, i = 1, 2, ..., K$ % the class that x' belongs to.

The output class shows extracted feature of both image and numerical data. Abnormal and normal data has been decided through the decision tree algorithm. A decision tree based on a examples of training set $\{(x1, y1), ..., (xn, yn)\}$ where feature vectors are $x1, ..., xn \in Rd$ the and labels are $y1, ..., yn \in [1, ..., c]$ are constructed. Two ordered child node are present in each internal node of tree and rule for decision forms $x(i) < \alpha$, in which ith attribute is denoted by x(i) and real number is denoted by *a*. Left child node are directed with the feature vectors and right child node is directed with other vectors. Therefore, **x** every example possesses the path to any one of the leaves from the root, and it is represented by $l(\mathbf{x})$. *t* is the label associated with each leaf, $t\ (l(\mathbf{x})$ represents the **x** example assigned to the label. On executing the 3rd line every time a new iteration is started. A large number of samples is present then it is only possible to read a number of samples which are predefined, or else the entire dataset is used. In every iteration new node levels are attached to the tree. The decision of splitting of labeling the leaf *v* is taken in line 5 based on the criterion of stopping. This criterion may be samples count or few thresholds attaining the node, or impurity of node which is denoted as G and it is used to measure the label's homogeneity present in samples attaining the node. Algorithm of tree construction is described in succeeding sections.

10.3.3 DECISION TREE ALGORITHM

Input Training set $\{x_1, y_1, ..., (x_n, y_n)\}$

1. Start T to be a single unlabeled node.
2. **While** there are unlabeled leaves in T **do**
3. Navigate data samples to their corresponding leaves.
4. **for all** unlabeled leaves v in T **do**
5. **if** v satisfies stopping criterion **or** there are no samples reaching v **then**
6. Label v with most frequent label among samples reaching v
7. **else**
8. Select candidate splits for v and evaluate D for each of them.
9. Split v with highest estimated D among all possible candidate splits.
10. **end if**
11. **end for**
12. **end while**

Constructing decision tree for one node for one iteration.

➢ **Input:** Primary dataset values of training as $\{(x_1, y_1)... (x_n, y_n)\}$.
1. Single node T is initialized.
2. **while** T is with unlabeled leaves **do**
3. **for all** T *with* unlabeled leaves v **do**
4. **if** stopping criterion is satisfied by v **or** samples are not attaining v **then**
5. Label v is labeled with the utmost common label amongst samples attaining v
6. **else**
7. For splitting v select the candidate and D is estimated.
8. **end if**
9. **end for**
10. v unlabeled leaf is split so the value of nvD is maximum amongst all unlabeled leaves and every candidate possible are split, where nv is the samples count attaining v.
11. **end while**

When normal data is obtained, it has been updated to the hospital database, when the data is abnormal, then initiating of treatment. Then the MRI images of the heart and lungs have been collected for prediction of cardiac attack and respiratory problem. This image has been classified using architecture Hybrid CNN with VGG-16 and algorithm of inception V3.

10.3.4   ARCHITECTURE OF HYBRID CNN WITH VGG-16 AND ALGORITHM OF INCEPTION V3-BASED CLASSIFICATION

Three main layers present in CNN are convolution layer, the pooling layer and the fully connected layer. Model's knowledge is provided by pooling and convolutional layer and classification is obtained by the full connected layer. VGG-16 and inception V3 algorithm is used along with CNN. VGG-16 is a modest model which is applied to the CNN model due to in-depth structure and double or triple convolution layers associated with it. The parameters 138 million are computed by this model approximately. An efficient feature eliminator uses the benefits of pertained models.

The implementation architecture of VGG-16 is given in Figure 10.4.

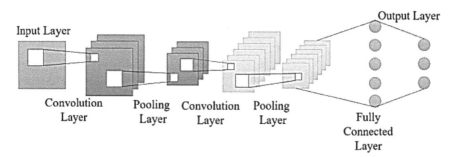

FIGURE 10.4   Implementation architecture of VGG-16.

Three convolution layers are present in the architecture of VGG-16 for extracting features, ReLU layer having maximum pooling layers are followed by every convolution layer. Classification is performed by fully connected layer which possesses three layers, in which two of it is aided as hidden layer. Categories of images are represented in 1,000 units which is present in the last fully connected layer. Advantages of small size filters are preserved in large filters in this structure. As compared to the models exist before this VggNet performs well by the usage of some special parameters. A ReLU layer is replaced by two ReLU layers and act as a convolution layer. Because of the decrease in the input volume's spatial size, volume depth is increased because of the increment in the filter count. VGG16 network model is finely tuned and used in this architecture having the dataset with samples of m number $\{(x(1), y(1)), ..., (x(m), y(m))\}$ for training. The cost function of the entire network is described as follows:

$$J(W,b) = \left[\frac{1}{m} \sum_{i=1}^{m} \left(\frac{1}{2} \| K_{w,b}(x^{(i)}) - y^{(i)} \|^2 \right) \right]$$
$$+ \frac{\lambda}{2} \sum_{l=1}^{nl-1} \sum_{i=1}^{sl} \sum_{j=1}^{sl+1} \left(W_{ji}^{(l)} \right)^2 \quad (1)$$

Where the model of NN is described as $K_{w,b}(x^{(i)})$, Layer l j^{th} element and layer $l + 1$ i^{th} element's weight of connection is represented by $W_{ji}^{(l)}$, and neuron of hidden layer's bias term is denoted by b. The issue of overfitting, weight reduction is prevented by the right side regulation item present in Eqn. (1) and cost function λ's relative importance (before and after λ) is adjusted. The optimization algorithm of Gradient descent is adopted for getting the solution $J(W, b)$ having minimum value in Eqn. (1) and W and b 's partial derivatives are calculated for the algorithm of back propagation.

Figure 10.5 shows the structure of Inception architecture core with three inception modules. Inception module process are described as: 1st layers of 1×1 reduces the previous layer's feature map dimensions; 1×11×n, 3×3 convolutional layers are used to extract features, Filter Concat layer is the final layer comprising Depth Concat layer and LRN (local response normalization) layer. Extracted features from the convolutional layers are fused by this Depth Concat layer. If the depth of the network is increased, then the feature channel numbers will also increase. On selecting the huge kernels of convolution like 3×3, 5×5, computation amount will have increased accordingly. Rather than using fully connected layer, average pooling layer is used in this architecture and for the forward propagation it uses auxiliary softmax layer.

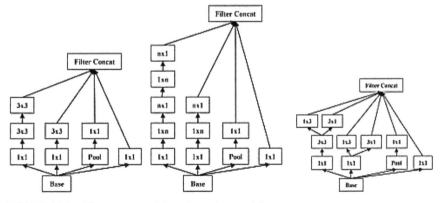

FIGURE 10.5 The structure of three inception modules.

An additional 1×1 convolution layer is used in front of 3×3 convolution layer and 5×5 convolution layer in Inception modules network, because of this, the computation process is robust and cost effective. The model of pre-trained inception V3 is introduced in this chapter. The model's classification portion is replaced by 128×1 dense layers. Feature extraction is better processes by fine-tuning of MRI. 224×224×3 is the size of the input image provided for training Inception V3, Different inception modules process the input values. The cost of computation and overfitting issue are prevented by this model. 128×1 and 3×1 or 2×1 is the dimension of the dense layer through which the input image is passed. In this layer segmentation is performed. The inception V3 architecture is shown in Figure 10.6.

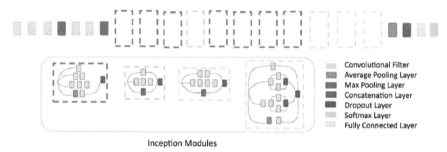

Inception Modules

FIGURE 10.6   Inception V3 architecture.

10.4   PERFORMANCE ANALYSIS

In this experiment, samples of count 6,936 are used totally and every case uses 2,313 samples. Wearable sensor with samples of 1,850, hospital database with the samples of 1,851 and normal cases uses 1,850 samples are used for dataset training and testing by dividing the entire dataset into 80%–20%, The enduring samples of 463 as wearable sensors, samples of 462 as hospital database, and samples of 463 as normal cases were utilized for the testing.

Figures 10.7–10.10 show comparative analysis of accuracy, precision, recall, and F1-score. The Confusion matrix for abnormal and normal data detection has been given in Figure 10.11.

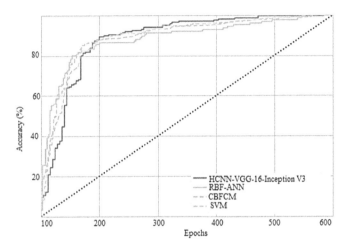

FIGURE 10.7   Comparative analysis of accuracy.

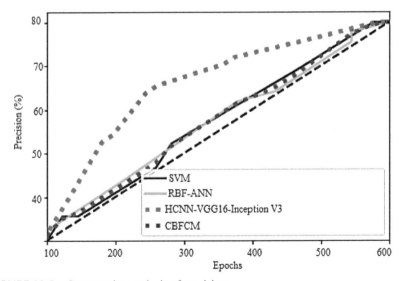

FIGURE 10.8   Comparative analysis of precision.

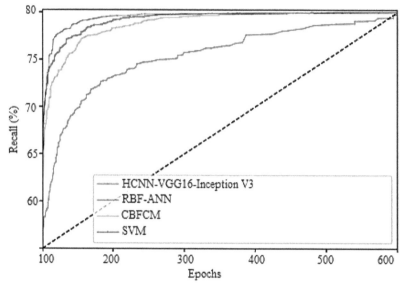

FIGURE 10.9   Comparative analysis of recall.

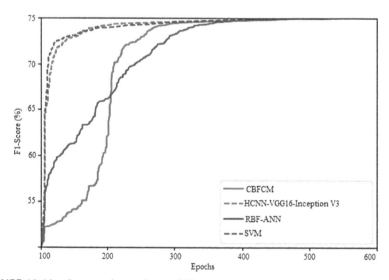

FIGURE 10.10   Comparative analyzes of F1-score.

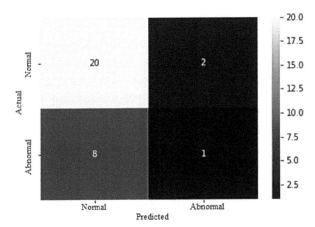

FIGURE 10.11   Confusion matrixes for abnormal and normal data detection.

Table 10.1 and Figure 10.12 shows the comparative analysis for proposed and existing technique for parameters.

TABLE 10.1   Comparative Analysis Table

Parameters	SVM	CBFCM	RBF-ANN	HCNN-VGG16-Inception V3
Accuracy	90	92	93	95
Precision	74	75	78	80
Recall	76	79	80	82
F1-Score	70	72	73	75

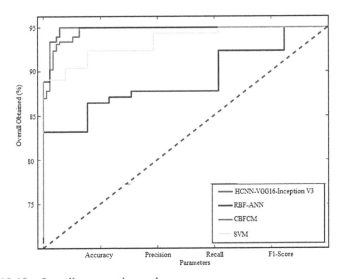

FIGURE 10.12   Overall comparative analyzes.

10.5   CONCLUSION

ML algorithms significantly encourage the growth of personalized medicine in regions like drugs development, disease characteristics and identification, and prediction of therapeutics effect. So, this chapter proposes the personalized medicine The created data has been pre-processed and segmented for numerical data, and then the features have been extracted and separated the numerical data and image data. Here both features have been extracted using Pre-trained RCNN, for the patients with abnormal numerical data range, the treatment has been initiated. There we obtain image data of the patients, and it has been classified for prediction and stage of the disease. Here we examine for range of diabetes, cardiac disease and respiratory rate based on lung movement. The data has been classified using hybrid Convolutional Neural Network architectures of VGG-16 and Inception V3 algorithm. The simulation results provided the best outcomes as compared with other algorithms of ML achieved accuracy of testing by 96.2%.

KEYWORDS

- Atrial Fibrillation
- Case Based Fuzzy Cognitive Map
- Deep Neural Networks
- Electronic Health Records
- Inception V3
- Internet of Things
- Monitoring Systems
- Pre-Trained RCNN
- VGG-16
- Wearable Devices

REFERENCES

1. Fröhlich, H., (2018). From hype to reality: Data science enabling personalized medicine. *BMC Medicine, 16*(1), 1–15.
2. Cirillo, D., & Alfonso, V., (2019). Big data analytics for personalized medicine. *Current Opinion in Biotechnology, 58*, 161–167.

3. Lambin, P., (2017). Radiomics: The bridge between medical imaging and personalized medicine. *Nature Reviews Clinical Oncology, 14*(12), 749–762.
4. Battineni, G., (2020). Applications of machine learning predictive models in the chronic disease diagnosis. *Journal of Personalized Medicine, 10*(2), 21.
5. Suo, Q., (2018). Deep patient similarity learning for personalized healthcare. *IEEE Transactions on Nanobioscience, 17*(3), 219–227.
6. Berrouiguet, S., (2018). From eHealth to iHealth: Transition to participatory and personalized medicine in mental health. *Journal of Medical Internet Research, 20*(1), e2.
7. Ahamed, F., & Farnaz, F., (2018). Applying internet of things and machine-learning for personalized healthcare: Issues and challenges. In: *2018 International Conference on Machine Learning and Data Engineering (iCMLDE)*.
8. Suwinski, P., (2019). Advancing personalized medicine through the application of whole exome sequencing and big data analytics. *Frontiers in Genetics, 10*, 49.
9. Lin, E., & Hsien-Yuan, L., (2017). Machine learning and systems genomics approaches for multi-omics data. *Biomarker Research, 5*(1), 1–6.
10. Ahmed, Z., (2020). Artificial intelligence with multi-functional machine learning platform development for better healthcare and precision medicine. *Database, 2020*.
11. Nithya, B., & Ilango, V., (2017). Predictive analytics in health care using machine learning tools and techniques. In: *2017 International Conference on Intelligent Computing and Control Systems (ICICCS)*.
12. Alfian, G., (2018). A personalized healthcare monitoring system for diabetic patients by utilizing BLE-based sensors and real-time data processing. *Sensors, 18*(7), 2183.
13. Walinjkar, A., & John, W., (2017). ECG classification and prognostic approach towards personalized healthcare. In: *2017 International Conference on Social Media, Wearable and Web Analytics (Social Media)*.
14. Alam, M. M., (2018). A survey on the roles of communication technologies in IoT-based personalized healthcare applications. *IEEE Access, 6*, 36611–36631.
15. Ho, D. S. W., (2019). Machine learning SNP based prediction for precision medicine. *Frontiers in Genetics, 10*, 267.
16. Devarajan, M., (2019). Fog-assisted personalized healthcare-support system for remote patients with diabetes. *Journal of Ambient Intelligence and Humanized Computing, 10*(10), 3747–3760.

CHAPTER 11

PERSONALIZED PHYSIO-CARE SYSTEM USING AI

ARUNA DEOSKAR,[1] SHILPA PARAB,[2] and SHUBHANGI PATIL[1]

[1]ATSS College of Business Studies and Computer Application (CBSCA), Affiliated to SP Pune University, Pune, Maharashtra, India

[2]CMF College of Physiotherapy, Maharashtra, India

ABSTRACT

Artificial intelligence (AI) describes techniques that allow computer to perform the sequence of tasks in the absence of human beings. AI cannot replace the human mind but can create the virtual presence of human mind. This chapter will talk about the Personalized Physio-care system and how the technology has impacted the physiotherapy treatments. Telerehabilitation is the need of today's era. Physiotherapy is the area where patient need to be treated under constant supervision and physical presence of Physiotherapist. Telerehabilitation has made it possible to support all patient's physio treatment through distant location as well. But there are many challenges that are discussed in this chapter. This chapter also suggests technical recommendations to ease-out such challenges. Many AI and IoT based healthcare models are in existence for the basic healthcare systems. Physiotherapy can be executed through telerehabilitation mode and can be strengthened with AI based models as suggested in this chapter. The predictive model using decision tree classifier covers data sets like BP, Barthel index, pain, etc. The outcome of this model gives the results indicating the deviation from normal and the suggestive treatments. The reader can take this suggestive prototype for enhancing the digitized physiotherapy treatment on various parameters.

Handbook of Research on Artificial Intelligence and Soft Computing Techniques in Personalized Healthcare Services, Uma N. Dulhare, A. V. Senthil Kumar, Amit Datta, Seddik Bri, Ibrahiem M. M. El Emary, (Eds.)
© 2024 Apple Academic Press, Inc. Co-published with CRC Press (Taylor & Francis)

11.1   INTRODUCTION

Artificial intelligence (AI) has played a significant role in minimizing the human intervention in daily operational activities. In this Information technology era, many activities are automated using AI and machine learning (ML) algorithms. The healthcare system is supporting patients for their medical requirements. This medical field has grown up significantly over the years. With advancements in medicine and technology the patients are facing various challenges. Patients are preferring the personalized guidance and treatment. The personalized medicine is helping the patient to gain the confidence of receiving the correct treatment as per their need and diagnosis. The major role of personalized healthcare is to get the correct diagnosis of individual depending upon the patient data and providing the customized treatment best suited to the patient. The use of AI in personalized medical system is important in terms of correctness, accuracy, and exact treatments, preventive measures and suggestive medications to the patient. AI algorithms can be applied for the detecting the patient's health status, can predict the criticality if any, and accordingly can generate the customized suggestive medical care (Figures 11.1 and 11.2).

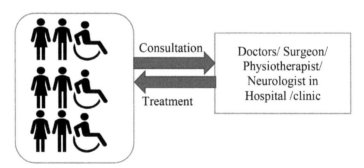

FIGURE 11.1   General healthcare system.

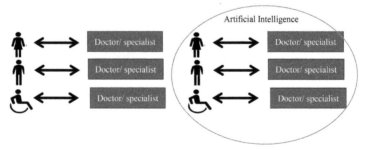

FIGURE 11.2   (A) Personalized healthcare system; and (B) technology-based personalized healthcare.

11.1.1 HEALTHCARE SYSTEM OF INDIA AND PHYSIOTHERAPY

Indian healthcare system involves four levels of services. Public primary community healthcare center, Primary Health Centers and Sub-Centers, Secondary Sub-District, Tertiary District level hospitals. India's Healthcare system is centrally controlled by the Union Ministry of Health and Family welfare [1]. Various states are responsible for the functioning of the health-care delivery system through their State Department of Health and Family Welfare. Each regional set-up covers 3 to 5 districts. Indian healthcare system is deficient in the rural sector due to lack of infrastructure and trained health-care professionals. Figure 11.3 reflects various core and allied branches of healthcare area.

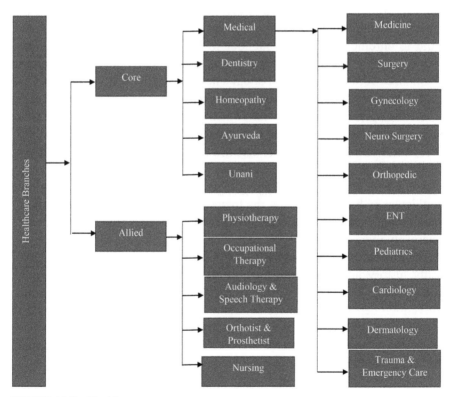

FIGURE 11.3   Healthcare areas.

Presently Physiotherapy services are confined at tertiary care level of the Indian healthcare system. Physiotherapists play a vital role as rehabilitation specialist to improve the health status of the patient all throughout life span. Physiotherapy services include assessment, treatment, and follow up. Considering the huge population of India and 60% residing in rural areas, several national level programs are implemented through Primary Healthcare system. There is huge potential and opportunities for delivering Physiotherapy services through all levels of the healthcare system [1, 2].

11.2   PERSONALIZED PHYSIO-CARE SYSTEM

Physiotherapists are rehabilitations specialists providing their services to people with disabilities due to numerous and varied causes to make them functionally independent and improve their quality of life. Physiotherapy treatments are very important in specialties like musculoskeletal conditions, after surgery, medicine, pediatric, fitness, women's health pre- and post-delivery, Intensive care, oncology, geriatric, etc. They treat patients from Acute to chronic stage all throughout life span. Physiotherapy treatment when given to a Particular patient is unique in its own way, i.e., becomes personalized for that particular Patient's need.

Physiotherapy treatment usually comprises of exercises and modalities for treating specific condition wise clinical presentation. Every intervention has a specific objective or goal to achieve. The therapy keeps on varying from patient to patient as well as depends on functional needs of the patient and the clinical condition. For example, a person with a knee injury may have only walking and stair climbing as goal for treatment to achieve, while an athlete may have to run after the treatment. Situations like these create a space for personalized physiotherapy care [3]. The Personalized healthcare system involves detailed assessment of patient including physical examination, assessment individual patients' lifestyle, comorbid disease factor, family history and also assessment of their metabolic processes through investigations. Every patient may respond in a different way to the same intervention depending on these factors. Physiotherapist needs to do necessary changes in treatment for each individual patient. Figure 11.4 describes the conceptual map to synthesize the relationship between a person-centered care and physiotherapist [4].

11.3   TECHNOLOGY AND HEALTHCARE

Technology has gripped the healthcare system in all fields. The use of AI in healthcare is an immense need in today's digital world. AI can make the personalized healthcare system more user specific and customized as per

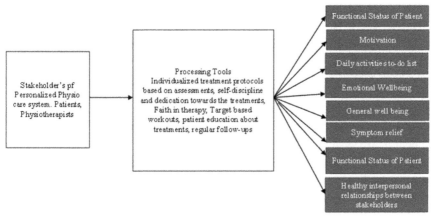

FIGURE 11.4 Personalized physio-care – conceptual map.

the user's need. AI using machine algorithms overcomes some of the challenges of traditional healthcare system like geographical boundaries, cost, expert's availability, and many more. In this virtual world the personalized medicine is fulfilling the user's medical need by customizing the healthcare plan. Healthcare areas are automated with the use of technology. IT tools, healthcare software is designed to boost the hospital and administrative productivity (Figure 11.5).

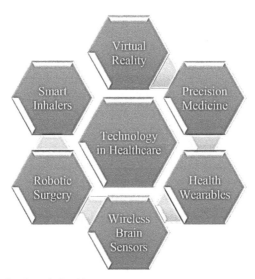

FIGURE 11.5 Technology in healthcare system.

11.3.1   IMPACT OF TECHNOLOGY ON HEALTHCARE

Technology has brought lot many positive changes to the healthcare industry. Many technologies based diagnostic tools, treatment suggestive applications, basic health plan information are now available to patient on their fingertips through AI based applications. This is a positive change in the healthcare sector where patient do not require to wait for the doctor or visit the doctor personally. In this digital world now, AI can make the personalized healthcare system more user specific and customized with respect to the patient's need. In this virtual world the personalized medicine is fulfilling the user's medical need through customized healthcare plan. The use of AI in healthcare system overcomes many healthcare system challenges but faces many new challenges as well.

Healthcare system requires real time data to get the patient's actual and accurate information. This includes about the basic information regarding their medical history, if any they have, their family medical history, ongoing treatments or previous treatments, test reports along with observed symptoms and lab results. Many technological devices are involved in the healthcare system. Some of the common technological devices used in healthcare system are related to tele-support as medical assistance remote treatment tools, wearable gadgets for continuous monitoring, and other electronic health record (EHR) devices. AI along with virtual reality are the most promising and upcoming technological involvements in the healthcare system.

11.3.2   AI IN HEALTHCARE

AI creates the virtual intelligence through specialized algorithms and software. The use of AI concept in the medical area has changed the patient and doctor's look out towards the health checkup. AI with ML algorithm resembles the human thoughts while analyzing the data and accordingly suggests the treatments. Some of the major problems which a user found in traditional healthcare system is the wastage of time, money, distance, and unavailability of qualitative medical experts. To get the better treatment the patient and user starts thinking of personalized treatment. But it involves a lot of cost and most of the time it is not affordable. AI combined with cloud computing, robotics, and internet of medical things (IoMT) has the potential to address the problems of traditional healthcare system.

AI can find immediate partial but required solutions. It can help in early detection and diagnosis and accordingly the decision and treatments would be prescribed by the experts (Figure 11.6).

Personalized Healthcare (PH) = Healthcare system and healthcare plan customized as per the user's need and individual's medical history and data. This included the personalized healthcare plans, personalized suggestive treatments, and personalized diagnosis system.

AI-based PH – Artificial intelligence based personalized healthcare system.

FIGURE 11.6   AI-based personalized healthcare system stages.

AI gives ease to patients and doctors by performing human tasks in less time and at minimum cost. AI in personalized healthcare works on patient's personal data sets and accordingly can provide the suggestive treatments after diagnosis. AI can play a crucial role in early detection, based on patient's data and investigation reports of individual patients. AI's ability in personalized healthcare system critically depends on the stored valid data sets.

AI gives the prediction and suggestive measures after processing the heterogeneous patient data received as input from the healthcare system. A preliminary investigation and data collection through AI based healthcare system can save a lot of time. This preliminary investigation reports can be used by the doctor for clinical examinations and patient's physical visit to the doctor as per the need. AI based healthcare system will be having the actual acceptable data values of all common medical examination parameters. The user's collected and observed information is compared with acceptable stored values, and accordingly, the system will generate the suggestive treatment and measures for the patient. The system can also suggest in case of any emergency and accordingly to whom the patient should meet for immediate consultation along with the contact details of the clinics and doctors. Many AI based healthcare system are now in the market. Patient's do not want to feel like neglected and so prefer the personalized service which helps them for getting the right healthcare solutions. Table 11.1 gives the details of such AI based healthcare systems that are used for some specific investigations.

TABLE 11.1   AI-based Healthcare Systems [5, 6]

Sl. No.	Healthcare System	Details	
1.	Buoy Health [5]	AI based symptom and cure checker.	Uses algorithm to diagnose and treat illness.
2.	Nethra by Forus Health	An AI based portable device to screen out common eye problems.	AI powered device used by doctors even at remote places with nil or intermittent connectivity to the cloud.
3.	Narayna Netraylaya and Sankalpa Nethralaya	AI system for diabetic retinopathy detection.	AI driven healthcare solutions.
4.	Enlitic	Deep learning medical tool.	Used to streamline radiology diagnosis.
5.	Freenome	Earlier cancer detection with AI.	Uses AI in screenings, diagnostic tests and blood work to test for cancer.
6.	BenevolentAI	Uses AI to produce a better target selection and gives undiscovered insights through deep learning.	Used to get the right treatment to the right patients at the right time.
7.	One Drop App	AI based app allows people to manage their conditions through interactive coaching from real world professionals.	Used for managing diabetes, heart health, BP, and weight management.
8.	Kaia Health	Uses AI technology to ensure that patients receive the best therapist care possible and integrated with best medical professionals.	It is a digital therapeutics platform and act as a live physical therapist.
9.	Babylon-Health	Uses AI to provide personalized and interactive healthcare with anytime face to face appointments with doctors.	Powered with chatbot to get patient's symptoms. Then gives medical recommendations.

Source: https://builtin.com/artificial-intelligence/artificial-intelligence-healthcare.

1. Lloret presented an architecture and protocol for smart e health monitoring system. It collects patient information through dynamic signs. The data is processed using a machine learning algorithm to observe the intelligent responses. An alarm is raised whenever any abnormality is observed.

2. Chen et al. has proposed a mobile health system for continuous monitoring of diabetic patients.

3. Xiao et al. has proposed an IoT-based solution based on RFID. IAAS: Indoor anti-collision alarm system to help blind users to avoid obstacles, LWLR algorithm log-normal distance pass loss.

11.4 ROLE OF PHYSIOTHERAPY IN TELEREHABILITATION

Telerehabilitation allows patients to connect with the therapist through remotely. Here we will talk on the Physiotherapist roles while treating a patient in a personalized way or in the group. It also covers the technological need and challenges faced by Physiotherapist while doing telerehabilitation.

11.4.1 WHAT IS TELEREHABILITATION

Telerehabilitation is an electronic form of rehabilitation given to the patients using E-tools like mobile phones, laptops, tablets, etc., to remotely located patients. Physiotherapy services can be delivered through telerehabilitation just like other healthcare services like occupational therapy, neuropsychology, speech pathology, etc. Telerehabilitation is equally beneficial to doctors as they deliver virtual care and knowledge to their patients from their own clinic providing them the flexibility and convenience to reach their patient [7].

Tele-rehabilitation can be delivered by three different modes [7]:

i. By giving real-time by the clinician, via the use of video platforms (synchronous telerehabilitation);
ii. By giving the patients access to material such as videos and guides (asynchronous telerehabilitation); and
iii. Individual therapy carried out directly with the clinician, associated with a program of activities performed in asynchronous mode (Mixed or hybrid tele-rehabilitation).

Benefits of telerehabilitation includes:

- Treatment protocols adapted to specific patient's health condition;
- Real time monitoring and control over patient's treatment by the therapist;
- Cost effective and time saving;

- Patient can interact with the therapist;
- Patient is empowered as he is taking part in his own treatment execution;
- Patient can perform exercises at his own comfortable place, i.e., from home;
- Real time immediate feedback received from the patient.

11.4.2   PHYSIOTHERAPY AND TELEREHABILITATION

Musculoskeletal Physiotherapist are treating predominantly pain related to acute and chronic orthopedic conditions along with post-surgical conditions like arthroplasties, soft tissue repairs, etc. They use hands-on and hands-off interventions to take care of patient's pain and making them functionally independent as well as improving their quality of life. Manual therapy techniques are hands on treatment where in response to treatment is important to adjust it as per individual patients need. While hands off interventions like education, therapeutic exercises can be rendered to improve patient's self-efficacy, confidence, and compliance to the treatment.

11.4.3   COVID PANDEMIC CASE STUDY

11.4.3.1   MUSCULOSKELETAL PHYSIOTHERAPY WITH TELEREHABILITATION

The intense nature of corona disease 2019 forced a near total lockdown in many countries including India. There was limited mobility of people to avoid widespread infection spread. All the establishments comprising of large community presence, namely Schools, shopping malls, entertainment venues, restaurants were closed. This measure was implemented to avoid collapse of the healthcare system due to inadequate facilities. The steps taken helped to some extent to control the infection spread, but on the other hand service industry which also includes Physiotherapy was not easily available to people who needed them. To ensure safety World Health Organization (WHO) postponed all rehabilitation services which were not urgent, only essential services were available. Musculoskeletal physiotherapy, neuro-physiotherapy, and fitness are few services which were affected due to these restrictions. During the pandemic, the patient's suffered with pain and disability due to non-availability of these treatments as Musculoskeletal Physiotherapy was considered to be non-essential service. The need of the hour is helping these patient's needing musculoskeletal Physiotherapy by tapping the potential of telerehabilitation for treating Patients. Clinical evidence on telerehabilitation in musculoskeletal conditions have positive outcomes. Researchers have recommended the use of physiotherapy treatments through telerehabilitation are equally effective in treating a few Musculoskeletal conditions. Especially clinical signs of Pain, Range of motion and functional abilities of patients have shown improvements. The only limitations of these evidences are studies with small sample size, so results cannot be generalized to other populations. Secondly, much attention is not drawn towards barriers and limitations of implementing telerehabilitation effectively for patients' treatments. Short follow up period was also observed by researchers as one of the factors regarding the effect of interventions [8].

11.4.3.2 NEUROPEDIATRIC PATIENTS

Social isolation was used as a tool to keep high risk population from getting infected by the pandemic. Among them neuropediatric patients were badly impacted due to unavailability of drug treatment and physical therapy. The middle-income population of developing countries with limited income was badly impacted financially in this pandemic. This resulted in negative impact on this population healthcare due to high cost medications, inadequate techno-logical support and Physical therapy. Pediatric neuro Physiotherapy patients are in constant need of Physiotherapy treatments. They are functionally independent due to these treatments. Social isolation to avoid contamination to these patients led to disruption in their treatment protocol leaving with numerous Physical disabilities. Telerehabilitation has been widely discussed as an option for facing this limitation of reaching the patient population. During this period telerehabilitation has been chosen as an option to reach patient population who were confined to their homes to keep them away from getting infected. The neuro physiotherapy treatment sessions comprise of monitoring and doing alterations in movement execution while the patient is moving. Most of the time, patient needs to be handled manually to do this. Tools like virtual reality, machines, gaming apps can be utilized in pediatric patients who are home bound. Recent evidence does mention the beneficial effects of telerehabilitation for neuropediatric patients but are reflecting limited use in clinical practices [9].

Numerous systematic reviews conclude that patients will be having residual functional disabilities in the post-acute phase of COVID-19. These problems are to be addressed by using the rehabilitation tools. The studies on telerehabilitation reveal several barriers to effective implementation along with benefits reported by patients. Researchers are doing extensive meta-analysis to prove the efficacy of telerehabilitation. If it is proved to be as effective as face to face treatment session, it will be useful in any such future crisis like COVID-19 pandemic. The new normal is the new mantra of today's world's functioning. It's time that telerehabilitation should be adapted by Physical therapist as a mean to reach all patients who need their care. Removing technological barriers and making use of smart user-friendly tools for their patient's use is the way by which patient receives the care at the right time and right place [10].

11.4.3.3   TELEREHABILITATION IN CARDIOPULMONARY PHYSIOTHERAPY

According to evidence use of telerehabilitation in the field of cardiopulmonary dates back to 2012. The US Department of Veteran affairs was one of the first to report the use of telehealth for rendering Physical therapy services to cardiac patients. The cardiac rehabilitation after surgical and nonsurgical interventions for people with cardiovascular disease (CVD) is a vital part of medical management. Due to the high cost of rehabilitation and the need to visit the hospital in the immediate post-operative period, many times it becomes a constraint for continuing the treatment. Home-based cardiac rehabilitation integrated with telerehabilitation is an effective, feasible, and safe way for cardiac rehabilitation [11]. Patients with low or medium risk can be safely given this homebased exercise protocol. A physical therapist and a nurse should be continuously monitoring the patient through telerehabilitation for any adverse effects. Emergency medicines are to be in accessible range of the patient. In spite of having few barriers still patients who could benefit by this home bound care appreciated the service.

While urban patients find it easy to take full advantage of this homebased cardiac rehabilitation, but on other hand for reaching patients living in rural areas, trained personnel, i.e., exercise Physiologist, Physical therapist or a nurse play pivotal role in hospital during tele-support. Online monitoring of program through live observation or through recorded activities are done by the expert while assisting patients who are treated at home. Continuous supervision is very important while rendering telerehabilitation in cardiac physiotherapy to the patients at their home. Different researchers have used various modes to give telerehabilitation to cardiac patients like voice contact, video conferencing, etc. Recent advances in the field of medical technology have resulted in the use of virtual platforms, apps with specific function and sensitivity with accurate measuring functions for cardiac telerehabilitation.

Physiotherapy services given through telerehabilitation in the period of a pandemic have very effective results in presence of few barriers. The need to assess the patient in person for planning dosages of exercises and adjusting the interventions still remains a challenge for few therapists. But clinicians can always keep themselves updated with patient-friendly tools to reach their patients when patients do not have access to their centers due to many reasons. Reaching the rural population with these simple tools would be possible.

Extensive research trials have been conducted during COVID-19 pandemic for reaching out to patient population to give treatment to patients through telerehabilitation. The treatments were offered to all specialties of Physiotherapy namely musculoskeletal, neurosciences, and cardiopulmonary. Almost all clinical conditions have been covered, ranging from acute to chronic. The patients from all age criteria, i.e., Pediatric, adult, and geriatric have been treated with telerehabilitation. The evidence suggests that Physiotherapy treatment through Online mode is at least better than no treatment. Few have experienced barriers especially from patient's perspective. Technological limitations are at the epicenter of all the problems faced by the clinicians in having effective treatment rendered to their patients. There is a need to have cost effective, easy to use and accessible tools for having efficient Physiotherapy sessions in online mode. Home cardiac rehabilitation has been proven to be highly effective in comparison to hospital-based protocol. Patients do have apprehension about receiving cardiac rehabilitation through telerehabilitation in fear of adverse events. Structured technological assessment while patient is performing the protocol like continuous BP measurement, pulse monitoring, breathlessness tracking will help patient to perform cardiac rehabilitation on their own. Monitoring is possible via telerehabilitation. COVID-19 pandemic has drastically changed the way healthcare delivery used to be given. Digital health is the new tool which helped the therapists reach out to their patients. When social isolation and safe distance were acting as constraints for giving care to the patients. Researchers conclude that telerehabilitation is effective and feasible but less resource intensive in Indian scenario due to lack of required infrastructure and especially in rural areas [12].

To take care of any pandemic like situation it is need of the hour that Physical therapist should collaborate with technology experts and other healthcare professionals to conduct evidences with research in field of tele-rehabilitation as well as implement in their clinical practice. In future technology is to be used in clinical practice to overcome few barriers of contact practice Physical therapist should integrate telehealth in their routine clinical practice to promote telerehabilitation [13]. COVID-19 pandemic has placed many challenges for safe and effective physiotherapy services for their patients. The physiotherapy profession had to embrace and make use of digital tools to give physiotherapy services available to their patients in this pandemic. There is need to create space for digital physiotherapy for emergent and nonemergent situations [13].

Outcome and effectiveness universally drive healthcare services and Physiotherapy services are an important part of this system. In this pandemic Physiotherapist have explored this viable option of telerehabilitation to offer consultations to non-COVID patients. The physical presence of Physiotherapist while treating a patient is an immense need in some of the cases. Such need is an integral part of treatment and assessment. Thus, telerehabilitation is not suitable for all categories of patient.

The contact practice is a key component of Physiotherapy evaluation and management. The advanced technological tools have proved to be effective in rendering Physiotherapy interventions to render services to patient in remote location, still technology cannot replace "touch" component of Physiotherapy management and assessment [11].

In spite of limitations Physical therapist must embrace technology into their daily practice so that in future where virtual reality is going to be normal, they should not lose their societal identity due to lack of untrained staff, inadequate infrastructure and technological illiteracy. Physical therapist are rehabilitation experts whose role in patients life continues even after patient's disease is cured. Due to the long duration of their interventions, they should be ready for change and updation for their patients and their own benefit.

11.5   CHALLENGES AND OPPORTUNITIES

Technology has impacted the traditional systems. In healthcare system the therapist are experts in their respective fields. Neither Doctor nor patients might not be expert in handling the technology. This chapter will talk on all such challenges. These will be based on the primary data collected from patients and Doctors while treating through telerehabilitation.

11.5.1   CHALLENGES AND OPPORTUNITIES WHILE RENDERING PHYSIOTHERAPY VIA TELEREHABILITATION

COVID-19 pandemic saw many physiotherapists turning to digital technology to reach their patients. Lock down and need of social isolation and distancing kept many patients needing physiotherapy treatment away from it. Physiotherapy being considered non-essential services till now, came into the limelight due to its importance in managing COVID patients. Due to its infectious nature, the therapist had to isolate themselves after treating infected patients. This resulted in deprivation of physiotherapy services to non-COVID patients. Different specialties have faced various types of challenges while giving Physiotherapy treatment via telerehabilitation. For example, Musculoskeletal physiotherapy known for manual therapy interventions for their patients faced constraints in delivering their services. Other than the interventions factors like therapy interventions, interaction with other patients, sound of modalities, environment in therapy room were also missed by some patients [8]. They also observed that the use of free commercial applications did not provide data privacy guarantee, which might be a very crucial factor. Physiotherapy in neurological conditions require continuous monitoring and correcting the patients postures while interventions are being given to the patients. Quick instructions and supporting postures are the main components of treatment. Though elderly population received these treatments online without any trouble, they still missed the therapist's presence when they were doing exercises on telerehabilitation sessions. Some older adult patients found telephonic conversations better than digital communication due to lack of understanding and training technology. In Indian scenario, the elderly were more comfortable with actual face to face conversations rather than online communication. Some researchers also found that teleconsultation needed more time [14].

Researchers have conducted numerous studies on various non-COVID clinical conditions like stroke. They observed barriers like equipment setup, internet network issues and availability and need of supporting care giver [14]. Perceived barriers for study conducted on smartphone based telerehabilitation on Chronic pulmonary disease Patients. It has been found that poor health literacy, financial burden, Physiotherapist are not technological experts so whenever they are using technology for rendering their services, they have to learn first and then use it. This takes extra time and effort on their part. Lack of incentives, no technology support, lack of resources for running the tools and no separate guidelines and schemes from the government are additional constraints for effective use of technology to give Physiotherapy services, Patient beliefs and lack of family support were also found to be important constraints for patients as well as healthcare professionals [15].

Though globally telerehabilitation and rendering Physiotherapy through it is normally practiced, still developing countries like India are still facing a lot of constraints like technological barriers, cultural issues, untrained healthcare personnel, patient's literacy status, financial implications to both patients and physiotherapists, and many more. There is limited evidence which speak of success with online therapy. The Pandemic has given a way for introduction of technology to replace in person Physiotherapy care which was totally impossible due to social distancing. Though the Indian Government has announced guidelines for the practice of Telemedicine, still they are without any legislation. The clinicians do not have a clear idea whether to follow or not. This further makes the effective implementation of telerehabilitation more difficult [16] (Figures 11.7 and 11.8).

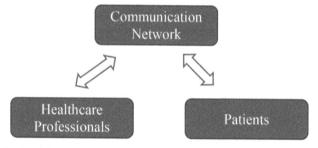

FIGURE 11.7   Healthcare, patient connection through communication network.

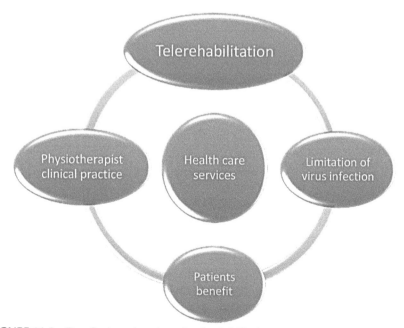

FIGURE 11.8   Benefits to patient through telerehabilitation.

Telemedicine works at three ends, communication network being the key component of the chain which connects the patient to the healthcare worker. In India due to lack of IT infrastructure in many urban and rural areas, Telemedicine or Telerehabilitation suffers major barriers. Rural patients do not have access to basic healthcare, leave alone Rehabilitation. All the facilities with the latest technology are based in urban set ups. Telemedicine can be used to make rural population accessible to urban super specialty services. Telemedicine is a tool which can facilitate healthcare delivery system in an effective way in spite of physical, technological constraints on part of Healthcare service provider making it easy for the patients to use. Technological literacy and access to smart phones will be needed to achieve this.

Throughout the world what 2020 showed us was the importance of embracing digital technology by healthcare professionals to reach their patients [16]. Time has come to identify the constraints in rendering telerehabilitation and find workable solution for effective inventions, research, and extensive use of patient friendly tools. We need to identify those constraints which are acting as barriers and try to find opportunities for the benefit of Professionals and patients. Opportunities which are available for rendering physiotherapy services through online mode are as under:

- Maintaining education of patient through remote consultation in their own home;
- Online physical assessment and planning of treatment;
- Monitoring patient's progress, feedback can be given for motivation;
- Supervised treatment protocols can be given;
- According to patients need duration, frequency, and intensity of exercises can be planned;
- Cost effective treatment;
- Continuous, effective, and adequate care to all categories of patients;
- Rural patient can take advantage of expert and standard care available in urban set ups;
- Reaching out to remotely located patients, senior citizens, immobile patients.

Challenges faced during telerehabilitation to patients needing physiotherapy services:

Internet speed and data privacy issues;

- Reluctance to accept telerehabilitation in patients who are not motivated;

- Lack of skill and knowledge for using e-health services;
- Availability of uninterrupted internet service was the biggest challenge with both urban and rural patients;

Monitoring the treatment was the biggest constraint;

- Cost concerns in economically weak patients;
- Lack of awareness about telerehabilitation;
- Lack of e-resources;
- Dependence on electricity and internet broadband width to run the tools, usually patients faced this difficulty.

Outcome and effectiveness form two major drivers while rendering physiotherapy services to patients. It is important to touch the patient while assessing, giving intervention and assisted techniques. In COVID pandemic the major limitations were found in assessment maneuvers like measuring range of motion, assessing strength, Assessing tone of the muscle. Around 90% of Musculoskeletal Physiotherapy services had these limitations while providing these services online to their patients. There is lack of appropriate technological tools to assess these parameters at least in India.

Many physiotherapy techniques are to be provided to patients via manual touch which cannot be done through tele-rehabilitation Physiotherapy. At least 60% of our OPD patients suffered due to non-availability of these treatment facilities online.

On the other side we have many positive results obtained when we conducted online Physiotherapy sessions for geriatric (senior) citizens. Three online sessions were conducted for senior citizens during January 2020 to December 2020. Geriatric fitness camp, Diabetes awareness camp, COPD awareness drive and organ donation awareness seminar. We had an enormous response from senior citizens for these events. All participants were registered via google forms, and their health-related problems were studied, and seminars were based on those problems. The organizers have given them videos with safe exercise protocols and termination criteria. The online mode of this program reached to all those senior citizens who had limitations to move out of house due to the pandemic. Around 250 patients participated in the above-mentioned telerehabilitation webinar sessions. The efficacy of the interventions and overall impact are as under (Table 11.2).

TABLE 11.2   Patients Perceptions, Treated Through Telerehabilitation

Parameters	Observed Results
Ease of using technology	30% found it easy while 70% faced difficulties
Comfortable communication	Only 25% were comfortable
Satisfaction with management	80% liked the management
Satisfaction with online treatment	95% were satisfied
Safety while doing prescribed exercises	65% found it unsafe
Recommendations to friends and family	87%
Likely to choose the sessions in future	75%

11.6   TECHNOLOGY-BASED HEALTHCARE SYSTEM

ML algorithms are like Blackbox. Decisions are predicted through AI using ML based on the input data and their accuracy. ML algorithms need to be applied based on the data sets. Table 11.3 gives the different ML algorithms and the relevant data processing tasks [17].

TABLE 11.3   AI Algorithms and Data Processing Tasks

Sl. No.	Algorithm	Data Processing Tasks	Description
1.	K-nearest neighbors	Classification/ regression	KNN is a supervised nonparametric classification method. Used for the classification and regression problems. Has input with k closest training data sets.
2.	Naïve Bayes	Classification	A supervised ML algorithm based on Bayes theorem used for classification problem. Used for making fast predictions. Prediction is based on probability.
3.	Support vector machine	Classification	A supervised ML algorithm. Used for classification problems. It divides the space into classes. We can put the new data set in to respective and correct set.
4.	Linear regression	Regression	This model represents the relationship between dependent and independent variables through a sloped straight line.
5.	Decision tree classification	Classification/ regression	Supervised learning technique for classification and regression problems. Here the decisions are performed on the basis of given data sets. Also called CART algorithm – classification and regression tree algorithm.
6.	Random forests	Classification/ regression	A supervised ML algorithm which uses multiple classifiers. Random forests take the prediction from each tree and then gives the output and predictions.

We will be proposing a model using decision tree classifier technique. This will talk on the probable solutions based on AI and ML algorithms for monitoring the patient health system on a regular basis. Accordingly, the patient telerehabilitation schedule can be planned.

11.6.1   TELE-BASED PERSONALIZED SYSTEM – CONCEPTUAL AI-BASED MODEL

Regular monitoring of patients can help in better treatment and fast recovery. Technological advancements and involvements of the internet of things (IoT), AI, smart systems, and intelligent devices can support the better monitoring and guidance in the healthcare system. These have made it possible for patient as well as Doctors to provide personalized and remote health services. Intelligent healthcare system is an economical solution to ease out the personalized healthcare challenges. Intelligent architecture for monitoring the Physio-care patient while treating remotely. ML algorithms are applied for proposing a smart architecture for telerehabilitation. Data classification can be done using ML based on physio-care parameters. Expected values (values within range) will not trigger any abnormal behavior. But as soon as the algorithm records any of the parameter values beyond range, the intelligent monitoring system should advise and alert for the Physical attendance of experts.

A conceptual solution based on AI and ML algorithms for monitoring the patient health system on a regular basis can be considered to support the tele-based personalized system. Accordingly, the patient telerehabilitation schedule can be planned (Figure 11.9).

Patient observed data is entered into the system and is checked with the standard data set values. If any deviation is observed by the system, then accordingly virtual doctor prescribes the suggestive measures. In case of emergency/alarming situation due to excess deviations of observed set against the standard data set values, then the system will provide the suggestive measures with emergency medication plans.

11.6.1.1   TELEREHABILITATION REAL TIME CASE STUDIES

The model is trained for four different cases and accordingly the results are monitored using ML algorithm. Decision tree classifiers are used for generating the suggestive measures. Decision tree algorithm is used for two reasons (Figure 11.10):

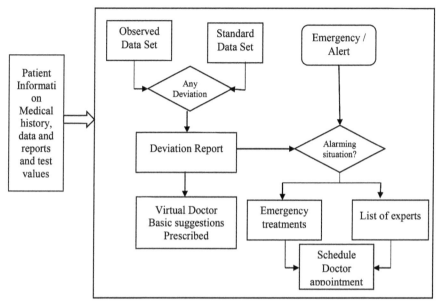

FIGURE 11.9   Block diagram of tele-based (AI) healthcare system.

- It reflects the human thinking ability while making any decisions; and
- Algorithm asks a question and based on the answer yes/No the subtrees with leaf and nodes are generated.

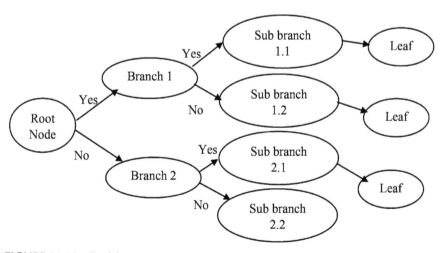

FIGURE 11.10   Decision tree concept.

Steps used with decision tree classifier for predicting the values are (Figure 11.11 and Table 11.4).

FIGURE 11.11   Decision tree algorithm stages.

TABLE 11.4   Physio-Care Case Study and Parameters

Case	Particulars	Observed Parameters	Patients Data
A	General	BP, pulse rate	30
B	Balance scale	Berg balance scale	23
C	Functional status of patient	Barthel index	23
D	Pain with functional status	Oswestery back pain scale	40

A. **General Data Set:** Patients' Blood Pressure and Pulse Rate is observed. Depending upon BP value, the model is trained for Systolic and Diastolic BP values with suggestive treatments. Pulse rate values are also interpreted for bradycardia, normal and tachycardia stages (Tables 11.5 and 11.6).

TABLE 11.5   Blood-Pressure Classification

Blood Pressure	Diagnosis	Suggestive Treatment
80–120	Normal	No treatment needed
80–89, 120–139	Prehypertension	Consultation with physician physiotherapist for exercises
90–99, 140–159	Stage 1 hypertension	Consult physician, medications, exercise prescription with physiotherapist
>=100, >=160	Stage 2 hypertension	Consultation with cardiologist mandatory

TABLE 11.6   Pulse Rate Classification

Pulse Rate	Interpretation	Suggested Action
>50	Bradycardia	Immediate consultation with cardiologist
50–75	Normal	No intervention needed
75–100	Tachycardia	Consultation with cardiologist and physiotherapist. medicines needed and exercises as well

B. **Balance Scale:** An observational study was conducted on 23 blind individuals aged 20–45 years for understanding their balancing level. Their functional status was assessed using a scale called Barthel index and balance was assessed using Modified Berg Balance Scale. It is observed that there is a greater risk of falls, impaired balance and moderate dependency for performing daily activities in individuals with complete blindness (Table 11.7).

TABLE 11.7   Berg's Balance Scale

Score	Interpretation	Action
45–56	Good balance	No treatment needed
>45	Greater risk of fall	In person physiotherapy needed

C. Functional Status of the Patient (Barthel Index) (Table 11.8):

TABLE 11.8   Barthel Index

Score	Interpretation	Action
0–20	Total dependency	Active physiotherapy management needed on regular basis
21–60	Severe dependency	Regular progressive face to face personalized physiotherapy management
61–90	Moderate dependency	Telerehabilitation and once or twice weekly in person physiotherapy sessions.
91–99	Slight dependency	Caretaker monitored physiotherapy exercises at home. regular consultations once a week with physiotherapist

D. Pain with Functional Ability Status of the Patient (Oswestray Low Back Pain Scale) (Table 11.9 and Figures 11.12–11.16)

TABLE 11.9   Functional Ability Status of the Patient

Score	Interpretation	Action
0–20%	Minimal disability	Telerehabilitation
20–40%	Moderate disability	In person physiotherapy needed
40–60%	Severe disability	Consultation with physician and physiotherapy management
60–80%	Crippled	Physiotherapy and vocational training
80–100%	Bed-bound	Home bound continues career, palliative care

FIGURE 11.12   Set A – SBP, DBP interpretation of model through decision tree algorithm.

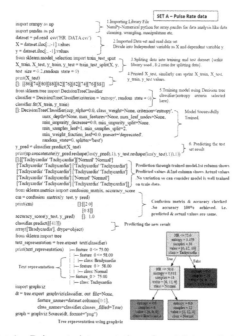

FIGURE 11.13   Set A – Pulse rate interpretation of model through decision tree algorithm.

FIGURE 11.14   Set B – Balance interpretation of model through decision tree algorithm.

FIGURE 11.15   Set C (a) – Barthel index interpretation of model through decision tree algorithm.

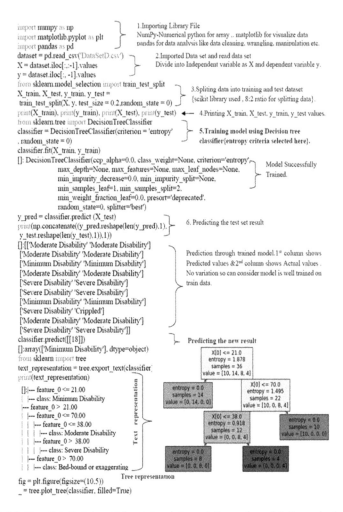

FIGURE 11.16   Set D (a) – Pain status interpretation of model through decision tree algorithm.

11.6.2   APPLICATIONS AND CHALLENGES OF AI-BASED HEALTHCARE SYSTEMS

AI based healthcare system can provide the quick support to the user. Patient do not require to visit the doctor and the clinic physically. They can connect from anywhere and can get the support any time. But some of the challenges are:

- AI-based healthcare system requires a basic level of digital literacy, which is very low;
- We have diversity of population. And it is a big challenge;
- Every geographical location has different geographical based unique challenges due to poor data sets, network connectivity and many more such technological challenges;
- Medical data is highly unstructured data. Extracting information from such variety of unstructured data is a big challenge;
- Illiteracy of people of using internet-based applications;
- Data and information security is a very big challenge;
- Development costs;
- Data privacy and security. Big threat to patient's personalized data and information;
- Data exchange between various telemedicine stakeholders. Need proper training for understanding the working and actual implementation of the system;
- Awareness among patients and staff need to be provided for the better analysis and predictions.

11.7 CONCLUSION

The digital physiotherapy task force of World Physiotherapy defined digital practice as "Healthcare services, support, and information provided remotely via digital communication and devices" [21]. Digital Physiotherapy is practiced by Physiotherapist but with limitations. There is a need to give specific education and training to Physiotherapist about digital technologies like AI which can help them. Educational strategies should include incorporating specific education programs in undergraduate and post-graduate programs which will ensure trained therapist availability for successful implementation of digital physiotherapy. Decision tree classification algorithm is used in this chapter for understanding the tele-based personalized healthcare system with basic data sets related to health like BP, Pulse Rates. For decision related problems this algorithm is very useful. But it also has some limitations. This may be very complex if the decision tress contains a lot of layers. This problem can be resolved by using the random forest (RF) algorithm for predicting the patient's health in a quick manner.

KEYWORDS

- **Artificial Intelligence**
- **Decision Tree Algorithm**
- **Healthcare System**
- **Machine Learning**
- **Physio-Care System**
- **Physiotherapy**
- **Telerehabilitation**

REFERENCES

1. Danigond, A., (2021). *5 Reasons Why Indian Healthcare System is Struggling*. The Hindu Business line. [online], Available: https://www.thehindubusinessline.com/news/national/5-reasons-why-indias-healthcare-system-is-struggling/article34665535.ece (accessed on 24 January 2023).

2. AMAZ Post Editorial Team, (2020). *What is the Structure of Healthcare System in India?* Health A-Z. Magazine Blog. [online].

3. Team of Experts, (2017). *Pro Health Asia Physiotherapy and Rehabilitation, Healing from Within with Personalized Physiotherapy*. Economic times health world [online], Available: https://health.economictimes.indiatimes.com/news/industry/prohealth-asia-world-class-physiotherapy-and-rehab-center-launched-in-delhi/57300493 (accessed on 24 January 2023).

4. Dukhu, S., Purcell, C., & Bulley, C., (2018). Person-centered care in the physiotherapeutic management of long-term conditions: A critical review of components, barriers and facilitators. *International Journal of Developmental Practice, 8*(2). https://doi.org/10.19043/ipdj.82.002.

5. Daley, S., (2021). *37 Examples of AI in Healthcare, AI Health Care System Tool*. builtin.com, [online]. Available: https://builtin.com/artificial-intelligence/artificial-intelligence-healthcare (accessed on 24 January 2023).

6. Awwalu, J., Garba, A., Ghazvini, A., & Atuah, R., (2015). Artificial intelligence in personalized medicine application of AI algorithms in solving personalized medicine problems. *International Journal of Computer Theory and Engineering, 7*(6). doi: 10.7763/IJCTE.2015.V7.999.

7. Gayatri, (2021). *What Are the Challenges of Telemedicine in Indian Healthcare Industry?* NYOOOZ My city My news [online]. Available: https://www.nyoooz.com/features/health/what-are-the-challenges-of-telemedicine-in-the-indian-healthcare-industry.html/5240/ (accessed on 24 January 2023).

8. Turolla, A., Rosettelli, G., Viceconti, A., Palese, A., & Geri, T., (2020). Musculoskeletal physical therapy during the COVID-19 pandemic: Is telerehabilitation the answer? *Physical Therapy, 100*(8), 1260–1264. doi: 10.1093/ptj/pzaa093.

9. Meireles, A. L. F., & Ferreira De, M. L. C., (2020). Impact of social isolation due to the COVID-19 pandemic in patients with pediatric disorders: Rehabilitation perspectives from a developing country. *Physical Therapy, 100*(11), 1910–1912. doi: 10.1093/ptj/pzaa152.

10. Suso-Martí, L., La Touche, R., et al., (2021). Effectiveness of telerehabilitation in physical therapy: Umbrella and mapping review with meta-meta-analysis. *Physical Therapy, 101*(5). doi: 10.1093/ptj/pjab075.

11. Sari, D. M., & Wijaya, L. C. G., (2021). Cardiac rehabilitation via telemedicine in COVID-19 pandemic situation. *The Egyptian Heart Journal, 73*(1), 31. *Sari and Wijaya the Egyptian Heart Journal,* (2021). doi:org/10.1186/s43044-021-00156-7.

12. Meeka, K., Guru, S. G., Bagevadi, V. I., Gupt, A., Kulkarni, K., Shyam, R. P. S., Basavaraju, V., et al., (2018). Feasibility and utility of tele-neurorehabilitation service in India: Experience from a quaternary center. *Journal of Neurosciences Rural, Practice.* doi: 10.4103/jnrp.jnrp_104_18.

13. Aderonmu, J. A., (2020). Emerging challenges in meeting physiotherapy needs during COVID-19 through telerehabilitation. *Bulletin of Faculty of Physical Therapy, 25.* Article no: 16. Available: https://bfpt.springeropen.com/articles/10.1186/s43161-020-00018-4 (accessed on 24 January 2023).

14. Chandre, H., & Ganvir, S., (2020). Identifying the challenges of 6 months telerehabilitation program on non-COVID patients during COVID-19 through patient's perception. *VIMS J. Physical Therapy, 2*(2). https://doi.org/10.46858.VIMSJPT.2206.

15. Bairapareddy, K. C., Alaparthi, G. K., Jitendra, R. S., Prathiksha, P., Rao, P., Shetty, V., & Chandrasekaran, B., (2021). We are so close; yet too far: Perceived barriers to smartphone-based telerehabilitation among healthcare providers and patients with chronic obstructive pulmonary disease in India. *Heliyon, 7*(8), e07857. ISSN 2405-8440. https://doi.org/10.1016/j.heliyon.2021.e07857; https://www.sciencedirect.com/science/article/pii/S2405844021019605 (accessed on 24 January 2023).

16. Marchand, J., (2020). *India the Opportunities and Challenges of Telerehabilitation During COVID-19 And Longer Term.* ITU news, online]. Available: https://news.itu.int/in-india-the-opportunities-and-challenges-of-telemedicine-during-covid-19-and-longer-term/ (accessed on 24 January 2023).

17. *Machine Learning Algorithms.* https://www.javatpoint.com/machine-learning-decision-tree-classification-algorithm (accessed on 24 January 2023).

18. Kamal, J., & Vinita, S. (2020). *Artificial Intelligence for Precision Medicine and Better Healthcare.* https://www.kdnuggets.com/2020/09/artificial-intelligence-precision-medicine-better-healthcare.html (accessed on 24 January 2023).

19. Schork, N. J., (2019). Artificial intelligence and personalized medicine. *PMC, Published in Final Edited form as: Cancer Treat Res., 178,* 265–283. doi: 10.1007/978-3-030-16391-4_11.

20. *Artificial Intelligence in Healthcare,* (2019). Academy of Medical Royal Colleges. [online], Available: https://www.aomrc.org.uk/wp-content/uploads/2019/01/Artificial_intelligence_in_healthcare_0119.pdf (accessed on 24 January 2023).

21. Rausch, A. K., Baur, H., Reicherzer, L., Wirz, M., Keller, F., Opsommer, E., Schoeb, V., et al., (2021). Physiotherapists' use and perceptions of digital remote physiotherapy during COVID-19 lockdown in Switzerland: An online cross-sectional survey *Archives of Physiotherapy, 11,* Article no. 18. [online]. Available: https://archivesphysiotherapy.

biomedcentral.com/articles/10.1186/s40945-021-00112-3 (accessed on 24 January 2023).

22. Mohan, K. S., & Darpan, M., (2020). Healthcare solution based on machine learning applications in IoT and edge computing. *International Journal of Pure and Applied Mathematics, 119*(16), 1473–1784.

23. Dinesh, B., Animesh, M., & Moumita, M., (2021). *Amalgamation of Blockchain Technology and Internet of Things for Healthcare Applications.* doi: 10.1007/978-3-030-67490-8_22, Blockchain for 5G-Enabled IoT.

24. Pradeep, K. V., & Randeep, S., (2021). A review on IoT assisted ECG monitoring framework for healthcare applications. In: *2021 Fourth International Conference on Computational Intelligence and Communication Technologies.* doi: 10.1109/CCICT53244.2021.00047.

25. Vahideh, H., (2021). Edge Intelligence for Empowering IoT-Based Healthcare Systems. IoT Evolution and Security Challenges in Cyber Space: IoT Security, pp. 99–127, Countering Cyber Attacks and Preserving the Integrity and Availability of Critical Systems, IGI Publisher.

CHAPTER 12

AN APPROACH FOR THE IMPLEMENTATION OF MULTILEVEL TECHNIQUE OF GA FOR CARDIAC DISEASE DETECTION

NEERAJ BHARGAVA,[1] RITU BHARGAVA,[2] KAPIL CHAUHAN,[3] PRAMOD SINGH RATHORE,[3] and VISHAL DUTT[4]

[1]Department of Computer Science, School of Engineering and System Science, MDS University, Ajmer, Rajasthan, India

[2]Sophia Girls' College, Ajmer, Rajasthan, India

[3]Assistant Professor, Aryabhatta College of Engineering and Research Center, Ajmer, Rajasthan, India

[4]Assistant Professor, Department of Computer Science, Aryabhatta College, Ajmer, Rajasthan, India

ABSTRACT

Artificial intelligence (AI) procedures have fundamentally advanced and transformed into a reality in the neural organization of our regular day-to-day existence. In the clinical consideration field, different frameworks are used for AI advancement for clinical treatments. For cutting edge strategies in AI calculations and work on the presentation, the AI innovation is to assume an imperative part in viably dissecting and using broad measures of wellbeing and clinical information.

The rationale behind of AI security system for various applications is included for the future help in light of the fact that numerous applications

Handbook of Research on Artificial Intelligence and Soft Computing Techniques in Personalized Healthcare Services, Uma N. Dulhare, A. V. Senthil Kumar, Amit Datta, Seddik Bri, Ibrahiem M. M. EI Emary, (Eds.)
© 2024 Apple Academic Press, Inc. Co-published with CRC Press (Taylor & Francis)

identified with computerized reasoning like bioinformatics and picture examination.

In this chapter the meaning of genetic algorithm (GA) to streamlining of result utilizing MATLAB capacity, and utilization of capacity as enhancement issue to comprehend various keywords like mutation. The action could be a target one that is a factual system or a reenactment, or it tends to be an emotional one where we pick better arrangements over most noticeably.

GA essentially carried out in various clinical region including cardiology, medical procedure, radiology, radiotherapy, and irresistible infections, nervous system science, pharmacotherapy. In the medical care framework, this calculation is utilized to tackle complex clinical issues.

12.1   INTRODUCTION

Genetic algorithm (GA) is a program-based procedure which is frames its premise from the organic advancement [6]. GA is in a general sense used as a basic suspecting method to offer an optimal plan. They're the simplest thanks to affect tackle the difficulty that little is understood. They're going to work splendidly in any request space since they structure an amazingly expansive estimation. The singular thing to be known is what the real circumstance is the place where the game-plan performs well really, and a GA will make a dumbfounding explanation. GA utilize the standards of determination and advancement to create a few answers for a given issue:

1. **Individual:** Any conceivable arrangement.
2. **Population:** Group, everything being equal.
3. **Search Space:** All potential answers for the issue.
4. **Chromosome:** Copy (blueprint) for a person.
5. **Trait:** People attribute value.
6. **Allele:** Attribute setting (possible).
7. **Locus:** The situation of a quality on the chromosome.
8. **Genome:** Number of chromosomes.

Thusly, the commitment to GA may be a bunch of anticipated responses for that issue, encoded in some style, and an action called the wellness work that permits all likelihood to be evaluated observational. These applicants may obviously be realized frameworks to figure, along with the purpose in GAs creating them further, albeit all the more frequently they emerge unpredictably [11].

12.2 FUNCTIONALITY OF GA

There is an honest scope of frameworks that a GA can be used to settle on the people to return:

1. **Determination:** During this capacity, the fittest people from each age are sure to be picked.

2. **Determination of Wellness Proportionate:** Healthier persons are more probable, anyway uncertain, to be chosen.

3. **Determination Roulette-Wheel:** A kind of wellness balanced decision during which the shot at a person's being picked is comparative with the mixture by which its health is more important or not the maximum amount as its adversaries' wellness.

4. **Scaling Choice:** Along these lines, the standard wellness of the overall population constructs, the strength of the actual squeezing think about like manner increases and therefore the wellbeing work finishes up being genuinely isolating. This procedure is usually valuable in making the only assurance afterward when the health of all persons is generally high and there is a slight difference in health, remember each other.

5. **Competition Choice:** Subgroups of people have perused the greater people, and other people from each subgroup go facing one another. Simply a solitary individual from each subgroup is picked to duplicate [23].

Following operators are mentioned:

i. **Selection Procedure:** Along these lines, the deal tendency to individuals with extraordinary wellness scores and license them to pass their characteristics to the reformist ages.

ii. **Crossover Procedure:** The instrument addresses mating between individuals. Two individuals are picked to use the determination administrator and hybrid objections are picked self-assertively. Then, the characteristics at these crossbreed objections are exchanged this manner making an absolutely new individual (posterity) as shown in Figure 12.1.

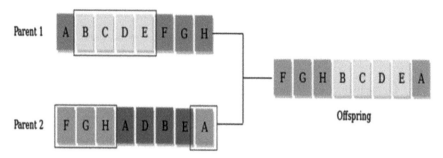

FIGURE 12.1   Crossover procedure.

iii. Mutation Procedure: The key factor of two offspring depends on the strong arbitrary value of populace to keep up with the variety in to stay away from the untimely assembly as shown in Figure 12.2.

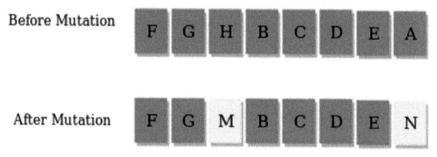

FIGURE 12.2   Crossover mutation.

Key factor of algorithm:

- Randomly introduce populaces p;
- Calculate fitness of populace;
- Assembly rehash:

  - Select guardians from populace;
  - Crossover and create new populace;
  - Perform change on new populace;
  - Calculate readiness for new populace.

12.3   GA MODEL

A GA is worked from different specific sections. are often ">" this is often a specific strength since it infers that standard parts can be re-used, with unimportant variety during a wide scope of GAs, appropriately working with execution. The many parts are choice, chromosome encoding, the wellness work, and therefore the improvement plot [7].

12.3.1   REPRESENTATION OF CHROMOSOME

In this way, the GA controls populaces of chromosomes, which is string indication of answers for a specific issue. A chromosome is a reflection of a natural DNA chromosome. A specific position or locus in a chromosome is indicate to as a gene and the letter happening by then in the chromosome is presented to as the allele point or basically allele. A specific portrayal utilized for a given issue is indicating to as the GA encoding of the issue. The old-style GA utilizes a bit-string representation to encode arrangements. Bit-string chromosomes comprise of a series of qualities whose allele point are characters from the letters in order {0,1} [17].

12.3.2   REPRESENTATIONS OF FITNESS

The main mechanism of fitness function is a calculation that assesses the nature of the chromosome as an answer for a specific issue. By relationship with science, the chromosome is indicating to as the genotype, while the arrangement it addresses is known as the phenotype. The interpretation cycle can be very complex. In timetabling and assembling planning GAs, for instance, a chromosome is converted into a schedule or set of booked exercises including enormous quantities of interfacing assets. The fitness calculation will then, at that point proceed to gauge the achievement of this timetable as far as different rules and targets, for example, finishing time, asset usage, cost minimization, etc. This intricacy is suggestive of natural development, where the chromosomes in a DNA atom are a bunch of directions for building the phenotypical organic entity. A complicated series of compound cycles changes a little assortment of undeveloped cells containing the DNA into a completely mature organic entity, which is then, at that point, "assessed" as far as its achievement in reacting to a scope of natural factors and impacts [19].

12.3.3   REPRESENTATIONS OF SELECTION

The procedure utilizes fitness as a discriminator of the nature of arrangements addressed by the chromosomes in a GA populace. The choice a part of a GA is meant to utilize wellness to direct the advancement of chromosomes by particular pressing factor. Chromosomes are during this manner chose for recombination supported wellness. Those with higher fitness need to have a more prominent possibility of determination than those with lower fitness, along these lines making a selected pressing factor towards all the more exceptionally fit arrangements. Determination is typically with substitution, implying that profoundly fit chromosomes get an opportunity of being chosen more than once or even recombined with themselves. The conventional choice strategy utilized is Roulette Wheel (or wellness corresponding) choice [21]. This assigns each chromosome a probability of being picked compared to its relative wellbeing, which is its health as a degree of the amount of fitness of all chromosomes within the general population [15]. There are different assurance plans:

1. **Discretionary Stochastic Selection:** This unequivocally picks each chromosome on different events like its supposition for being picked under the wellbeing relative strategy.

2. **Rivalry Selection:** This initially picks two chromosomes with uniform probability and a short time later picks the one with the foremost raised wellbeing.

3. **Truncation Selection:** This basically picks capriciously from the overall population having first discarded a legitimate number of the un-fit chromosomes [14, 24]. This assigns each chromosome a probability of being picked compared to its relative wellbeing, which is its health as a degree of the amount of fitness of all chromosomes within the general population [15].

4. **Contest Selection:** This initially picks two chromosomes with uniform probability and subsequently picks the one with the foremost raised wellbeing.

12.3.4   REPRESENTATION OF RECOMBINATION

In the GA mechanism recombination is the interaction that is chromosomes chose from a main populace is rejoined to frame individuals from a replacement populace. To simulate the blending of genetic material that can happen when life forms replicate. The selection for recombination is one-sided for higher fitness, the equilibrium of ideally is that all the more exceptionally strong chromosomes will advance therefore [18].

In this recombination interaction, the hybrid director measures the blending of genetic hypothesis from two picked parent chromosomes to form two or three youth chromosomes. After two parent chromosomes are decided for recombination, hit or miss number within the range [0,1] is delivered with uniform probability and stood out from not actually settled " hybrid recurrence." If the self-assertive number is quite the hybrid rate, no hybrid occurs and one among the 2 gatekeepers offers unaltered to the accompanying stage or recombination. If the hybrid rate is more unmistakable than or just like the discretionary number, then, the hybrid director is applied. One for the foremost part used half breed manager is one-point crossover. A mixture point among 0 and n is picked with uniform likelihood. Child chromosomes are then advanced from the characters of the central parent happening before the crossover point and consequently the characters of the next watchman happening after the mixture point [11].

12.3.5   PROCEDURE OF EVOLUTION

Finally above procedure, output of chromosomes is replaced into the replacement populace. The cycles of determination and recombination are then iterated until a total replacement populace is created. By then the replacement populace turns into another source populace (the next generation). The GA is iterated through various generations until suitable rules are reached. These can incorporate a proper number of generations having passed, noticed intermingling to a best-fitness arrangement, or the generation of an answer that completely fulfills a bunch of imperatives. There are a few developmental plans that can be utilized, contingent upon the degree to which chromosomes from the source populace are permitted to pass unaltered into the replacement populace [23].

12.3.6   PROCEDURE OF GA DESIGN

In the GA design, there are numerous decisions that must be made in planning a GA for a given application. The decision of encoding will rely upon the idea of the issue. As the size of the allele set extends, for instance, where the strings comprise of floating point numbers, the arrangement of potential chromosomes turns out to be significantly more prominent. Numerous cutting edge (or non-classical) GAs utilize a scope of illustrative ways to deal with guarantee that the arrangement of potential chromosomes is a nearby counterpart for the arrangement of potential arrangements of the issue. Having chosen an encoding, there are numerous different decisions to make. These include: the type of the wellness work; populace size; hybrid and change administrators and their separate rates; the transformative plan to be applied; and fitting halting/ re-start conditions. The standard plan approach is a blend of involvement, issue explicit demonstrating and experimentation with various advance-ment plans and different boundaries. A normal plan for a traditional GA utilizing total supplanting with standard genetic administrators may be as per the following [16]:

- Arbitrary production of source populace of P chromosomes.
- Maintain the fitness, P(S), of every chromosome S in the source populace.
- Design a procedure for replacement populace and afterward rehash the accompanying strides until S chromosomes have been made:

  - By utilizing wellness determination, select S1 and S2 as 2 chro-mosomes, from the provider populace.
  - Operate one-guide hybrid toward d1 and d2 with hybrid rate pc to urge a teenager chromosome c.
  - Confirm uniform change to c with change rate pm to form c'.
  - Add s' to the new people.

- By utilizing this supplant the source people with the new people.
- If ending rules haven't been met, return to Step 2.

12.4   CLASSIFICATIONS OF GAS

A metaheuristic is a system which means to track down an adequate arrangement in extremely complex improvement and search issues [2]. In contrast with different heuristics, metaheuristics make utilization of low-level heuristic or search calculations. In this way, metaheuristics utilize substantial heuristics or calculations which are more dynamic. In contrast with streamlining calculations and iterative techniques, recovered arrangement is subject to the arrangement of irregular factors created. Contrasted with streamlining calculations and iterative techniques, metaheuristics don't ensure that a universally ideal arrangement can be found on some class of issues. Numerous metaheuristics carry out some type of stochastic streamlining, with the goal that the arrangement found is subject to the arrangement of arbitrary factors created. Metaheuristics, for example, GA are described by the facts [19].

Metaheuristics guide search measure with characterized systems. Albeit randomized, metaheuristic calculations, for example, GA are not irregular quests.

They will probably productively look through the state space to discover close ideal arrangements. Along these lines metaheuristic look incorporate basic nearby pursuit calculations and difficult learning calculations.

Metaheuristic calculations are rough and normally deterministic. Metaheuristic calculations are not issue explicit. They make not many suppositions about the advancement or search issue being tackled, and hence they can be utilized for an assortment of issues [12].

12.5 DIFFERENTIATE GA AND HEURISTIC SEARCH

Sl. No.	Representation of GA	Heuristic Search
1.	GA is routinely applied to issues that require only the region of a hub.	Heuristic pursuit regularly requires the development of a way.
2.	An issue tended to by GA doesn't indicate a beginning space or/and objective state.	An issue tended to by informed Search frequently indicate a beginning area.
3.	GA is consistently executed to issues that don't decide how a sufficient course of action can be seen.	Heuristic Search is frequently implemented to issues that do indicate equal perceived.
4.	Connectivity is not defined.	The charts looked by means of heuristic calculations frequently have some not really settled.
5.	GA navigates with several graphs.	State space search calculation will in general explore on a solitary chart.

12.6   DIFFERENTIATE OF GA WITH HILL CLIMBING

Factor	GA	Hill Climbing
Working	GA have start with input data with numerical value.	Hill climbing is a numerical streamlining strategy which has a place with the group of nearby inquiry.
Throughput	Performance is based on strong input value.	Every move of input value is dependent on logical value, so each new example has everything except one of similar pieces as the past example.
Representation	Bit-string portrayal is basic.	MoveSet configuration is basic
Technique preferred	Worldwide optimum	Nearby optimum
Dispersion of populace is different and enormous	GA makes a huge, helpful, and organized leap even after fractional assembly.	Hill climbing isn't great when contrasted with GA when the circulation of the populace is assorted and enormous.
Least assorted populace	GA doesn't acquire advantage in the least different populace.	Hill climbing search work productively creates great outcome.
Search through Sampling for example Blind search.	GAs accomplishes a lot of their broadness by disregarding data aside from that unsettling result.	Depend vigorously on such data, and in issue where the fundamental data isn't accessible or hard to acquire, these strategy separates.
Search mechanism	The output calculated in terms of search mechanism.	HC utilizes a looping mechanism to improve task.
Examples	Chemistry, electrical engineering, financial markets, game playing, geophysics, materials engineering.	The eight-queens problem, circuit design.

12.7   EXPERIMENTAL METHOD AND MATERIAL

In this study, we used the dataset of some cardiac patients. The dataset has 303 records with 14 different attributes. The dataset consists of the patient age, sex, chest pain, resting blood pressure, cholesterol, fasting blood sugar, resting electrocardiography, heart rate, exercise angina, fluoroscopy, heart status, slope, and oldpeak.

We have divided the dataset into two parts; one for training and another for testing. The training dataset has 84% and the remaining 16% of data has been included to testing dataset.

In the GA, the underlying stage begins with tons of game plans (oversaw by chromosomes) referred to as a general population. Plans from one people are taken and wont to outline another general population. This is often convinced by an assumption, that the new people are going to be better than the previous one. Plans that are picked to stipulate new courses of action are picked by their wellness – the more suitable they're the more potential outcomes they have to breed. In the GA, the fitness value is dependent on the genes value. So we have use the strong genes are consider for apply functionality.

In this way, the main piece of the genetic calculation is the crossover and mutation. The exhibition is affected mostly by these two administrators. The chromosome ought to somehow or another contain data about arrangement which it addresses. The most utilized method of encoding is a parallel string. Every chromosome has one double string. Each bit in this string can address some trait of the arrangement as shown in Figure 12.3.

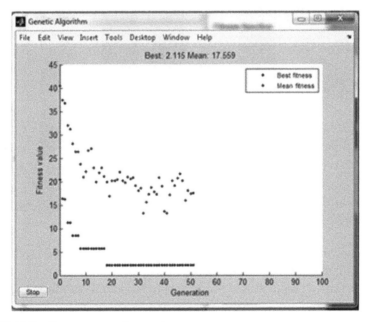

FIGURE 12.3   Crossover mutation result.

In the GA we arrange the issues and showing the outcomes with various phrasing like best individual, best fitness, Expectation, Range, Score, Selection, Max Constraint.

We utilize the rastrigin capacity to compute the imperative and plot stretch. To show the plot stretch and requirement, we utilize the quantity of variable for direct disparity, Bounds (lower and upper), Linear uniformity, Nonlinear limitation work as shown in Figure 12.4.

A fitness capacity ought to have the accompanying qualities:

- The wellness capacity ought to be adequately quick to process;
- It should quantitatively gauge how fit a given arrangement is or how fit people can be created from the given arrangement.

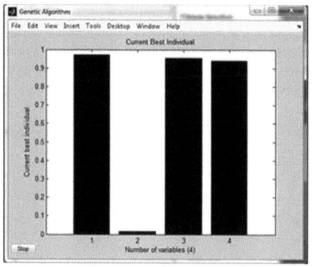

FIGURE 12.4   Best individual in GA.

For the most part the minimization method ought to fulfill the accompanying prerequisites:

- Capacity to acquire usable outcomes in a sensible measure of time (as fast as could really be expected).
- Usability, i.e., scarcely any control factors to deal with the minimization.
- Steady assembly to the worldwide least in sequential autonomous preliminaries.

An ordinary GA with a parallel pursuit to discover the crossing points of a line with the limit of the attainable district to wrap the hunt space more like an achievable area as shown in Figure 12.5.

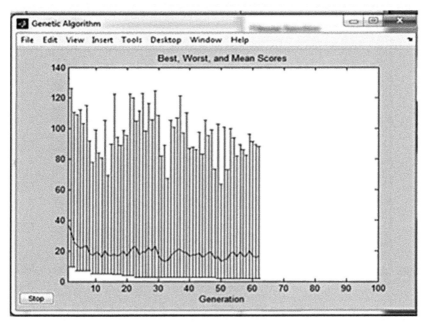

FIGURE 12.5   Range in GA.

Two strategies for keeping up with genetic variety in a populace of organic entities being followed up on by a genetic calculation. In the two cases, the organisms are on a square matrix and just cooperate with their closest neighbors. The quantity of communications depends on the fitness. Different cases are shown in Figure 12.6. One strategy brings about environmental specialties in sizes from a couple of creatures to a few dozen. In the second technique, pretty much every living being in the populace stays in a novel natural specialty looking through the fitness scene. The two techniques can be utilized in discovering different arrangements. The pictorial portrayal shows that the score variety exists between a number of individual and score (range). In this figure, the tallness of individual is rely upon the score worth and property estimation. The strategies included the information with testing reason which is impart the information being followed up on strategy results for not many cooperation which depends on score variety followed up on different arrangement of score variety. The strategy is discovering numerous answers for acknowledge the score variety of creatures being followed up on by a genetic calculation.

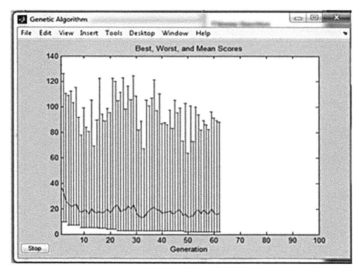

FIGURE 12.6   Range in GA.

Chromosomes are chosen from the populace to be guardians to hybrid. The issue is the means by which to choose these chromosomes. As indicated by advancement hypothesis the best ones ought to endure and make new posterity. Guardians are chosen by their wellness. The better the chromosomes are, the more opportunities to be chosen they have. The selection function is shown in Figure 12.7.

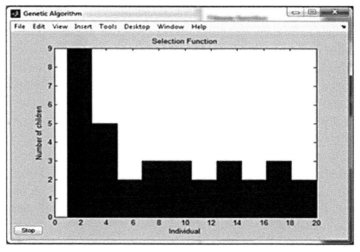

FIGURE 12.7   Selection in GA.

12.8 APPLICATION OF GA

GAs has many applications, some of them are:

1. **Recurrent Neural Network (RNN):** This technology performing calculations continuously for repeated statistics and most popular voice search services like Apple's Siri and Google's voice search are using this information. RNN are a class of neural organizations that are useful in demonstrating grouping information. Derived from feedforward networks, RNNs display comparable conduct to how human minds work.

2. **Mutation Testing:** Each mutant is changed over into a various leveled chart, which addresses the program's stream, factors, and conditions. Based on this diagram structure an extraordinary chart part is characterized to ascertain closeness among programs. It is then used to foresee if a given test would recognize a mutant. The forecast is completed with the assistance of a classification calculation.

3. **Code Breaking:** An improvement issue is one in which we have a machine for certain handles that we can go to change the machine's settings and an approach to gauge how well the machine is performing with the current settings. We need to track down the most ideal settings, which will be those that expand some basic proportion of how well the machine is performing. That point will be known as the ideal. Arriving at it will be called streamlining.

4. **Filtering and Signal Processing:** Processing of digitized discrete-time tested signs. Handling is finished by broadly useful PCs or by computerized circuits like applied explicit incorporated circuits (ASICs), field-programmable gate arrays (FPGAs) or specific digital signal processors (DSPs) or Advanced RISC Machines (ARM chips). Advanced handling permits in numerous applications for a few benefits over simple preparing, like mistake recognition and revision in transmission just as information pressure.

5. **Learning Fuzzy Rule Base:** The principle part in fuzzy framework is the standard base and the outcomes in a fuzzy order framework rely upon the fuzzy standards.

12.9   CONCLUSION

GAs finishes up being better find spaces of intricate and certifiable issues. GAs is adaptable to their environmental factors, as this type of procedure may be a phase appearing within the advancing environment. In Present these estimations are more suitable. A few of upgrades need to be made all at once that GAs might be even more all-around relevant. In this research, more prominence is set on representing the essential of the GA, its handiness. The varied issues that are looked at by GA are in like manner related to this chapter. Its supportiveness and sophistication of handling concerns has chosen it the more most adored choice among the normal techniques, explicitly point search, subjective chase, etc. GAs is especially helpful when the specialist doesn't have definite region authority, since GAs has the power to research and acquire from their space.

In future work, we on a really basic level spotlight on the varied issues associated with the GA, what all methodology are needed to are done to beat these issues to form GA extensively more noteworthy and capable.

KEYWORDS

- Advanced RISC Machines
- Applied Explicit Incorporated Circuits
- Artificial Intelligence
- Crossover
- Field-Programmable Gate Arrays
- Genetic Algorithm
- Healthcare
- Machine Learning
- Mutation

REFERENCES

1. Cheng, J. R., & Gen, M., (2020). Parallel GAs with GPU computing. *Impact on Intelligent Logistics and Manufacturing.*

2. Metawa, N., Kabir, H. M., & Mohamed, E., (2017). GA based model for optimizing bank lending decisions. *Expert Systems with Applications, 80*, 75–82.
3. Coello, C., (2000). An updated survey of GA-based multiobjective optimization techniques. *ACM Computing Surveys, 32*(2), 109–143.
4. Haoze, L., (2012). Research on artificial intelligence optimization based on GA. *Light Industry Science and Technology*, 77–79.
5. Hui, W., (2008). Application of GA in the field of artificial intelligence. *Computer Knowledge and Technology*, 2040–2042.
6. Huailiang, L., & Miao, L., (2005). A hybrid genetic simulated annealing algorithm and its application. *Journal of Guangzhou University*, 141–145.
7. Amin, D., Suhaimi, I., & Reza, M., (2016). Effect of GA on artificial neural network for intrusion detection system. *International Journal of Computer Sciences and Engineering, 04*(10), 10–18.
8. Shrivastava, A., & Singh, R., (2014). An implementation of hybrid GA for clustering-based data for web recommendation system. *Int. J. Comput. Sci. Eng., 2*(4), 6–11.
9. Sangari, F. E., & Mehrdad, N., (2014). *Efficacy of Different Strategies in Graph Coloring with Parallel GAs*, 138–141.
10. Li, J., & Xinbo, G., (2003). A GA-based clustering algorithm for large data sets with mixed numeric and categorical values. *IEEE, Proceedings of the Fifth International Conference on Computational Intelligence and Multimedia Applications (ICCIMA'03)*. 0-7695-1957-1/03.
11. Haldurai, L., & Vinodhini, V., (2015). Parallel indexing on color and texture feature extraction using R-tree for content-based image retrieval. *International Journal of Computer Sciences and Engineering, 03*(11), 11–15. E-ISSN: 2347-2693.
12. Sreedharamurthy, S. K., & Sudarshana, R. H. R., (2015). Feature subset selection using GAs for handwritten Kannada alphabets recognition. *International Journal of Computer Sciences and Engineering, 03*(06), 94–99.
13. Noraini, M. R., & John, G., (2011). A GA performance with different selection strategies. *Proceedings of the World Congress on Engineering* (Vol. II).
14. Gaidhani, C. R., Vedashree, M. D., & Vrushali, N. B., (2014). *Image Steganography for Message Hiding Using GA. 2*(3), 67–70, E-ISSN: 2347–2693.
15. Burchardt, H., & Salomon, R., (2006). Implementation of path planning using GAs on mobile robots. *IEEE International Conference on Evolutionary Computation* (pp. 1831–1836). Vancouver, BC.
16. Chen, R., Liang, C. Y., Hong, W. C., & Gu, D. X., (2015). Forecasting holiday daily tourist flow based on seasonal support vector regression with adaptive GA. *Appl. Soft Comput., 26*, 434–443.
17. Liu, D., Dongxiao, N., Hui, W., & Leilei, F., (2014). Short-term wind speed forecasting using wavelet transform and support vector machines optimized by GA. *Renewable Energy, 62*, 592–597.
18. Cheng, H., Yang, S., & Cao, J., (2013). Dynamic GAs for the dynamic load balanced clustering problem in mobile ad hoc networks. *Expert. Syst. Appl., 40*(4), 1381–1392.
19. Chouhan, S. S., Kaul, A., & Singh, U. P., (2018). Soft computing approaches for image segmentation: A survey. *Multimed. Tools Appl., 77*(21), 28483–28537.
20. Chuang, Y. C., Chen, C. T., & Hwang, C., (2016). A simple and efficient real-coded GA for constrained optimization. *Appl. Soft Comput., 38*, 87–105.

21. Das, A. K., & Pratihar, D. K., (2018). A direction-based exponential mutation operator for real-coded GA. *IEEE International Conference on Emerging Applications of Information Technology.*

22. Dash, S. R., Dehuri, S., & Rayaguru, S., (2013). Discovering interesting rules from biological data using parallel GA. In: *3ʳᵈ IEEE International Advance Computing Conference (IACC)* (pp. 631–636). Ghaziabad.

23. Datta, D., Amaral, A. R. S., & Figueira, J. R., (2011). Single row facility layout problem using a permutation-based GA. *European J. Oper. Res., 213*(2), 388–394.

24. De Ocampo, A. L. P., & Dadios, E. P., (2017). Energy cost optimization in irrigation system of smart farm by using GA. In: *2017 IEEE 9ᵗʰ International Conference on Humanoid, Nanotechnology, Information Technology, Communication and Control, Environment and Management (HNICEM)* (pp. 1–7). Manila.

25. Deb, K., & Deb, D., (2014). Analyzing mutation schemes for real-parameter GAs. *International Journal of Artificial Intelligence and Soft Computing, 4*(1), 1–28.

PART III
Telemedicine and Personalized Healthcare Services

CHAPTER 13

A TELE-HEALTHCARE SYSTEM FOR DIAGNOSIS AND TREATMENT OF PATIENTS DURING A PANDEMIC

DISHA M. DHABARDE,[1] MONIKA P. MASKE,[1] JAGDISH R. BAHETI,[1] and HITESH V. SHAHARE[2]

[1]Kamla Nehru College of Pharmacy, Butibori, Nagpur, Maharashtra, India

[2]Shriman Sureshdada Jain College of Pharmacy, Chandwad, Nashik, Maharashtra, India

ABSTRACT

This chapter deals with the significance of telehealth and various technologies used to implement artificial intelligence (AI) in the virtual health management system. Telehealth is the diagnosis and treatment of patients at a distance during a pandemic. The main advantage of telehealth is to reduce travel costs, waiting time and improve the quality of care. It could be very useful, particularly in rural regions or where the healthcare system is not available. The important aim of telehealth is to enhance chronic diseases management, notably in times of emergency. Due to the unavailability of physicians for patients at the time of the pandemic, readers get aware of the models which will be beneficial to take care of the patient for self-management of chronic diseases and meet the expectation of the healthcare system. Telehealth plays a direct and indirect role in eliminating the spreading of infections by maintaining physical distancing. The far-flung prognosis and remedy of sufferers by way of telecommunications technology is very helpful during COVID-19, cardiovascular diseases (CVDs), mental disorders, diabetes. Hence,

Handbook of Research on Artificial Intelligence and Soft Computing Techniques in Personalized Healthcare Services, Uma N. Dulhare, A. V. Senthil Kumar, Amit Datta, Seddik Bri, Ibrahiem M. M. El Emary, (Eds.)
© 2024 Apple Academic Press, Inc. Co-published with CRC Press (Taylor & Francis)

there is a requirement for the development of new strategies by hospitals and healthcare systems to develop their own digital transformation.

13.1   INTRODUCTION

The terminology of telemedicine came into existence in the late 1970s and its means "recovery from a distance." The far-flung prognosis and treatment of sufferers by telecommunications technology are very helpful during pandemic diseases. Telehealth and Telemedicine from the decade brought a major change in healthcare structures to make sure that network stays healthful well as hospitals are available to those who are unwell or in need [1]. By using technology and telecommunication, patients get safe, effective, timely treatment. Telemedicine the time period changed into coined in overdue 1970s and actually way "restoration from distance." The faraway prognosis and remedy of sufferers by telecommunications era. The application of generating and telecommunication systems to manage healthcare for patients who are geographically distanced from the issuer [2].

Various technologies are mHealth or cellular fitness, video, and audio technology, virtual photography, and remote patient monitoring (RPM). mHealth consists of smartphones, tablets, laptops which include devices to sell higher fitness effects and growth get right of entry to care. These programs permit the sufferers to tune fitness measurements, set medicine and appointment reminders, percentage data with clinicians [3].

Videoconferencing, video-scopes, and High-decision cameras take care of inmates, patients, and sufferers in rural locations. Video scopes and high-decision digital digicam for diagnosing and dealing with inmates remotely [4].

Remote patient monitoring (RPM) – it includes the reporting, collection, transmission, and assessment of affected person fitness facts via digital devices. Technologies used for store and in advance telehealth encompass stable servers and routes [5].

13.2   TYPES OF TELEHEALTH

- Live videoconferencing;
- Asynchronous video (AKA store-and-forward);
- Remote patient monitoring (RPM);
- Mobile health (mHealth).

13.2.1   LIVE VIDEO CONFERENCING

Synchronous video conferencing is another name for it. It is a very fast normalized part of healthcare. This kind of telehealth is usually utilized by each health practitioner in neighborhood hospitals for presenting offerings to patients [6]. The stay videoconferencing is extra useful for rural areas.

13.2.2   ASYNCHRONOUS VIDEO

Asynchronous video is the healthcare supplier for electronic delivery of patients' documented health history outside of real-time. Largely employed in rural areas once healthcare suppliers are consulted with a specialist in an alternative location. It helps to bring healthcare to areas wherever it. This method involves exploiting medical data like medical images, biosignals, and so on and transferring the information to a healthcare provider, medico or doctors at a convenient time for assessment offline. Common store and forward technologies used embrace secure messaging, email, and web-based self-management programs [7].

13.2.3   REMOTE PATIENT MONITORING (RPM)

This is also referred to as a self-examination or self-monitoring system. This technology is used for observing the health and clinical signs of patients remotely. It manages chronic diseases like cardiovascular, asthma, and diabetes mellitus. Remote monitoring is cost-effective, frequent, and more patient satisfaction. Simply healthcare providers monitor patients remotely by using various technological devices. RPM may be an answer of which can fill care gaps for chronic sickness and drugs of patients who are unable to go to the clinic. It provides care to manage and monitor patients with many conditions remotely by exploiting virtual channels like smartphones, email, video calls, and remote strategies of assembling specimens, moveable medical devices, and health kits for patients to remain safe at their habitation [8].

The person who suffers is going to be provided with wireless home medical devices like deliberation scale or sign monitor or different devices for information assortment, particularly for the not itinerant patient. Subsequently, data was sent to the hospital data server for additional analysis. These systems send alerts to the doctor and additionally the patient if the measurements are out of the traditional range [7, 8].

If any affected person calls for therapeutic drug monitoring (TDM) to hint drug awareness of their blood level, the group will require care and pattern taken at unique intervals. Remote blood series is feasible with the transportable tool and in-domestic healthcare kits like Mitra micro-sampler or Mitra Blood series kit. Doctors can deliver to sufferers, and then sufferers switch their self-gathered pattern with the aid of using mail for lab testing [9]. The lab document passes directly to the scientific report of the patient. The device gets the right of entry with the aid of using a care provider, who can connect with the affected person through a telecall smartphone to speak about any extrude in medicine.

RPM is made for concurrent for supplying transmission of physiological size including weight, coronary heart rate, blood pressure, etc., to decorate via way of means of channels without a doubt and self-control of sufferers. By the use of era and transportable devices, healthcare company video display units the fitness reputation of sufferers and manipulate remedy routine remotely.

RPM allows monitoring physicians:

- For better results, the dose was adjusted, and regular treatment was required;
- To keep watch on patient's progress;
- To reduce hospitalization by timely check-ups and care;
- To understand biometric of patients relative to prescription and lifestyle behavior;
- For boosting, data analysis reduces manual data collection and data entry;
- Give priority and attention to those who need more or serious patients [9, 10].

13.2.4   MHEALTH (MOBILE HEALTH)

The usage of smart devices such as smartphones, tablets, computers, note-books, and other similar devices, as well as health-based entire software programs developed for devices, is referred to as m health. These heath-primarily based totally apps can display the entirety like diabetic affected person blood sugar level, and water intake daily. It also helps and encourages lifestyle behavior and integrates with patients' personal health records (PHRs). Healthcare provider uses a various range of mobile health solutions for improving the quality of care and access to critical wellness recourse:

1. **Remote or Online Consultations:** In online or remote consultations uses video conferencing software, digital tools provided by a healthcare provider, or mobile apps.

2. **Electronic Health Recorders (EHRs):** It helps patients a healthcare provider for transfer and update information. EHRs are the best instrumental in determining healthcare treatment. Tracking of Mobile Data helps to track their personal health data like insulin level, body temperature. The internet-connected medical devices also collect data and transfer it to healthcare providers and EHRs.

3. **Wearable Gadget:** In wearable gadgets, smartwatches, are more widely used. iTBra detects the most cancers in breast tissue and the apple watch tracks atrial traumatic inflammation primarily based totally on heartbeat data.

4. **AliveCor App:** It's the mobile health app that provides heart electrocardiograms (ECG) from their mobile device with a sensor. The device is used fast, automatically, affordable to find out health issues like tachycardia, atrial fibrillation (AF). Patients regularly get reviews on their cardiologist's ECGs.

5. **HealthKit App:** This app connects with sufferers' or customers' iPhone and apple watch to tune their fitness, fitness files environmental stressors to reveal coronary heart disease, and file their fitness on time.

6. **IExaminer App:** Welch Allyn's I Examiner app permit healthcare to click pictures of eyes and retinal nerves properly from their Smartphone. The mobile is connected to a PanOptic ophthalmoscope and takes an image in high-resolution to store and send when needed. This images study by the healthcare provider undergoes treatment and suggests the medication.

7. **Glucose Buddy App:** Its diabetes management app for tacking insulin, blood sugar, weight, food intake, and physical activity. Record the reading data send to healthcare providers who provide help, advice, and treatment for managing and regulating diabetes [10, 11].

8. **Fitbit App:** The Fitbit app and wearable gadgets present human beings to set health and well-being progress. It additionally facilitates sleep monitoring to reveal how plenty of time is spent in sleep

healthcare issuer advocate how they enhance their sleep higher or recover.

9. **Strava:** The Strava app used by athletes to build their performance, tracking. Strava also syncs to a device like a global positioning system (GPS), coronary heart video display units to offer extra complete view progress.

10. **Mobile Image Monitoring (MIM) Software:** MIM Software gives doctor centers cell photos for radiation oncology, neuroscience, cardiac, and radiology images. Remote get admission to healthcare company and without problems stocks with patients, offer remedy and remedy plans.

11. **Medisafe App:** It facilitates sufferers to without difficulty fill their prescription and their medicinal drug dosage and apply. The enterprise companions with main pharmaceutical manufacturers and healthcare carrier's non-public solutions facilitates sufferers [12] (Table 13.1).

TABLE 13.1   Types of Telehealth, Time, Applications, and Technology

Types	Time	Applications	Technology
Synchronous	• Real-time interaction with health checker.	• Clinical assessments; • Ongoing care; • Treatment and emergency service's needs.	• Video calls; • Web-conferencing; • Telephone.
Asynchronous	• Sharing data to direct patient's treatments; • Methods can be interactive or passive.	• Clinical assessment; • Symptoms management.	Web-based portals, email, text, mobile application, symptoms management tracking, electronic medical recorder.
Remote patient monitoring	• This method observing the health and clinical signs of patients remotely.	• Adjust dosing and monitoring; • Monitor patients regularly; • Provide manual data collection; • Data entry and understanding patient's biometrics.	• Mitra micro-sampler; • Virtual channels like smartphone, e-mail, video consults, home health kits.

TABLE 13.1 *(Continued)*

Types	Time	Applications	Technology
Mobile health (mHealth)	• Electronic record-keeping; • Real-time information collection, tracking symptoms and treating them.	• Tracking symptoms quickly; • Get health information; • Record-keeping; • Reducing the spread of diseases; • Providing reminders for medicine to patients.	• Online or remote consultations; • Electronic health records; • Wearable devices; • Mobile tracking data.

13.3 IMPORTANCE

The importance of telehealth is to enhance chronic disease management, especially in emergencies. In the epidemics or pandemics has behavior the employment of growing new virtual era strategies, which brought on the usage of telemedicine throughout the various degree of contamination an awful lot greater frequently, such as severe acute respiratory syndrome (SARS) pandemic, middle east respiratory syndrome coronavirus (MERS-CoV), and most recently coronavirus disease 19 (COVID-19) which minimizes the spread of infections.

Telehealth is beneficial and sustainable for precaution; prevention and treatment to stop the spread of diseases. Benefits are:

- It also increases the quality of care;
- Cost-saving;
- Minimizes exposure for patients and staff;
- It helps to increase the range of care and education [13].

13.3.1 IMPORTANCE TO PATIENTS

- To remove the barricade like waiting rooms, parking, and time of traveling;
- To advance protection for sufferers who're critical to travel;
- Approach to physiotherapy services that are not available in a faraway location;

Patients self-manipulate their fitness with the aid of using the use of online self-control and monitoring;

- It is more flexible for patients and cost-effective.

13.3.2 IMPORTANCE TO THERAPIST OR PHYSIOTHERAPIST

- To improve efficiency in between travel and locations;
- Chance to improve creativity in care of standards with the use of technology;
- Patients are self-control at domestic and tracking care and outcomes.

13.3.3 IMPORTANCE TO SOCIETY

- The patients/society is more independent and informed;
- Satisfaction of people to be a more digital connection;

Decreased independence on the clinical device and expanded the encouragement for sufferers to self-manipulate their health;

- Reduction in traveling;
- more time is saving;
- Very well used of public resources;
- Various approaches to healthcare.

13.4 CHALLENGES

In every technology there are some challenges, telehealth also faces challenges like money, regulation, hype, acceptance, technology, proof, and success:

1. **Money:** It's a huge project for telemedicine due to the fact there's no assured fee among telehealth or telemedicine and sufferers. Some sufferers do not avail the facility of this remedy or care due to cost.

2. **Regulation:** Licensing is a small problem due to the fact ordinarily telemedicine structures operated. There are multistate structures with multi-nation practices. Another undertaking is the Social Security Act, which limits the use of telemedicine to sure providers.

3. **Hype:** There is a few programs of telehealth that have very excessive value, and a few aren't working.

4. **Technology:** Technological demanding situations like software or hardware program failure that break down the additionally poses a

task to the utilization of telehealth and telemedicine. It is used for numerous generations to create greater facts a few instances that aren't beneficial.

5. **Evidence:** Telemedicine required more studies, evaluation, and their evidence is needing cost-saving.

A lack of studies showing the economic benefits and cost effectiveness of telemedicine programs has hampered efforts to persuade policymakers to invest in the field. Confidentiality and private's problems can also pose an undertaking. Issues encompass breaches of private fitness statistics which can arise on unsecured networks, in addition to unlocked and unencrypted hardware that may be accessed. Still, it has more potential, and the network of telehealth is very vast. People used this technique very easily because it's saving time and stop the spread of infection.

13.5 STRATEGIES

1. **To Support from the Government:** In this address legal and regulatory considerations require secure approvals.
2. **Identify Telemedicine Users:** In this healthcare providers and patients are familiar with these advancements.
3. **Train Health Workers:** In these healthcare workers trained and empowered treatment in the community.
4. Engage patients self-manage and take care.
5. The person care should be appropriate and includes language interpretations.
6. Encourage digital ready mindset and culture.

13.6 MODELS

Due to the unavailability of physicians for patients at the time of the pandemic, there is some model which will be beneficial to take care of the patient and meet the expectations. The neurosynaptic paradigm enables remote diagnosis and consultation hardware and software solutions. Apollo Telehealth Services promoted by the Apollo chain of hospitals provide services like telecardiology. Global Digital Dispensary provides consultation, medication, and basic diagnostics. Yolo health carries out health check-up at the doorstep.

Medical on go gives services through its medicine dispensers. Voice, video chat, email, instant messaging, discussion forums, and social media are all available through e-Vaidya. World Health partners provide mainly for reproductive health services whereas Welfare gives remote ophthalmology services [14, 15].

13.7   SAFEGUARDS

13.7.1   VOICE CONFERENCING AND VIDEO CONFERENCING

The use of technology such as telephones, video-gadgets connected by LAN (local area network), WAN (wide-area network), Internet, cell phones, e-mail, fax, and other means to diagnose, medicate, educate, and counsel patients about their health [15].

13.7.2   HIPAA (HEALTH INSURANCE PORTABILITY AND ACCOUNTABILITY ACT)

The HIPAA recommendations on telehealth have an effect on any clinical expert or healthcare machine that gives a far-flung carrier to patients. Under HIPAA, any information that can be used to identify a patient is called electronically protected health information. According to HIPAA, electronically protected health information requires special safeguards to prevent breaches. The HIPAA technical safeguards include a unique account for each user, passwords, providing each user minimum electronically protected health information, and recording all access and changes to electronically protected health information [16].

13.7.3   PATIENT PERMISSION

It is vital for sessions of telehealth. The consent may be implied or expressed. If the affected person initiates the telemedicine session, then its miles are referred to as implied while an express affected individual consent is wanted if a fitness worker, Registered Medical Practitioner or caregiver initiates a Telemedicine session. Registered Medical Practitioner would gather information of patient required for proper medication [15, 16].

13.7.4 SAFEGUARD FOR TELEHEALTH UPTAKE

To recognize approximately the kingdom planes, restrictions, transient mandates, directives, and expiration dates, it consists of up-to-date regulatory moves for healthcare machines and fitness care persons. Training is supplied to staff, practice approximately policies, protocols at the same time as the use of telehealth offerings consists of appointment scheduling, documentation, and billing, pressing, and emergency care laboratory offerings, prescriptions, scientific gadgets, and visits. Telehealth is used to circulate anywhere in elements of healthcare shipping structures like pharmacies, clinics, labs, etc. [17].

13.8 FOCUS ON DISEASES

Telehealth plays a direct and indirect role in eliminating the spreading of infections by maintaining physical distancing. It helps for self-management with chronic diseases surviving to old age. Patients at a better chance of contamination, particularly the ones who have chronic, autoimmune, and immune suppressant sicknesses save the contamination chance through e-fitness with medical doctors or specialists. Telehealth also helps to regulate diabetic patients.

13.8.1 TELEHEALTH DURING COVID-19

Telehealth is a powerful preference to lessen the eruption of COVID-19. The problems are considerably more urgent and extreme during outbreaks, pandemics, and failures when the health system is already overburdened, and infection transmission is a struggle. Telemedicine technology has additional capabilities to aid and address the issues. Telemedicine is the shipping of fitness care services, with the aid of using all healthcare experts the usage of ICTs (information and communication technology) the trade of records for diagnosis, research, assessment, and contributing schooling for the fitness care provider. Healthcare structures to make certain that networks stay healthful, and hospitals are to be had most effective the sick and needy. Telemedicine and digital care have ended up a critical device in worrying for sufferers at the COVID-19 pandemic [5]. The upward thrust in range of instances withinside the network with instances in domestic isolation, telemedicine is the handiest feasible choice to be had to screen them and make sure well-timed referral. For OPD services "Calldoc" and "DR YSR Telemedicine" are commenced via way of means of kingdom governments at some point of COVID-19. This pandemic has paved slightly at the significance of telehealth and telemedicine in provider shipping and the way its miles going to be widely widespread in the future [6].

13.8.2 TELEHEALTH IN CARDIOVASCULAR DISEASES (CVDS)

Cardiovascular diseases (CVDs) cause death because of poor lifestyles and disability in the world. CVD causes the death of around 17.9 million lives each year, and smoking is also responsible for nearly 10%. CVDs it's a set of coronary heart disease and blood vessels additionally consist of rheumatic heart diseases, etc.

13.8.2.1 RISK FACTORS OF CVDS

Most important is a behavioral risk factor of heart disease and stroke is the poor lifestyle like unhealthy diet, tobacco use, smoking, alcohol, physical inactivity. This affects increased blood pressure, blood glucose, blood lipids, obesity. It leads to heart attack, stroke, heart failure, and other complications.

For those suffering from cardiovascular illnesses and stroke, telehealth will revolutionize the approach and provide a new level of comfort. This is especially true for patients with cardiovascular illnesses or stroke who would otherwise be unable to access specialty healthcare services due to their geographic location, physical impairment, advanced chronic disease, or difficulty obtaining transportation. In CVD, telehealth provides primary, acute care, rehabilitation, chronic disease management.

13.8.2.2 ACUTE CARE

The telehealth application is used for diagnosis as well as treatment of acute cardiac. The patient's ECGs are transferred to the healthcare provider then the specialist interprets the ECG and started the treatment and care. The rural areas paramedics, hospital staff of rural areas can send data to telehealth providers for care and interpretation.

Acute stroke – the acute stroke for which thrombolysis produces good results in patients. The thrombolysis gives in a combination of brain images and clinical assessment from a neurologist, with tele-stroke services which is implemented all over the world. It also includes rural as well as remote for accessing radiological and neurological expertise. Telehealth provides safety, efficacy in patients [18].

13.8.2.3   REHABILITATION

1. **Cardiac Rehabilitation:** The people do not go for telehealth at the complication of cardiac rehabilitation is very less. The main problem is cost, distance, and patients not having information about the healthcare provider or telehealth. Telehealth in cardiac rehabilitation is internet and home-based as well as effective.

2. **Stroke Rehabilitation:** Telehealth has the ability to extend rehabilitation to home and make more efficient use of resources [19].

13.8.2.4   CHRONIC DISEASE MANAGEMENT

Telehealth manages chronic CVDs through the home and decreases inequalities. The patient sends information to the healthcare provider by video conferencing or manual entry or automatic via devices like blood pressure machine, watches, etc., the healthcare provider monitor and regulates, medication is provided.

13.8.2.5   HYPERTENSION

It's the most useful application of telehealth for managing chronic cardiovascular conditions because of accurate measurements of blood pressure and improves adherence to treatment. This data goes to a healthcare provider or is stored in records, and they regulated by continuous monitoring.

13.8.2.6   HEART FAILURE

To treat chronic heart failure patients, direct hospitalization is required, but due to delay in treatment, high mortality rates occur. In telehealth involves a combination of vital sign monitoring, weight, detection of fluid retention in a timely as well as symptom reporting. This data is regulated and managed by healthcare providers treated according to the patient.

13.8.2.7   ISCHEMIC HEART DISEASE

The cardiologist used the app, software for continuous monitoring, regulation of patients. It is home-based monitoring for patients with coronary artery disease. The Healthcare provider monitors and changes the medication according to change in the situation, condition of patients. Recently the heart attack detection instrument also available like Mobisense test instrument. The Mobisense test app is a fourth-generation app in which a Troponin test is done which is very sensitive for heart attack prevention. It gives results within 10 minutes with only one drop of blood on the finger stick. This app is available by healthcare providers anywhere at any time. RPM facilitates to the preservation of coronary heart health. The heart specialist used high-tech equipment including a wearable coronary heart screen that's related to smartphones to screen and manipulate the sufferers with persistent coronary heart diseases. The affected person coronary heart electric interest is recorded whilst working, drowsing, or excising, and this information is given to the physician to outlook the affected person's health [18–20].

13.8.3   TELEHEALTH IN DIABETES

Diabetes is an insulin hormone problem in which the body produces high blood sugar. It is characterized by frequent urination, increase thirst and appetite. The three kinds of diabetes are Type I, Type II, and gestational diabetes:

1. **Type I Diabetes:** This often known as juvenile diabetes, occurs when the body's ability to produce insulin is compromised.

2. **Type II Diabetes**: It affects the way the use of insulin, while the still body makes insulin. This is also known as non-insulin-dependent diabetes. It increases obesity and physical inactivity.

3. **Gestational Diabetes:** It occurs during pregnancy because the body becomes less sensitive to insulin [21].

   i. **Self-Management Diabetes:** It involves self-management activities like blood sugar monitoring, tracking.

   ii. **Medication Adherence:** The prescribed medication is important for the management of diabetes. Telehealth helps to manage the medication correctly with dose and frequency. Text messaging is one of the ways for remembering the medication.

    iii. Care Consultations: Telehealth helps rural area people for their care remotely. The regulation and monitoring are done with the help of telehealth.

Telehealth involves a wide range of technologies like live video, RPM, computers, etc. It helps to deliver diabetes-related education, management, and monitoring services. The various apps are available for monitoring and regulation of diabetes such as glucose buddy, sugar sense, Mysugr, and diabetes connect [22]. Diabetic sufferers self-take a look at their blood glucose each day at domestic through the usage of finger-stick method. The strip test and portable glucose meter store the reading of glucose. Daily glucose meter stores the reading and that data sheared with healthcare provider team remotely or during the visit. RPM inspires sufferers with diabetes to be extra accountable approximately fitness and the way it impacts via way of means of food plan and exercise. By using RPM monitoring improvement in diabetic regular care [21, 22].

13.8.4 TELEHEALTH IN MENTAL ILLNESS

Mental illness is also known as a mental health disorder. There are various conditions of disorders like change in thinking, behavior, and also effect on mood and it also involves depression, anxiety, eating disorders, addictive, and schizophrenia. Mental illness causes problems in our daily life. Sometimes is a neurological disorder. Signs and symptoms of mental illness vary from person to person. Symptoms like confusion, feeling sad, fear, worries, staying away from people; a sudden change in mood, thinking of suicide, anxiety, etc.

The 'telepsychiatry' is involved various services like evaluation therapy, patient education, and medication. It involves direct interaction with a healthcare provider that is a psychiatrist with the patient. The use of telehealth helps patients for consulting directly, monitoring via video conferencing or another digital device. Telepsychiatry also involves medical information recording like images, videos, and transfer to the healthcare provider for review [22].

13.8.5 TELEHEALTH REMOVES BARRIERS

Telehealth helps to remove barriers with digital devices. These devices monitor and regulate patients. Telehealth gives reminders of appointments, information about condition, mental illness. The copying technique like distress methods which have low bandwidth text messages for patient's care. The remote patient sensor is also used for monitoring patients' symptoms in real time by app.

Telehealth changes the access of mental health services. Psychiatrists and mental healthcare provider use various tools like Talkspace, Bluelce app, 7 cups app, Teladoc app, eating disorder management app, etc. The mental health component provides selecting and seeing the healthcare providers [22].

13.8.6   DIFFERENT TYPES OF MENTAL HEALTH APPS

1. **Mental Health App (Bluelce):** It is designed for various age groups, genders. The Bluelce app deals with health issues, physiological characters. General Mental Health App (7 Cups app): It enhances self-awareness, control mood, good habits, thinking pattern changes, and help to recognize feelings. It involves 7 Cups app and help physiologically.

2. **Addiction Recovery App:** It helps to prevent bad habits like smoking, drinking, and taking drugs.

3. **Stress and Anxiety App:** It helps patients for dealing with anxiety and stress by giving toolkit, diaries 24/7 hours.

4. **Mental-Self Improvement App:** This app helps for monitoring patients' mood swings, bad habits [22, 23].

13.8.7   TELEHEALTH IN CONJUNCTIVITIS

The conjunctivitis is infection of eyeball of outer membrane as well as inner membrane of eyelids. It may case irritation, inflammation in the conjunctiva which involves white part of eyeball. It may be caused by bacterial, viral infection or by allergies. It may be spread by contact with eye secretions from any infected persons. Some common symptoms are itching, redness, and tears in eyes [23].

The telehealth includes virtual visits, videoconferencing, and RPM for diagnosis and management of eye conditions. The technology allows healthcare (ophthalmologist) to take care of eye to patients in rural areas. The Cradle app for eye disease detector, these types of apps are used by healthcare provider [23–25]. Conjunctivitis is also called Pink Eye infection. The eyeball as well as inside of eyelids get infected. Symptoms of pink eye involve itching, burning sensation, tear production is increases. In telehealth the healthcare provider examines by video conferencing they examine eyelids, lashes, and anterior segment exam for the lens. For examination they can use Google Duo, Face Time app. In the dry eyes body does not produce sufficient tears to lubricate the eyes. The common symptoms of dry eye are pain, burning sensation, this condition is very uncomfortable but not harmful. In telehealth services healthcare professionals monitor patients' symptoms, regulate and manage disease in time. The virtual services used such as Doxy.me, Eyecare live, etc. The dry eyes detector is also available. Blepharitis is the eyelids inflammation of both eyes, and it is a chronic condition. The symptoms are swelling of eyelids, red eyes, burning sensation, crusted eyelashes, light sensitivity and blurred vision. Diabetic retinopathy (DR) causes blindness. In early diagnosis it's preventable. The people with diabetes have a disease known as DR and when blood sugar level is high. It damages blood vessels within side the retina. Hence, blood vessels swell, leak, near, and preventing passage of blood. There is also possibility of formation of abnormal blood vessels on retina ad its affect eye vision. Patient with diabetes undergo the dilated eye exam in once year. Telehealth offers in primary care images obtained from special retinal camera from healthcare provider. There are various image technologies such as digital retinal images, digital retinal scanner, etc. Glaucoma is excessive strain internal the attention which damages the optic nerve. Telehealth healthcare makes use of far-off tracking to test sufferer eye strain in among visits. The telehealth makes use of intraocular strain domestic tracking device, glaucoma tracking, and many others for tracking and regulating the sufferers.

13.8.8 TELEHEALTH IN SKIN DISEASES

Skin disorder having various symptoms and severity. The skin disorder may be permanent or temporary as well as painful or painless. Sometimes it is genetic. By using telehealth some skin diseases are cure. Due to allergies, rashes and hives symptoms are observed. The Amwell device is used for telehealth treated for allergen sensitivity test and tracking down the causes of allergies [24].

13.9   LIMITATIONS

- Some types of care need for physical examinations and laboratories to check the sample.
- They need to afford the cost to of telehealth.
- Need to convey about sensitive topics when person not comfort. Simply it means poor patient and doctor relationship.
- Acceptance about digital visit.
- Not everyone has internet or comfortable with digital technology.

Some limitations related patients, technology, education, and medical aids are discussed in subsections.

13.9.1   LIMITATIONS RELATED TO PATIENTS

- Patients go to shop and bring – it may lead to confusion and disturbances in services or healthcare provider.
- Sometimes language is also a problem to understand the healthcare interpretation.
- Need of strong communication with healthcare provider.
- Decision with old and young people related to dose.

13.9.2   LIMITATIONS RELATED TO TECHNOLOGY

- Sometimes internet connectivity is poor then communication disturbances.
- The proper set up of proper light, camera, audio, background needs to increase telehealth services.
- Everyone does not use the technology.
- Virtual or Online behavior is totally different from face-to-face care like eye contact, etc.
- The software is used also play an important role in the fulfillment of consultation and safeguard.
- The healthcare provider and patients need to be familiar with technology, so it makes it easy.

13.9.3   LIMITATIONS RELATED TO EDUCATION

- All members of healthcare provider (staff of hospital) should have information about telehealth.

- All members of healthcare provider should have proper knowledge and be well trained to successively handle telehealthcare services.

13.9.4   LIMITATIONS RELATED TO MEDICAL AIDS (INSURANCE, FUNDS)

- The healthcare provider and patients should be aware about health-care insurance, funds.
- Reimbursement is a challenge in rolling out telehealth services [24, 25].

13.10   SUMMARY

Telehealth is referred to as the supply and facilitation of fitness and health center which include scientific care, fitness services, and self-care through telecommunications and virtual communication technology. Some technology utilized in telehealth stay video conferencing, cellular fitness apps, "keep and forward" digital transmission, far-flung affected RPM, affected person portals. Telehealth and Telemedicine from the decade delivered a chief extrude in healthcare structures to make sure that network stays healthful, and hospitals are for the sick and needy. Each type of telehealth is much more important in healthcare when it is used properly way, and it has much more benefits. The important aim of telehealth is to enhance chronic disease management, especially in emergencies. In the epidemics or pandemics has behavior the employment of growing new virtual era strategies, which brought on using telemedicine at some point of the numerous levels of contamination a lot greater frequently, like SARS pandemic, MERS-CoV, and most recently COVID-19. In every technology there are some challenges, in telehealth challenges are money, regulation, hype, acceptance, technology, proof, and success. Due to unavailability of physicians for patients at the time of the pandemic, there are some models which will be beneficial to take care of the patient and meet the expectation of the healthcare system. Telehealth is a boon to combat epidemic diseases to treat patients. This digital health technology is especially helpful in Covid 19 when geriatric patients, pregnant women, chronically ill and immunosuppressant patients are treated virtually and gets less exposure to other infected patients. Although it has a few boundaries associated with patients, technology, schooling, and clinical aids. Still, telehealth provides better healthcare in emergency conditions.

This pandemic indicates the significance of telemedicine when transportation is not possible from remote areas. It improves the supply of fitness care machines for the duration of a pandemic.

KEYWORDS

- **Cardiovascular Diseases**
- **Diagnosis**
- **Electronic Health Recorders**
- **Remote Patient Monitoring**
- **Telecommunication**
- **Telehealth**
- **Therapeutic Drug Monitoring**

REFERENCES

1. TeleHealth, (2017). *The Health Resources and Services Administration*, 04–28.
2. Birthe, D., Brandie, N., & Thomas, N., (2016). Personalized telehealth within side the future: A global research agenda. *J. Med. Internet Res.*, e53. doi: 10.2196/jmir.5257.
3. Zundel, K. M., (1996). Telemedicine: History, applications, and impact on librarianship. *Bull. Med. Libr. Assoc., 84*, 71–79.
4. McConnochie, K. M., Conners, G. P., & Brayer, A. F., (2006). Differences viruses in-person evaluation of acute illness. *Ambulatory Paediatrics, 6*(4), 187–195.
5. Suneela, G., Navya, G., Nidhi, B., Singh, M. M., Raina, S. K., & Sagar, G., (2020). Telemedicine: Embracing digital care in the course of COVID-19 pandemic. *J. Fam. Med. and Pri. Care.*
6. India, (2019). *Ministry of Health and Own Circle of Relatives' Welfare*. National Digital Health Blueprint.
7. Elham, M., & Alireza, H., (2020). The position of telehealth in the course of COVID-19 outbreak: A scientific evaluation primarily based totally on modern-day evidence. *BMC Public Health, 20*, 2–9.
8. Canady, V. A., (2020). COVID-19 outbreaks represent a new way of mental health service delivery. *Mental Health Weekly, 30*(12), 1–4.
9. Bokolo, A. J., (2020). Use of telemedicine and digital take care of faraway remedy in reaction to COVID-19 pandemic. *J Med Syst., 44*, 132.
10. Bardford, N., Caffery, L., & Smith, A., (2016). Telehealth services in rural and remote Australia: A systematic review of models of care and factors influencing success and sustainability. *Rural and Remote Health, 3808*, 1–23.

11. Enfield, K., Mehring, B., & Carpenter, R., (2015). Application of telemedicine platform, isolation communication management system, for the care of dangerous diseases: A case series. *Open Forum Infection Diseases, 2*, 1, 2.

12. Alvandi, M., (2017). Telemedicine and its role in revolutionizing healthcare delivery. *Am J Accountable Care, 5*, 1.

13. Mishra, S. K., Ayyagari, A., Bhandari, M., Bedi, B. S., & Shah, R., (2004). Telemedicine application in "Maha Kumbh Mela" (Indian festival) with large congregation. *Telemed. J. E Health, 10*, 107, 108.

14. Kennedy, C. A., (2005). The challenges of economic evaluations of remote technical health interventions. *Clin Invest Med., 28*(2), 71–74.

15. Blandford, A., Wesson, J., Amalberti, R., AlHazme, R., & Allwihan, R., (2020). Opportunities and challenges for telehealth within, and beyond, a pandemic. *Plum Metrics, 8*(11), 1364–1365.

16. Valerie, J., Leming, Z., & Linda, M., (2015). A systematic review of telehealth privacy and security research to identify best practices. *Int. J. Telerehabilitation, 7*(2), 15–22.

17. Scholl, J., Syed-Abdul, S., & Ahmed, L. A., (2011). A case study of an EMR system at a large hospital in India: Challenges and strategies for successful adoption. *J. Biomed Inform., 44*, 958–967.

18. American Medical Association, (2020). *Digital Health Research: Physician's Motivation and Requirements for Adopting Digital Health-Adoption and Attitudinal Shifts.*

19. Hjelm, N. M., (2005). Benefits and drawbacks of telemedicine. *J. Telemed. and Telecare, 11*, 60–70.

20. Zundel, K. M., (1996). Telemedicine: History, applications, and impact on librarianship. *Bull Med. Libr. Assoc., 84*, 71–79.

21. Tuckon, R. V., Edmunds, M., & Hodgkins, M. L., (2017). Telehealth. *N. Engl. J. Med., 377*, 1585–1592.

22. Bashshur, R. L., Shannon, G. W., Bashshur, N., & Yellowlees, P. M., (2016). The empirical evidence for telemedicine interventions in mental disorders. *Telemedicine and e-Health, 22*(2), 87–113.

23. Powell, R. E., Henstenburg, J. M., & Cooper, G., (2017). Patient perceptions of telehealth primary care video visits. *Ann. Fam. Med., 15*, 225–229.

24. Wechsler, L. R., Demaerschalk, B. M., & Schwamm, L. H., (2017). Telemedicine quality and outcomes in stroke: A scientific statement for healthcare professionals from the American heart Association/American stroke association. *Stroke, 48*, e 3–25, 10.1161.

25. Siwicki, B., (2020). *Telemedicine During COVID-19: Benefits, Limitations, Burdens, Adaptation.* Healthcare IT News.

CHAPTER 14

PERSONALIZED TELEMEDICINE UTILIZING ARTIFICIAL INTELLIGENCE, ROBOTICS, AND INTERNET OF MEDICAL THINGS (IOMT)

KIRAN SHARMA

Assistant Professor, KIET School of Pharmacy, KIET Group of Institutions, Delhi-NCR, Meerut Road (NH-58), Ghaziabad, Uttar Pradesh, India

ABSTRACT

The technical advanced artificial intelligence (AI) and robotics with the aid of the internet of medical things (IoMT) is extremely needed for the development of capacity for the future needs of in-person care across geographies and health professional organizations. Both AI and telemedicine were versatile and flexible and offered an unending opportunity to produce improved health services. Trends in the use of this technology may be grouped into four: patient monitoring, information technology in the field of healthcare, intelligent assisted diagnostics, and collaboration in information analysis. These can be utilized in shifting medical services from healthcare centers and organizations to houses and smart devices with increased convenience and lower costs. As AI has an immense potential to support doctors in their everyday schedule of image investigation and alleviate their occupational load. In addition, the operating room (OR) is presently an advanced combination of medical robots, workstations for telepresence, software-integrated surgery, and powerful imaging equipment. Robots have enhanced surgeon dexterity and offered the least intrusive procedures and have increased the

Handbook of Research on Artificial Intelligence and Soft Computing Techniques in Personalized Healthcare Services, Uma N. Dulhare, A. V. Senthil Kumar, Amit Datta, Seddik Bri, Ibrahiem M. M. El Emary, (Eds.)
© 2024 Apple Academic Press, Inc. Co-published with CRC Press (Taylor & Francis)

access to the target organ. However, the use of AI may also be controversial in relation to a number of legal, ethical, and societal questions.

14.1 INTRODUCTION

The utilization of medical information to enhance patient's health is telemedicine or telehealth. The reorganization of medical services, funding of electronic health records (EHRs) and support systems for clinical decisions can speed up the incorporation of telecommunications into the provision of healthcare as shown in Figure 14.1. In this regard, the usage and delivery of telemedicine can play a significant role for artificial intelligence (AI) and robotic technology. Even though the idea of AI was primarily created some 60 years ago, the fast development of AI-centered technology and applications took place after the graphical treating units were improved in 2010. As it currently stands, AI-based algorithms can imitate the judgment and behavior of people in the highest level with equal or even greater precision. The fourth industrial revolution of the human race has now been led and our everyday lives are gradually changed by AI, as have several other technical breakthroughs including the internet of things (IoT) [1].

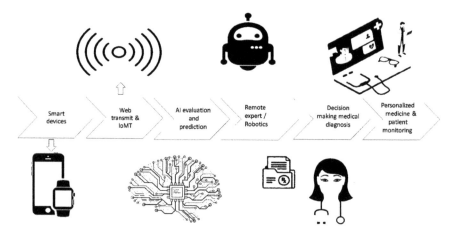

FIGURE 14.1 Artificial intelligence (AI)-based personalized telemedicine approach is shown starting from smart devices data collection to patient monitoring.

Many IT and researchers spend a lot of time and money studying novel AI algorithms and applications and apply them in the field of health sciences using different devices. These devices are generally divided into two primary classes: Machine learning (ML) and natural language processing (NLP) [2].

14.1.1   MACHINE LEARNING (ML)

The most popular AI technology now utilized is ML. In 1959, the first ML programs were launched. With ML, the mathematical models are built on massive data sets utilizing train algorithms in order to forecast correctly. This approach analyzes the structured data given in the form of images, genetic information or EP data. Here ML techniques try to complement the patients' features or deduce their likelihood that the illness results would be achieved in the medical application. Three types of ML algorithms may be divided into: supervised learning, unsupervised learning, and reinforcement learning (RL). Deep learning (DL) is an ML subset that has developed into the largely favored method for further AI study. In the DL algorithms, the programs learn from multi-layer feedback and modify themselves regularly and automatically, until the highest and most stable forecast result is achieved [3]. The main element of DL is that scientists are not participating in the middle layer learning progression.

14.1.2   NATURAL LANGUAGE PROCESSING (NLP)

Natural language processing (NLP) comprises the second group method of extracting data from unstructured information such as clinical remarks/health newspapers to harmonize and augment prepared medical information. The NLP processes aim to transform texts to structured data which can be read from the machine, and then analyzed using ML technology.

In order to expedite test interpretations, to increase the accuracy of the diagnosis and to decrease the consumption of work and time, AI algorithms were examined and developed in several medical domains. Modern medicine not only utilizes binary information and numerical information (e.g., positive or negative outcomes), but also a tremendous quantity of patient images [4]. For these last reports, standard computer programs cannot simply read complex information. Modern AIs, however, have proved themselves to be able to interpret and interpret visual data efficiently.

14.2   AI IN MEDICAL SCIENCE

AI is a wide field of computer discipline that is focused on creating intellectual computers that can perform normally just like a human brain. As a result, AI aspires to imitate human cognitive processes and bring about a paradigm change in healthcare, aided by increased access to healthcare data and significant advancements in analytics techniques. Artificially intelligent systems in healthcare typically follow a pattern in which a system begins with a huge amount of information and then uses ML algorithms to attain required values from that data, and then uses that information to create a helpful output to answer a well-defined problem in the health sector. Matching patient symptoms to the proper physician, patient diagnosis, patient prognosis, drug discovery, and both assistants that can translate languages, transcribe notes, and arrange photos and information are all examples of AI in the medical sciences [5].

14.2.1   BIG DATA ANALYTICS

The requirement to evaluate huge amounts of formless data created each second from numerous data bases gave rise to the phrase "big data." Conventional analytics solutions are typically not designed to analyze such formless data and extract insights. Speed, a vast volume of data, and a range of data sources are all characteristics of big data. The problem with large data is determining how to do an investigation as rapidly as feasible while maintaining a reasonable level of accuracy. The real-time monitoring and prediction of occurrences is an advantage of big data analytics. Big data is now generating new tools for data analysis that integrate ML models.

Modern medicine makes use of not only binary (+ve or –ve) and arithmetical data, but also a large quantity of picture images from patients. Detail reports cannot be simply comprehended by typical computer systems in this case. Modern AI, on the other hand, has been shown to be capable of effectively processing and analyzing such picture data. Automated interfaces for pictorial perception, speech identification, judgment-making, and linguistic conversion are illustrations of AI applications. Artificial neural networks (ANNs) are a kind of computing scheme that is intended to imitate how the humanoid brain analyzes and processes data. On this basis, AI evolute, and it resolves glitches that are hard or challenging to solve using individual or statistical measures. Because ANNs are self-discovering, they may improve their functioning as further data becomes obtainable.

Thousands of artificial neurons termed processing units are connected via nodes to an ANN. These processing units are constituted of input, hidden, and output units as shown in Figure 14.2. The input units accept various forms and structures of data via an internal weighting mechanism, and the neural network is concerned with learning about the information supplied so as to create a single output report. Hidden layers are present between the input and output layers where 3 or more layers are present as deep network. Back-propagation, the abbreviation for retroactive error spreading, is a number of learning regulations employed by ANNs to develop outcomes, since human beings want laws and guidelines for achieving results [6].

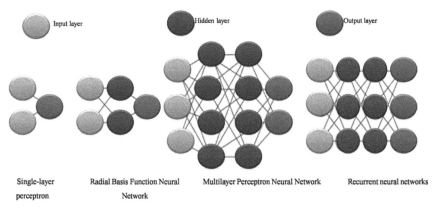

FIGURE 14.2   Different types of neural networking connection with input, hidden, and output layers.

14.2.2   TYPES OF NEURAL NETWORKS

Neural networks mimic human brain function, allowing computer programs to identify patterns and solve common issues in AI, ML, and DL. They are a subset of ML and provide the foundation of DL algorithms. Particular type of neural networks exists, each of which is utilized for a different purpose, such as in subsections.

14.2.2.1   SINGLE-LAYER PERCEPTRON (SLP) NEURAL NETWORK

It was the first and basic model with no hidden layers; a neural network has two input units and one output unit. The perceptron here is a single processing unit to detect a linear assessment. The single-layer perceptron (SLP) operates on the basis of threshold transfer between nodes. This is the most fundamental type of ANN, and it is commonly employed in linearly based ML tasks.

14.2.2.2   RADIAL BASIS FUNCTION NEURAL NETWORK

These systems are similar to feed-forward neural networks, apart from that the activation function for these neurons is the radial basis function. Radial basis function networks differ from other neural networks in that they have a universal approximation and a quicker learning pace. An RBF network is a form of feed forward neural network that is made up of three layers: the input layer, the hidden layer, and the output layer. Each of these levels is responsible for a separate set of duties.

14.2.2.3   MULTILAYER PERCEPTRON (MLP) NEURAL NETWORK

In contrast to the single layer, these networks employ more than one buried layer of neurons. These are also called Deep Feed-forward Networks. Although most real-world issues are nonlinear, feed-forward neural networks, also known as multi-layer perceptrons (MLPs), are made up of sigmoid neurons rather than perceptrons. These models provide the cornerstone for computer vision, NLP, and former neural networks, and they are typically given data to train them. The back-propagation process includes two phases: the forward phase, in which activations are transmitted from the input layer to the output layer, and the backward phase, in which the weights and bias values are modified.

14.2.2.4   CONVOLUTIONAL NEURAL NETWORK (CNN)

The CNN is a deep neural network, mainly used for the processing and analysis of visual images. There are several processing levels in the network. It converts the picture into the output layers from many unrestricted parameters in the input layers to the hidden ones, which can significantly minimize the number of parameters. In the field of medical science, CNNs were frequently employed to identify images and classify illnesses [7].

14.2.2.5   RECURRENT NEURAL NETWORKS (RNNS)

Recurrent neural networks (RNNs) may be used for time-series, and feedback loops can be discovered. These learning algorithms are used largely to anticipate future results, such as forecasting by analyzing time series data.

Neural network technologies are developed to handle many challenging problems, for example starting with diabetes where clinical symptoms are dependent on the kind of illness, gender, age, insulin level, arterial pressure, and many other parameters. This is due to the fact that researchers are frequently presented with a huge quantity of factual information for which no mathematical model exists. Models of ANNs have shown promising results in the diagnosis of such diseases and others like nerve diseases, Parkinson's disease, Huntington's disease, etc. For forecasting the risk of osteoporosis, multilayer perceptron (MLP) models are also utilized. Thus modern neural networks evolved as a collection of devices and programs created for models and specialized equipment that use a set of algorithms and object recognition theory to solve a wide variety of diagnostics jobs [8].

14.3 ROBOTICS IN MEDICAL SCIENCE

Robotics is a potentially cutting-edge technology that has the prospective to change physical exams and medical treatment, as well as patient monitoring in faraway locations. As the population ages, neurological disorders worsen, resulting in impairment among the elderly. This circumstance necessitates the development of innovative techniques to increase rehabilitation efficacy and efficiency. It also offers an once-in-a-lifetime chance to use cutting-edge technologies like robots to aid in the healing process. So that rehabilitative and assistive robotics as shown in Figure 14.3 can

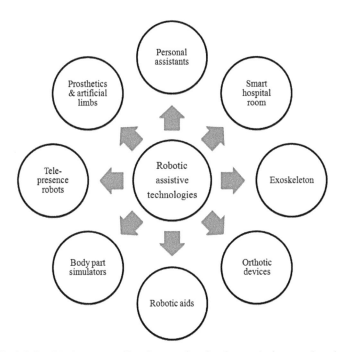

FIGURE 14.3 Various applications of robotic assistive technologies for use in different areas.

enhance the lives of older people, aid their recuperation, and/or assist them in doing daily activities.

Medical robots may be divided into three categories: (i) surgical robotics, diagnostics, and medication delivery devices; (ii) assistive robotics, like wearable robots and rehabilitation devices; and (iii) robots that mimic the individual body [9].

Rehabilitation robotic devices, therapeutic robots, exoskeletons, prosthetic devices, orthotic devices, and companion robots are among the most popular ones. Rehabilitation robots are gadgets that actively help and/or oppose the movements of a stroke patient, increasing effectiveness and lowering costs by reducing the quantity of one-on-one time spent by an analyst with the patient. Whereas therapeutic robots persistently gather information that can be utilized to quantify a patient's development all the way through the healing process, allowing therapists to fine-tune treatment approaches. Robotic orthotics are devices that help or support joints, muscles, or limbs that are weak or inefficient [10].

Exoskeletons are machines which are used in orthotics. It is a power-driven anthropomorphic suit weared by the patient with human-like linkages and joints, as well as actuators that help the patient in turning their body part or raising heavy weights. When a limb is lost, a prosthesis robotic device is used that replaces the lost portion of the human body, giving movement and manipulation skills.

Robotic assistive technology can be used to help people with special requirements, such as youngsters and the elderly, get back on their feet. Indeed, in adding up to their learning responsibilities, robots have been introduced to aid youngsters with autism disorder; a neuro-affected disease marked by deficits in social-communication abilities as well as limited and repetitive behaviors. The majority of them are shaped like animals (cats, dogs, rabbits, seals, and so on), but others are humanoid robots. They can listen, respond to speech, speak in limited situations, identify touch, and perceive sound and light. Companion robots are frequently employed in cases of social separation, but not so often in cases of medical or mental illness. They can be useful in addressing a lack of activity in a few instances. Telepresence robots are primarily employed to allow two-way conversation with elderly individuals; they can provide a better communication experience than speech alone due to their visual content. A sense of connectivity is one of the most crucial components of communication, since it helps people avoid feeling lonely. These robots may also be beneficial to those suffering from cognitive impairment, allowing them to remain in their homes [11].

14.3.1   MEDICAL ROBOTS AS BODY-PART SIMULATORS

Quite a few commercial practical body-part simulators have been available for the teaching of medical students, motivated by the necessity for standardized medical procedures and the need to eliminate animal and patient experiments. Soft materials, contractile actuators, and flexible sensors have opened up a lot of possibilities for developing body-part simulators for studying physiology and creating realistic healthcare scenarios. Surgical simulators that employ computer images, rubber phantoms, and harvested animal organs are now available for educating young, inexperienced surgeons. The phantom imitates the small intestine, advanced VR-based cardiac life support (ACLS) simulators, and bronchoscopy simulators are just a few examples.

14.4   AI AND ROBOTICS ASSISTED TELEMEDICINE

AI and robotic technologies are delivering a range of creative solutions to improve the quality of patient care as the latest technological trends sweep the global healthcare business. These technical advancements are demonstrating their usage in telemedicine and in developing the ability to reply to potential epidemics ahead of the COVID-19 period like the "Da Vinci Intuitive Surgical System." It is the most widely used surgical robot. This surgical robo can link to the cloud to help physicians in the operating theater by mining massive amounts of open MRI data from patients with comparable medical problems. In the event of an emergency, robots will be able to access the individual Cloud data stream from a patient's activity band or mobile locations. This robotic system is made up of three parts: a physician's station, a patient side robotic cart with four arms that the physician may move and a HD 3D vision system. The robotic arms, which are inserted into the body through cannulas, are equipped with articulated surgical tools.

Biocompatibility and biomimicry are important factors to consider while designing such medical robots. It's important to keep in mind that these robots operate inside the human body in surgery and endoscopy, as they interact with the patient's body physically. The artificial limbs and organs that substitute human limbs and those medicine-delivery robotic devices which are integrated inside or on the skin of patients should be biocompatible. To minimize allergies and touch reactions, as well as rapid immunological responses and rejection, medical robots must be well-matched with the human body and tissues in order to ensure system performance and body acceptability. The materials used for these robots must also have mechanical characteristics that are similar to those of human tissues to some extent.

Many clinical sub-domains of surgery, such as neurosurgery, orthopedic surgery, throat surgery, abdominal surgery/laparoscopy, radio surgery, and so on, now employ robot-assisted surgery. Another example is the 'i2 Snake robot,' which is a prototype of an articulated endoscopic robot with two tiny arms that are equipped with a camera, light, and a suction/irrigation channel that allows the surgeon to do surgery remotely. It can get to deep-seated lesions by navigating via the mouth.

14.4.1   EXPERT SYSTEM

The expert system is computer software that mimics the decision-making abilities of human experts. It is one of the earliest effective AI programs because it uses an existing knowledge system to reason and solve a series of complex problems. The expert system displays a high level of clinical decision-making capability, as well as improvements in the identification and diagnosis of disease. However, improving the system's accuracy, combining it with the patient's medical history, and incorporating the doctor's clinical experience all at the same time is critical [12]. Furthermore, in order to provide doctors with cutting-edge diagnoses and treatment plans, medical knowledge and outcomes must be updated on a regular basis.

14.5   TELEMEDICINE ORGANIZATIONAL FRAMEWORKS

Telemedicine is a two-way telecommunication between a healthcare practitioner and patients who are geographically separated, yet because to its organizational frameworks, it enables for the delivery of high-quality healthcare regardless of location. Telemedicine and its associated technologies, in essence, substitute human transportation with digital transmission. Telemedicine demands secure, high-quality connection equipment with no audio or visual interruptions for the best patient experience. In addition, the telemedicine provider needs seamless connection between the telemedicine platform and the EHR, as well as timely, easily accessible medical data to aid clinical decision-making. Construction of a full, dynamic telemedicine system that attempts to connect diverse healthcare institutions is a problem in the absence of a regional or state wide telemedicine network.

14.5.1   ORGANIZATIONAL FRAMEWORKS

Various organizational frameworks used are discussed in subsections.

14.5.1.1 CENTRALIZED TELEMEDICINE FRAMEWORK

In the healthcare system, data management is a common method for storing and managing patient data, which lead to the provision of medical information for the construction of a timely and effective treatment plan. This sort of information is now kept as electronic healthcare records (EHR) in healthcare organizations to manage personal health records (PHRs) via a cloud-based architecture. A centralized system with standard tools is necessary if the aim is for the company to be strongly aligned, standards, and best practices for analytics. When everyone uses the same tools, analysts may share their knowledge of those tools as they gain experience with them. Rather of having isolated pockets of knowledge, the organization as a whole becomes wiser. It also implies that someone is always available to run a certain report, even if the person who typically handles that department is sick, on vacation, or otherwise unavailable. Analysts and data architects will be able to move across domains much more readily if the tools are standardized. When we employ an analyst at one provider with a decentralized strategy, it can take a data architect six to nine months to get up to speed in a new area since he or she is unfamiliar with the technology. Finally, while different groups may be focused on their particular concerns, management is concerned with the larger picture. It's incredibly difficult, time-consuming, and expensive to roll up reports generated using multiple technologies into a single report that can be read in its entirety. The use of a common set of reporting tools guarantees that it may be completed quickly. With all the advantages of centralized systems, there are some obstacles and concerns also, particularly on the administrative side of healthcare. A lot of us have seen firsthand, heard from friends and family, or read in the press how central authorities are reducing coverage, restricting networks, and even excluding some patients [13].

14.5.1.2 HUB-AND-SPOKE FRAMEWORK

The hub-and-spoke system comes out from traditional and hierarchical positioning system. It entails a centralized hub that acts as a point of contact and education for numerous care-deliveries spoke locations. This arrangement is appropriate for the setup and incorporation of telehealth networks, but it delays decision-making, inhibits novelty, making it hard for spokes to interact, and not everyone in the spoke has the hub's capabilities. Along with this not every spoke will have treatment capabilities due to cost-effective and infrastructure considerations, as well as a scarcity of neuro-interventionalists. Barriers to healthcare access that affect socially and lingually miscellaneous groups, as well as those from marginalized background or in short-resource settings, deserve distinct attention [14].

14.5.1.3 DECENTRALIZED TELEMEDICINE FRAMEWORK

A decentralized healthcare platform powered by AI access and authenticated use of different devices while also instilling confidence and transparency in patient health records. The technique relies on AI-enabled intelligent programs and the creation of a community block-chain system. A block-chain-based solution is intended to improve data availability in the medical sector, particularly for patients and physicians. Complex operations and clinical trials based on block-chain technology for improved data management are among the many workflows for the healthcare system. To achieve privacy in the PHR, a structure is utilized that aid in retaining the patient's personal data while also allowing the patient to regulate it. In comparison to EHR (electronic medical record) wearable devices or remote patient monitoring (RPM) are very susceptible since they rely on third parties to maintain the PHR. Furthermore, tracing rogue and malfunctioning devices in the network is challenging.

Even though a patient-centered health organization is like the one explained here would most likely start off centralized, it should gradually decentralize the decision-making procedure, leaving it in the hands of the healthcare professionals and patients who engage with it on a daily basis. Staking and voting procedures can be used to accomplish this. We can facilitate patients to get advantage financially from investing in their individual health and wellness and save on the fee of their care by incorporating block-chain technology into the described system, and we can allow innovators from all over the world to contribute to the platform's growth and improvement by incorporating block-chain technology into the described system. It also enables consumers and doctors to drive healthcare decision-making by allowing them to control and potentially monetize their own health data (together with medical records and genetic data) [15].

14.5.1.4 KHOJA–DURRANI–SCOTT (KDS) ASSESSMENT FRAMEWORK

Some of the writers that created the e-health readiness assessment tools established KDS Assessment Framework. The importance of this framework is that it recognizes the necessity for several assessment techniques throughout the deployment lifetime. The steps of the e-Health process make up the column headers, while the topics for the analysis lists make up the row captions. A set of assessment questionnaires is another component of the KDS architecture. These surveys, like the e-health promptness estimation tools, contain of a sequence of data connected to a Likert scale. While the previous were graded on a scale of not prepared to be prepared. There are three types of questionnaires accessible, depending on the respondent's point of view. A few sets of questionnaires were created, comparable to the e-health readiness valuation techniques. The assessor's point of view, i.e., management or healthcare provider, decided the appropriateness set. The KDS now has a third perspective category, namely client [16].

14.6   RECENT TREND OF AI UTILIZATION IN TELEMEDICINE

The usage of telehealth facilities has improved dramatically as a consequence of COVID-19. In the recent past, telehealth technologies were used in place of in-person appointments for 50% of Medicare primary care visits. More significantly, telehealth's development is expected to continue long after the epidemic is gone, because patient acceptance is the highly essential element in telehealth's success. Because maximum patients are comfortable with telemedicine alternative, the sector undoubtedly has a vivid potential. Telemedicine applications are the most effective and reliable service. WebRTC, the framework used for linking web browsers with mobile applications, is the technology powering the telemedicine app. WebRTC's flexibility is one of the best significant characteristics that make it best for telemedicine apps. This can facilitate capabilities such as text and video chat, screen sharing, file transfer, and EHR exchange, among others. Incorporating EHRs into the telemedicine app is crucial since it gives access to patients and healthcare professionals to view patient medical information in the same app. Interactive voice response (IVR) is an important aspect of the app that permits the communication between patients and physicians through the use of digital voice.

14.6.1   PATIENT MONITORING

One of the primary and most popular uses of telemedicine is patient monitoring. This enables a more efficient and cost-effective method of carrying out usual doctor-to-patient consultations at a distance to examine the patient's present status and clinical outcomes. Through video conferencing and the attachment of smart medical devices to capture and record the patient's health information, this has been evolved to mimic face-to-face consultation. When opposed to physical patient monitoring, the goal of this development is to give accessibility, convenience, effectiveness, and cost savings. Tele-presence robots in recent designs have been developed to be able to walk about halls and rooms independently utilizing a software interface that connects the client to the robot via a Wi-Fi connection. This model has recently been refined by including the use of AI and vision technologies to aid navigation and obstacle recognition. For example, one commercially used robot is made out of a mobile body and a screen enabling patient-doctor interaction. It has a micro-projector for combined examination and operations, as well as an intuitive vision method that tells the cameras to pursue the doctor's motions and gestures. This robot, as well as other telepresence robot designs, has already been used in a number of hospitals. AI will be integrated into a ML concept that includes simultaneous mapping and interior navigation utilizing sensors, allowing software to create a course for the robot using just the user's intention as input [17]. The similar expertise may be utilized to have the robot modify its physical setup for the patient's comfort, such as the elevation and slant of the camera lens.

14.6.2   HEALTHCARE INFORMATION TECHNOLOGY

Medical data will be complicated to access and retain as a result of the huge amount of healthcare information being captured in hospitals, not just via human register but also throughout the growing use of self-diagnosing technologies. Furthermore, because the objective of telemedicine is to link health professionals and patients from all over the globe, a common record coordination for all participating institutions is required. The currently popular method of combining big data analytics and neural networks to maintain and retrieve EHR is insufficient. The development of using AI to automate data retrieval and evaluation also sought out the problems experienced in medical data retrieval operations [18].

14.6.3   INTELLIGENT ASSISTANCE AND DIAGNOSIS

Another popular aspect of AI and robotics is the integration of aiding mechanical components, as well as the utilization of medical data and outcomes for intellectual diagnosis. Both characteristics are designed to help patients physically or through studying early patient evaluations to help the present hospital system. These technologies can work with neural networks and ML that have been designed. This will allow the technology to evolve over time as new data and outcomes are added to the system. Existing technologies are starting the use of intelligent diagnosis in a variety of softwares and smart phone applications for telehealth self-diagnostic.

14.6.4 INFORMATION EVALUATION AND COLLABORATION

This is the area where telemedicine is used in medical research as well as academic training or consultations. Utilizing the available technologies, telemedicine help to connect medical professionals from different nations so that they could stimulate collaboration on medical data as well as viewpoints and information for diagnosis. This will change the way pharmaceutical research is done, particularly in terms of using big data analytics to consolidate clinical test findings and genetic neural networks to recognize patterns and analyze data. This section of the chapter discusses how AI is being used to diagnose the patient's condition and treatment using provided clinical data. This trend will heavily rely on AI's pattern recognition feature, as healthcare data must not only be saved and accessed, but also be evaluated. Because the program will work only on the basis of the findings using computer analysis that will eliminate prejudice and views about the results but interpretation should use neural networks to assess a patient's conditions, behaviors, and other aspects using an algorithm.

14.6.5 AI IN OPHTHALMOLOGY

The study's goal is to develop prediction tools for improved comprehension and interpretation that may be used in home-based care. In ophthalmology, AI research focuses largely on diabetic retinopathy (DR), glaucoma, and other disorders. True color and particular color sorting photography, fluorescence angiography, ecograms, and optical coherence tomography are all used in clinical ophthalmology (OCT). Each picture type includes different types of information that can be used to diagnose eye disorders or predict patient outcomes [19].

The most well-known example of this research arm is Google Brain, which shows how DL algorithms can utilize retinal pictures to recognize a patient's oldness, sex, smoking prominence, and systolic blood pressure; compute cardiovascular risk factors; and forecast the likelihood of significant adverse cardiac events in the following five years, according to a study published by Google Brain. Google Brain discovered that a retinal fundus image alone was sufficient to predict a variety of cardiovascular risk factors. The anatomical feature patterns were extracted using a convolutional neural network, a computational model that specializes in understanding images. Researchers used retinal scans from 2,84,335 individuals to train models, which were then verified on two separate datasets of patients. The trained model correctly recognized patients' ages with a 3.26-year margin of error, correctly identified gender and a smoker most of the time and correctly calculated blood pressure with a low margin of error. After that, Google Brain made a step ahead. The trained model could accurately estimate a patient's risk of cardiovascular disease (CVD) over the following five years 70% of the time, reaching the correctness rate of known risk calculators without all the extra data inputs.

DL is frequently criticized for its lack of transparency and interpretability, which has hampered the technology's adoption in fields such as medicine and law. Google Brain, on the other hand, feels its technique is sound. It uses attention techniques to figure out which pixels are most essential for forecasting a certain cardiovascular risk factor, such as blood vessels, which are a key characteristic in calculating blood pressure [20].

14.7 CHALLENGES IN IMPLEMENTATION

One of the most noteworthy advantages of telehealth over in-person options is that it minimizes the contact between patients, healthcare providers, and other patients. Wearable gadgets provide healthcare personnel access to real-time patient data while they're still at home. With all of these advantages, telemedicine has also faced a number of challenges, including accessibility, cost, legal concerns, medical treatment quality, and so on as shown in Figure 14.4.

14.7.1 LICENSURE BARRIERS

Telehealth practitioners can deliver medical services to patients and other healthcare professionals across the world while sharing medical knowledge. Because researchers must obtain and sustain the license (together with the accompanying education and financial needs) in numerous jurisdictions, the short of multistate licensure leads to a barrier in telehealth. In recent times, healthcare professional licensure will be under the control of each state,

FIGURE 14.4 Different types of challenges faced while implementing the telemedicine practically.

necessitating several distinct state licenses for multistate practices. During a telehealth interaction, the provider must follow both the state licensing rules and regulations for the patient and the state licensing rules and regulations for the provider. The licensing procedure is lengthy and costly, and varied continuing medical education requirements add to the administrative complexity of maintaining several state licenses [21].

14.7.2 BILLING AND REIMBURSEMENT BARRIERS

The inability of proper remuneration is often cited as a foremost obstacle in telemedicine adoption. Despite serving a large number of patients, there is small proof that managed care organizations employ telemedicine to save funds. Furthermore, Medicare reimburses relatively little in the fee-for-service organization, and that remuneration is mainly restricted to non-metropolitan areas, particular institutions. A lot of these limitations originate from the doubts that telemedicine would permit providers to exploit the healthcare system, or that technology will direct to misuse and increased expenditure. Many technological firms that aren't well-versed in the healthcare industry are investing in telemedicine because of the lucrative revenue prospects. As a consequence, numerous technologies are being developed by people who are drawn to the probable market of healthcare but do not fully comprehend telemedicine's application [22].

14.7.3   CONNECTIVITY BARRIERS

To facilitate the transfer of data, pictures, and sound, e-healthcare technologies require patients to use a computer with a broadband internet connection and/or a cellular-enabled smartphone or tablet. Although the number of linked devices and services are continuously rising but patients' age, geography, race/ethnicity, and income also have a role in connection. Some individuals may find participation in telemedicine efforts difficult, and they will require education in the usage of recent internet-connected equipment and software. Another aspect creates difficulties for those who live in rural regions, those who do not have access to the internet, or susceptible populations who cannot manage to pay for it [23].

14.7.4   CHANGES IN IN-PATIENT E-CONSULT SERVICES

Inpatient e-Consult services, on the other hand, were restricted, with only two use cases backed up by successful pilots in infectious illness and dermatology. There was a drop in eConsult volume in the early months of the pandemic, which corresponded to a fall in practice and new patient volumes. Inpatient e-Consults, on the other hand, were made available to all hospital specialties and locations, and the service was well-used.

14.7.5   PATIENT PRIVACY AND CONFIDENTIALITY

The success of telemedicine and e-healthcare is also dependent on data privacy and protection. Telemedicine utilization is mainly subject to privacy and security issues than face-to-face meetings. Although most telehealth systems are heavily secured and adhere to HIPAA standards and laws, but no platform is completely secure from hackers. Robotics' ongoing development, as well as their usage of Big Data and Cloud computation technology, will exacerbate safety and confidentiality concerns. Thus, to increase telehealth's adoption and implementation, concerns regarding privacy and security must be addressed carefully so that both clinicians and patients may trust that information sent during telehealth encounters is kept private and safe.

14.7.6 DATA ACCURACY AND MISDIAGNOSIS

Data transmission accuracy is another potential stumbling barrier to successful telehealth practice. According to a study looking into the precision of physical function tests, Internet access has an impact on the legality and dependability of fine motor task evaluations. If healthcare providers are ignorant of technological inconsistencies, they may make medical treatment decisions and recommendations based on potentially imprecise patient facts. The greatest danger arises when the medical practitioner heard or saw information that was insufficient during the contact, or when technological faults, such as a brief glitch in the visual or auditory interface, cause the doctor to hear or see the wrong thing, resulting in a misdiagnosis [24].

14.7.7 PROVIDER-PATIENT RELATIONSHIPS

The requirements for establishing provider-patient relationships vary by country and may involve a healthcare provider's examination or evaluation of a patient. Understanding the prerequisites for building a provider-patient connection is very crucial before any medication is provided.

14.7.8 MEDICAL LIABILITY

Informed consent, practice principles and procedures, management needs for non-physician providers, and the condition of professional liability insurance coverage are just a few of the issues that telehealth poses when it comes to malpractice liability. It's not easy to apply current malpractice liability standards to telehealth, particularly when it's uncertain what constitutes an acceptable "quality of care." Professional liability plans might not cover telemedicine. Errors and omissions, inattentive credentialing, breaches of privacy, and service disruptions due to equipment or technological failures should all be avoided with special attention [25].

14.7.9   FRAUD AND ABUSE

As the use of telehealth expands, vigilance and care should be exercised to ensure that it does not violate set standards and any other law statutes. These rules make it illegal for providers to be paid for accepting or making recommendations to other institutions or providers in whom they have a financial interest. Fines, imprisonment, and/or prohibiting from healthcare may be imposed for violations of these statutes [26].

14.7.10   PRESCRIBING OF CONTROLLED SUBSTANCES

One area of interest and potential concern as telehealth increases is the prescription of prohibited medicines. This has an especially severe effect on medical and surgical specialties that rely on medications to treat chronic illnesses. Telemedicine prescribing regulations and guidelines should be considered while developing service process and procedures that fulfill patient requirements while also complying with the numerous layers and stages of linked state and country regulations on telehealth, health practice, controlled drug prescribing, scam, and/or mistreatment [27].

Finally, numerous telemedicine opportunities for e-healthcare are emerging and most of them have the prospective to assist patients, healthcare staff, and healthcare organizations, but proper and proper utilization is critical to reaping the benefits of these services. Residents, patients, medical specialists, and healthcare organizations all benefit from incorporating telemedicine into healthcare procedures during the COVID-19 epidemic. We encourage policymakers throughout the world to use the telemedicine experiences recorded during this outbreak to allow e-healthcare practices to be covered by privacy and data protection legislation [28].

14.8 THE FUTURE AND NEXT GENERATION OF AI

AI approaches have reverberated across the healthcare organizations, triggering a lively debate about whether AI practitioners will sooner or later substitute human physicians. Human doctors and all medical practitioners believe that it will not be swapped by computers soon, but AI may indeed assist physicians to make good quality clinical decisions or they can substitute human reasoning in some specific regions of Medicare. Medical robots have also demonstrated their capability for application in a broad range of health concerns by completing an increasing number of health functions. Medical robotics has progressed to the point where it will be feasible to use technology to develop both our healthcare structure and the medical world. In the realm of surgery, the operating room (OR) is now a complex combination of micro-robots, telepresence workstations, computer-integrated surgery, and modern imaging equipment. As a result, medical robots should be extra precise than traditional robotic procedures and include sensor techniques that offer security precautions and a rudimentary understanding of biological processes.

The emergence of "big data" is another significant development in modern research. It typically refers to the gathering of a significant number of complicated data quickly, not just for insurance compensation but also for any additional research or non-research objectives. Although the application of big data in healthcare robotics is still in its early stages, algorithms that leverage Cloud technology to acquire HIPAA-compliant data that will enhance healthcare robotics use and robotic process automation (RPA).

Another important use of AI in the medical area is the provision of easily available screening tools in parts of the world where healthcare systems are less developed. On the other hand, the current trend in AI development is to build increasingly complicated networks in order to get higher diagnostic sensitivity, so that patients may be able to decrease their visit intervals in half while still obtaining the highest level of individualized medical treatment. Due to the advancement of portable gadgets, patients may now capture basic data and submit it to a healthcare institution to be analyzed by a clinician. As a result, the use of AI in medicine is inevitable, and its integration with big data and IoT makes it even more accessible and relevant. AI would undoubtedly advance to a new level with the advancement and integration of other technologies.

KEYWORDS

- **Artificial Intelligence**
- **Internet of Medical Things**
- **Khoja–Durrani–Scott**
- **Machine Learning**
- **Natural Language Processing**
- **Robotic Process Automation**

REFERENCES

1. Ohno-Machado, L., (2017). Understanding and mitigating the digital divide in health care. *J. Am. Med. Inform. Assoc., 24*, 880, 881.
2. Acs, B., Rantalainen, M., & Hartman, J., (2020). Artificial intelligence as the next step towards precision pathology. *J. Intern. Med., 288*, 62–81.
3. Heinrichs, B., & Eickhoff, S. B., (2020). Your evidence? Machine learning algorithms for medical diagnosis and prediction. *Hum. Brain. Mapp., 41*, 1435–1444.
4. Jakhar, D., & Kaur, I., (2020). Artificial intelligence, machine learning and deep learning: Definitions and differences. *Clin. Exp. Dermatol., 45*, 131, 132.
5. Davenport, T., & Kalakota, R., (2019). The potential for artificial intelligence in healthcare. *Future. Healthc. J., 6*, 94–98.
6. Jiang, F., Jiang, Y., Zhi, H., Dong, Y., Li, H., & Ma, S., (2017). Artificial intelligence in healthcare: Past, present and future. *Stroke. Vasc. Neurol., 2*, 230–243.
7. Kayri, M., (2010). Data optimization with multilayer perceptron neural network and using new pattern in decision tree comparatively. *J. Comput. Sci., 6*, 606–612.
8. Sharma, A., & Chopra, A., (2013). Artificial neural networks: Applications in management. *J. Bus. Manag., 12*, 32–40.
9. Beasley, R. A., (2012). Medical robots: Current systems and research directions. *J. Robot., 11*, 1–14.
10. Bakas, T., Sampsel, D., Israel, J., Chamnikar, A., Ellard, A., & Clark, J. G., (2018). Satisfaction and technology evaluation of a telehealth robotic program to optimize healthy independent living for older adults. *J. Nurs. Scholarsh., 50*, 666–675.
11. Avgousti, S., Christoforou, E. G., Panayides, A. S., Voskarides, S., Novales, C., & Nouaille, L., (2016). Medical telerobotic systems: Current status and future trends. *Bio. Med. Eng. Online, 15*, 96.
12. Loh, E., (2018). Medicine and the rise of the robots: A qualitative review of recent advances of artificial intelligence in health. *BMJ. Leader., 2*, 59–63.
13. Downing, N. L., Bates, D. W., & Longhurst, C. A., (2018). Physician burnout in the electronic health record era: Are we ignoring the real cause? *Ann. Intern. Med., 169*, 50, 51.

14. Ekeland, A. G., Bowes, A., & Flottorp, S., (2010). Effectiveness of telemedicine: A systematic review of reviews. *Int J Med Inform., 79*, 736–771.

15. Eland-De, K. P., Van Os-Medendorp, H., Vergouwe-Meijer, A., Bruijnzeel-Koomen, C., Ros, W., (2011). A systematic review of the effects of e-health on chronically ill patients. *J. Clin. Nurs., 20*, 2997–3010.

16. Khoja, S., Durrani, H., Scott, R. E., Sajwani, A., & Piryani, U., (2013). Conceptual framework for development of comprehensive e-health evaluation tool. *Telemed. J. E Health, 19*, 48–53.

17. Bashshur, R., Doarn, C. R., Frenk, J. M., Kvedar, J. C., & Woolliscroft, J. O., (2020). Telemedicine and the COVID-19 pandemic, lessons for the future. *Telemed. J. E Health, 26*, 571–573.

18. Goldstein, B. A., Navar, A. M., Pencina, M. J., & Ioannidis, J. P., (2017). Opportunities and challenges in developing risk prediction models with electronic health records data: A systematic review. *J. Am. Med. Inform. Assoc., 24*, 198–208.

19. Polisena, J., Tran, K., Cimon, K., Hutton, B., McGill, S., & Palmer, K., (2009). Home telehealth for diabetes management: A systematic review and meta-analysis. *Diabetes. Obes. Metab., 11*, 29, 30.

20. Silva, P. S., Cavallerano, J. D., & Aiello, L. M., (2011). Telemedicine and diabetic retinopathy: Moving beyond retinal screening. *Arch Ophthalmol., 129*, 236–242.

21. Uma, N. D., & Mohammad, A., (2016). Extraction of action rules for chronic kidney disease using naïve bayes classifier. *IEEE International Conference on Computational Intelligence and Computing Research (ICCIC)*, 1–5.

22. Uma, N. D., (2016). Prediction system for heart disease using Naive Bayes and particle swarm optimization. *J. Biomed. Res., 29*, 2646–2649.

23. Gogia, S. B., Maeder, A., Mars, M., Hartvigsen, G., Basu, A., & Abbott, P., (2016). Unintended consequences of tele health and approaches for their solutions. *Yearb. Med. Inform., 1*, 41–46.

24. Veinot, T. C., Mitchell, H., & Ancker, J. S., (2018). Good intentions are not enough: How informatics interventions can worsen inequality. *J. Am. Med. Inform. Assoc., 25*, 1080–1088.

25. Ajami, S., & Lamoochi, P., (2014). Use of telemedicine in disaster and remote places. *J. Educ. Health. Promot., 3*, 26.

26. Drake, C., Zhang, Y., Chaiyachati, K. H., & Polsky, D., (2019). The limitations of poor broadband internet access for telemedicine use in rural America: An observational study. *Ann. Intern. Med., 171*, 382–384.

27. Hjelm, N. M., (2005). Benefits and drawbacks of telemedicine. *J. Telemed. Telecare, 11*, 60–70.

28. Bender, W., Hiddleson, C. A., & Buchman, T. G., (2019). Intensive care unit telemedicine: Innovations and limitations. *Crit. Care Clin., 35*, 497–509.

CHAPTER 15

CYBER-PHYSICAL SYSTEM-BASED SECURE ONLINE MEDICATION SYSTEM

KUNDANKUMAR RAMESHWAR SARAF[1] and P. MALATHI[2]

[1]*PhD Research Scholar, Department of Electronics and Telecommunication Engineering, D.Y. Patil College of Engineering, Akurdi, Pune, Maharashtra, India*

[2]*Professor, Department of Electronics and Telecommunication Engineering, D.Y. Patil College of Engineering, Akurdi, Pune, Maharashtra, India*

ABSTRACT

Due to heavy rush at the clinic, on-time patient diagnosis is difficult. It may spread the contagious disease among the people which may lead to the death of patients. Hence quick and on-time diagnosis is prime important part of healthcare. This can be possible using cyber physical system (CPS) prepared by integration of Splunk software, networking, and sensing devices. One bed equipped with health monitoring sensor detect the various health conditions of the patient. In case of any unusual health condition Splunk alert notify to physician who will save the patient's life. In case of any cyber-attack on any CPS component Splunk alert will notify to the CPS admin. Both the alerts are received in the form of phone call, SMS, and E-mail. Using artificial intelligence (AI), user behavior analytics and machine learning (ML). Splunk has the capability to detect any unusual health conditions 30 to 45 minutes before its actual occurrence. This system can monitor the

Handbook of Research on Artificial Intelligence and Soft Computing Techniques in Personalized Healthcare Services, Uma N. Dulhare, A. V. Senthil Kumar, Amit Datta, Seddik Bri, Ibrahiem M. M. El Emary, (Eds.)

patient's health as well as cyber-attacks on CPS. This chapter explains the use of Splunk for the implementation of smart and secure online medication system against the unwanted cyber-attacks. Reader will understand the effective integration of Cyber Physical Components to treat the remotely located patient.

15.1   INTRODUCTION

This chapter introduces the use of Splunk software platform to monitor the patient's health from remote location. Doctor can simultaneously diagnose the health of multiple patients without actual physical contact with all of them.

One chair or bed equipped with all the sensors should be placed in every village. These sensors will generate the logs according to the health condition of the patient. These sensors may include temperature sensor, oxygen level monitoring sensor, blood pressure sensor, pulse rate sensor. These logs will be sent to Splunk. Using machine learning (ML) algorithm this system can collect and diagnose all the logs generated by the sensors. Using artificial intelligence (AI), this system can anticipate the health issue of patient prior to its actual occurrence and major harm to the patient's body. In case of any unusual health condition of any patient, this system will generate the alert and notify this report to the patient relative as well as to the physician. This alert is generated in the form of phone call, SMS as well as email. Based on this report, the physician can recommend the appropriate medical treatment to the patient.

15.2   PROBLEM DEFINITION

This section explains the need of this system in detail. Quick diagnosis of disease can save the life of many patients. The mortality-rate of human being is still high due to unavailability of skilled physicians, remote location of hospitals, lack of health awareness, huge number of patients affected by same disease and deficiency of essential diagnostic equipment's. This mortality rate can be decreased if early health diagnostic can be performed by using AI. All available IoT Heath care systems can diagnose the issue with patient health only after any parameter goes outside of threshold limit. These systems are helpful to overcome the danger caused by disease after its actual occurrence. Hence these systems may cause harm to the patient's health.

To avoid this issue, the healthcare monitoring system must recognize the symptoms of illness before the actual manifestation of disease. This can be possible using Splunk Industrial IoT platform. This software can predict the health issue before its actual occurrence.

To simplify the working of Splunk for Industrial IoT one can consider the COVID-19 disease diagnosis. Normally COVID-19 patients suffer from a symptom such as body pain, headache, fever, cough, low oxygen level, etc. To diagnose all these symptoms the chair or bed equipped with various sensors can be created once the victim seat on this chair. This chair will calculate all these parameters and send the corresponding logs to Splunk for Industrial IoT platform. In this platform threshold of oxygen level, blood pressure, temperature, etc., already set by the doctor. User will store the phone number and email id of a doctor. After the occurrence of any symptoms beyond the threshold limit, generate the alert. This alert sends the notification to the doctor through phone call, SMS, and email. Doctor can understand the future health issue on patient's health and suggest the medicines to avoid the serious effect of COVID-19.

15.3 LITERATURE REVIEW

In December 2014 Anish Hemmady has introduces the significance of big data in healthcare and data security. He has also suggested the use of Splunk to filter this data to smoothen the information retrieval system for efficient and effective output [1]. This research can be extended by demonstrating detail Splunk use to overcome the big data issue in the healthcare sector.

According to the news given by Splunk website, many in April 2015, many healthcare institutions use Splunk Operation Intelligence for healthcare [2]. This research has not considered the cyber security aspect of the entire CPS.

Splunk news in February 2017 explains that, Molina leadership team has used the Splunk IT service intelligence (ITSI) to monitor the health of patients [3]. The Splunk ITSI can be used for predictive analysis of patients' health condition. It can also be used to secure the entire healthcare system against the cyber-attacks. But as compared to Splunk Enterprise it is a costly solution.

In 2017, internet of medical things (IoMT) has predicted the use of Splunk for health monitoring and diagnosis [4]. Security and privacy of healthcare data is the biggest challenge in using IoMT for healthcare monitoring. Interoperability is another challenge to implement this system in practice.

Also, difficulty in updating and upgrading the IoMT devices is the biggest hurdle of this technology.

In October 2019, Venketesh et al. has explained the 20 different tools to analyze the big data of healthcare system [5]. The significant tool must be considered to manage, analyze, and process the big data.

In December 2019, .Conf19 has shown the single dashboarding framework for monitoring the health of sports person in real time [6]. The alerting system is essential and should collaborated with a single dashboarding framework for the comprehensive healthcare monitoring system.

In March 2021, Atef Kouki has informed the use of Splunk to simply the work of medical staff [7]. The alerting mechanism used in this research can be extended to secure the CPS and diagnose the health issues faced by patients.

In March 2021, Angelina et al. has uses Splunk for extended log analysis during the healthcare process [8]. This research can be extended by exploring the aggregated events for the treatment such as chemotherapy. The user access record of patient pathway manager (PPM) Splunk should be combined with the treatment record in PPM database to analyze the system functionality effect on the treatment.

The white paper named "Using Healthcare Machine Data for Operational Intelligence." This paper has used the Splunk to minimize the billing error in hospitals, real time fraud detection and drug dispensing monitoring [9]. Any serious health issue is expensive in the form of diagnosis, treatment, traveling, and service. These systems reduce all these expenses incurred by patient. Hence it is in turn reduces the mortality rate of the country.

Medigate has created a document showing used the use of Splunk to deliver the complete visibility and control over the medical devices and IoT devices [10].

The research described in Refs. [2, 3, 9, 10] has used Splunk for healthcare monitoring. They have not considered the use of Splunk to reduce the cyber-attacks on entire system. As all components of intelligent healthcare monitoring system are connected by the internet, these systems have threat of cyber-attacks. Hence threat monitoring and detection must be established to prevent these attacks on CPS.

15.4   DESIGN OF SYSTEM

This section includes the schematic of the system in the form of a block diagram. It has also included the details of each sensor used in CPS. Working of the system is briefly described by algorithm and flowchart.

15.4.1 BLOCK DIAGRAM OF SYSTEM

Figure 15.1 shows the block diagram of the intelligent health monitoring system. This system is a cyber physical system (CPS) which contain the bed equipped with various health status monitoring sensors. Patient can sleep on this bed to diagnose themselves for any health criticality. The sensors connected to this bed sends the data to Splunk Heavy Forwarder. Splunk heavy forwarder parse the received logs from the sensors and delete unwanted logs. These parsed logs then transferred to Splunk Indexer. Splunk Indexer creates the indexes based on the logs received from sensors. Splunk Indexer and Splunk Search Head connected by internet. Splunk search head can monitor all the indexed logs. The dashboard and alert are created based on the received logs.

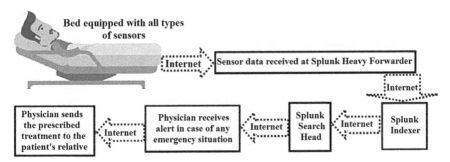

FIGURE 15.1 Intelligent health monitoring system.

As shown in Figure 15.2, the intelligent health monitoring system monitors the health issue as well as cyber-attacks on the system. This system can be prepared using a chair. The patient needs to sit on a chair which is equipped with various sensors to monitor the health of patient. As shown in Figure 15.2, the weight sensor (load sensor) measures the weight, blood pressure sensor BMP180 measures blood pressure, temperature sensor TMP36 measure body temperature of the patient. The oximeter connected over the middle finger of the patient can measure the heart rate (pulse rate), oxygen level in blood and perfusion index (PI) level of the patient. The output of all these sensors is transmitted to a syslog server. This syslog server is situated in the similar room near the chair and connected over the internet. Syslog server collects the logs and send them to Splunk Heavy Forwarder. This forwarder parses the logs and filter the unwanted logs. These filtered logs transferred to Splunk indexer. This indexer segregates the received data into various Splunk indexes. Splunk search head can monitor the data available on Splunk indexer. In this figure only the syslog server is placed near the chair. Splunk heavy forwarder, indexer, and search head are placed away from the chair and all these four servers connected with each other through the internet. This connectivity over the internet is shown by the dashed line in Figure 15.2.

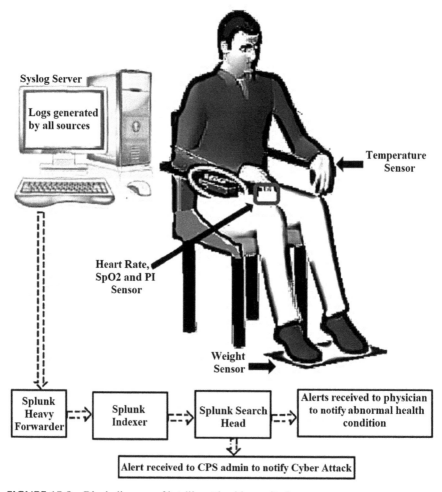

FIGURE 15.2   Block diagram of intelligent health monitoring system.

15.4.2 HEALTH STATUS MONITORING SENSORS

The bed of this system equipped with temperature sensor, weight sensor, oxygen level monitoring sensor, pulse rate measurement sensor. The details of all these sensors are given as below:

1. **Temperature Sensor:** This system uses digital thermistor temperature sensor Module to measure the body temperature of the patient. This module uses NTC type of thermistor. This module provides both analog and digital form of output. Thermistor is less affected by shocks or vibration and provide stable reading in any adverse condition. Also, thermistor has enough accuracy to measure the body temperature. Table 15.1 shows the comparison of all available temperature sensors.

TABLE 15.1 Comparison of Temperature Sensors

Parameter	Thermocouple	RTD	Thermistor	Silicon
Temperature range	−454°F to 3,272°F	−418°F to 1,652°F	−148°F to 842°F	−67°F to 302°F
Accuracy	±0.5C	±0.01°C	±0.1°C	±0.15°C
Ruggedness	It rugged in nature due to use of large gauge wires	Susceptible to damage by vibration	Not affected by shock and vibration, most stable sensor	Ruggedness is like the dual in line IC package

2. **Weight Sensor:** This system uses compression load cell connected at the bottom of the bed. This load cell uses the principle of strain gauge or Wheatstone Bridge to measure the weight of the patient. This load cell is rugged in nature and less affected by adverse environmental conditions. It has the capacity to measure a weight up to 1,000 Kilogram (Kg).

3. **Oxygen Level Monitoring Sensor:** This system uses a pulse oximeter to measure the pulse rate, oxygen level and PI index of the patient. This system uses transmissive technology to measure the oxygen level of the human body. In this method, the middle finger of the patient must be placed at between the pulse oximetry sensor device as shown in Figure 15.3. This sensor can measure the oxygen saturation of a patient's blood which is also called SpO2 level in percentage. If the SpO2 level is below 94%, the patient needs a quick treatment. This sensor can also measure the PI of the patient. PI is

the ratio of pulsatile blood flow to the static blood flow. PI shows the pulse strength of the patient. For normal patient, its value is the range of 0.02% to 20%. The beats per minute (BPS) for the normal patient must be between 70 and 100. Hence if the heart rate of the patient is beyond this range shows the critical health of the patient. Figure 15.3 shows the oxygen level measuring sensor. According to this figure, the heart bits of patients are 79, SpO2 level of patient is 97%, and the PI index is 5.8%. It shows that the patient has a normal health condition.

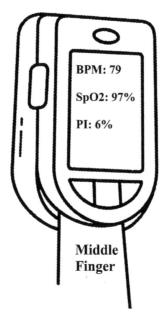

FIGURE 15.3   Oxygen level monitoring sensor.

15.4.3   ALGORITHM

Remote health monitoring issue can be solved by below given research algorithm. This algorithm also shows the steps to detect the cyber-attacks on entire CPS:

- Patient located in village visits the healthcare center.
- Patient or their relatives provide their general details to the technician appointed at this center. They can also insert the details by themselves into the interactive syslog server.

- Patient seats on health monitoring chair and technician connects all the sensors to the patient body.
- Sensors measure the physical condition of the patient and send the details to the syslog server.
- Syslog server collects the general details of patient along with readings of sensors and forward them to the Splunk heavy forwarder.
- Splunk heavy forwarder parses and filters the incoming data and sends these details to the Splunk indexer.
- Splunk indexer segregates the incoming data in the form of multiple indexes.
- User can observe the logs data of Splunk indexer using Splunk search head.
- User creates the dashboard to visualize the patient's present health status. User also creates an alert to notify the criticality of any health issue. User also creates the alert to detect any cyber-attack on CPS infrastructure.
- If the health status of the patient is normal and not crosses the pre-decided threshold level, no alert will be triggered.
- If the CPS is not affected by any cyber-attack, no alert will be triggered.
- In both the above cases, user can see the health monitoring and cyber-threat monitoring dashboards to understand the present status of patient health and CPS infrastructure security, respectively.
- Splunk search head detects the incoming logs and if the physical parameter of patient crossed the threshold levels it creates the alert and send it to the physician through phone call, SMS, and email. The physician understands the emergency and monitor the health status dashboard. Depending on the health criticality, physician contacts to the patient relative to suggest the required treatment to them.
- Splunk search head detects the cyber-attack and immediately notify to the CPS admin by alert through phone call, SMS, and email. CPS admin immediately monitor the cyber-threat detection dashboard and block the IP address from where the attack has started.

15.4.4   FLOW CHART OF SYSTEM

Figure 15.4 shows the flowchart of the system.

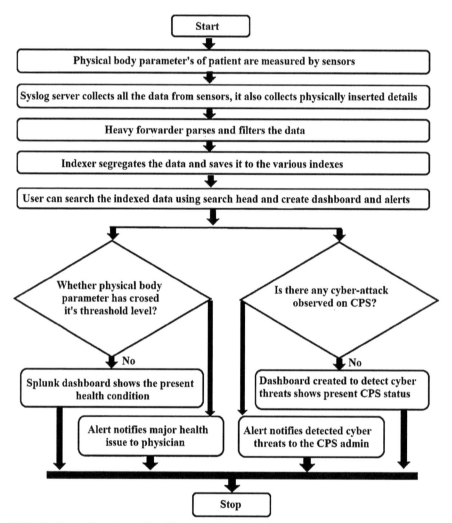

FIGURE 15.4   Flowchart of intelligent health monitoring system.

As shown in Figure 15.4, sensors measure the physical body parameter of the patient. Syslog server situated near the chair collects all the sensors data to determine the physical status of the patient's health. Patient or their relative also insert the general details of patient in the syslog server. These general details include name, gender, age, phone number, email id, medical history, and present health issue of patient. Syslog server transfers the general details along with the present health status of the patient to the Splunk heavy forwarder. Splunk heavy forwarder parses and filter the received data and send it to Splunk indexer. Splunk indexer segregates the data in the form of multiple indexes. Splunk user can monitor the received data and create dashboards and alerts through the Splunk search head. 'Health monitoring dashboard' created by the user shows the general details of patient's health along with various physical parameters.

If any physical parameter goes beyond the pre-decided threshold level, the Splunk creates the respective alert and notify to the physician regarding the same. Dashboard named 'Detection of cyber threats on intelligent health monitoring system' detects the cyber-attacks on CPS. Splunk creates alert and notifies to the CPS admin in case of detection of any cyber-attack on CPS.

15.5 DASHBOARD OF INTELLIGENT HEALTH MONITORING SYSTEM

This research has created the Splunk application named 'Kundan's CPS Security Research.' This Splunk contain the two dashboards as below:

- Intelligent health monitoring; and
- Detection of cyber-threats on intelligent health monitoring system.

The first dashboard shows the present health status of each patient. The second dashboard shows the security status of complete CPS.

15.5.1 INTELLIGENT HEALTH MONITORING DASHBOARD

This research has created the Intelligent Health Monitoring dashboard to monitor the health status of patient. To diagnose the health of patient, this chapter has created one intelligent health monitoring dashboard as shown in Figure 15.5. This dashboard has a dropdown menu which shows the names of the four patients. The first panel of this dashboard shows the general details of the patient. These general details include the name of patient, gender, age, contact details, three options to enter their medical history. One computer must be placed near the health status monitoring bed. On this computer operator enters the general details of the patient. Also, the physical status of the patient measured by sensor and stored in this computer. This computer connects to the internet and sends all these data to heavy forwarder for the further processing. This health status is mainly measured by the sensors which are equipped with the bed or chair. This status includes the parameters such as weight of patient, height, body mass index, pulse rate in rpm, blood oxygen level (SpO2%), body temperature (in °F) and PI.

FIGURE 15.5   Dropdown menu of intelligent health monitoring dashboard.

This dashboard has below given panels:

1. **General Patient Details:** This panel shows the patient's name, age, gender, patient relatives phone number and email id. This detail needs to be entered by patient or their relative in a syslog server. One technician can be placed near the syslog server to make this process easy.

2. **Present and Past Health Issue:** This dashboard shows any medical history of the patient along with present health related issues suffered by the patient. These details should be inserted into the syslog server by the patient or their relative or by technician situated near the server.

3. **Patient Weight in Kilogram:** This dashboard shows the body weight of the patient. The load sensor located near the chair measures the weight of the patient. This sensor transfers these details to the syslog server.

4. **Patient Height in Feet:** The patient height can be measured by stadiometer available in the health monitoring center. In the serious situation patient cannot stand straight, which leads to the inaccurate height measurement. To avoid this issue, the relative of patient can measure their height by portable height measurement tape. This height is details should be entered in the syslog server by a technician.

5. **Body Mass Index:** This parameter measures a body fat of adult based on their height and weight using below formula:

Body Mass Index = (Body weight in kilogram)/(Height in meter)^2 (1)

Underweight, normal weight, overweight, and obesity can be decided based on the BMI as given below:

- Underweight if the BMI is less than or equal to 18.5;
- Normal weight if the BMI is between 18.5 and 24.9.

Overweight if the BMI is between 25 and 29.9. Obesity if the BMI is more than 29.9.

6. **Pulse Rate in BPM:** The oximeter measures the pulse rate of the patient shows this pulse rate in this panel. Pulse rate is between 60 and 100 indicate normal pulse rate. A pulse rate below 60 and above 100 indicates abnormal pulse rate.

7. **Oxygen Level SpO2 in Percentage:** This panel shows the oxygen level in blood. This level can be measured by oximeter and shown in the form of percentage. SpO2 level for normal middle-aged adults is 94% to 100%. SpO2 level beyond this indicates the abnormal health condition.

8. **Body Temperature in °Fahrenheit:** The temperature sensor TMP36 measures the body temperature and send these details to the syslog server. For normal people, the body temperature (in °F) 97°F to 99°F. The temperature is beyond this limit shows the abnormal body condition.

9. **Perfusion Index in Percentage:** This index is the is the ratio of the pulsatile blood flow to the non-pulsatile blood flow in peripheral tissue. PI thus represents a noninvasive measure of peripheral perfusion that can be continuously and noninvasively obtained from a pulse oximeter. Normally PI value ranges between 0.2% and 20% but 0.2% PI indicates extremely weak pulse strength and 20% indicates extremely strong pulse strength. Normally PI should be above 3% and below 15% to indicate the normal health condition.

As shown in Figure 15.6, a patient named Raj Patil aged 34 has medical history of asthma and high blood pressure as shown in the dashboard panel 1 of the same figure. Currently, he does not face any health issue. Dashboard panel 2 shows the weight of Raj Patil is 72 kilograms. This weight is measured by a load sensor. The body temperature of Raj Patil is 98°F which is normal temperature and shown in the dashboard panel. The %SpO2 level of Raj Patil is 97%. The heart rate of Raj is 79 beats per minute. The PI of Raj is 6%. Raj Patil has 5.8 feet height with body mass index is 24. As shown in Figure 15.6, all the present health conditions of patient Raj Patil are normal. Hence no alert will be sent to the physician as well as to the relative of the patient. The Raj can take a medicine from the local physician in case of any mild health issue.

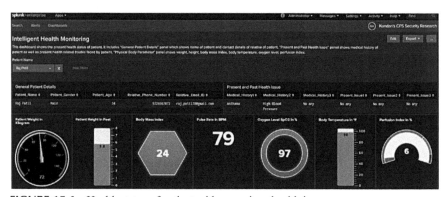

FIGURE 15.6   Health status of patient with no serious health issue.

Figure 15.7 shows the dashboard with the health status of one female patient Simran Singh. This dashboard also contains the similar 6 panels the first panel of this dashboard shows the general details of patient such as patient name is Simran Singh with 28 years of age and has medical history of low blood pressure. Currently facing breathing issue as well as fever. The 2nd and subsequent panels show that the weight of Simran is 56 kilo grams. Body temperature of Simran is 101°F. SpO2 oxygen level is 91%. The heart rate of Simran is 64 beats per minute (BPM). The PI of Simran is 1%. Simran has 5.3 feet of height with 22 body mass index. As per the data received by the 3rd panel to the 6th panel of this dashboard, it can be concluded that the Simran needs urgent medical treatment to save her life. In this case, the body temperature is beyond the predefined temperature range (above 98.5°F). The SpO2 level is also beyond the predefined range of below 94%. The heart rate has also crossed its threshold limit of 70 to 100 beats per second. PI is also very low than the normal expected value of 4% to 10%.

FIGURE 15.7 Health status of patient with serious health issue.

Table 15.2 gives the values of various physical parameters for two patients. Values of all parameters shown by the dashboard for Raj Patil indicates that the patient is not affected by any health issue. In this case no alert triggered.

Values of all parameters shown by the dashboard for Simran Singh indicates that patient is moderately affected serious health issue. The patient has low pulse rate, oxygen level and PI. Patient also has high body temperature. This situation creates the alert and notify to the physician through email, phone call and SMS. Physician immediately observe the dashboard and contact to the relative of the patient. Physician can recommend the required treatment to solve the further harm to the patient's body.

TABLE 15.2 Values of Physical Parameters for Two Patients

Physical Parameter	Value for Raj	Value for Simran
Medical history	Asthma, high blood pressure	Low blood pressure
Present issue	No	Breathing issue, body pain
Body weight in kilogram	72 KG	56 KG
Height	5 feet 8 inch	5 feet 3 inch
Body mass index	24	22
Pulse rate in beats per minute	79 BPM	64
Oxygen level SpO2	97%	91
Body temperature	98°F	101
Perfusion index	6%	1

15.5.2 CYBER THREAT DETECTION BY INTELLIGENT HEALTH MONITORING CPS

This dashboard detects the occurrence of cyber threats on intelligent health monitoring CPS. This chapter mainly concentrates on denial-of-service attacks, network, and port scanning threat, and brute force attacks.

Figure 15.8 shows dashboard which can detect the DoS attack, Port Scan attack and Brute Force attack by internal or external intruder. This dashboard was mainly created to monitor all these attacks on Splunk Search Head. The similar dashboard can be created to monitor the attacks on Splunk Indexer, Splunk Heavy Forwarder, and syslog server.

FIGURE 15.8   Dashboard to detect DoS attack, network, and port scanning, brute force attack on intelligent health monitoring CPS.

Figure 15.9 shows the detection of DoS attack on Splunk search head:

1. **DoS Attack Description:** In this attack attacker floods the network or server by sending a huge number of illegitimate traffic. This flooding makes the server inaccessible to the legitimate user.

2. **Splunk Dashboard Panel to Detect DoS Attack:** This dashboard panel counts the number of requests received to the Splunk search head in last 30 seconds. If the number of requests from any host is below 1,000 in last 30 seconds, it will reflect the normal scenario without any attack. But if the number of requests in the last 30 seconds is above 1,000, it may be the reason of Denial-of-Service attack. On detection of this attack, the CPS administrator monitor the reputation of the source IP address from where the huge requests are coming to the search head. If the reputation of this source IP address is bad, then the CPS admin block it immediately. If the reputation is good as well as internal, then the CPS admin contact to the owner of the IP address and ask the reason of huge requests in a short span. In this way DoS attack can be detected and mitigated by Splunk.

FIGURE 15.9 DoS attack detection by cyber threat detection by Splunk.

Figure 15.10 shows the network and port scan detection by Splunk:

1. **Network Port Scanning Attack Description:** In this attack, the attacker scan the IP address of network or server. By this scanning attacker gets the details of open ports on the server along with the services running on each port. The attacker creates the exploit based on the services running on the open port. Attacker can establish their full control over network/server by applying this exploit.

2. **Splunk Dashboard Panel to Detect Network Port Scanning Attack:** This Splunk search continuously monitor the firewall logs. If more than 500 access requests received in the last 5 minutes to any specific port in a network lead to the possibility of network port scanning attack. In this case the Splunk notifies to the CPS admin by alert through phone call SMS and email. CPS admin monitors the dashboard as well as search results and block the source IP address which performs the scanning of Splunk search head. This will mitigate the further harm to the entire CPS.

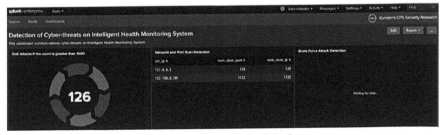

FIGURE 15.10 Network and port scan detection by Splunk.

Figure 15.11 shows the detection of brute force attack on Splunk search head:

1. **Brute Force Attack Description:** In this attack, the attacker tries to access the server. During this access attempt attacker may enter wrong credentials more than 3 times within 10 minutes time span.

2. **Splunk Dashboard Panel to Detect Brute Force Attack:** This panel detects the brute force attack on network/server. This search counts the login failure attempt by user in last 10 minutes. The Splunk creates the alert if the number of access failure attempts are more than 3 within the last 10 minutes. After receiving this alert, the CPS admin can observe the Splunk dashboard and verify whether the access attempt is performed by the legitimate user or not. If this attempt is illegitimate the CPS admin immediately remove the access attempt and change the password of server to avoid further harm.

FIGURE 15.11   Brute force attack detection by Splunk.

15.6 SPLUNK ALERT TO NOTIFY THE EMERGENCY HEALTH ISSUE TO PHYSICIAN

Figures 15.12–15.15 shows the alert created in Splunk. This alert notifies the physician through phone call, email, and SMS. After receiving this alert, the physician can contact to the patient's relative and provide the prescribed treatment to control the critical health condition of the patient. Figure 15.8 shows the first part of the alert. It shows that this alert is triggered after each and every emergency case (Per Result). This alert continuously monitors the health status of all patients (Real Time). It triggers only when the physical health parameters go beyond the expected predetermined threshold level.

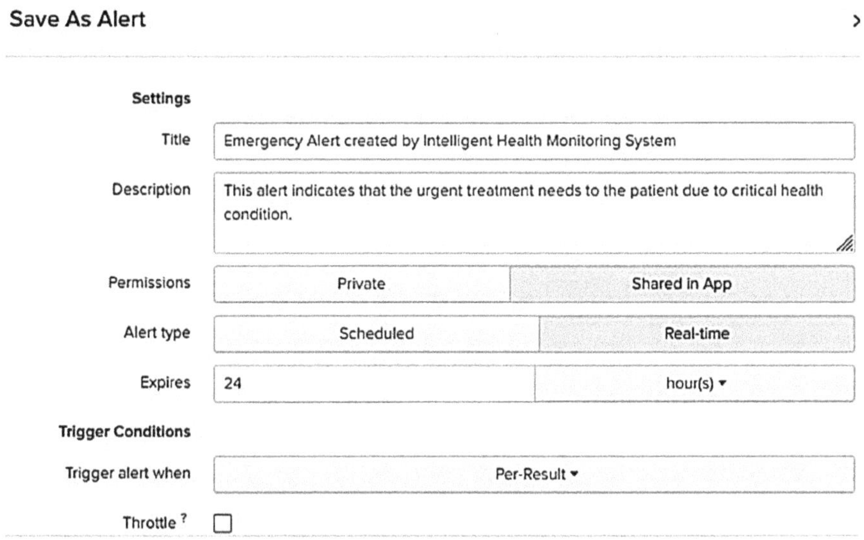

Save As Alert   >

Settings

| Title | Emergency Alert created by Intelligent Health Monitoring System |

| Description | This alert indicates that the urgent treatment needs to the patient due to critical health condition. |

| Permissions | Private | Shared in App |

| Alert type | Scheduled | Real-time |

| Expires | 24 | hour(s) ▼ |

Trigger Conditions

| Trigger alert when | Per-Result ▼ |

| Throttle ? | ☐ |

FIGURE 15.12   First part of alert.

Figure 15.13 shows the configuration of the second triggered action of this alert. As shown in the figure, Splunk sends the email to the physician and notify the complete all 6 dashboard panels as shown in Figure 15.13. By observing all these panels, physician come to know the criticality of patient's health.

Figure 15.14 shows the third part of alert configuration. In this part using www.zenduty.com website one can enter the phone number and email id of a physician. The token provided by this website must be entered in the webhook option of the alert. In case of every emergency situation, this configuration makes a phone call and sends the SMS to the physician.

Figure 15.15 shows the triggered alert configuration of Splunk alert. By setting up this configuration, the Splunk user can see all the notified alert in the triggered alert tab of Splunk. This configuration helps the Splunk user as well as physician to count the total number of triggered alerts by the Intelligent Health Monitoring System.

15.7 INTEGRATION OF HEALTH MONITORING SYSTEM WITH SPLUNK FOR INDUSTRIAL IOT

This system can be integrated with Splunk for Industrial IoT to monitor the health status of patient before the occurrence of any major health issue

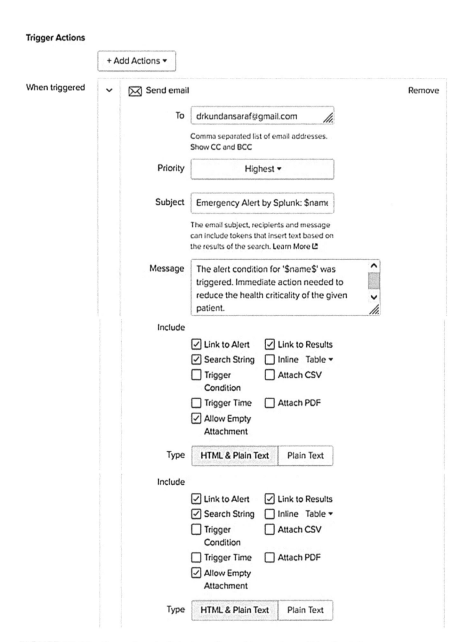

FIGURE 15.13   Second part of alert configured to send email to physician.

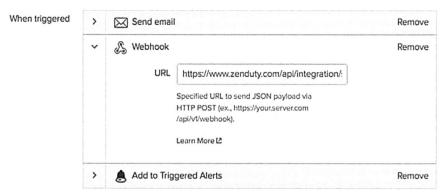

FIGURE 15.14   Webhook option configuration for phone call and SMS alerting.

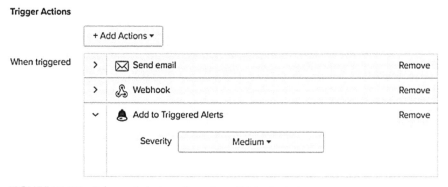

FIGURE 15.15   Triggered alert configuration of Splunk alert.

to the patient's body. Splunk for industrial IoT provides comprehensive solution and performs real time monitoring of any IoT based system. This single technology can help to achieve the security of CPS against the cyber threats along with predictive analysis of any undesired behavior by the CPS. Integration of intelligent health monitoring system with Splunk for industrial IoT provides the cyber security to the complete CPS. Because of predictive analysis feature, it monitors the behavior of the system. If any physical parameter goes beyond the predefined threshold limit this system will create a notable event using AI technology used by Splunk for Industrial IoT app. This system can diagnose various cyber-attacks on CPS before their actual occurrence and harm to the CPS. It immediately triggers a notable event and send alert to the CPS admin. Various cyber-attacks and the condition for creating notable events by Splunk for industrial IoT is shown in Figures 15.8–15.11.

15.8   MERITS, DEMERITS, AND APPLICATIONS

15.8.1   MERITS

- Patient located in small village can diagnose their health in less time by visiting the nearby healthcare center;
- In a cheaper cost patient can get the accurate health diagnosis and treatment;
- On time diagnosis and treatment can be easily possible by use of this automated system;
- This system can detect the major cyber-threats without any human intervention;
- Use of this system reduces the burden on physician to diagnose the huge number of patients in a pandemic situation.

15.8.2   DEMERITS

- This system needs good internet connectivity for its uninterrupted working;
- CPS admin and Splunk admin are needed to maintain the persistent working of this system.

15.8.3   APPLICATIONS

- This system can be used during the pandemic situation when the number of patients is too high as compared to number of physicians;
- This system can be permanently implemented and used by villagers to get accurate and quick diagnosis of their health.

15.9   CONCLUSION

This research has implemented the intelligent health monitoring system using CPS, sensors, and Splunk enterprise. This system detects the health condition of remotely located patient. In case of abnormal health condition of patient, this system creates the alert and notifies to the physician regarding the same. This system also monitors the cyber threat on the entire CPS. In case of cyber-threat detection this system notifies to the Splunk CPS admin regarding the same. This performs the task of remote health monitoring and secure the CPS against the cyber-threats.

ACKNOWLEDGMENT

Researcher have used 60 days trial version of Splunk Enterprise 8.2.1 version. Head of D. Y. Patil college of engineering, Akurdi, Pune have supported to achieve the objectives of this research.

KEYWORDS

- **Artificial Intelligence**
- **Cyber-Physical System**
- **Internet of Medical Things**
- **IT Service Intelligence**
- **Online Medication System**
- **Splunk**

REFERENCES

1. Anish, H., (2014). Significance of big data on healthcare and data security. International *Journal of Scientific & Engineering Research, 5*(12).
2. Press release by Splunk, (2015). *Splunk Builds Strong Traction in Healthcare.* https://www.splunk.com/en_us/newsroom/press-releases/2015/splunk-builds-strong-traction-in-healthcare.html (accessed on 24 January 2023).
3. Press release by Splunk, (2017). *Splunk IT Service Intelligence Helps Molina Healthcare Deliver Innovation to Patients.* https://www.splunk.com/en_us/newsroom/press-releases/2017/splunk-it-service-intelligence-helps-molina-healthcare-deliver-innovation-to-patients.html (accessed on 24 January 2023).
4. Data insider, (2017). *What is the Internet of Medical Things (IoMT)?* https://www.splunk.com/en_us/data-insider/what-is-the-internet-of-medical-things-iomt.html (accessed on 24 January 2023).

5. Venketesh, P., & Ramkumar, T., (2019). Implications of big data analytics in developing healthcare frameworks: A review. *Journal of King Saud University – Computer and Information Sciences*, *31*(4), 415–425.

6. Splunk, (2019). *Reintroducing Splunk Dashboards*. https://www.splunk.com/en_us/ blog/platform/reintroducing-splunk-dashboards.html (accessed on 24 January 2023).

7. Splunk, (2021). *Splunk at the Service of Medical Staff.* https://www.splunk.com/en_us/ blog/platform/splunk-at-the-service-of-medical-staff.html (accessed on 24 January 2023).

8. Angelina, P. K., Geoff, H., David, H., & Owen, J., (2021). Process mining on the extended event log to analyze the system usage during healthcare processes (case study: The GP tab usage during chemotherapy treatments). *International Conference on Process Mining, ICPM 2020: Process Mining Workshops* (pp. 330–342).

9. White paper, (2012). *Using Healthcare Machine Data for Operational Intelligence*. https://davidhoglund.typepad.com/files/splunk_for_healthcare.pdf (accessed on 24 January 2023).

10. Medigate Splunk, (2021). *Clinical SOC Solution Delivering Complete Visibility and Control Over Medical and IoT Devices*. https://medigate.pathfactory.com/medigate-and-splunk (accessed on 24 January 2023).

11. Geetha, S., Uma, N. D., & Siva, S. S. S., (2018). Intrusion detection using NBHoeffding rule-based decision tree for wireless sensor networks. *Second International Conference on Advances in Electronics, Computers and Communications (ICAECC)*.

CHAPTER 16

DURBHASHAN: A HEALTHCARE GUIDING BOOTH FOR RURAL PEOPLE

G. SUNIL, SRINIVAS ALUVALA, AREEFA, S. PRAVEEN KUMAR, K. PRAGATHI, AND K. RISHITHA

Department of Computer Science and Engineering, SR Engineering College, Warangal Urban, Telangana, India

ABSTRACT

Nowadays, neglecting health issues will lead to further complications, and when it comes to rural areas, it is more miserable. Technology can only facilitate the challenges like low-quality care, lack of awareness, and limited access to health facilities that are availing in the rural areas. Thus this chapter depicts the proposed system named DurBhashan, a healthcare guiding booth for rural people which has been implemented using technologies like AI, Web technologies, used for connecting the rural people with the healthcare facilities, an Audio Bot in DurBhashan interacts and guides the rural people in their local language and helps them to connect to the healthcare providers. The Audio Bot resembles a doctor and help people in identifying their health issues based on their symptoms. It helps in easy appointment booking in hospitals that provide affordable healthcare services. Once the user wants to consult the hospital, the Bot passes general information to the hospital management system to review the appointment request and once confirmed an SMS of appointment details will be sent to the respective patients. It even helps in the functioning of Anganwadis in auto recording the BMI and analyzing the status of nourishment in children.

Handbook of Research on Artificial Intelligence and Soft Computing Techniques in Personalized Healthcare Services, Uma N. Dulhare, A. V. Senthil Kumar, Amit Datta, Seddik Bri, Ibrahiem M. M. El Emary, (Eds.)
© 2024 Apple Academic Press, Inc. Co-published with CRC Press (Taylor & Francis)

16.1   INTRODUCTION

The main reason for healthcare complications in the rural areas is due to lack of 3 A's, i.e., Availability, Accessibility, and Affordability. Thus, we could improve healthcare access only by making possibilities to ensure these 3 A's. Emerging technologies like AI have such an impact that their implementation for real-world problems can make lives better. As we know how vast the AI applications are in any field which has gained popularity in mimicking human intelligence. Thus, in various situations, it became a dire need to enable a system that could assist the rural people in diagnosing their health issues, giving the awareness, precautions, guiding them to consult the specialist with easy appointment and coordinating all these with the help of AI and web technologies. The basic idea about our project named as DurBhashan, A healthcare guiding booth for rural people, was generated by taking the STD booths in the olden days that served by connecting the people all over. What if the same idea would be used in connecting the rural people with the healthcare facilities was the fascinating thought that made us implement an Audio Bot which interacts and guides the rural people in their language and helps them to connect to the healthcare providers.

The Audio Bot developed by us is an AI-based trained model such that it could resemble a doctor and help people in identifying their health issues based on their symptoms. This Bot model is trained on the datasets which we downloaded from Kaggle which consists of various symptoms and followed by the disease corresponding to those symptoms. We trained our model with different algorithms like decision tree, SVM, logistic regression, random forest (RF) algorithms and compared the results where all were giving an accuracy of 100% but the logerror was very low in the case of the Decision tree Algorithm. Hence, we model trained with a Decision Tree Classifier which applies the search tree method where when 1 symptom is given by the user, it asks whether other sets of symptoms present and through traversal based on the symptoms responded as yes by the user, prediction is done.

Our system also helps in easy appointment booking in the hospitals that provide affordable healthcare services to rural people. Once the user willing to consult the hospital, the bot passes on the general information including the user's phone number that the user gives to a website portal that we have created where we provide services to the hospital appointment booking staff to review the appointment request and once confirmed, the automatic SMS of appointment details including the hospital name, address, phone, timings, the date will be sent to the respective patient's mobile. According to the census, all over India, there are about 900 million mobile users including remote areas. Thus, our system is reliable. On the other hand, we even created portals on the same website that helps in recording the health camps' data and storing them safely over the sheets such that we could encourage the medical colleges for conducting health camps practical for students with ease. Our Audio bot even helps in the functioning of Anganwadis in automatically recording the BMI data and analyzing the status of nourishment in children.

The data required will be transferred from our Audio bot in the rural areas into the Google sheets powered by Google cloud which would be only accessed to the respective hospitals or respective medical colleges who have registered through our Web portal. The data of google sheets is displayed over web portals with help of JavaScript and the Google Sheets API from where the JSON data would be accessed and with the help of CSS and HTML portrayed over the web portals. This is a brief overview of the project.

16.2 LITERATURE SURVEY

In the present scenario, to ensure rural health, many advancements are being made like Telehealth. Though it could help to overcome the shortage of specialists, it takes time in implementation for covering rural areas due to the challenges of regulatory and the prevailing licensing restrictions. Thus, an immediate medium is required to serve in this case. Many research papers depict different models and approaches concerning healthcare, and most of them proposed the healthcare chatbots applications.

Setiaji & Wibowo [1] described their work on the chatbot that they created which works based on the knowledge base (KB) that they defined. As the KB designing includes the static entering of the data like the QNA bot, it might not work in real-time applications. It will only be able to address based on the knowledge that has been defined. This model is unintelligent as no algorithm is defined and trained for the model. If any new instance or input other than the KB is given, then it will not be able to produce output, and it must be again trained with that similar kind of dataset. There is one more similar kind of work in another research paper where they designed a chatbot that takes the inputs from the user in the form of symptoms and tries to match the tags or the keywords of the disease and if it is not present then it would consider the suggestions from the user and feed it [6].

In this device, the data stored in form of XML which displays different symptoms that are stored and ask the user to select the symptoms that he/she is facing and based on that it gives a prediction [3]. The system has no decision-making capacity, and no algorithm has been trained for categorizing the data [3]. The user gets annoyed to select among symptoms as it is time-consuming and in the case of rural areas, we cannot implement this in real-time.

One research paper [2], describes their work on creating an AI healthcare application where the decision tree algorithm is applied which predicts the disease and prescribes the medicines to be taken. But they had mentioned that their model was trained with a limited KB for getting more accuracy [4]. The hyperparameters were not tuned, and a limited dataset would not lead to effective prediction for new symptoms [5] (Figure 16.1).

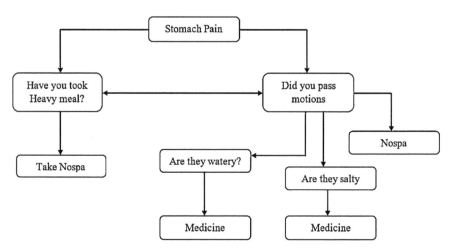

FIGURE 16.1   Decision tree login limited to fewer symptoms search due to limited knowledge base.

Moreover, this chapter [2], mentioned in the conclusion part the scope of the extension which includes the improved database to be used to train the model for efficient predictions, and enabling the audio or voice inputs would help people to use the bot easily.

16.3   PROPOSED METHODOLOGY

As we had seen the drawbacks of the existing systems and the possible scope of the extension of their work, which specifies the need for a system that could be more efficient in terms of predictions of the health issues. Moreover, as we are implementing this system for the rural people access, we should consider the audio inputs, and more specifically it should be language specific for interaction with the rural people in their language. We are not limiting our model to the symptoms prediction, instead, we are expanding the use cases of the Audio bot in different aspects like easy appointment booking system for the rural people to aware them not to neglect their health issues but to consult the specialists. We are suggesting the hospitals which would give more affordable health services to the rural. Thus, one form of way to encourage the hospitals to come up to serve rural people. These audio bots can be used in the functioning of Anganwadis and even for easy conducting of health camps. These all aspects of implementation are discussed in the form of modules in succeeding sections.

16.4 HEALTHCARE AUDIO BOT FOR RURAL PEOPLE

The healthcare audio bot is designed in such a way that the users would be able to communicate in their language. The use case diagram (Figure 16.2) describes the services provided by the bot and the flow of interaction between the rural people and the audio bot to use it.

The healthcare audio bot is an Audio-based bot that communicates with the user in their language and predicts the health issues based on the algorithm that we have trained the model.

16.5 AI-BASED MODEL USING DECISION TREE ALGORITHM

The development of this model includes various key elements of AI like NLP, ML algorithms, KB-datasets in training and testing the model. The implementation of the model involves various steps:

> **Step 1: Read Dataset:** We have downloaded the dataset from the Kaggle site. The dataset consists of various symptoms and their corresponding disease. By importing the pandas library, we were able to read the dataset as a data frame (Figure 16.3).

Overall, the dataset of symptoms consists of about 4,920 rows and 18 columns (17 symptoms, 1 disease) (Figure 16.4).

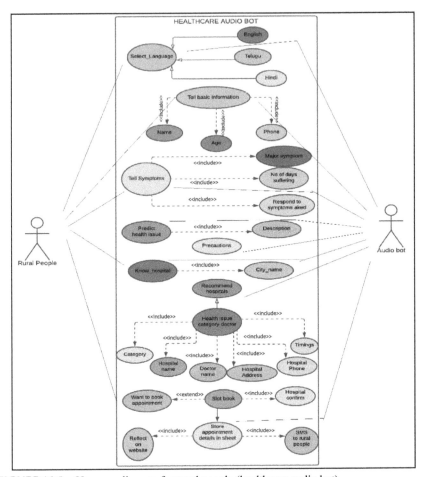

FIGURE 16.2   Use case diagram for rural people (healthcare audio bot).

	Disease	Symptom_1	Symptom_2	Symptom_3	Symptom_4	Symptom_5	Symptom_6	Symptom_7	Symptom_8	Symptom_9	Symp
867	Drug Reaction	itching	skin_rash	burning_micturition	spotting_urination	NaN	NaN	NaN	NaN	NaN	
3975	Psoriasis	skin_rash	joint_pain	skin_peeling	silver_like_dusting	small_dents_in_nails	inflammatory_nails	NaN	NaN	NaN	
3999	Hepatitis D	joint_pain	vomiting	fatigue	yellowish_skin	dark_urine	nausea	loss_of_appetite	abdominal_pain	yellowing_of_eyes	
3418	Malaria	chills	vomiting	high_fever	sweating	headache	nausea	diarrhoea	muscle_pain	NaN	
1115	Heart attack	vomiting	breathlessness	sweating	NaN	NaN	NaN	NaN	NaN	NaN	

`[4] df.sample(n=5)  #dataset_symptoms.csv`

FIGURE 16.3   Displaying the random records of the dataset.

```
#show all diseases
print("Total Diseases count in the dataset: ",len(df['Disease'].unique()))
print()
df['Disease'].unique()

Total Diseases count in the dataset:  41

array(['Fungal infection', 'Allergy', 'GERD', 'Chronic cholestasis',
       'Drug Reaction', 'Peptic ulcer diseae', 'AIDS', 'Diabetes ',
       'Gastroenteritis', 'Bronchial Asthma', 'Hypertension ', 'Migraine',
       'Cervical spondylosis', 'Paralysis (brain hemorrhage)', 'Jaundice',
       'Malaria', 'Chicken pox', 'Dengue', 'Typhoid', 'hepatitis A',
       'Hepatitis B', 'Hepatitis C', 'Hepatitis D', 'Hepatitis E',
       'Alcoholic hepatitis', 'Tuberculosis', 'Common Cold', 'Pneumonia',
       'Dimorphic hemmorhoids(piles)', 'Heart attack', 'Varicose veins',
       'Hypothyroidism', 'Hyperthyroidism', 'Hypoglycemia',
       'Osteoarthristis', 'Arthritis',
       '(vertigo) Paroymsal  Positional Vertigo', 'Acne',
       'Urinary tract infection', 'Psoriasis', 'Impetigo'], dtype=object)
```

FIGURE 16.4   Diseases whose symptoms were recorded in the knowledge base.

In addition to this, as our audio bot also tells about the disease and gives the precautions based on the severity of the disease predicted, we have even considered other three datasets as shown in Figure 16.5.

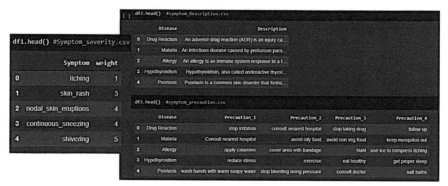

FIGURE 16.5   Other datasets – symptom severity, disease description, and disease precaution.

> ➤ **Step 2: Preprocessing the Data:** It is very important before feeding the data to the model. Thus, first of all, we tried to visualize the data in the symptom dataset.

From Figure 16.5, we can observe there are heatmaps depicted which describe the presence of NaN values. Hence, we need to remove them before training the model.

Thus, we preprocessed the data by replacing all the NaN values with 0 as it indicates the absence of the symptom for that corresponding disease. As our Model can only understand binary values, we need to give either 1/0. Thus, the symptoms that indicate the disease are replaced by 1 as follows (Figure 16.6).

	itching	skin_rash	nodal_skin_eruptions	continuous_sneezing	shivering	chills	joint_pain	stomach_pain	acidity	ulcers_on_tongue	muscle_wasting	vomit
3923	0	0	0	0	0	0	0	0	0	0	0	
3342	0	0	0	0	0	0	0	0	0	0	0	
1364	0	0	0	0	0	0	0	0	0	0	0	
4548	0	0	0	0	0	0	0	0	0	0	0	
844	0	0	0	0	0	0	0	1	1	1	0	

5 rows × 133 columns

FIGURE 16.6   Dataset after preprocessing.

As the prediction column – y, i.e., disease column is still in the form of a string, we need to encode it with the help of NLP tools. Here, we used Label Encoder that maps the categorical variables to unique integers on basis of the alphabetical ordering. It is imported from the scikit library (data cleaning).

> **Step 3: Splitting the Data:** Generally, we follow the steps of Cross-validation before feeding the dataset directly to the model. Cross-validation is very important to find out the performance of our model fitted with a specific algorithm. Thus, according to it, the dataset is split into a Training dataset and Testing dataset with the help of Train-Test Split.

Train-Test split is a technique that is usually used for cross-validation for evaluating our model via the performance of the ML algorithm applied. Training Dataset: used to fit the ML model (for training model). Test Dataset: used to validate the fitted ML model.

> **Step 4: Applying the Algorithm:** Now it's time to fit our model by the classifier over the training dataset.

We can observe that we got 100% accuracy on the dataset by Decision Tree Classifier with the least logerror. We even applied different algorithms like RF classifier, logistic regression, SVM to compare the results. The graph of logerror is portrayed in the results section of the chapter.

From all, we got log-error = 0 in the case of the Decision Tree Classifier. Thus, we proceeded with this algorithm (Figure 16.7).

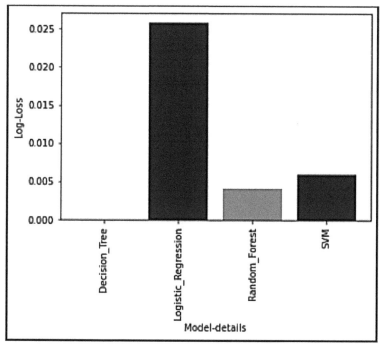

FIGURE 16.7   Log loss comparison.

16.6   MAKING OUR BOT CAPABLE TO TAKE AUDIO INPUTS

The bot designed by us is an audio bot that takes the audio inputs from the user and replies with audio. Figure 16.8 shows the mechanism proposed, which depicts the functioning of the audio bot.

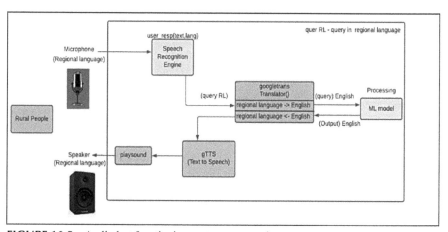

FIGURE 16.8   Audio bot functioning system proposed.

1. **Speech Recognition (Version = 3.8.1):** In the project, this is very important to enable the interaction between the audio bot and the rural people. Thus, we used the Speech Recognition Engine that takes input from the microphone and recognizes the speech using Google Speech Recognition by which our Audio bot can listen and understand the user's speech.

2. **Google Trans (Version = 3.0.0):** One more challenge is that the bot must be able to communicate in the same language which the rural people communicate. Thus, we need to interface a translator in between the speech recognition system and the ML model and in between the ML model and the Text to Speech Synthesizer as shown in Figure 16.8. Again, once processed, the output from the model is in form of English text which needed to be translated back to the regional language so that we could pass it to the Text to Speech Synthesizer which gives the audio output to the user in the translated language only.

3. **gTTS (Google Text to Speech) Synthesizer (Version = 2.2.2):** It is the python library that establishes a connection with Google Translates Text to Speech API for the synthesis of the text into the audio file – speech by which our Audio Bot now can speak. The output from the ML model which is translated into the specified user's language is converted into speech in the same language and stored as an audio file.

4. **PlayAudio (Version = 1.2.2):** The model plays the audio file generated by the text to speech synthesizer to the rural people.

16.7   AUDIO BOT SUGGESTING HOSPITALS TO CONSULT

The Audio Bot is programmed in such a way that, based on the prediction of health issues of the rural people, to encourage them to consult the proper specialist, it suggests affordable hospitals to the rural people and gives the details of the hospital and the doctor. All the health services or the hospitals willing to provide the better affordable services come under our suggesting system where we map the category doctor to be consulted based on the health issue to the category specialized hospitals that collaborated to the rural people. For this, we created two KBs as shown in Figure 16.9.

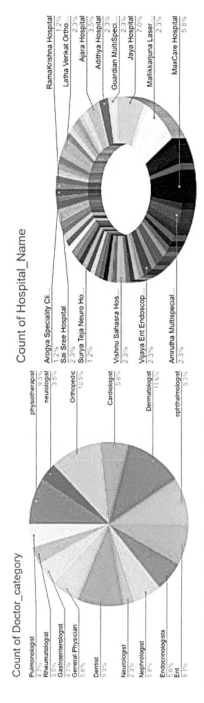

FIGURE 16.9 Data visualization of the knowledge base.

We programmed the bot with the general python code that maps the category of the predicted health issue's category from KB 1 and then maps the category in the KB 2 and returns the corresponding record which would be given as audio output from the bot.

16.8   WEB PORTALS INTERFACED WITH AUDIO BOTS (SERVICES)

16.8.1   *HOSPITAL APPOINTMENT BOOKING SYSTEM AND HEALTH CAMPS*

If the user (rural people) wants to consult the doctor, our bot automates the appointment booking by sending the general data of the user and store in the Google sheets which reflect on the web portal accessible by the respective hospital appointment desk staff through our proposed system depicted in the use case diagram.

Once the data as the appointment requests gets stored in the sheet, it would be displayed on the web portal of the respective hospital access where we provide a login gateway for data security. Only the respective hospital appointment staff can login and view the appointment requests and confirm, then SMS would be automatically sent to the user's mobile in rural areas consisting of the hospital details, phone, and the appointment date and time.

Thus, we are automating this process for easy access of appointments for people in rural areas to ensure the availability of health services and on the other side, encouraging hospitals to support affordable healthcare to get into our recommendation system.

We even created the portals for the medical colleges for conducting health camp practicals with ease by recording the data through the portal into the sheets system proposed by us. Login gateway is provided for accessing the respective sheets recorded by respective medical colleges (Figure 16.10).

16.8.2   *FUNCTIONING OF ANGANWADIS (VIA AUDIO BOT)*

The audio bot takes the weekly surveys at the Anganwadi's to facilitate the functioning and analyze the growth of children. Thus, the audio bot helps in recording the inputs from the Anganwadi staff regarding the BMI data and stores them directly into the google sheets which would be displayed on the Anganwadi's functioning portal designed by us (Figure 16.11).

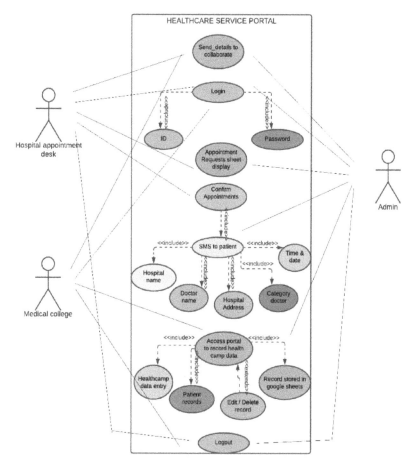

FIGURE 16.10 Use case diagram for hospitals and medical colleges (healthcare service portal).

As shown in Figure 16.11, the bot run a python program where we provided code for analysis of the BMI data and generate the report of categories whether severely underweight or healthy or underweight or overweight.

16.8.3 TECHNOLOGY OVERVIEW OF THE WEB PORTAL – AUDIO BOT SYSTEM

1. **HTML and CSS:** The web portals are created with the help of HyperText Markup Language and styled with the help of cascading style sheets (CSS). HTML is majorly used to create the actual content

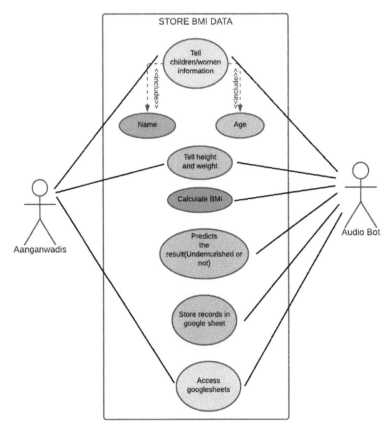

FIGURE 16.11   Use case diagram (via audio bot).

to be displayed over the website whereas CSS is used to customize the content and styling the website. Thus, with the help of these, we had designed the various elements of the website.

2. **Data Storage – Google Sheets:** The data from the audio bot will be automatically stored into the google sheets which have access to only those organizations associated. Google sheets are secure because we need not give edit access to anyone except the respective organization (hospital/medical college) to access their sheet data through the portal. For this, we designed the secure gateway in the form of logins for the registered ones only. The ER diagram in Figure 16.12 represents the Google sheets and their attributes (columns) in which the data is stored from the audio bot and represents the relationship between the entities.

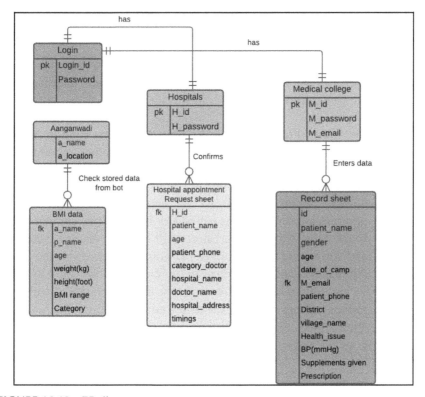

FIGURE 16.12   ER diagram.

Thus, whole data that needed to be stored from the audio bot is connected to their respective google sheets, and these sheets are accessed over the portals with the help of the following next technologies which we depicted here.

3. **JavaScript:** As our web portals deal with the real-time data being reflected from the sheets, they should be more dynamic and interactive.

In our project, there are many functionalities where we used JavaScript like:

*   Retrieving the data from the google sheets when clicked over the cards in form of tabular format over the web portal.
*   All the changes made over the google sheets by the access holders to reflect over the website.

- Web App that we created for the medical colleges that help them to record the health camps data by entering the form and submitting.
- Enabling the CRUD (create, read, update, delete) operations by one click on the respective buttons of the records displayed on the web portal.

4. **Google Cloud Platform (For Writing Data from Python Audio Bot to Sheets):** Implemented for storing hospital appointment requests from audio bot and BMI data from Anganwadis.

   i.   **Google Sheets API v4:** As we know that API (application program interface) acts as a mediator between two applications, In the same way, Google Sheets API helps in reading, writing, and formatting the data over the google sheets from the Web Applications and vice versa. In our case, we have used Python for programming as our Audio bot is also programmed with the same language such that the data from the user and the hospital appointment request data would be stored from the bot to the google sheets.

   ii. **Google Client Library:** We need to install packages that would be required to access the Google Client Library which helps in calling the Google Cloud APIs and utilize the services.

   iii. **Google Cloud Platform – Developers Console:** Developers console of the Google cloud platform gives insights into the traffic over the web application, databases, data analysis, and networking that has been deployed and uses the services of the Google cloud.

   iv. **Enable Google Sheet API:** Hence, we need to create a new project and activate it. Then once activated, we find a button to Explore and enable APIs, where we will be redirected to the Services API. Select Google Sheet API and Enable it.

   v.   **Create Credentials:** As we are going to send the data from the bot to the Google Sheets, we need to create the unique credentials for the bot by which the bot would be able to have access to the google sheet. To create the credentials we need to create a service account.

    vi. Create Service Account: Creating service account automatically creates an identity that our application (in our case audio bot) uses to send the requests for the services provided by the Google Cloud (in our case Google Sheets) on our behalf.

    vii. Google App Script (Creating Web Apps for Data Entry – Health Camps Data Portal): Google app script is the development environment that helps in the fastest development of the applications and publishes them in one click. This can be accessed from the tools tab in the google sheets. We need to do the coding by creating the files.

  5. XMLHttpRequest – Sending SMS on One Click: With the help of XMLHttpRequest, we can get the data or the message data from the server-side and in our case, we are calling the Google Sheets API and getting the data from the columns in form of JSON which is being appended to the text message. All the credentials – the API key would be generated which helps to access the data and with the help of SMS Rapid API, the text message would be sent to the phone number in the phone column in the google sheet.

Thus, in the appointment booking system proposed by us, once the appointment staff of the hospital review the appointment requests on the portal and confirm by clicking the confirm button, the SMS would be sent with all the column details of that particular row to that user's mobile in rural areas.

16.9 RESULTS

16.9.1 AUDIO BOT – HEALTHCARE

Thus, the Audio bot only suggests the hospitals concerning the health issue category to the rural people and asks whether to book an appointment in that hospital (Figures 16.13–16.15). If the user is willing to book an appointment, the details of the user as shown in Figure 16.16 stores into the sheet as shown in Figure 16.17 automatically.

FIGURE 16.13   Audio bot interaction with the user (rural people) in their selected language.

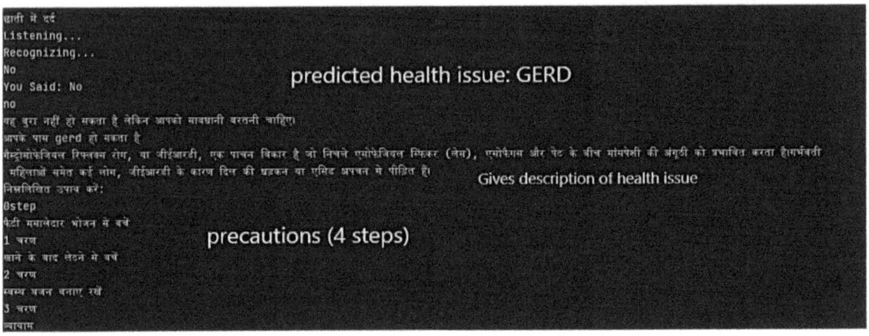

FIGURE 16.14   Audio bot tells details about the predicted health issue and precautions to be taken.

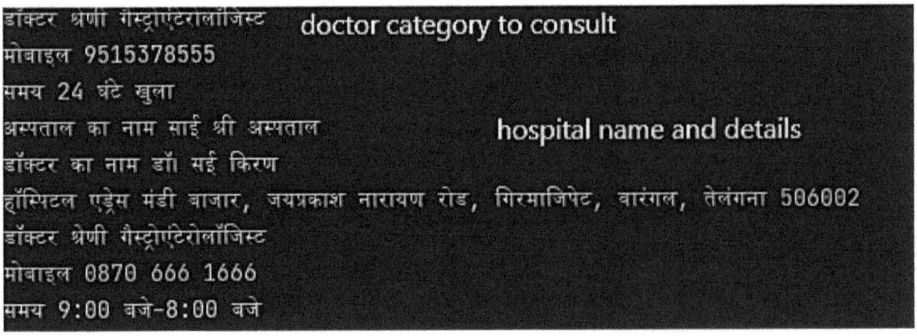

FIGURE 16.15   Audio bot suggests the hospitals based on doctor category (on health issue).

By this sheet it is secure, it is accessed by respective hospitals only. The Hospital Appointment staff approve the requests on the web portal and SMS would be sent.

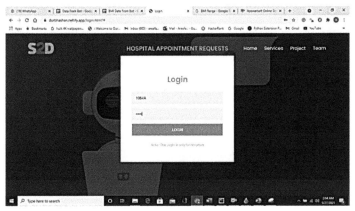

```
ANALYSIS DATA OF PATIENT - FINAL
ID:  1064A
Patient Name:  Chandana Verma
Patient Age:  35
Patient phone:  8466961585
Doctor Category to consult:  Gastroenterologist
Hospital Name:  Sai Sree Hospital
Doctor Name:  Dr.Sai Kiran
Timings:  9:00AM-8:00PM
Hospital Phone:  08706661666
Successfully Stored!
exited
```

FIGURE 16.16   Details recorded.

FIGURE 16.17   The record data from the bot get stored into the Google sheet through API.

16.9.2 WEB PORTAL – HOSPITAL APPOINTMENT REQUEST (FIGURES 16.18 AND 16.19)

FIGURE 16.18   Login page for the hospitals.

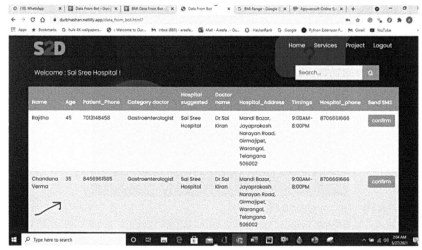

FIGURE 16.19   The newly added record is reflected over the web portal.

16.9.3   BMI BOT

The Audio Bot helps in recording the BMI data at the Anganwadis automatically such that the manual writing would be saved, and the progress of the growth and analysis can be made (Figures 16.20 and 16.21).

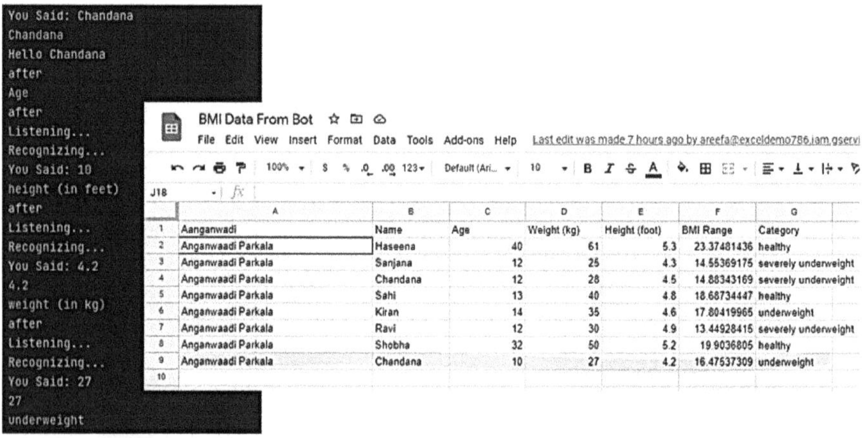

FIGURE 16.20   The BMI data gets stored from the bot into the sheet.

Aanganwadi	Name	Age	Weight (kg)	Height (foot)	BMI Range	Category
Anganwaadi Parkala	Haseena	40	61	5.3	23.37481436	healthy
Anganwaadi Parkala	Sanjana	12	26	4.3	14.55369175	severely underweight
Anganwaadi Parkala	Chandana	12	28	4.5	14.88343169	severely underweight
Anganwaadi Parkala	Sahi	13	40	4.8	18.68734447	healthy
Anganwaadi Parkala	Kiran	14	35	4.6	17.80419965	underweight
Anganwaadi Parkala	Ravi	12	30	4.9	13.44928415	severely underweight
Anganwaadi Parkala	Shobha	32	50	5.2	19.9036805	healthy
Anganwaadi Parkala	Chandana	10	27	4.2	16.47537309	underweight

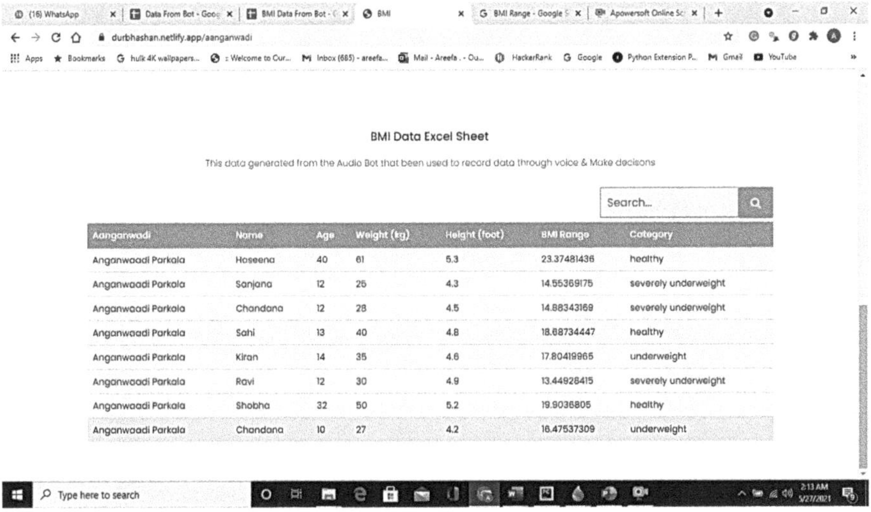

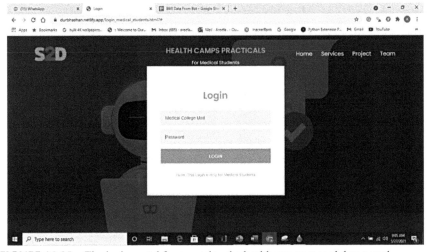

FIGURE 16.21 The data is reflected on Anganwadis service on the web portal.

16.9.4 MEDICAL COLLEGES (HEALTH CAMPS PORTAL)

The web portal designed for the medical colleges to conduct the practicals in the rural areas helps in recording the data through form into the sheet as shown in Figure 16.22 once after successful login by the registered medical colleges as per login portal in Figure 16.23.

FIGURE 16.22 The login portal for accessing the health camps record data portal.

FIGURE 16.23   Data recorded from health camps through CRUD operations.

16.9.5   *HOSPITAL APPOINTMENT REQUESTS APPROVAL*

The hospitals have login data to access their portal (Figures 16.24 and 16.25) to confirm requests and automatically send SMS as shown in Figure 16.26.

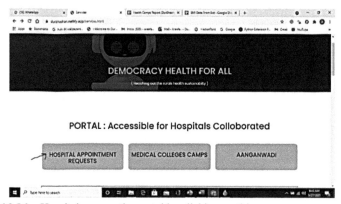

FIGURE 16.24   Hospitals access the portal by clicking on this.

FIGURE 16.25 Hospitals login and confirm the appointments.

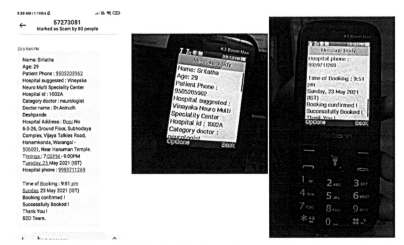

FIGURE 16.26 SMS sent to that patient's phone whose appointment was confirmed.

16.10 CONCLUSION

The end system will be a working model with complete coordination between the audio bot and the web portal. The audio bot is trained with more than about 100 health issues and corresponding symptoms with the tree traversal Decision tree algorithm with 100% accuracy. It is an audio bot, which could communicate with the people in their regional languages, which will be very useful to create awareness about the health issues and connect them to the health services. On the other hand, we have expanded the use cases by creating an automatic appointment booking system by sending the confirmation requests from the audio bot to the web portals from where the hospitals could view, confirm, and an automatic SMS would be sent to the user's mobile about the confirmation details. Our portals also help in easy conducting of the health camps and record the data directly through portals and the Anganwadis functioning, in recording the BMI and comparing the growth status of the children. Our audio bot as tested with different slang in the languages with rural people and it performs well in recognition and giving prediction. Thus, one system helps in bringing the change in the society by involving the organizations to collab and reach out to the rural.

16.11   FUTURE ENHANCEMENT

Future advancements include increasing the levels in the decision tree by increasing the data, more specifically the real-time data for the real-time implementation. This Audio Bot can be made to run over the raspberry pi 4 to make it into the product and implement in rural areas. The audio libraries can be changes to offline libraries that help in working the bot even without the internet. We can collect the tribal slangs of the people and train our model with NLP concepts for better expansion of the project even in remote areas.

Moreover, it is just a beginning, the system and our proposed approach can be utilized for many other use cases that can make lives better (https://durbhashan.netlify.app/index.html).

KEYWORDS

- **Anganwadis**
- **Appointment Booking System**
- **Decision Tree Algorithm**
- **Healthcare Audio Bot**
- **Rural Healthcare**
- **Web Portals For Medical Camps**
- **Web Technologies**

REFERENCES

1. Setiaji, B., & Wibowo, F. W., (2016). Chatbot using some knowledge in database: Human-to-machine conversation modeling. In: *2016 7th International Conference on Intelligent Systems, Modelling and Simulation (ISMS)* (pp. 72–77). IEEE.
2. Rida, S. K., Ali, Z. A., & Zeeshan, B., (2018). Artificial intelligence based smart doctor using decision tree algorithm. *Journal of Information & Communication Technology – JICT, 11*(2).
3. Chetan, B., Chinmay, P., Akshata, T., Samiksha, A., & Sachin, K., (2020). A review of AI based medical assistant chatbot. *Research and Applications of Web Development and Design, 3*(2).
4. Jha, S., & Eric, J. T. (2018). Adapting to artificial intelligence: Radiologists and pathologists as information specialists. *JAMA, 316*(22), 2353–2354.
5. Abel, D., MacGlashan, J., & Michael, L. L., (2016). Reinforcement learning as a framework for ethical decision making. *Workshops at the Thirtieth AAAI Conference on Artificial Intelligence.*
6. Ruotsalainen, M., Ala-Kleemola, T., & Visa, A., (2007). GAIS: A method for detecting interleaved sequential patterns from imperfect data. In: *Proc. IEEE Symp. Comput. Intell. Data Mining* (pp. 530–534).
7. Ahmed, I., & Singh, S., (2015). AIML based voice enabled artificial intelligent chatterbot. *International Journal of u-and e-Service, Science and Technology, 8*(2), 375–384.

CHAPTER 17

INTERNET PHARMACY BRANCH IN POLAND AND ITS LOGISTICS SUPPORT MANAGEMENT

MARTA KADŁUBEK

Department of Logistics and International Management,
Czestochowa University of Technology, Czestochowa, Poland

ABSTRACT

The chapter presents the issues of identifying the condition and structure of the Internet pharmacy branch in Poland and logistic solutions supporting the management areas of the analyzed industry. The essence of e-commerce and the conditions of logistic support for the e-commerce industry were indicated. The condition of Polish e-commerce and its logistics in statistical data, the condition and structure of the pharmaceutical market in Poland, as well as the condition and structure of the Polish e-pharmacy market were identified. The conditions for the use of logistic solutions for the Polish e-pharmacy sector were also analyzed and improvements in the management of logistic support for e-pharmacy were indicated.

17.1 INTRODUCTION

Undoubtedly, in the modern turbulent economy, a significant influence of new technologies resulting from the rapid pace of scientific and technical progress is noticeable. The dynamics of e-commerce development is also determined by the logistics solutions used. Online shopping is very popular in the EU. According to the Eurostat report [1] on e-commerce statistics for individuals, around two-thirds of Internet users in the EU in 2019 with

Handbook of Research on Artificial Intelligence and Soft Computing Techniques in Personalized Healthcare Services, Uma N. Dulhare, A. V. Senthil Kumar, Amit Datta, Seddik Bri, Ibrahiem M. M. El Emary, (Eds.)

Internet help made their purchases. On the other hand, online pharmacies, as an element of the pharmaceutical industry, intended mainly for individual customers, have already become an important and popular channel of distribution and marketing communication in the modern digital economy [2]. Polish e-pharmacies set the future direction for the dynamic development of the next e-commerce sector. One of the important areas enabling the implementation of the assumed development strategies is logistics and its support for the management processes of economic entities. Appropriate logistics solutions, allowing for the delivery and ordering process to be carried out at the time, place, and cost specified by the consumer, significantly influences building the experience of buyers, including mobile customers. The purpose of the chapter is to identify the condition and structure of the online pharmacy segment in Poland and to identify logistics solutions supporting the management areas of the analyzed segment.

17.2   THE CONCEPT AND THE ESSENCE OF E-COMMERCE

The development of the e-commerce sector has created new prospects for companies and individuals in terms of low-cost sales of a large range of products on the local and global market. Enterprises from many industries operating all over the world had to implement the advantages of e-commerce in their strategies. More than once it contributed to the expansion of their activities and forced them to adapt the company to service on new markets. The effect of this approach is to increase the level of complexity of the supply chain service, as the traditional model of logistics services is more and more often insufficient for the needs of the current customer and company.

The meaning of the terms e-commerce and e-business is often used interchangeably because they define the same range of activities and conditions that must be obtained in the electronic trading process. To classify a transaction as e-commerce, the customer must place an order via the Internet, electronic data exchange system or extranet [3]. The participants of these transactions are not only individual customers, but also enterprises that trade with a greater sales volume than in the case of a single order.

E-commerce solutions can be broadly divided into business-to-business (B2B) and business-to-client (B2C) [4]. The B2C model is used when the entire transaction is carried out directly between the buyer and seller on the websites. Meanwhile, the seller, after receiving the order, starts packing it and hands over the goods for shipment. In order to receive a large number of orders, companies must operate on a wide scale of the marketing sphere, invest in new IT infrastructure and software, and also guarantee the appropriate quality of customer service. On the other hand, B2B is distinguished by transactions of much greater value, and their venture itself carries a much greater risk. The purchase of unsuitable goods or goods of insufficient quality may place the buyer in a very difficult situation [5].

In addition to the development of the e-commerce market, the situation in the field of distribution solutions is developing very dynamically. Recently, large logistics companies focused on servicing the B2B segment. As the transport and storage processes were organized, this was how the system functioned. However, the B2C service process is completely different [6]. Currently, a consumer ordering a product wants to have it on the same day. So, the standard is a 24-hour service, companies more and more often use services that guarantee the delivery of goods on the day of ordering. Delivery within 48 hours is becoming unacceptable for a growing number of customers.

Nowadays, mobile customers make an online purchase from a place of their choice, at a convenient time, using portable devices. They smoothly move between the online and offline worlds to search for suitable offers, verify opinions, and complete a transaction. Communities are increasingly using mobile devices in the transaction process. E-retailers who want to develop a company in the mobile sphere must properly adapt their websites to mobile devices, as well as create dedicated mobile shopping applications.

Therefore, the development of e-commerce has a key impact on the functioning of trade in general. The continuous increase in demand in this area exerts the development of e-commerce on enterprises. Logistics and courier companies try to meet the expectations of consumers by offering them the shortest possible delivery time and a high level of service provision. Therefore, the future of logistics will be closely related to the development of the e-commerce industry.

17.3 LOGISTICS SUPPORT FOR THE E-COMMERCE INDUSTRY

The global conditions for the functioning of organizations and the constantly increasing complexity of logistics processes mean that today's market mechanisms are characterized by high dynamics of changes in the business sphere. The measure of their adaptation is the opportunity to shape the competitive advantage of intelligent organizations through the use of many factors that will enable the implementation of the assumed development strategies [7]. Logistics, carrying out the delivery and order at the time, place, and cost specified by the consumer, significantly influences building the experience of buyers, including mobile consumers. Modern solutions in the field of information and communication technologies (ICT) infrastructure play a fundamental role in organizations. They are based on ICT in the area of supporting logistic processes with the use of organizational and IT solutions called e-logistics.

The essence of e-logistics and its key components cannot be considered without a brief diagnosis of electronic business, which, like e-banking, e-work, e-marketing or e-finance, is closely related to it. The basics of e-commerce are becoming a crucial element in the development of all sectors of the modern economy. Overall, e-commerce is based on the widespread use of information, telecommunications, and information technologies in the area of business process management (BPM).

Along with the dynamic development of the Internet, computer networks and logistics systems, a new area of logistics has emerged, called e-logistics [8]. This term appears more and more frequently in contemporary literature, however, no uniform definition of it has yet been developed. E-logistics can be interpreted in various ways:

- as the use of e-business solutions to improve supply chains and logistics processes implemented on network platforms;
- as the use of websites, e-mail, and data exchange protocol to accelerate the exchange of information in the sphere of supply chain operation;
- as the application of modern IT solutions in the implementation of logistics processes.

The specificity of e-logistics therefore relates to effective, fully automated communication and wireless telecommunications, as well as multidirectional support for logistics activities. The use of solutions offered by e-logistics provides a wide range of benefits on many levels. Distributors, producers, suppliers, and in particular retail customers profit from this. The use of innovative IT tools in enterprises is becoming an essential aspect of gaining market advantage. Organizations, through an efficiently operating IT system, are able to define optimal solutions in the area of transport, supply, and distribution.

17.4   THE CONDITION OF POLISH E-COMMERCE AND ITS LOGISTICS IN STATISTICAL DATA

Statistical data describing the Polish e-commerce industry in the Gemius report [9] clearly confirms its development trends. In 2019, the number of e-stores in Poland amounted to almost 32,000, and in 2020, according to estimates, the number of newly created online stores exceeded 10,000. The expected increase in revenues generated by Polish e-commerce will reach as much as 40%, which will translate into generating a value close to PLN 100 billion [10]. Moreover, the analysis carried out by PricewaterhouseCoopers [11] shows that in 2026 the gross value of the Polish e-commerce market will be at the level of PLN 162 billion. This means an average annual increase of 12%.

New legal regulations and changes in stationary trade, resulting from actions aimed at limiting the spread of the COVID-19 pandemic, caused the purchasing structure to shift to the Internet network. This trend is expected to be continued. Activities that can help in-store shops encourage consumers to switch from online to offline form are certainly new services desired by e-customers, e.g., the possibility of sending and collecting courier parcels. The increase in e-commerce directly influenced the number of sending and receiving points across Poland, which are more and more often indicated as the preferred form of parcel collection. According to Polish Post's data, partner stores belonging to the company's network accounted for 48% of the total share. They recorded the highest growth dynamics, which amounted to over 18% year to year.

According to the results of the KPMG Advisory research [12], in the case of non-food purchases, only 29% of Poles make them in stationary stores during the COVID-19 pandemic (Figure 17.1). As many as 71% indicated a situation in which, however, they gave up traditional purchases and made them via the website, and 43% using the mobile application. However, only

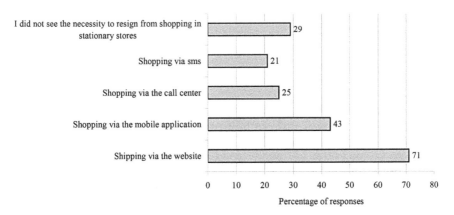

FIGURE 17.1 Poles' non-food shopping habits during the COVID-19 pandemic.
Source: Ref. [12].

1/3 of consumers rate their online shopping experience better than in-store pre-pandemic statements. Similarly, only a quarter of Poles decided that they are now better at shopping with the mobile application than before the pandemic in the store.

The main criterion for choosing an online seller is convenience, which is noted by 66% of Poles [12]. The price of the offered products came the second, while the third place was the safety that consumers began to pay more attention to during the COVID-19 pandemic. In the near future, Poles expect online sellers to be more flexible in the method of parcel delivery, which is the factor with the highest number of responses – 73%, which significantly differs from other aspects indicated by consumers (Figure 17.2).

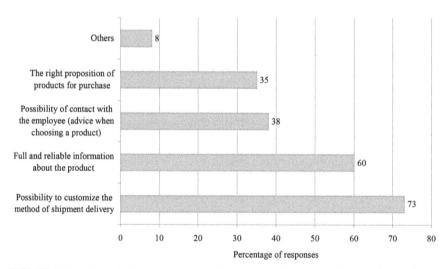

FIGURE 17.2 Aspects that consumers believe should focus on online retailers offering non-food products.

Source: Ref. [12].

During the pandemic, 1% of Poles started shopping online for the first time (Table 17.1). In turn, 34% of Poles admitted that during the pandemic they started buying new products online that they had not previously bought online. About 15% of respondents said that the outbreak of the COVID-19 pandemic changed nothing in their online shopping habits. On the other hand, 42% of consumers bought products in the same product categories as in the period preceding COVID-19, but the frequency of these purchases for individual categories has changed.

TABLE 17.1   Customer Segments – Attitudes Towards Online Shopping

No Purchases	8%	No online purchases	4%
		No online purchases during the pandemic	4%
New Purchases	35%	New customers of online stores	1%
		Customers who started buying online new product categories during the pandemic	34%
No Changes	15%	No changes in consumer behavior	15%
Change of the Purchases Frequency	42%	No changes or increase in the frequency of purchases of selected products	6%
		No changes or decrease in the frequency of purchases of selected products	4%
		No changes or different changes in the frequency of purchases for different assortment categories	32%

Source: Ref. [12].

On average, from the perspective of individual product categories, during the COVID-19 pandemic, online stores in Poland gained 6% of new customers who, before the outbreak of the pandemic, did not buy products in these categories online. The largest percentage of new customers was gained by stores offering groceries – 9% of Poles made their first grocery shopping online during the pandemic (Figure 17.3). Similarly, 8% of Poles surveyed

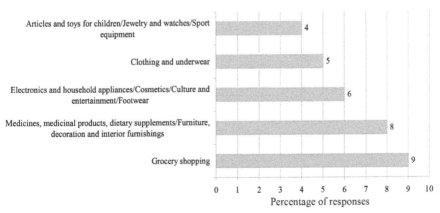

FIGURE 17.3   New online shoppers who started shopping online during COVID-19.
Source: Ref. [12].

declared that they had made purchases online for the first time in the category of drugs, medicinal products or dietary supplements. It can be argued that the genesis of these increases was related to the fear that other customers do not comply with the applicable rules of social distance, and the places of purchase (especially pharmacies) were perceived as a particular threat.

According to the report "E-commerce in Poland" [9], a change in parcel collection preferences can be noticed. The most frequently chosen form is delivery to the parcel machine (61%) slightly before delivery by courier to home (55%). Nevertheless, still the most desirable and motivating form of delivery is home courier delivery, slightly before delivery to the parcel machine. In the area of delivery, two brands of courier services achieve much better results than others – DPD and DHL. InPost is slightly behind them. People who like to use direct home or work delivery services often wish the goods they purchased to be brought home by courier. This preferred option is marked by as many as 89% of online shoppers. About 46% of those who prefer this form of delivery consider it motivating that it should be a delivery and assembly. More than half (52%) of online buyers declare that the form of return that encourages them to buy online is the possibility of free returning the product by courier (door-to-door), and 45% of respondents indicate the possibility of shipping via a parcel machine. It's worth noting that 30% of online shoppers have never returned a product.

The results of this year's report "E-commerce in Poland" [9] clearly confirm the continuation of the trend of changing the model of delivering online purchases – poles collect the parcels more and more often at the sending and receiving points (Figure 17.4). The leaders of this form, according to

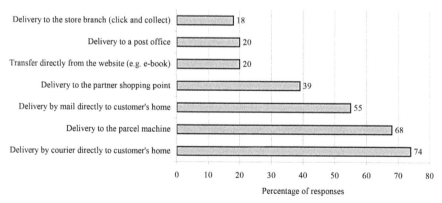

FIGURE 17.4   Forms of goods delivery motivating people to purchase via the internet.
Source: Ref. [9].

data from Sendit [13], there are InPost (parcel lockers) and Polish Post (own branches and partner stores). Consumers are gradually but permanently convinced to the new delivery model, which is the result of individual trials and purchasing experiences. Thanks to the option of point-to-point delivery, consumers gain greater flexibility in time and place (package waited for the recipient at the point, not the consignee to the courier with the package) and usually lower delivery costs.

The literature on the subject also provides analyzes of e-commerce in selected industries, in which the situation Polish market is intercorrelating with the global dimension [14]. Studies comparing the Polish market with the European market are available [15]. Many studies compare this phenomenon in the context of various markets in terms of geography (national). They are also presented in the form of summaries and comparisons in the dimension of international organizations (e.g., OECD), as well as third party logistics [16]. The factors conditioning the development of e-commerce applications are also presented from the perspective of its individual sectors. Although the vast majority of studies concern the classic e-commerce, i.e., the segment of relations between the customer and the enterprise (B2C sector), there are also studies concerning other sectors, such as the sector of trade between enterprises (B2B) [17].

17.5 THE CONDITION AND STRUCTURE OF THE PHARMACEUTICAL MARKET IN POLAND

The pharmaceutical market is a regulated market in which there is a significant influence of moderators. The functioning of enterprises, on the one hand operating in a turbulent environment with high competitiveness, and on the other hand subject to legal aspects resulting from the state policy, indicates the complexity of the general activity of pharmaceutical enterprises. Nowadays, the pharmaceutical market is thriving as one of the most developed sectors of the economy. Enterprises operating in this sector implement increasingly advanced management systems, organizational methods, and distribution processes, as the expectations of both customers and patients are constantly growing. Pharmaceutical companies, wholesalers, and pharmacies require from each other a specific level of service, terms of the contract, distribution, and high-quality services.

Poland is one of the largest markets in the pharmaceutical sector among the European Union countries. In this sector, the effective functioning of distribution is particularly important, as it must meet the requirements of pharmaceutical law and good practice in logistics solutions to respect customer needs.

A pharmacy is a public health facility where authorized persons, in particular, provide pharmaceutical services [18]. An institution whose name is reserved solely for the provision of these services is a participant in the healthcare system, including the healthcare system with social activity focused on healthcare [19]. The pharmacy provides so-called health benefits in kind, which are drugs, medical devices and auxiliaries related to the treatment process, as well as intangible services in the form of, inter alia, informing about medicines and conducting sales.

Already in 2011, Poland was the sixth largest pharmaceutical market in Europe, amounting to over PLN 20 billion in net producer prices [20]. Due to the relatively low prices of drugs, compared to the prices of other European countries (the average Polish price is approx. 44% of the European average), export significantly exceeds import. The latest forecasts permanently indicate the dynamic development of this market at an average rate of 5% per year.

The total value of the Polish pharmacy market in 2020 amounted to PLN 37.2 billion gross, recording an increase of 2.2% compared to 2019. The structure of this market according to the share in value when sold by pharmacies is [21]:

- 45.1% for reimbursed prescription drugs (Rx ref);
- 35.3% for non-reimbursed prescription drugs (Rx non-ref);
- 19.6% for over-the-counter products (Consumer Health, CH).

The largest increase was recorded in the CH segment (3.9%). This was largely due to: the growth dynamics of the e-commerce channel safe during the pandemic, growing consumption resulting from self-medication by patients with limited access to medical care, new products (increase in quantity by 23%) and an increase in prices on average to the level of PLN 15.9 for the package.

On the other hand, the increases in the Rx ref and Rx non-ref segments were lower, by 0.4% and 1.5%, respectively, which was related to the decrease in their consumption and the reduction in the number of packages in circulation, which significantly decreased: by 10% for Rx ref and as much as 30% for non-ref. Rx drugs. Packaging prices for these segments were PLN 28.30 and PLN 29.80, respectively – according to the IQVIA report [21].

The total value of sales of stationary pharmacies in December 2020 amounted to PLN 3.08 billion, recording a decrease of 3.5%. In 2020, 147.1 million packages were sold – 9.2% less than the year before.

In total, the number of pharmacies in Poland in December 2020 amounted to 13,432 and decreased on an annual basis by 345 pharmacies, including 205 for individual pharmacies and 140 for chain 5+.

In turn, the 18 largest 50+ chains in December 2020 (2,877 pharmacies) generated sales representing 33% of the total market value, and 11.6% for 11 virtual networks, respectively.

During the pandemic, very high dynamics characterized the still small, but dynamically growing, sales channel through e-pharmacies, which generated PLN 1.07 billion in sales in 2020, 44% more than in 2019.

17.6   THE CONDITION AND STRUCTURE OF THE POLISH E-PHARMACY MARKET

The importance of the online pharmacy sector is significant, and in the coming years it will increase even more [22], which is confirmed by the systematically increasing number of pharmacies and the aging of the Polish society [23].

The USA remains a pioneer in the mail order sale of drugs. Mail-order sale of drugs in the USA has a long, more than 40-year history, and currently constitutes a significant part of the drug retail channel. The development of e-commerce in the area of pharmacy is also noticeable in the territory of the countries forming the European Union, although due to the lack of uniform regulations in this area, the aforementioned development is uneven. Poland belongs to the category of countries where mail order sale of drugs is allowed only under OTC drugs, and for example, Germany and the United Kingdom allow, apart from selling OTC drugs, also the sale of prescription drugs.

Internet portals usually constitute a strong price competition for traditional entities, thanks to the lower costs of running a business, although in the case of legally operating Polish online pharmacies, they must be based on a traditional outlet. However, the capacity of the market varies considerably, as e-pharmacies cover the entire territory of the country, often offering shipment of goods abroad.

The key to the success of the online market is also often effective and cheap distribution – articles distributed via e-pharmacies are cheaper by nearly 10% compared to prices in traditional pharmacies.

The term online pharmacy does not exist in Polish law, although it is used in everyday language and in the documentation kept by provincial pharmaceutical inspectorates. Pharmacies operating on the Internet are defined as generally accessible pharmacies or pharmacy outlets that conduct mail-order sales of drugs based on an order submitted using the form available on the facility's website. The activity of mail order sale of medicinal products is regulated by the provisions of the Act of 6 September 2001 – Pharmaceutical Law [18] and the Regulation of the Minister of Health of March 26, 2015 on mail order sale of medicinal products [24]. Pursuant to the provisions of Polish law, the mail-order sale of medicinal products may only be carried out by generally accessible pharmacies and pharmacy outlets, which is tantamount to the need for these entities to meet all requirements and have the necessary permits provided for by the legislator for this type of entities.

With a view to ensuring the appropriate quality, the regulation specifies the conditions for the mail-order sale of medicinal products without prescription and the method of delivering these products to recipients. Thus, e-pharmacies are not typical online stores, but only new distribution channels for products offered for sale in a traditional pharmacy under the conditions set out in the regulations.

Since 2004, when the first online pharmacies appeared in Poland, the online drug market was organizing and developing, and the rules for the operation of pharmacies on the Internet were shaped. In recent years, various entities have appeared and withdrawn from the market, the balance of power and regulations concerning the online sale of drugs have changed. Despite the complexities and turmoil of legal nature, the interest in buying medicines online is growing, in line with the upward trend in total Internet trade turnover.

At the moment, 143 online pharmacies are actively operating in Poland [25], and there are as many as 321 registered in the Central Health Information System (CSIOZ) as mail-order ones. The discrepancies result from the fact that the lists contain many inactive domains. Additionally, some chains report several or a dozen traditional pharmacies as mail order pharmacies – but they sell under one internet domain.

In 2011, there were about 165 active online pharmacies (out of 180 registered in CSIOZ). In 2016, the number of active e-pharmacies increased by over 30 entities to 197 pharmacies. In May 2019, although the number of pharmacies entered in the register as mail order pharmacies increased to 326 entities, the number of active and selling websites decreased by as many as 40 entities.

Last year (in February 2020), although the number of pharmacies entered into the register as mail order pharmacies was 317 entities, the number of active and selling websites dropped to 139 entities (Figure 17.5).

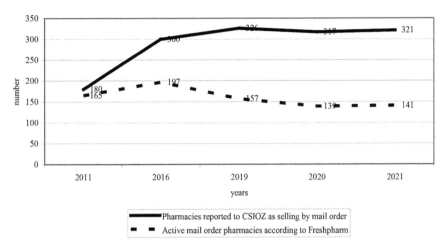

FIGURE 17.5 Number of pharmacies reported to CSIOZ as selling by mail order and number of active mail order pharmacies according to Freshpharm.

Source: Ref. [25].

In the area of the physical location of active pharmacies selling by mail order, the clear leaders are the Łódzkie (25 pharmacies) and Mazowieckie (22 pharmacies) voivodeships. In the remaining voivodships, the number of e-pharmacies is smaller, ranging from a few to a dozen or so entities (Figure 17.6).

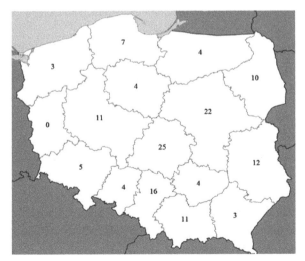

FIGURE 17.6 Number of e-pharmacies in voivodships of Poland.

Source: Ref. [25].

According to the report "E-commerce" [9], as in the case of cosmetics and perfumes, also when it comes to pharmaceutical products, Internet users first reach for various types of information sources. The search engine is important, but also the websites of online stores and price comparison engines (Figure 17.7).

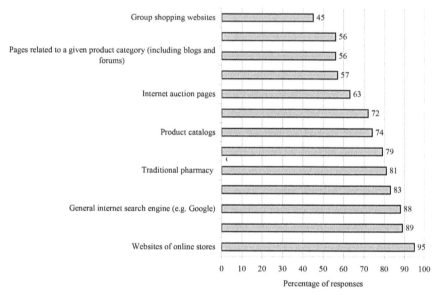

FIGURE 17.7   Sources of information used for e-purchases of pharmaceutical products.
Source: Ref. [9].

According to experts on the online pharmaceutical market, in the near future it can be expected [26]:

- Consolidation of the online pharmacy market, caused by acquisitions of small entities and traditional pharmacies by "large players."
- Slowdown in the increase in the number of new pharmacies, mainly due to the introduction of a new, more restrictive law and the related difficulty in building a competitive advantage.
- Reducing competition and increasing prices, because the introduced regulations reward leaders and reduce the chance of success for new websites.
- An increase in the costs of promotion and business activities.
- Creating new solutions to circumvent unfavorable legal provisions.

- Slowdown of the market growth dynamics, which so far has been growing at a pace of 15–20% annually, several times faster than the traditional market.

Online pharmaceutical trade is highly controversial, and the views of the participants in this debate can be extremely polarized. On the other hand, the literature on the subject [27–29] indicates numerous benefits for buyers of online pharmacies related to this form of distribution. Undoubtedly, however, the Internet offer facilitates access to goods, guarantees a 24-hour overview of the offer along with the price of products and delivery costs. It allows patients to read information materials, eliminates geographic restrictions, and facilitates comparisons between the offers of individual stores. Therefore, it favors the environment of disabled people with reduced mobility or territorially excluded people for whom access to this segment of the healthcare market has been limited so far. In addition, the portals, apart from the product offer, also publish information on selected disease entities, recommendations related to lifestyle, nutrition, prevention, and simple health counseling.

17.7 CONDITIONS FOR THE USE OF LOGISTICS SOLUTIONS FOR THE POLISH E-PHARMACY SECTOR

A number of obligations are imposed by law on a pharmacy or pharmacy point selling medicinal products by mail order. They concern the prerequisites for conducting mail order sales and its subsequent stages – concluding a contract, implementation, and documenting the order, as well as the obligations of pharmacies and pharmacy outlets towards buyers after the delivery of medicinal products [30]. According to the law, a pharmacist or a pharmaceutical technician must be appointed to process online orders, whose task is to check the preparation of shipment and transport conditions. The employee preparing the product for shipment should select the appropriate medicine, mark the outer packaging with the identification data of the facility, the recipient's details and the place of delivery. Each order should be subject to electronic records, ensuring that no entries will be deleted, and that each change will be marked with the personal data and position of the person making the amendment. The medicinal product should be protected against external factors, in particular against contamination, theft or mechanical damage. It should also be taken care of the appropriate storage temperature and the lack of access to light, water, and other factors harmful to the drug. The product should be transported in a separate part of the means of transport, preventing the access of unauthorized persons, as well as temperature control during transport.

The shaping and selection of transport solutions is undoubtedly a key element of logistics for e-pharmacy. A properly shaped and managed system for transporting and storing drugs and medical materials has a major impact on significant technical and economic parameters both in pharmaceutical wholesalers and the course of the processes of the services provided [31].

For several years, a strong trend in the development of the click and collect model has been visible on the market, in which the patient on the website of the online platform books products (medicines, supplements, cosmetics) and collects the order at a stationary pharmacy of his or her choice. Platforms based on pharmaceutical wholesalers and a network of cooperating pharmacies operate in this system.

There are also entities operating in the mixed model, which both ship orders and have a network of outlets for personal pickup. Entities operating in the classic click and collect model do not have to be registered as a mail-order pharmacy, because they do not actually run it. However, they are significant (and intensively developing) players on the online market for the sale of drugs, supplements, and dermocosmetics.

As at the study conducted by Głowiak [25] in February 2021, there were 143 active online pharmacies and click and collect platforms in Poland, with 5 active platforms operating in the click and collect model (Figure 17.8). The three platforms operate in a mixed model, offering mail order sales and personal pickup at the same time in a network of partner outlets. The other 2 platforms only allow for personal collection of ordered products.

In the study by Głowiak [25] it was assumed that an online pharmacy is:

- a pharmacy reported to the Provincial Pharmaceutical Inspectorate as conducting mail order sales and actively conducting this sale on a functioning website.
- a website where you can order drugs, regardless of whether they are sent by courier, by post or it is possible to collect them in person; this group also includes entities operating in a pure click and collect model.
- a website with a consistent visual identity and a price and assortment strategy – regardless of how many traditional pharmacies (e.g., associated in the network) sell goods using it.

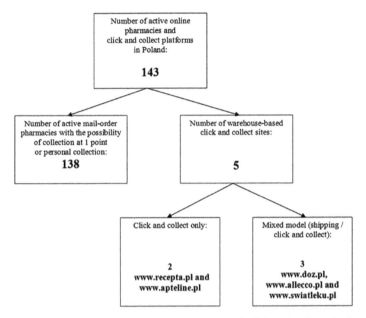

FIGURE 17.8 Division of active online pharmacies and click and collect platforms on the Polish e-pharmacy market.

Source: Ref. [25].

Ignjatović & Stanić [32] mention a number of advantages of the mail order sale of drugs, which include:

- Reduction of drug costs (benefit not only for the patient but also for the healthcare system in the case of extending the mail order sale with reimbursed drugs).
- Reducing the costs of running a business (no need to have an apartment in a good location, no network of premises and no costs of maintaining them).
- Increasing competition (possibility of instant, automatic comparison of product prices).
- Availability (home delivery) of medicines for the sick, the elderly, and those who have problems with moving.
- The possibility of placing an order for a drug around the clock, access to the hotline dedicated to the purchased products.
- Ease of reaching the patient in the event of a decision to withdraw or suspend a given drug from marketing, contact with a pharmacist by phone, e-mail, etc.

17.8 IMPROVEMENTS IN THE MANAGEMENT OF LOGISTICS SUPPORT CONDITIONS FOR THE POLISH E-PHARMACY

Logistics issues for e-pharmacy are gaining importance from the point of view of rationalization and management of its processes. For each drug has only a certain value if it can be disposed of at a time when it is needed. Therefore, there is a need to treat logistics support as a process related to the implementation of pharmaceutical services. Considering logistics in terms of a system allows for the rationalization of transport and storage systems, but also for the creation of close links in integrated distribution chains [33].

Logistics processes for e-pharmacy are an essential element of the integration of material flows, which require coordination and mutual adjustment of many parameters in the supply chain management of pharmacy entities. In addition, the following are integrally linked with the technical systems implementing physical material flows:

- Information flows (along with the sphere of integrated automatic identification activities);
- Decision flows (the sphere of control and management of material flows).

The logistics of pharmaceuticals, apart from pharmaceutical companies, are handled by proven, international third-party logistics for whom it is feasible to meet the relevant requirements. The legal requirements are also becoming more and more restrictive from year to year. In addition, each of the processes is supervised by the relevant state authorities, which strictly enforce the imposed procedures, and this forces a specific activity [34]. There has been a group of proven, usually international third-party logistics on the market for years, providing services to the pharmaceutical industry, who have gained the trust of customers, deal with the maze of regulations and meet legal requirements.

Restrictive legal regulations and the difficult issue of guaranteeing the safety of a medicinal product during transport and handling are the barriers that discourage other operators from serving this industry.

If a third party logistics is to distribute medicines in accordance with the law and ensure an adequate level of safety, it must use similar organizational and technical solutions as the manufacturer, and the logistics processes carried out must be planned, coordinated, and consistent in management process. Full identification of the goods must be carried out, including the batch number of the product, as well as efficient and effective supervision over the expiry dates of products and over products withheld or withdrawn from the market. Companies should also constantly monitor the side effects of drugs and reduce the logistic costs of warehouse operation by reducing the level of inventories and increasing their rotation. It is necessary to implement risk analyzes and identify the critical points of each stage of the logistics chain [35]. Attention should be paid to the high level of personnel qualifications and the development of the technical infrastructure used.

Thus, for pharmaceutical companies, the determinant of selecting a specific third-party logistics should be experience in servicing the pharmaceutical industry (process security), the comprehensive offer and the firm's specialization in servicing this industry [36]. It is a mistake made by producers to associate with a well-known logistics market tycoon, which has proven solutions in the field of warehousing and full truckload transport, but does not have a distribution system well managed that guarantees timely and safe delivery, an appropriate number of means of specialized transport, a system of transshipment chambers, the possibility of tracking and documenting transport conditions, etc.

A visible direction in the area of building the supply chain by carriers is looking for solutions that reduce the costs of shipment delivery. The last mile is one of the most important phases of the online order fulfillment process, which when properly managed can significantly reduce the operating costs of logistics and courier companies [37]. Multiple attempts to deliver the package when there is no recipient at the address indicated not only generate additional costs, but also result in the dissatisfaction of both parties to the process. By optimizing their own processes, including the emphasis on cost-effectiveness, as well as following the expectations of consumers, carriers develop the service of pick-up at the point understood broadly, not only through the prism of parcel machines. Thanks to this, the e-customer can pick up the parcel at any time, in the place of his or her choice.

The number of parcel collection points in Poland is constantly growing, as it is a response to the expectations of e-consumers in terms of convenience and ease of collection, as well as due to mass online shopping and the increase in the number of parcels appearing in the market. The possibilities of sending and receiving points, parcel machines or retail outlets, are limited, hence the need to launch new ones. This is done not only by building them from scratch (e.g., building new machines), but also by using the already available infrastructure of stationary trade. Today, thanks to the appropriate technology, each store or commercial network can become a sending and receiving point, increasing the scope of its services and expanding the group of potential customers [38].

The popularization of collection points as the preferred form of delivery and the customer's migration towards online shopping causes that the logistics industry is looking for optimal e-logistics solutions that are to combine all the components in management process, i.e., e-commerce consumer, retail network outlets and the courier industry – into one coherent whole. Carriers, diversifying their offer, focus on cooperation with chains and stationary stores – for this purpose, they use the already available facilities, instead of building new sending and receiving points or building their own parcel machines. It is the maximization of the market potential in the existing sales structure of stationary outlets. The combination of the online and offline world translates into a set of named and obvious benefits resulting from the resulting synergy [39].

The store or retail network must be visible on a map showing available pickup points for a shipment ordered online. Few companies still offer the service of locating a point on the map [40]. Thanks to this solution, e-customers who want to collect their parcel, in the online ordering process, will be able to choose not only popular parcel machines or partner networks known to them and present on the map, but, e.g., their local store, which they are closest to. When picking up the order, customers will most likely also make purchases there, contributing to an increase in the turnover of a given business. In a natural way, an additional influx of e-customers in a given network facility is built, without the necessity to incur additional, paid marketing activities.

The recently introduced smart-points systems have become a modern e-logistics solution, bringing benefits to all entities of the purchase and sale transaction. The project combines the needs and expectations of both the e-customers striving for the convenience of picking up the parcel at the time and place of their choice, the e-store that cares about the satisfaction and loyalty of the consumers, and the traditional offline store, which by joining smart-points, introduces a new service. Thus, acting as a post office, traditional trade gains the opportunity to acquire a group of new customers and generate additional income resulting from the very fact of serving an e-customer – both in the context of the collection service and the sale of products from its own offer. Smart-points with its idea naturally fits in the trend of popularizing the collection of parcels at the point. Perhaps this management model is a "business vitamin," thanks to which traditional trade will reduce losses or, moreover, improve its condition caused by the loss of customers during the pandemic.

Currently, innovative ways of handling parcels are being tested, which do not involve the seller, who is able to deliver or send a parcel in a few seconds. A machine dedicated to the convenience chain was developed, which will enable customers to send and collect parcels on their own. The device is able to handle up to 140 shipments per day and takes up only 0.6 sq m of retail space. The rest of the installation can be located behind the shelves on which the goods are placed. The use of retail space, so valuable in stores, is therefore minimal. Shipment delivery is handled by the latest generation Cartesian robot, operating in several axes and moving with remarkable precision and speed. Thanks to this solution, an even better response to the needs of customers is assumed, who will be able to send or collect a package quickly and comfortably on their way to work or home.

Linking online commerce with traditional commerce is part of the omnichannel concept, i.e., multi-channel customer management in the form of design, implementation, coordination, and evaluation of channels in order to increase customer value through effective customer acquisition, maintenance, and development [41–44]. The effective functioning of the omnichannel strategy is determined by certain conditions, e.g., warehouse logistics management, the possibility of returning goods purchased online at a stationary point and vice versa, fast and effective exchange of information between customer databases, orders, products, and standardization of payment methods in all used channels.

17.9 CONCLUSION

The challenges of logistics support for the e-pharmacy industry are subordinated to the most important – meeting the growing demands of the customers. Research shows that customer satisfaction largely depends on the convenience of the "first mile," simplicity of the process management, and low costs. Hence the huge pressure of e-pharmacies to reduce logistics costs while maintaining the quality of service. When joining a logistics support organization, e-pharmacies basically have two options. They can do it themselves or outsource the entire process or its individual stages to external companies. The vast majority of e-pharmacies decide to take advantage of the offer of specialists who prepare the infrastructure together with the IT system, design processes, employ employees and build competencies in the area of optimal logistics solutions. Modern logistics solutions, such as, for example, parcel machines, parcel collection and shipping points, the click and collect system and the most innovative solutions that optimize last mile costs, allow for effective improvement of entity management processes in the area of liquidity of deliveries, which in today's extremely competitive e-pharmacy can determine the survival of the entrepreneur.

KEYWORDS

- **e-Commerce**
- **e-Pharmacy**
- **Goods Delivery**
- **Internet Pharmacy Branch**
- **Logistics**
- **Management**
- **Polish Pharmacy Market**

REFERENCES

1. Eurostat, (2020). *E-commerce Statistics for Individuals.* https://ec.europa.eu/info/departments/eurostat-european-statistics_pl (accessed on 24 January 2023).
2. Szymański, G., (2018). The essence and development of online pharmacies as a trend of contemporary economic reality – implications for the management process. *Przegląd Organizacji, 9*, 41–46. doi: 10.33141/po.2018.09.06.
3. Deges, F., (2020). *Grundlagen Des E-Commerce.* Wiesbaden, Springer. doi: 10.1007/978-3-658-26320-1.
4. Faraoni, M., Rialti, R., Zollo, L., & Pellicelli, A. C., (2019). Exploring e-loyalty antecedents in B2C e-commerce: Empirical results from Italian grocery retailers. *British Food Journal, 121*(2), 574–589. doi: 10.1108/BFJ-04-2018-0216.
5. Hua, N., Hight, S., Wei, W., Ozturk, A. B., Zhao, X. R., Nusair, K., & DeFranco, A., (2019). The power of e-commerce: Does e-commerce enhance the impact of loyalty programs on hotel operating performance? *International Journal of Contemporary Hospitality Management, 31*(4), 1906–1923. doi: 10.1108/IJCHM-02-2018-0168.
6. Yu, Y., Wang, X., Zhong, R. Y., & Huang, G. Q., (2017). E-commerce logistics in supply chain management. *Industrial Management & Data Systems, 117*(10), 2263–2286. doi: 10.1108/IMDS-09-2016-0398.
7. Lim, S. F. W. T., Jin, X., & Srai, J. S., (2018). Consumer-driven e-commerce: A literature review, design framework, and research agenda on last-mile logistics models. *International Journal of Physical Distribution & Logistics Management, 48*(3), 308–332. doi: 10.1108/IJPDLM-02-2017-0081.

8. Gołembska, E., Bentyn, Z., & Gołembski, M., (2017). *Service Logistics*. Warszawa, Wydawnictwo Naukowe PWN.

9. Gemius, (2020). *E-commerce w Polsce*. Warszawa, Gemius.

10. Central Statistical Office, (2021). *Internet Retail*. Warszawa, Główny Urząd Statystyczny.

11. Pricewaterhouse, C., (2021). *Prospects for the Development of the e-Commerce Market in Poland.* Warszawa, PricewaterhouseCoopers.

12. KPMG Advisory, (2020). *A New Reality: The Consumer in the Age of COVID-19*. How the shopping habits of Poles have changed during the coronavirus. Warszawa, KPMG Advisory.

13. Sendit, S. A., (2021). https://sendit.pl (accessed on 24 January 2023).

14. Śliwczyński, B., Komorowska, M., Statkiewicz, W., & Horzela, A., (2019). The new silk road: An opportunity and a challenge for Poczta Polska in handling the import and transit of e-commerce cargo from China to Europe. *Logistics, 6*, 20–27.

15. Jędrzejczak-Gas, J., Barska, A., & Sinicakova, M., (2019). Level of development of e-commerce in EU countries. *Management, 23*(1), 209–224. doi: 10.2478/manment-2019-0012.

16. Konopielko, Ł., Wołoszyn, M., & Wytrębowicz, J., (2016). Handel elektroniczny, ewolucja i perspektywy (Warszawa, Oficyna Wydawnicza Uczelni Łazarskiego. E-commerce, evolution and prospects (Warszawa, Oficyna Wydawnicza Uczelni Łazarskiego.)

17. Strzębicki, D., (2016). Czynniki rozwoju rynków elektronicznych B2B [Factors of development of B2B electronic markets]. *Handel Wewnętrzny, 3*, 329–340.

18. Dziennik, U., (2001). Act of September 6, 2001: Pharmaceutical law. *Journal of Laws, 126, 1381*.

19. Stankiewicz, R., (2016). Instytucje rynku farmaceutycznego [Pharmaceutical Market Institutions] (Warszawa, Wydawnictwo Wolters Kluwer).

20. Instytut Badań nad Gospodarką Rynkową; Strategia rozwoju krajowego przemysłu farmaceutycznego do roku 2030 [Institute for Market Economics Research; National industry development strategy pharmaceutical industry by 2030] (Warszawa, Instytut Badań nad Gospodarką Rynkową,, 2018).

21. IQVIA, (2020). Struktura i dynamika rynku farmaceutycznego, zachowań lekarzy i pacjentów oraz dystrybucji leków w roku 2020 – kluczowe fakty [The structure and dynamics of the pharmaceutical market, the behavior of doctors and patients and drug distribution in 2020 – key facts]. https://iqvia.com (accessed on 24 January 2023).

22. Taylor, D., (2016). The pharmaceutical industry and the future of drug development. In: Hester, R. E., & Harrison, R. M., (eds.), *Pharmaceuticals in the Environment* (pp. 1–33). Cambridge, The Royal Society of Chemistry.

23. Adamczyk, M. D., (2017). The aging of the polish society is a challenge for sustainable development. *Scientific Journals of the Silesian University of Technology, series: Organization and Management, 106*(1981), 105–113. doi: 10.29119/1641-3466.2017.106.

24. Dziennik, U., (2015). Regulation of the minister of health of 26 March 2015 on mail order sales of medicinal products. *Journal of Laws, 481*.

25. Głowiak, G., (2021). *Ile Jest Aptek Internetowych w Polsce?* https://eapteki.info (accessed on 24 January 2023).

26. IPSOS, (2018). *Badanie Polski Konsument 2018*. https://ipsos.pl (accessed on 24 January 2023).

27. Prashanti, G., Sravani, S., & Noorie, S., (2017). A review on online pharmacy. *IOSR Journal of Pharmacy and Biological Sciences, 12*(3), 32–34. doi: 10.9790/3008-1203043234.
28. Soboń, M., (2016). Methods of operation and market success factors of online pharmacies. *Internal Trade, 362*, 291–304.
29. Arif, M. J., El Emary, I. M. M., & Koutsouris, D. D., (2014). A review on the technologies and services used in the self-management of health and independent living of elderly. *Technology and Health Care, 22*(2), 677–687. doi: 10.3233/THC-140851.
30. Łapińska, J., & Kądzielawski, G., (2018). Bariery zakupu produktów farmaceutycznych przez internet. [Barriers to the purchase of pharmaceutical products via the Internet.] *Handel Wewnętrzny [Internal Trade], 4*(375), 190–199.
31. Yılmaz, E. S., Kockaya, G., Yenilmez, F. B., Saylan, M., Tatar, M., Akbulat, A., Gursoz, H., & Kerman, S., (2016). Impact of health policy changes on trends in the pharmaceutical market in Turkey. *Value in Health Regional Issues, 10*, 48–52. doi: 10.1016/j.vhri.2016.07.002.
32. Ignjatović, D., & Stanić, M., (2019). Contemporary marketing in pharmacy with the focus on the e-pharmacy concept. *FINIZ 2019 – Digitization and Smart Financial Reporting* (pp. 78–84). Serbia. doi: 10.15308/finiz-2019-78-84.
33. Tsang, Y. P., Wu, C. H., Lam, H. Y., Choy, K. L., & Ho, G. T. S., (2021). Integrating internet of things and multi-temperature delivery planning for perishable food e-commerce logistics: A model and application. *International Journal of Production Research, 59*(5), 1534–1556. doi: 10.1080/00207543.2020.1841315.
34. Mangiaracina, R., Perego, A., Seghezzi, A., & Tumino, A., (2019). Innovative solutions to increase last-mile delivery efficiency in B2C e-commerce: A literature review. *International Journal of Physical Distribution & Logistics Management, 49*(9), 901–920. doi: 10.1108/IJPDLM-02-2019-0048.
35. Grima, S., Spiteri, J. V., & Thalassinos, E., (2020). Risk management models and theories. *Frontiers in Applied Mathematics and Statistics, 18*, 6–8. doi: 10.3389/fams.2020.00008.
36. Vipin, J., Arya, S., & Gupta, R., (2019). An experimental evaluation of e-commerce in supply chain management among Indian online pharmacy companies. *International Journal of Recent Technology and Engineering, 8*(3S), 438–445. doi: 10.35940/ijrte.C1092.1083S19.
37. Ren, S., Choi, T. M., Lee, K. M., & Lin, L., (2020). Intelligent service capacity allocation for cross-border-e-commerce related third party forwarding logistics operations: A deep learning approach. *Transportation Research Part E: Logistics and Transportation Review, 134*, https://doi.org/10.1016/j.tre.2019.101834.
38. Seaton, H. S., (2018). The new e-commerce/home delivery retail distribution paradigm. *Journal of Transportation Management, 29*(1), 7–25. doi: 10.22237/jotm/1530446520.
39. Ying, Y., Wang, X., Zhong, R. Y., & Huang, G. Q., (2017). E-commerce logistics in supply chain management: Implementations and future perspective in furniture industry. *Industrial Management & Data Systems, 117*(10), 2263–2286. doi: 10.1016/j.procir.2016.08.002.
40. Goldmann, M., (2021). E-logistics in 2020 and 2021 – increasing importance of last mile logistics. *Logistics, 5*, 4.
41. Abramek, E., (2019). Wiedza o kliencie podstawą strategii i komunikacji omnichannel. Prace Naukowe Uniwersytetu Ekonomicznego w Katowicach, Procesy modelowania danych i podejmowania decyzji w architekturze systemowej przedsiębiorstwa [Customer

knowledge as the basis of omnichannel strategy and communication. Works Research at the University of Economics in Katowice, Data modeling processes and-decision-making in the system architecture of the enterprise], 11–27.

42. Kemendi, A., Michelberger, P., & Mesjasz-Lech, A., (2021). ICT security in businesses–efficiency analysis. *Entrepreneurship and Sustainability Issues, 9*(1), 123–149. doi: 10.9770/jesi.2021.9.1(8).

43. Illes, C. B., Nowicka-Skowron, M., Horska, E., & Dunay, A., (2017). *Management and Organization: Concepts, Tools and Applications.* Harlow, Pearson.

44. Piotrowicz, W., & Cuthbertson, R., (2019). *Exploring Omnichannel Retailing: Common Expectations and Diverse Realities.* Switzerland, Springer.

CHAPTER 18

EFFECTIVE EMERGENCY TRANSPORTATION AND COMMUNICATION FOR SAVING HUMAN LIVES DURING DISASTER

WALUNJKAR GAJANAN MADHAVRAO[1,2] and V. SRINIVASA RAO[3]

[1]Research Scholar, Computer Science, and Engineering, Vel Tech Rangarajan Dr. Sagunthala R&D Institute of Science and Technology, Chennai, Tamil Nadu, India

[2]Assistant Professor, Army Institute of Technology, Pune, Maharashtra, India

[3]Professor, Vel Tech Rangarajan Dr. Sagunthala R&D Institute of Science and Technology, Chennai, Tamil Nadu, India

ABSTRACT

When any disaster like earthquake, fire or flood situation occurs then to save people lives communication among civil protection forces such as rescue team should be faster. Providing effective healthcare services in disasters is at most important. A lifetime of the network and various other parameters such as time to travel packets to the destination and communication with acknowledgment plays vital role. It is difficult to trust on any infrastructured network hence ad hoc networks are most trusted here. A mobility model specifies the movement of rescue team members and its specific patterns inside the network. Areas are classified into distinct zones in the Disaster Mobility Model, such as IL, CCS, PWT, TOC, and APP. In DM model, the area is divided based on the method of separation of rooms. Leader in TOC

Handbook of Research on Artificial Intelligence and Soft Computing Techniques in Personalized Healthcare Services, Uma N. Dulhare, A. V. Senthil Kumar, Amit Datta, Seddik Bri, Ibrahiem M. M. El Emary, (Eds.)
© 2024 Apple Academic Press, Inc. Co-published with CRC Press (Taylor & Francis)

guides the movements within the areas. Various transport troops are present between PWT and CCS which are pedestrians to carry patients. Optimal path is selected using machine learning (ML) especially reinforcement learning (RL) to reach in shortest amount of time and also avoids obstacles. Hospitals are not a part of the disaster area network. APP transports the patients to the hospitals. All nodes should avoid obstacles and perform communication to the destination nodes. In this chapter, optimized RL method is proposed and analyzed using disaster scenario. The main intention is to minimize the losses of human lives by proper and faster communication and transportation among various units in disaster scenario, which will also reduce the healthcare consequences of natural disasters.

18.1   INTRODUCTION

Natural disasters like earthquake, tsunami, and typhoons occur every year. Proper and planned rescue operations will save numerous lives [1]. Maximum chances to save the human lives are considered to be 48–72 hours after disaster occurs. When any disaster like earthquake, fire or flood situation occurs then to save people lives, communication among the rescue team should be faster. Lifetime of the network and various other parameters such as time to travel packets to the destination, communication with acknowledgment plays a vital role. It is difficult to trust on any infrastructured network which might be partially or fully destroyed. It is also not possible to deploy such fixed network in a short time. This signifies the importance of ad hoc networks which are easily deployed in such situation. Ad hoc network does not require infrastructure like internet or any fixed networked line. More flexible and robust communication is established using ad hoc networks. Such types of networks are not only useful in natural disasters but also useful in man-made disasters. Nodes which are closer (visible) can transmit the packets directly else multi-hop communication takes place to communicate among far (invisible) nodes [2]. In disaster situation, the first 72 hours are treated as golden hour because maximum lives can be saved within this period. For proper and uninterrupted disaster management operation, network lifetime should be high. Due to the node's mobility, MANET's faces lots of routing problems and communication issues. Routing is a mechanism which forwards the packets hop by hop through intermediate mobile nodes. In single hop, nodes can communicate directly. In multi-hop communication, nodes communicate through intermediate nodes.

This chapter is constructed as follows: Section 18.2 explains the need for ad hoc networks and the use of various mobility models in ad hoc networks. Section 18.3 describes the importance of reinforcement learning (RL) and its use in designing network models and algorithms. Section 18.4 analyzes the survey of various routing protocols and RL algorithms implemented so far to evaluate the network. Section 18.5 describes the research methodology which will describe adaptive routing, reinforcement-based routing and design of new routing algorithm and various optimization done to achieve the better results. This section also explains the need of RL mechanism for disaster area scenario to find the path dynamically. Section 18.6 shows results and analysis which compares the proposed algorithm with existing protocols and evaluate the performance against the loss of packets, delay, and average energy utilization.

18.2 CHARACTERISTIC OF MANET, ROUTING, AND MOBILITY MODELS

In this section, we will discuss the various characteristics of MANET, routing process and use of various mobility models.

MANET characteristics are as follows:

1. **Multi-Hopping:** There is no such predefined router instead, packets go through various intermediate nodes and finally reaches to the destination.

2. **Mobility:** There will be random movement of nodes. Analysis of topology is used to analyze the simulation design, protocol analysis, and analysis of various QoS parameters.

3. **Self-Organization:** There is no external entity in a network to give directions to other nodes in the network, instead, nodes generate this information intelligently and configures without any external entity.

4. **Limited Energy:** All nodes are of having limited energy as they are operated using batteries. Energy of nodes decides the lifetime of the whole network. Lifetime of such mobile network is an important issue in such a scenario.

5. **Reconfiguration:** Such ad hoc networks are reconfigurable and self-recoverable.

Figure 18.1 shows how sender mobile nodes communicate with destination using multiple hops presents inside a network. Nodes use multi-hop communication in case of far nodes while direct communication takes place in closer nodes. Nodes are powered by batteries. Energy is required to remain in the network. Energy consumption management is also required for below reasons:

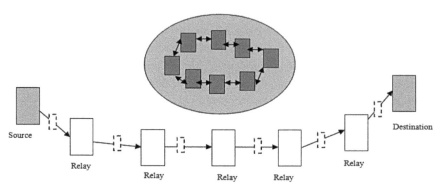

FIGURE 18.1   MANET.

1. **Limited Energy Storage:** The nodes have limited battery power.

2. **Battery Replacement Limitations:** In disaster situations, battery replacement is very difficult. Each node in MANET consumes energy in four states, send and receive, ideal and sleep states. Energy aware criteria that affect the energy aware routing are as follows:

    i. **Minimizing the Energy Consumed per Packet:** This measure minimizes the average energy consumption per packet.

    ii. **Maximizing Network Partitioning Time:** The purpose of this measure is to increase the network lifetime.

    iii. **Minimizing Difference in Power Levels of Nodes:** This is to make sure that nodes stay alive and work in collaboration.

    iv. Minimizing the cost of sending a packet.

    v. Minimizing the maximum cost of the node.

18.2.1 ROUTING PROTOCOLS

Routing in MANET is two steps process – forwarding packet to the next node and routing packets to the destination. Performance of any routing protocol is very important, and which can be evaluated using various QoS parameters. Routing protocols are classified into two groups – pro-active and on-demand. Paths are always available in proactive routing protocols and will direct the packets to flow from one node to other nodes. DSDV and OLSR are pro-active protocols. It is observed that more delay occurs in DSDV protocol due to its proactive nature. AODV gives good performance in such a scenario. In on-demand routing protocols communication path is obtained when there is a need. DSR, AODV, AOMDV are on-demand protocols. DSDV protocol is energy expensive with an increase in mobility of nodes but having less delay. In ADOV protocol, each node sets a reverse path on forwarding the request next hop neighbor. Energy efficient periodic update is not required as compared with DSDV. In DSR, every node store path information in route cache such that if another source node request path to the same destination, the intermediate node can reply immediately. If there is any change in the path, it updates cache information periodically. AODV, DSR, and AOMDV are more suitable in such scenario to prevent the loss of packets due to its reactive nature.

18.2.2 MOBILITY MODEL

A mobility model specifies the movement patterns inside the network. It specifies the random patterns to realistic patterns of movement of nodes. Mobility models are classified as random movement, temporal dependencies, and spatial dependencies and based on geographic restrictions. Figure 18.2 shows the classification of different mobility models.

RWP specifies random movement of nodes inside the network. In Manhattan mobility model, nodes move to selected or pre-decided paths like vehicles. Group behavior simulation is done using RPGM model where node belongs to a group and follows the path directed by a group leader. Initially, all nodes are randomly distributed across a single reference point and follow the instructions of a group leader. In post-disaster scenarios, all rescue members are divided into groups and follow communication and coordination among rescue members. In DM model, area is divided based on the method of separation of rooms such as IL, PWT, CCS, APP, and TOC (Figures 18.3 and 18.4) [3, 4].

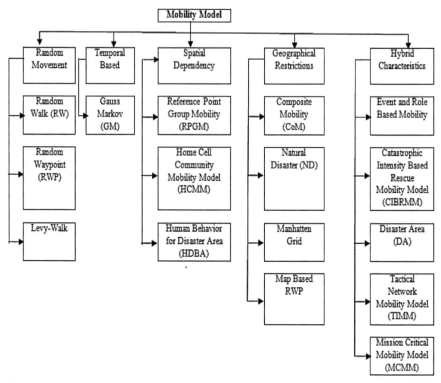

FIGURE 18.2   Different mobility models.

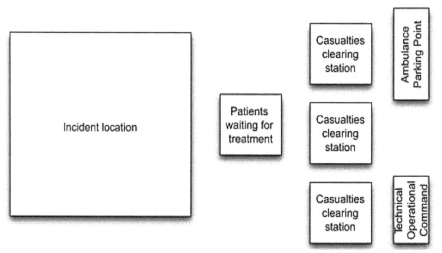

FIGURE 18.3   Zones in DM.

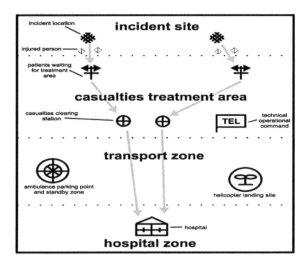

FIGURE 18.4.   IL, PWT, CCS, APP, and TOC.

18.2.3   DM MODEL

In DM model, the area is divided based on the method of separation of rooms such as IL, PWT, CCS, APP, and TOC. In this model, obstacles are also considered and hence it is a challenge to overcome the obstacles. Mathematical model for DM models is described as follows:

$$r = (l_r; P_r; e_r; a_r; N_r^{stat}; V_r^{stat}; T_r^{stat}; G_r^{stat}; N_r^{trans}; V_r^{trans}; T_r^{trans}; G_r^{trans}; Z_r^{trans}) \quad (1)$$

where; $l_r \in \{IL, PWT, CCS, APP, TOC\}$; P_r is the area; e_r and a_r are the border points; N_r^{trans} and N_r^{stat} are the nodes; velocities of the sets of N_r^{trans} and N_r^{stat} at V_r^{trans} and V_r^{stat} intervals $[v_{min}; v_{max}]$; T_r^{trans} and T_r^{stat} intervals $[t_{min}; t_{max}]$ pause time of N_r^{trans} and N_r^{stat}; G_r^{trans} and G_r^{stat} are the group size; Z_r^{trans} is the transport node movement cycle.

The IL contains rescue teams along with volunteers and victims. PWT contains medical teams along with volunteers and patients. CCS contains specialized medical teams which will do the first aid and then victims carried towards TOC. The TOC contains various transport nodes including vehicles and ambulance. Team leader located at TOC guides the complete operation. The RWMM and GM models are not suitable in this situation due to its random mobility nature. Also, movement of nodes is throughout the complete simulation area. In DM, the movement of nodes are more restricted and controlled by the controller.

Both victims and rescue teams such as firefighters, police, and medical teams are present at the scene of the disaster. Disaster happens at Incident location. People injured at incident locations are carried to CCS location. Nodes in CCS and TOC are fixed. Leader in TOC guides the movements within the areas. The gray arrows show the movement of patients. In IL, nodes are moving as patients are carried to the CCS locations. Search and rescue (SAR) operations are very crucial in this scenario. There are entry and exit points of IL and PWT locations. The PWT is much closer to IL to minimize the disaster (Figure 18.5).

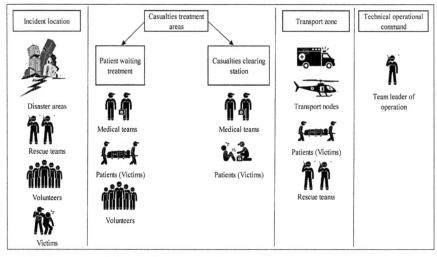

FIGURE 18.5   Detailed area of disaster incident location.

Between PWT and CCS, there are numerous transport troops carrying patients. The best route is chosen to get there in the lowest period of time while avoiding obstacles. The disaster area network does not cover hospitals. The patients are transported by APP to the hospitals. Thus nodes go outside of a network also whenever required nodes come inside a network. All nodes should avoid obstacles and perform communication to the destination nodes. Disaster area mobility models and RL based routing protocols plays a vital role not only in disaster scenario but also useful in post-disaster scenario. Exchange of information between various entities in a minimum amount of time and without any loss of data plays an important role in saving the human lives. Proper network connectivity even in dynamic mobility environment is at most important. Figure 18.6 shows the pseudo-code of DM model.

Require: VG - compute visibility graph with obstacles H and areas R

foreach area r in R do

while nodes in area r ¡ $N_r^{trans} + N_r^{stat}$

assign new node n to area r

$y \leftarrow 1$

if nodes in area r ¡ —N_r^{trans}— then

  $n = N_r^{trans}$

else

  $n = N_r^{trans}$

  $t := 0$

end if

while $t \leq d$ do

  if $n = N_r^{trans}$ then

    W_n path based on movement cycle Z_r and VG using Dijkstra

  else

    $n = N_r^{trans}$

    $v := rand([v_{min}; v_{max}])$

    $p := rand([t_{min}; t_{max}])$

    add waypoints for Wn to the trace based on r and p

    $t := t + time\text{-}needed(W_n)$

  end if

end while

FIGURE 18.6 Pseudo-code of DM model.

18.3 REINFORCEMENT LEARNING (RL)

In the previous section, we discussed the routing protocols and various mobility models used in routing. Also, we discussed the use of DM model in disaster scenario. This section describes the importance of RL and its use in designing network models and algorithms various existing routing algorithms are non-static algorithms where the routing tables are created, and packets are transferred using the shortest path. While calculating the shortest path, these algorithms only verify the number of hops parameter and do not take into account, actual traffic on a network. Once the shortest path is selected, all packets follow this path and packets reach to the destination [5]. But the shortest path is not optimum as there might be few alternate paths or subsequent paths which delivers the packet in minimum time when there is an increase in traffic on the shortest path. Researchers always concentrate on designing such adaptive routing algorithms where the path followed by the packets must consider the actual traffic on the network.

Shortest path algorithms always assume that topology never changes and select predetermined shortest path which is in number of hops. But for any ad hoc network, shortest path algorithms are not suitable. Ad hoc network specifically designed for disaster scenario are highly dynamic, and their topology changes frequently. Shortest path policy is more suitable for low load network but in high traffic network, where the intermediate routes get flooded with packets and thus shortest route may not provide optimal path [6]. Performance of shortest path degenerates in high traffic network and popular nodes carry high traffic and more delay occurs at the destination. It is also possible that whole network get congested and complete setup of network fails. This situation give rise to adaptive routing policy where the path will be selected at run time and alternate path may be obtained and selected for transmission of packets.

The various challenges in designing routing algorithms include frequent changes in topology and frequent disconnection of links in a communication network. In this, all nodes are mobile and selection of shortest path may not always be effective considering the performance parameters like delay and energy for high traffic scenarios. The main difference between adaptive and conventional routing policy is that routing decisions are different in adaptive routing and decision takes place by considering the present state of the network. It means there is a need to sense the present state of the network every time when the packets are transmitted to the next node, and thus all subsequent packets will get an idea of the optimum path. Thus optimum path is based on the real traffic and does not depend upon the minimum number of hops.

The machine learning (ML) is make machines to behave intelligently. This includes to train machines from available information and resources and to take the decision and enhances their experiences [7]. More and more experience and information will return to the better and correct decisions.

ML is the development of a program or algorithm that accepts data from one or more sources, analyzes it, classifies it and uses the useful data to predict or take decisions to control the system. These algorithms are basically divided into two categories Supervised and unsupervised learning. Supervised learning divides the sets or samples into two pre-defined class, i.e., Class A and Class B. Unsupervised learning classifies the samples into groups by identifying the similarity   .

Various existing routing algorithms are non-static algorithms where the routing tables are created and packets are transferred using the shortest path. While calculating the shortest path, these algorithms only verify the number of hops parameter and do not considers the actual traffic on a network. The shortest route becomes popular in heavy traffic network and is flooded with packets. In RL, mobile agents are located at each node which learns from interacting environment. In this, reward-penalty policy (Figure 18.7) is used to gain more experience and to take more rewarding action and are used to design such dynamic routing algorithms [8].

The various qualitative metrics used for analysis of a network are centralized or distributed, adaptive or non-adaptive, pro-active or reactive, etc. The various quantitative metrics (QoS) are also used for analysis.

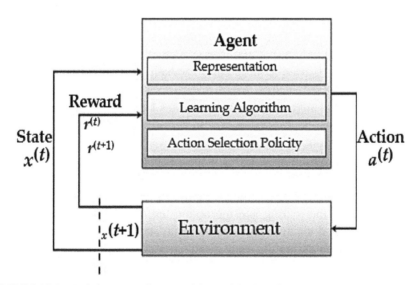

FIGURE 18.7 Reinforcement framework in machine learning.

The first adaptive routing algorithm, which was based on Q learning framework was designed in 1994. Every node contains Q tables, i.e., estimates of the remaining time of travel of packets and always get updated after packet transmission takes place. It is found that the quality and quantity of exploration is less and need to be improved to increase the speed of adaption to achieve good performance at high traffic networks. Every node is acting as an agent. Agent performs learning process. Learning process is executed periodically in the decision process. It is also observed that even in static network, RL based algorithms gives good results.

There are basically many Q-Routing protocols which are available today [9]. Q-routing is an adaptive routing for interconnection network which is unsupervised learning scheme is. In CQ routing, confidence values are used to improve the quality of exploration [10].

But still in order to tackle high mobility of network, this is not sufficient. Q Routing is a straightforward application of Q Learning, but at low loads, shortest path routing is always better then Q routing. CQ Routing shows a significant improvement in the quality of routing policy. Convergence of routing tables took less time in CDRQ routing as it includes backward exploration along with confidence measure values. At low loads, CDRQ routing gives the best performance. Average throughput is significantly high in case of CDRQ routing. Adaptive routing minimizes the delivery time of the packets. The major problem comes in CDRQ routing, that in low traffic network, CDRQ does not finds the shortest path. Hence these algorithms need to optimize further. One way of optimization is to use the memory to keep a history of Q values that are used to predict the Q values in advance. The Priority queue is used to keep best Q values in the network which are used further to predict Q values. Another optimization includes the propagation of significant changes in received estimates from the neighboring node throughout the network. It is necessary to compare the above optimization along with CDRQ routing.

Energy aware routing in MANET is also of great importance. The main objective of energy efficient routing protocols is reducing energy consumption in packet transmission, avoiding routing packets with low energy levels nodes, optimizing the routing and increasing the network lifetime. Energy efficient routing is done in several ways. Some approaches try to minimize energy consumption during the route discovery/reply/maintenance.

18.4   LITERATURE SURVEY

In the previous section, we discussed the importance of RL and its use in designing network models and algorithms. This section analyzes the literature survey of various routing protocols and RL algorithms implemented so far to evaluate the network.

In Ref. [11], authors did a performance comparison between AODV, DSDV, and ZRP. The simulation is done using NS2 and delay, PDR, throughput, and CO are used as a performance metrics. In this AODV performs better than DSDV. Simulation study on AODV is performed by Goyal et al. [12]. QualNet simulator is used for performance comparison. In Ref. [13], authors compared AODV and DSR and analysis is carried out against various QoS parameters. In Ref. [14], authors perform performance evaluation on wormhole attack in mesh networks. In Ref. [15], comparative analysis between pro-active routing protocol DSDV and AODV is done. AODV is always better than DSDV when PDR is used as a performance parameter. In this chapter, packet delivery ratio and delay are analyzed. Four routing protocols AOMDV, DSDV, AODV, and DSR are used for comparison and analysis in Ref. [16], WSN network is considered for comparison. The various performance parameters like packet delivery ratio, dropping ratio and delay are analyzed.

According to Harminder et al. [17], DSR gives good performance in TCP and medium load conditions. Different traffic and load patterns are tested and performance evaluation is done using group mobility model. Manickam et al. [18] compares DSDV, AODV, and DSR protocols and evaluation is done using NS2, which shows DSR routing protocol performs better in high mobility situations. Throughput, delay and PDR are analyzed.

Pragati et al. [19] compares AODV protocol with LEACH protocol using delay, dropping ratio and packet delivery ratio as a metric. Sathish et al. [20] showed that DSR is good to achieve high packet delivery ratio and less dropping ratio. Amith Khandakar [21] compares namely DSDV, DSR, and AODV using NS2 simulator. Number of nodes, speed, and pause time varies. PDR, delay, and CO parameters are used to judge the network performance. Kumar Prateek et al. [22] concluded that DSR and AODV protocols gives good performance in high mobility network. They also claim that DSDV gives poor performance as DSDV fails to adapt the network changes due to link or node failure. Nidhi et al. [23] compare the network performance of DSR and AODV protocols and uses delay, normalized CO and PDR as parameters. A number of nodes varies and they conclude that AODV gives better performance in a dense environment. Amer et al. [24] tested DSR protocol on 50 nodes network and using CBR traffic. Only DSR protocol is used against various network parameters.

Vyas et al. [25] concludes that pro-active protocols work better at low mobility and low traffic conditions. Adam et al. [26] shows that OLSR does not give good performance as compared with AODV/DSR protocols in case of PDR. Authors in [27] compare OLSR and TORA protocols using OPNET network simulator. Pankaj et al. [27] show that OLSR is better than TORA when the bandwidth is large. A good survey of adaptive routing protocol and their optimizations by considering network on chip is done by authors in Ref. [28].

In Ref. [29], MANET is considered with Q routing protocol. Various methodologies and constraints related with Q routing are discussed in short. Echo Q routing [30] is discussed by Kavalerov et al. This is proposed optimization carried out on Q routing.

18.5   RESEARCH METHODOLOGY

In the previous section, we discussed the survey of work done by various researchers in the analysis of various routing protocols and RL algorithms implemented so far to evaluate the network. In this section, we will discuss various optimizations done on Q routing and design of proposed method based on RL.

The route discovery process is the first step when a node enters a new network. This is required to identify the nodes and to configure it in a local network. Route discovery message is propagated to discover the new path for the destination. Also HELLO messages are frequently transmitted to keep up-to-date information.

Every node checks the Q tables and finds out the best path which will be an optimum path for the destination. Also, the packet includes backward exploration value inside the packet and the packet goes through the multiple hops. Every hop in the network transmits packets to the next hop and simultaneously updates the Q tables. Confidence tables are also used. The C values of other nodes are also decayed. Control packets are sent to nodes ahead of you.

Q and C tables are updated by all nodes by extracting reward and puts next node information along with destination node in the queue.

The proposed strategy doubles the amount of exploration. Backward exploration values, which are significantly more exact, are also useful. When C values are used, Q values are more reliable. All node Q values are updated. Learning rate is more reliable. It is observed less adaption time for frequent change in traffic. In link or node failure cases, it quickly reverts back to the original routing policy. Proposed method updates all Q values at a single instant. C values of selected nodes are also updated in order to reduce overhead (Figures 18.8 and 18.9). Variable decay constant approach is used to update C values of non-selected nodes.

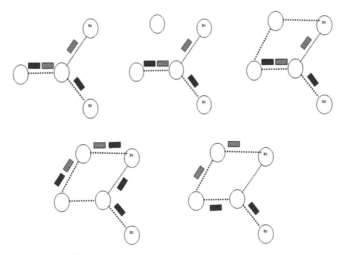

FIGURE 18.8   Proposed method optimization.

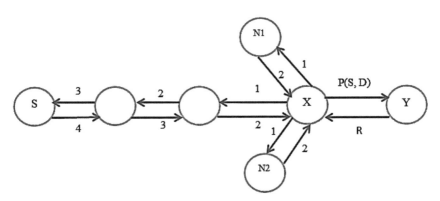

FIGURE 18.9   Another optimization.

18.6   RESULTS AND DISCUSSION

There are many simulators available on the Internet, and everyone is having their own pros and cons. Some of them are:

- NS (open source);
- OPNET;
- NetSim;
- OMNET++;
- JIST/SWANS;
- JSim.

Simulation approach is very useful to find out the realistic approach of node mobility and communication behavior. Different mobility models and different traffic patterns are generated to test the network and find out the realistic performance of the network. Performance evaluation largely depends upon the mobility models and mobility inside the network. BonnMotion is used to design different mobility patterns. The performance of a protocol is evaluated by testing them under reasonable conditions, particularly group of mobility nodes, data traffic and communication range. In fact, there are several mobility models that have been suggested which would accomplish a movement of rescue teams.

The first test is conducted to determine the suitability of the mobility model in a disaster scenario. Group mobility model is compared against DM model. The results are carried out to find out the delay and average energy utilization (Figures 18.10 and 18.11).

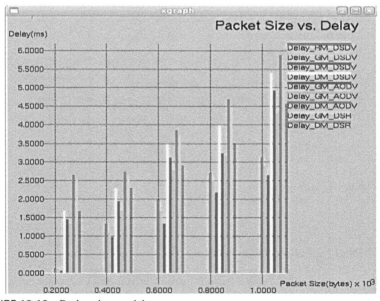

FIGURE 18.10   Packet size vs. delay.

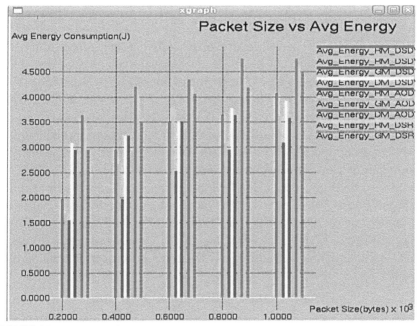

FIGURE 18.11   Packet size vs. average energy.

Delay and energy are important parameters, especially when dealing the communication between nodes in disaster scenario. Energy determines the lifetime of nodes while delay determines successful reception of data to the destination in optimum time for proper and uninterrupted disaster management operation. In random mobility model, as the nodes move randomly towards the random destination hence is not suitable for disaster scenario.

In comparison to AODV and DSR, DSDV is more suitable because of its proactive nature, which minimizes delays in disaster area mobility. For 1,000 bytes of packet, DSDV provides delay of 2.64 seconds while DSDV for group mobility, provides delay of 2.88 seconds. Also for small size of 200 bytes packet, DSDV provides a delay of 0.06 seconds as opposed to 0.108 seconds in group mobility. DSDV is also much suitable as far as average energy consumption is considered. Average energy consumed for 1,000 bytes of packet, for DSDV protocol using DM model is 3.08 joules while for group mobility, value is 3.62 J. Thus it is observed, total saving of 14% energy in simulation time of 300 seconds. Also for small packet of 200 bytes, average energy utilized in DSDV under DM model is 1.54 joules against

1.68 joules in RPGM model. Thus total saving of 7.5% energy is observed in simulation time of 300 seconds.

Packet rate also impacts the traffic on the network hence interval is also considered for evaluation. Figure 18.12 shows the analysis of delay by changing interval. Figure 18.13 shows the graph of energy utilization. For 0.10 seconds of interval, DSDV provides delay of 2.2 seconds while DSDV for group mobility, provides delay of 2.4 seconds. Also, for packet rate of 50 packets/sec, DSDV provides a delay of 0.05 seconds as opposed to 0.09 seconds in group mobility. DSDV is also suitable as far as average energy consumption is considered. Average energy consumed for 0.10 seconds of interval for DSDV protocol using DM model is 2.2 joules while for group mobility, value is 2.8. Thus it is observed, a total saving of 22% energy in simulation time of 300 seconds. Also for interval of 0.02 seconds, average energy utilized in DSDV under DM model is 1.1 joules against 1.2 joules in RPGM model. Thus total saving of 7% energy in simulation time of 300 seconds.

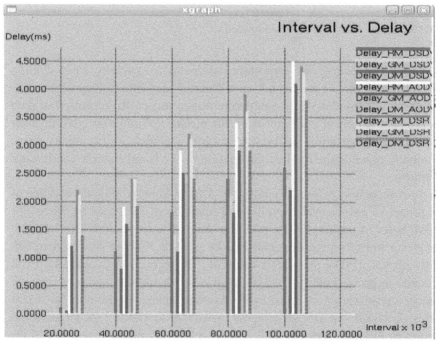

FIGURE 18.12   Interval vs. delay.

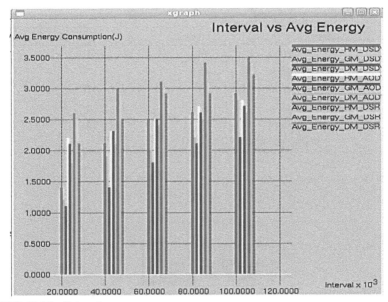

FIGURE 18.13 Interval vs. average energy.

Another experiment is also carried out to compare the proposed algo-rithm. For DM model evaluation, the proposed method is compared to routing protocols such as DSDV, AODV, DSR, and AOMDV. The parameters used to analyze the disaster area scenario are shown in Table 18.1. The time between subsequent packets ranges between 0.02 and 0.10 seconds. Figure 18.14 shows a simulation of the disaster area.

TABLE 18.1 Simulation Parameters in DM

Parameter	Value/Observations and Related Work
Interval	0.02 sec to 0.10 sec
Simulation time	300 seconds
Number of nodes	250
Mobility model	DM model
Area of simulation	285 m by 260 m
Energy	Energy per node is 100 Joule
Traffic	Constant bit rates

The size of area and number of nodes in each area are specified in Table 18.2.

TABLE 18.2   Disaster Area Scenario

Area	Size	Nodes	Transport Nodes
1 IL	35 m by 20 m	20	15
2 PWTA	90 m by 45 m	40	17
3 CCS	10 m by 40 m	15	0
4 APP	30 m by 15 m	30	25
5 TOC	15 m by 10 m	06	00
All	285 m by 260 m	111	–

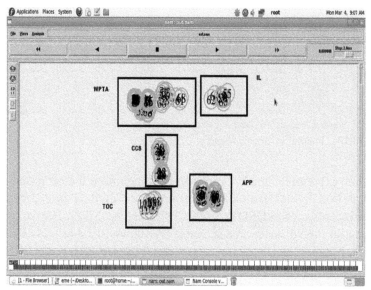

FIGURE 18.14   Simulation of DM model in NS2.

Figures 18.15–18.17 illustrate the network's performance in terms of PDR, latency, and average energy use. It is observed minimum communication loss with less time among the different zones in DM model. In addition, when compared to other routing protocols, average energy consumption is lower. Changing the size of the packets can also yield results. Similar results are also obtained here also. PDR and delay are comparatively improved in the proposed method. Experiment is also carried out to find out the control packets which might consume the bandwidth. Throughput and energy are comparatively improved in the proposed method. The sacrifice we have to make is control overhead, there is an increase in control overhead which could be reduced by eliminating extra control packets generated using various optimization techniques.

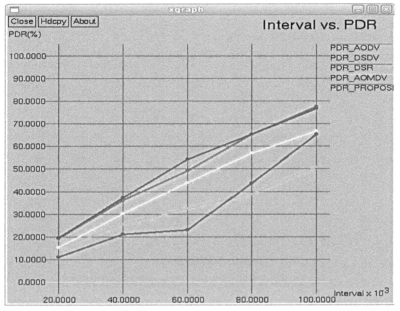

FIGURE 18.15   Interval vs. PDR.

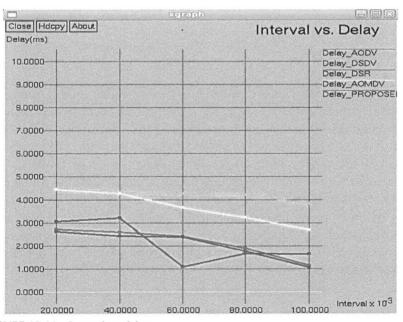

FIGURE 18.16   Interval vs. delay.

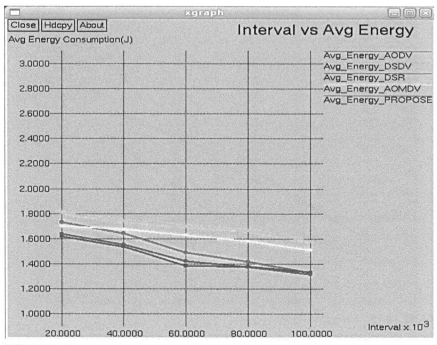

FIGURE 18.17   Interval vs. average energy.

18.7 CONCLUSION

The primary objective of the research is to investigate routing protocol for adaptive routing was achieved. RL is the balance between exploitation and exploration. From the above experiments, it is concluded that the DM model is much more effective and used in disaster scenario. The proposed method is the optimization on RL which gives good performance as compared with other routing protocols based on distance vector. A lifetime of the network and various other parameters such as time to travel packets to the destination and time to deliver the packets are analyzed here and show significant improvement in QoS parameters. Disaster area mobility models are well-suited to disaster scenarios and play a critical role in disaster lifesaving.

KEYWORDS

- **Communication Network**
- **Disaster Mobility Model**
- **Disaster Scenarios**
- **Mobility Model**
- **Quantitative Metrics**
- **Search And Rescue**

REFERENCES

1. Kim, N., Na, W., & Cho, S., (2020). Dual-channel-based mobile ad hoc network routing technique for indoor disaster environment. *IEEE Access, 8*, 126713–126724.
2. Shurman, M. M., Al-Mistarihi, F. M., & Khalid, D., (2016). Dynamic distribution of security keys and IP addresses coalition protocol for mobile ad hoc networks. *Automatika, 57*(4), 1020–1034.
3. Peer, M., Bohara, V. A., & Srivastava, A., (2020). Multi-UAV placement strategy for disaster-resilient communication network. *IEEE 92nd Vehicular Technology Conference (VTC2020-Fall)*, 1–7.
4. Gutierrez, D., (2015). A survey on multihop ad hoc networks for disaster response scenarios. *International Journal of Distributed Sensor Networks*. 10.1155/2015/647037.
5. Manogaran, G., Qudrat-Ullah, H., Bharat, S., & Rawal, K., (2021). *Intelligent Autonomous Cyber-Physical Systems and Applications*, 909, 910.
6. Desai, R., & Patil, B. P., (2018). Adaptive routing based on predictive reinforcement learning. *International Journal of Computers and Applications, 40*(2), 73–81.
7. Char, D. S., Michael, D. A., & Chris, F., (2020). Identifying ethical considerations for machine learning healthcare applications. *The American Journal of Bioethics, 20*(11), 7–17.
8. Al-Rawi, H. A. A., Ming, A. N., & Kok-Lim, A. Y., (2015). Application of reinforcement learning to routing in distributed wireless networks: A review. *Artificial Intelligence Review, 43*(3), 381–416.
9. Hwang, I., & Young, J. J., (2020). Q (λ) learning-based dynamic route guidance algorithm for overhead hoist transport systems in semiconductor fabs. *International Journal of Production Research, 58*(4), 1199–1221.
10. Walunjkar, G., & Anne, K. R., (2019). A reinforcement learning approach for evaluation of disaster relief. *International Conference on Cutting-edge Technologies in Engineering (ICon-CuTE)*, 22–27.
11. Gandhi, S., Chaubey, N., Tada, N., & Trivedi, S., (2012). Scenario-based performance comparison of reactive, proactive and hybrid protocols in MANET. *International Conference on Computer Communication and Informatics*, 1–5.

12. Goyal, A., Vijay, S., & Jhariya, D. K., (2012). Simulation and performance analysis of routing protocols in wireless sensor network using QualNet. *International Journal Computer. Application, 52*(2), 47–50.

13. Ahuja, R., Ahuja, A. B., & Ahuja, P., (2013). Performance evaluation and comparison of AODV and DSR routing protocols in MANETs under wormhole attack. *IEEE Second International Conference on Image Information Processing (ICIIP-2013)*, 699–702.

14. Arora, M., Challa, R. K., & Bansal, D., (2010). Performance evaluation of routing protocols based on wormhole attack in wireless mesh networks. *Second International Conference on Computer and Network Technology, 4*(2), 102–104.

15. Maleh, Y., & Ezzati, A., (2014). Performance analysis of routing protocols for wireless sensor networks. *Third IEEE International Colloquium in Information Science and Technology*, 420–424.

16. Paul, B., Bhuiyan, K. A., Fatema, K., & Das, P. P., (2014). Analysis of AOMDV, AODV, DSR, and DSDV routing protocols for wireless sensor network. *International Conference on Computational Intelligence and Communication Networks*, 364–369.

17. Harminder, S. B., Sunil, K. M., & Sangal, A. L., (2010). Performance evaluation of two reactive routing protocols of MANET using group mobility model. *International Journal of Computer Science Issues, 7*(3, No. 10), 38–43.

18. Rajagopalan, R., & Dahlstrom, A., (2012). Performance comparison of routing protocols in mobile ad hoc networks in the presence of faulty nodes. In: *2012 IEEE International Conference on Wireless Information Technology and Systems (ICWITS)* (pp. 1–4).

19. Pragati, E., & Nath, R., (2012). *Performance Evaluation of AODV, LEACH and TORA Protocols Through Simulation, 2*(7), 84–89.

20. Sathish, S., Thangavel, K., & Boopathi, S., (2011). Comparative analysis of DSR, FSR and ZRP routing protocols in MANET. *International Conference on Information and Network Technology, 4*, 238–243.

21. Amith, K., (2012). Step by step procedural comparison of DSR, AODV and DSDV routing protocol. *4ᵗʰ International Conference on Computer Engineering and Technology, 40*, 36–40.

22. Kumar, P., Nimish, A., & Satish, K. A., (2013). MANET-evaluation of DSDV, AODV and DSR routing protocol. *International Journal of Innovations in Engineering and Technology, 2*(1), 99–104.

23. Sharma, N., Rana, S., & Sharma, R. M., (2010). Provisioning of quality of service in MANETs performance analysis and comparison. In: *2ⁿᵈ International Conference on Computer Engineering and Technology* (pp. 243–248).

24. Amer, O. A. S., Ghassan, S., & Tareq, A., (2014). Performance analysis of dynamic source routing protocol. *Journal of Emerging Trends in Computing and Information Sciences, 5*(2), 97–100.

25. Vyas, K., & Chaturvedi, A., (2014). Comparative analysis of routing protocols in MANETS. *Proceedings of IEEE International Conference on Signal Propagation and Computer Technology*, 692–697.

26. Adam, G., Bouras, C., Gkamas, A., Kapoulas, V., Kioumourtzis, G., & Tavoularis, N., (2011). Performance evaluation of routing protocols for multimedia transmission over mobile ad hoc networks. *Proceedings of IEEE 4ᵗʰ Joint Conference on Wireless and Mobile Networking Conference*, 1–6.

27. Pankaj, P., & Sonia, G., (2012). Comparison of OLSR and TORA routing protocols using OPNET modeler. *International Journal of Engineering Research and Technology, 1*(5), 990–995.

28. Wang, L., Wang, X., & Mak, T., (2016). Adaptive routing algorithms for lifetime reliability optimization in network-on-chip. *IEEE Transactions on Computers, 65*(9), 2896–2902.

29. Haraty, R. A., & Traboulsi, B., (2012). MANET with the Q-routing protocol. *ICN the Eleventh International Conference on Networks*, 187–192.

30. Kavalerov, M. V., Shilova, Y. A., & Bezukladnikov, I. I., (2017). Preventing instability in full echo Q-routing with adaptive learning rates. *IEEE Conference of Russian Young Researchers in Electrical and Electronic Engineering (ElConRus)*, 155–159.

CHAPTER 19

RESOURCE ALLOCATION AND SCHEDULING OF PATIENT'S PHYSICAL ACTIVITY USING PSO

FAHMINA TARANUM, K. SRIDEVI, and MANIZA HIJAB

Computer Science and Engineering Department, Muffakham Jah College of Engineering and Technology, Hyderabad, Telangana, India

ABSTRACT

Healthcare-related resource management has been a challenge in view of varied requirements of the patients and effective resource utilization. COVID-19 pandemic is an example, which has brought to light the need for proper healthcare resource management and utilization. Few significant factors that aggravate the problem being size (resource, patient), allocation, response time, cost, etc. The work proposes an optimized approach for scheduling and allocation of the healthcare resources as per patient's physical activity needs. PSO is as an optimized algorithm, which works among others on the concept of minimizing cost and make-span. Each entity in the problem is represented in multi-dimensional space containing a mapping of parameters like activities and its prioritized assignment. The purpose of the design is to apply the different scheduling algorithm and select the efficient one that reduces the waiting time of a patient.

19.1 INTRODUCTION

19.1.1 TECHNIQUES

1. **Optimization:** The optimizations techniques are highly nonlinear and multimodal under various complex constraints in: Most of

Handbook of Research on Artificial Intelligence and Soft Computing Techniques in Personalized Healthcare Services, Uma N. Dulhare, A. V. Senthil Kumar, Amit Datta, Seddik Bri, Ibrahiem M. M. El Emary, (Eds.)
© 2024 Apple Academic Press, Inc. Co-published with CRC Press (Taylor & Francis)

different contexts, which are used to simplify high-quality solution with high convergence performance and low computational cost. It can be classified as deterministic or stochastic, trajectory-based or population-based, and gradient or derivative.

Deterministic algorithm works in a closed mechanical deterministic mode with static nature, whereas stochastic is dynamic in nature and open to adapt to all outputs. Trajectory based algorithms enhances strategic flow planning to reduce capacity-to-demand and manage a non-uniform path with fluctuating cost. Population based approach works on to identify the interest or risk of the entire individual in the community. Gradient-based algorithms use derivative information to converge to a minimum objective of obtaining linear decreasing dynamic inertia weight, with tightening factor weight and maximum possible velocity reduction. Derivative-free algorithms do not use any concept of any derivative information but use the values of the function itself. Some functions may work on discontinuities or continuous values depending on the input considered. Examples of computational techniques are the conjugate gradient approach, Fletcher Reeves, Newton's, and quasi-Newton method are used for un-constrained and non-linear optimization problems.

2. **Hybrid Method:** Combination of deterministic and heuristic can be used to optimize the results. It works on the concept of locating the most minimal global region.

19.1.2   PARTICLE SWARM OPTIMIZATION (PSO)

It is formerly identified by James Kennedy, Russell Eberhart and Shi while simulating social behavior for the movement of a cluster of birds. Further, the extensive review is done on its applications to know the swarm intelligence by Poli. Correlation of theoretical and practical aspects is explored by Bonyadi and Michalewicz.

The concept of PSO is to find the best optimized location, velocity, and fitness for randomly placed particles. An element is measured as a fact in multi-spatial dimensional with a state characteristic as location and speed. Each particle position is used to do the analysis and get the solution pertaining to its movement to a new location with certain speed for evaluating its fitness. To get an optimized solution in PSO the aspects used to make a decision includes its current velocity, the best position achieved and neighbors' position. PSOs are well suited and used to implement the non-convex nonlinear, continuous, or discrete strategy for problem related to integer variable type.

Each speck in the throng is designated by its location spotted and traversal swiftness. In broad-spectrum, speck spot signifies the resolution of optimization approach, and velocity denotes the exploration path with its direction, which monitors the hovering path of the speck. All the atoms hover through the spatial cluster by adapting the present best particles. The existing greatest particles contain the native best and the global best particle. The native finest speck represents the finest explanation for the speck's position, the particle has accomplished so far, and the global superlative particle denotes the preeminent assessment for the spot acquired by the swarm so far-off.

PSO is categorized as population-based, gradient based and stochastic algorithm. Gradient free approach is applied for global exploration and gradient centered pattern are used for perfect local investigation. Hybrid algorithm uses an amalgamation of heuristic and deterministic based optimization. Heuristic helps to get quick and efficient results. The entire swarm converges to yield an optimized position in search space on multiple iterations. The objective of the proposed approach is to reduce the lifespan and waiting time of any process in execution (Figure 19.1).

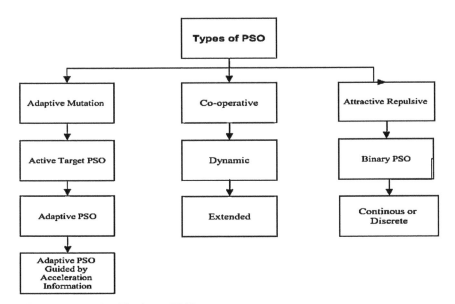

FIGURE 19.1   Classifications of PSOs.

Some of the types of PSO identified in implementation is listed out as follows:

1. **Active Target PSO:** The identified active target parameters are velocity, the best global position and a new target position as defined by Zhang.

2. **Adaptive PSO:** The adaptive behavior is obtained using the controlling parameters like evolutionary state and particle roles to enhance the speed by encouraging the exploitation ability as explained in Ref. [10].

3. **Adaptive Mutation PSO:** It uses the parameters of speed, velocity, and inertia to mutate as explained in ALFI.

4. **Adaptive PSO Guided by Acceleration Information:** The proposal is to design an algorithm that works for improving the optimization efficiency by finding spots for the global optimum.

5. **Attractive Repulsive Particle Swarm Optimization:** Used to improve the efficiency by exploring and exploiting particle behavior. It is applied for nonconvex economic dispatch and premature convergence problem.

6. **Binary PSO:** The position of the particle is defined in binary and its velocity is defined as the probability of changing its state from 0 to 1.

7. **Cooperative Multiple PSO:** Particles employ cooperative behavior to solve combinational optimization problem.

8. **Dynamic and Adjustable PSO:** Used to adjust and converge speed of dynamic adaptive to work in collaboration towards improving optimization.

9. **Extended Particle Swarms:** Apart from basic parameters, an integration of two paradigms of canonical is used to obtain optimized results.

19.1.3   RESOURCE ALLOCATION AND SCHEDULING

Allocating the suitable resource for the required amount of time is resource scheduling. The major confirmation is to schedule the process using fair scheduling concept and avoiding live and dead locks. The job here is to assign and recognize the unit of resource to be allocated for a specific duration of time by avoiding busy waiting and conflicts. The enhanced versions of the schedule are its integration with clouds environment in static as well as dynamic nature. An optimal source scheduling is to select the best suitable item for a defined specific time from the matched physical resources. Taking the resource availability and its capacity into consideration the scheduling can be done to work on metrics like latency time, work span and checking the real-time boundaries. It allows managers to check for firm or hard systems based on the outline of completion rates and time for tasks assigned in their teams. Primarily, resource allocation is an act of completing a task with the set of actions and methodologies used to efficiently assign the resources fairly without conflicting with each other and by meeting the deadlines.

Example: Depending on industrial requirement, resources can be people, equipment, and machines, or rooms and facilities. They may also be consumable or reusable resources like materials and parts.

Resource scheduling can be classified as shown in Figure 19.2:

1. **Earliest Deadline First (EDF):** It is a scheduling algorithm based on optimal dynamic priority approach in used in both dynamic and static real-time systems. EDF uses deadline priority to schedule the jobs, i-e. The earliest absolute deadline jobs are scheduled first. It's an efficient scheduling algorithm which guarantees maximum CPU utilization. Earliest deadline first (EDF) scheduling algorithm is preemptive in nature.

2. **Shortest Job First (SJF):** The jobs are selected based on the shortest processing time or execution time. It can be implemented both in preemptive and non-preemptive manner. It is known for reduced average waiting time algorithm. Advantage is its minimized waiting time and easy batch implementation. Drawback is its non-supportive implementation towards interactive systems.

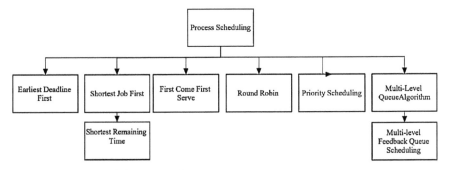

FIGURE 19.2   Scheduling approaches.

3. **First Come First Serve (FCFS):** It works by taking arrival time into priority for scheduling. The job is initially placed in a waiting queue if the resource is busy and then once the resource gets free, it is placed in a ready queue. The jobs are selected from the ready queue based on FCFS manner by the scheduler. The advantage is its easy implementation and understandability. The drawback of this algorithm is starvation if the first job takes longer time to execute among other ready jobs. The performance of the scheduling is poor as the average wait time of the jobs is high.

4. **Round Robin (RR):** It is one of the most widely used algorithms for process scheduling used by network schedulers. The algorithm works on the concept of assigning time slices (quantum) to each processor with equal portion in circular order to generate fair scheduling. On quantum expiry the process is preempted from the CPU and is allocated to the next process in the queue.

5. **Priority Scheduling:** The priority to set is generally a well-defined integer, which lies in between [1.10] and with the interpretation that the lesser the value the greater the priority. The CPU is allocated to the jobs with the higher priority first.

    It is classified as preemptive or non-preemptive. The priority is assigned to every processor for setting its execution turn, which may or may not vary in its state. In non-preemptive algorithm, jobs with the highest priority are executed foremost. Processes with the same priority are executed based on first arrived first delivered. In preemptive approach the executing jobs cannot be stopped even if some higher priority jobs arrive.

6. **Multi-Level Queue Algorithm:** It is classified as interactive or non-interactive processes. The interactive is beneficial over non-interactive in terms of faster execution or response time, hence interactive processes are given priority over non-interactive for quick scheduling. The multi-level queues used in the approach are system, interactive, interactive editing, batch, and student processes. When the job enters the system, it is placed in the correct level queue, which cannot be changed once allocated. The order of priority for multilevel queue goes from system level as highest to student level being the lowest.

7. **Multi-Level Feedback Queue Scheduling Algorithm:** The advantage of adaptability is an enhancement in this scheduling, i.e., the process can be swapped from one level to another based on a beneficial opportunity, higher priority or to satisfy the requirement. The parameters used in this scheduling algorithm includes the satisfactory working strategy listed below and the number of queues used to implement the system.

The working strategy required in this approach is a way to:

i. Recognize the scheduling algorithm at each level in the queue as each queue can have its own scheduling approach;

ii. Identify when to go with process upgradation and degradation or demotion, and also to determine which method is applied for the same;

iii. Determine the need and services required by the process to change its level.

8. **Shortest Remaining Time (SRT):** It is similar in characteristics to the preemptive version of SJF algorithm. Preemption is possible for the process allocated with the closest completion time, with the ready new jobs having shorter completion time. It cannot be applied for interactive systems, in which the CPU time is unknown. It works on the bases of batch scheduling whereas SJF uses priority concept for scheduling the jobs.

19.1.4 PHYSICAL ACTIVITIES OF THE PATIENT

Physical activities are suggested to patient to keep them fit, improve their health condition and maintain health fitness. These activities can base on every day, recreational or fitness training. Regular physical fitness can be practiced or maintained to condense the jeopardy of heart diseases, in elevation blood pressure, brain-stroke, diabetes, excess weight and other health related issues. The commonly used physical resources in real time includes raw material dispatch, building, and its facilities, machinery for dispatch on demand, energy utilization and resource supply. When the patient is admitted in the hospital the resource requirement is as listed: Beds, medical professionals for serving (viz. Doctors and Nurses), medical equipment or devices (e.g., respirators, B.P. monitor, medical equipment or and pulse oximeter, pedometer, thermometer, blood glucose monitor, weighing scale, Nebulizer and ventilators), medical supplies (e.g., facemasks, sanitizers, and plastic gloves), and diagnostics tests (as suggested by doctor).

The physical activities allocation to patients for scheduling is with respect to resource contention and demand. Commonly used physical units in the realistic scenarios include fresh ingredients, constructions, and facilities, apparatus, vigor, and supplies. Such corporeal resources are limited and reusable, proper allocation of which could result in efficient and effective utilization of resources with fair scheduling.

19.2   LITERATURE SURVEY

The concept is to move a group of nodes from space to another space looking for the connection for the base station for transmission. The path selected for transmission is the shorted path as a flock of birds move together searching for an optimal location. In PSO, the routing is not based on any routing algorithm, but the optimum path is selected for traversal. The author in Ref. [1] has applied the concept of position selection for movement of mobile nodes in the network as similar to movement of the birds in space using PSO to find an optimal position. The author has also used the velocity and the speed to search for the best optimum next node to move in the network searching for the shortest path.

Author in Ref. [2] proposes an improved PSO integration scheme with enhanced components to integrate mathematical logistics with inertia for getting enhanced control. Viz-a-viz uniform distribution, cubic spline, exponential reduction in inertia weight, interpolation gathering and learning rate.

The reduction of power consumption is the work targeted by the author in [3]. The nodes move in groups by connecting with the neighboring nodes in the closest vicinity as the birds move in the space to find an optimal best local and global position.

The proposal in Ref. [4] by the authors is to design a scheme of task processing framework for making decision to allocate appropriate resources to process at runtime. A set of experiments were conducted using distinct datasets over Cloud Sim to identify the most effective technique for designing a scientific application. The traditional optimum solutions are selected to improve various persuasive parameters like (speed, budget, duration, performance metric-throughput, and task acceptance rate). The target is to work with high velocity for better exploration and then to decrease the velocity after small iteration to perform better exploitation.

Authors has worked on the population diversity control problem to improve optimization in Ref. [5]. The approach is based on the dynamic selection using adaptive and diversity controlling parameters along with appropriate roles played by the particle. The dynamic assortment of particle role associates the evolutionary dynamic state of the particle using the estimation method for better optimization, and to encourage the exploitation ability for enhanced convergence speed. Author's concluded that the results have extra preferable probing for accuracy, probing-reliability, and convergence-speed of other variants of particle-swarm optimization.

The aim of the authors in Ref. [6] is the target of reducing the voltage used in harmonic distortion over a wide range of modulation index. The aim was to find an optimal switching angle for multilevel cascade inverters with less iterations. Further to reduce the overall class weighted sum, the concept used is to minimize the class variance and to go with automatic setting of image threshold.

Uma Dulhare has measured the performance in Ref. [7] using statistical tool R an Open source with caret to progress the accuracy of the Naïve-Bayes classifier algorithm using the particle-swarm optimization and has concluded that the classifier shows a tremendous improvement for running for 100 iterations, with a step increment of 10 each. The repository UCI is used for fetching data for heart disease analysis, the statistics are collected based on 14 features related to heart to check the severalty of the heart disease based on 270 generated instances.

Authors in Ref. [8] have worked for designing an optimal scheduling algorithm. In most applications of PSO, an approach of the continuous optimization problems is solved using the location of the particle, velocity, inertia weight, and global and local best positions. Scheduling of patients is performed using multiple permutations to find the most accurate solution.

An enhanced PSO for non-linear systems was proposed by Alfi in Ref. [9] to adapt the modifications done in the conventional PSO. The advancements were implemented with adaptive mutation approach to boost the global search aptitude and congregating the speed, further the accuracy of the system is improved using dynamism in the inertia weight. This proposal aims to implement two major aspects, namely dynamic inertia weight and adaptation using mutations, and the author has finally interpreted the results generated were with good performance and accuracy.

Zhihui et al. [10] have aimed to implement an approach of adaptive behavior by evaluating population distribution and its fitness. The parameters used to estimate the state of the particle is by using parameters like exploitation, jumping or skipping, exploration, and convergence. The efficiency and the convergence speed is improved by automatically controlling at run time the acceleration coefficients, random variable and inertia weights. To jump to local optima from global optima, an elitist learning strategy is applied, as soon as the state of the particle reaches a convergence state. The outcomes of parameter adaptation and elitist training with learning have shown substantial improvement in performance for terms like universal optimality, algorithm reliability, accurate, and safe solution with convergence speed.

In Ref. [11] authors have explained the working of an optimized algorithm using a novel binary approach for PSO. This algorithm uses a novel characterization for the vector velocity of binary-PSO. The interpretation of the author for the performance is the continuous approach of PSO outperforms discrete.

Researchers have targeted on weighted fusion rule with experimented threshold to integrate low-frequency coefficients for nurturing the excellent visual performance of fused image in Ref. [12] by Cheng et al.

In Ref. [13] authors aim to present an active approach to highlight particle swarm optimization (PSO) using three-targeted velocity updating formula calculating paramount previous position, global superlative position and active marked parameters. The proposed approach uses a complex method to find the active. The advantage is to jump off from the local optimum and to keep diversity in monitoring and disadvantage is extra computation expenses.

Authors in Ref. [14] have driven to improve the global convergent ability, the concept of acceleration has been added to the standard PSO algorithm. Author has also adjusted the influence of acceleration velocity using oscillation factor, this helps to globally optimize the validity. This logistics has shown an improvement in solving the premature validation cases with quicker convergent speed.

Kennedy et al. [15] have invented the perception for the optimization using non-linear functions with particle swarm methodologies. The progression of multiple distinct parameters and paradigms were highlighted, followed by its implementation. Benchmark paradigm recognition for testing is described along with its applications for optimization and neural network training using nonlinear function. The relationships between PSO and together integration of artificial life and genetic algorithms (GAs) are discussed.

19.3 PROPOSED APPROACH

The idea is to generate the finest solution for allocation and scheduling for the PSO algorithms. The algorithm works to generate the best position to adapt using parameters like velocity, inertia weight, acceleration constants, speed, distance, local and global position and direction. The local position is the place of each particle, and the universal position is the group's best position. The measure of the particle is in the course of superlative location value. The velocity is calculated using Eqn. (1):

$$V_i^{(z+1)} = wV_i^z + a_1 r_1 (Lbest_i^z - x_i^z) + a_2 r_2 (Gbest^k - x_i^z) \tag{1}$$

Lbest is the tiniest value of the calculated position of each particle, and the group's minimum value of experience position is Gbest. The movement is monitored using the kth step of the ith particle to get the next new place. The first term of Eqn. (1) gives the inertia with respect to previous velocity; second and third terms are used to fetch the direction of each particle and group position, respectively. An accelerating object is used to induce a uniform change in its velocity at each second. Acceleration constants used in Eqn. (1) are a1 and a2. The random numbers in a range of [0,1] are chosen as depicted in Eqn. (1) as r1 and r2. Velocity update and Position update is calculated using Eqn. (1) using its former velocity and parameter like the length of the route from its current position to its best native and universal optimums as defined by Kennedy & Eberhart [11].

$$x_j^{(z+1)} = x_j^z + V_j^{(z+1)} \tag{2}$$

Eqn. (2) is used to get the new position using the summation of the previous position and the velocity with which the particle is moving to go to a new position. After getting the best position, all the particles synchronize with each other to fly in the space by adapting the best selected particle path. The Lbest represent the best local particle and Gbest gives the best global particle solution or group's accurate position in the swarm. The original version of PSO is proposed in the year 1995 by Kennedy & Eberhart [15], PSO has been identified and fascinated many researchers considered as it uses simple concept with easy implementation and based on few parameters as explained by Ref. [13].

According to Kennedy et al., the search space is represented in a D-dimensional vector and the velocity and position update are calculated using Eqns. (1) and (2). The jth particle's position in D-dimensional vector is calculated using Eqn. (3). The local-best (Lbest) and the global-best (Gbest) of the jth item is denoted in Eqns. (3) and (4), respectively.

$$x_j = (x_{j1}, x_{j2}, x_{j3}, x_{jk}, ..., x_{jd}) \tag{3}$$

$$vx_j = (x_{j1}, x_{j2}, x_{j3}, x_{jk}, ..., x_{jd}) \tag{4}$$

$$l_j = (x_{j1}, x_{j2}, x_{j3}, x_{jk}, ..., x_{jd}) \tag{5}$$

$$g_j = (x_{1j}, x_{2j}, x_{3j}, x_{ij}, ..., x_{jd}) \tag{6}$$

For scheduling a job with a recourse, the problem here is to schedule n patients or n jobs competing for appropriate resource, each job has a list of successive responsibilities (functionalities), where i: is the indexed used to refer to the patient and is j the indexed task or the maneuver. The number of total operations completed or used in scheduling is depicted by d, with d being an aggregation of the total tasks in participation of entire active processors in execution, which is denoted in Eqn. (7).

$$d = \sum ni \tag{7}$$

$$y = \sum_{1=1}^{i-1} ni + 1 \tag{8}$$

19.3.1 PATIENT SCHEDULING USING PARTICLE SWARM OPTIMIZATION (PSO) APPROACH

An ideal solution to the PSO for patient-scheduling problem is done with multiple interpretations for particle depiction. In practice, most of the PSO applications uses the continuous optimization constants like particle location x_j, velocity v_j, acceleration coefficients c_1 and c_2, and inertia weight ω. Scheduling a patient is a conjunctional and feasible optimization with a sequence of resource selected operation. The aim is to find an optimal schedule where in which the patient is allocated resource without busy waiting.

19.3.1.1   PATIENT SCHEDULING WITH PSO

The scenario comprises of n-patients (or jobs) denoted as $P = \{P_1, P_2, \ldots, P_n\}$, sequential task $T = \{1.n\}$, resource $R = \{R_1, R_2 \ldots, R_m\}$, and O_{ij} are the operations of patients activity with i, j being the indices of the patient along with the operations, respectively. Every task of the V_{th} patient is numbered as V and for identical number of V tasks in Table 19.1, and y is defined in Eqn. (8). Some limited count of resources is taken into interpretation for better explanation. The resources could be selected as one defined in Section 19.1.4. For the appropriate assignment of resources to physical activity for a patient, many scheduling approaches are proposed by researchers. One sample representation of the particle for an optimization of scheduling is depicted in Table 19.1.

TABLE 19.1   Particle Representations for Resource-Scheduling

Task No.	1	2	–	V	–	n
Position $[X_{ij}]$	$[X_{i1}]$	$[X_{i2}]$	–	$[X_{iv}]$	–	$[X_{id}]$

1. **Phase I:** Initialization is performed for three patients scheduling with three resources as depicted in Table 19.2. The interpretation is done in multiple permutations (3p3 ways for 3:3 patients: resource allocation) giving in total 9 such task sequences. Table 19.2 uses one of the nine possible permutation representations for the resource allocations, where R_1, R_2, and R_3 are the distinct resources. The example for particle representation along with position and velocity vector initialization of scheduling is given in Table 19.3.

TABLE 19.2   Elements Scheduling Problem for 3:3 Patients and Resource Allocation

Patient-ID	Arrival Time	Sequence of the Task	Processing-Time			Age
1	2	R1-R2-R3	3	2	4	38
2	4	R3-R2-R1	4	2	3	40
3	6	R1-R3-R2	3	4	2	44

The assignment of the resources to the patient can be done in three phases: On Patients admission into the hospital, during his/her stay in hospital, when he was under the treatment and after he is discharged from the hospital. The facilities of patient's health monitoring is provided by some hospital, by means of which patient can utilize post-care services either by visiting a hospital or by calling a nurse to deliver the services. The scheduling of these services can be done by using the algorithms listed in Tables 19.5–19.7.

TABLE 19.3   Elements Representation with Configuration of Positional and Vector Velocity for the i_{th} Item

Task Id.	1	1	1	2	2	2	3	3	3
Position [x_{ij}]	[x_{i1}],	[x_{i2}],	[x_{i3}],	[x_{i4}],	[x_{i5}],	[x_{i6}],	[x_{i7}],	[x_{i8}],	[x_{i9}],
(Values)	1.13	0.83	1.85	0.32	1.09	0.75	1.95	0.65	0.55
Velocity v_{ij}	[v_{i1}],	[v_{i2}],	[v_{i3}],	[v_{i4}],	[v_{i5}],	[v_{i6}],	[v_{i7}],	[v_{i8}],	[v_{i9}],
(Values)	3.81	2.90	0.09	–2.79	1.35	3.25	–0.99	3.61	0.76

Initialization position of the Particle is selected with random number ranging from [x_{min} to x_{max}], and [x_{min}, x_{max}] is set as [0, 2]. During PSO execution, position and velocity vectors are set with no constraint. The velocity of the vector is configured with the randomized numbers limitation of [v_{min}, v_{max}] as [–4, 4] as interpreted in Table 19.3.

2. **Phase II:** Decoding Particles with PSO solutions: An integration of PSO for patient scheduling cannot be deployed directly as a solution to particle position. Hence indirect ways are adopted to decode particle representation as a solution to schedule patient problem. For decoding atoms into a schedule, the algorithmic steps are listed below:

    •   **Step I:** Sort in ascending order the values of the position vector.

    •   **Step II:** Organize the jobs in the consistent order of the standards of the position vector obtained from step I.

    •   **Step III:** The resultant is with sequential order of task along with the corresponding positions as shown in Table 19.4.

TABLE 19.4   Result Obtained for Sequenced Particles After Phase II

Task. Unit	2.1	3.1	3.2	2.2	1.1	2.3	1.2	1.3	3.3
Position P_{ij}	[x_{i4}]	[x_{i9}]	[x_{i8}]	[x_{i6}]	[x_{i2}]	[x_{i5}]	[x_{i1}]	[x_{i3}]	[x_{i7}]
(Values)	0.32	0.55	0.65	0.75	0.83	1.09	1.13	1.85	1.95
Order of Execution	1	2	3	4	5	6	7	8	9

Using the sequence obtained from the operation-based permutation is π = (2, 3, 3, 2, 1, 2, 1, 1, 3). An atom of π representing a value i for selected patient Pi. The jth incidence of ith in π denotes to operation O_{ij} for the jth-task (or operation) of ith speck. The antecedence of the selected task is firmed using the order of the atoms of π and the entirely ready task for scheduling as per the first row of Table 19.4. Based on the permutation, the first element selected for scheduling according to the permutation is 2, therefore first unit of the second patient is selected to process on resource R3. Followed with the first task of the third patient is administered on R1, followed with the third constituent is 3, to allow the second task of the third patient to be processed on. The obtained or resultant decoding table is shown in Table 19.5.

TABLE 19.5 Decoded Schedule with PSO

R3		[P 2.1]			[P 3.2]		[P 1.3]								
R2			[P 2.2]		[P 1.2]		[P 3.3]								
R1	[P 3.1]		[P 1.1]		[P 2.3]										
Time slot	1	2	3	4	5	6	7	8	9	10	11	12	13	14	15

The Patient 1, 2, and 3 completes the execution at 9, 6, and 7 time, respectively as concluded from Table 19.5 after applying PSO algorithm based on the Order of tasks is as depicted below:

O = {O11, O21, O12, O31, O13, O22, O23, O32, O33}

It is an optimal scheduling as all the processes have completed at time 9.

19.3.2 FIRST COME FIRST SERVE (FCFS) ALGORITHM

The working concept of FCFS is explained in Section 19.1.3, and results obtained after applying the scheduling is shown in Table 19.6.

TABLE 19.6 Decoded Schedule with FCFS

R3					[P 2.1]			[P1.3]			[P3.2]								
R2					[P1.2]		[P2.2]							[P3.3]						
R1			[P1.1]			[P3.1]			[P2.3]											
Time Slot	1	2	3	4	5	6	7	8	9	10	11	12	13	14	15	16	17	18	19	20

The Patient 1, 2, and 3 completes the execution at 12, 13, and 18 times, respectively, after applying FCFS scheduling algorithm as concluded from Table 19.6. The order is based on first in jobs would be the first to be out.

The selected operation of tasks is as depicted below:

$$O = \{O11, O21, O12, O31, O13, O22, O23, O32, O33\}$$

Hence the conclusion is drawn as FCFS is not optimal when compared to PSO algorithm. Patient 1 has arrived first, and he/she is processed for task 1 on resource R1 which is available. Next Patient 1 task 2 has to be processed on resource R2 and after completion of the task, Patient 1 has to get the resource R3 for task 3. But R3 is not available as it is allocated to Patient 2. So Patient 1 has to wait some time to get the R3 resource. Thus based on the FCFS description Table 19.6 decoded schedules is obtained. Based on FCFS total completion time for patient 1 is $12 - 2 = 10$. For patient 2 completion time is $13 - 4 = 9$. Patient 3 completion time is $18 - 6 = 12$.

19.3.3   BASED ON AGE PRIORITY (USING PREEMPTIVE MANNER)

The working concept of priority is explained in Section 19.1.3, and results obtained after applying the scheduling is shown in Table 19.7.

TABLE 19.7   Patient Decoded Schedule Using Priority

R3					[P2.1]		[P1.3]		[P3.2]			[P1.3]	[P2.1]						
R2					[P1.2]							[P3.3]		[P2.2]					
R1			[P1.1]			[P3.1]											[P2.3]		
Time slot	1	2	3	4	5	6	7	8	9	10	11	12	13	14	15	16	17	18	19	20

First Patient 1 is processed on task 1 requires resource R1. Next Patient 2 needs resource R3 for its first task and as it is available the resource is allocated for 3 minutes after that the same resource needed by patient 1 for task 2 whose priority is higher than patient 2. So, resource R3 is removed from patient 2 and given to patient 1 (based on age priority). Meanwhile patient 3 is arrived and processed on resource R1 for task 1. For patient 3 task 2 needs Resource R3 that is currently allocated to patient 1 and it is removed from patient 1 and given to patient 3 based on age priority. Table 19.7 represents a scenario for scheduling based on priority for 3 patients.

19.4   RESULTS AND DISCUSSION

The scheduling is performed using PSO, FCFS, and Priority scheduling algorithm to analyze the optimization based on performance metrics like completion time and resource utilization. The series labeled as series 1, series 2, and series 3 in the graph represents R1, R2, and R3, respectively.

The completion time of all the scheduling algorithms is depicted in Figure 19.3, based on the above comparison for three considered scheduling algorithms PSO has performed the best as it is completed promptly using less time. Resource Utilization is depicted in Figure 19.4, to show the results of the considered scheduling algorithms and do the analysis for best resource utilization. The units of the resources are allocated to guarantee the best utilization in resource utilization metrics. The final observation is the best resource utilization is achieved by PSO as it is utilizing the resources efficiently.

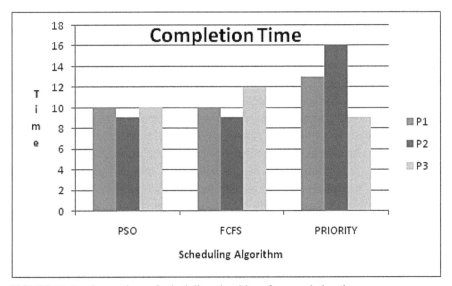

FIGURE 19.3   Comparison of scheduling algorithms for completion time.

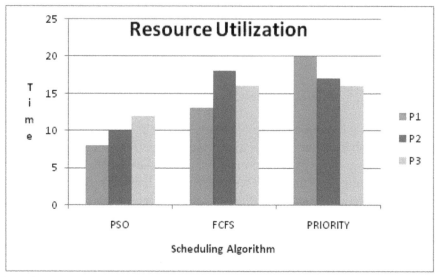

FIGURE 19.4   Comparison of scheduling algorithms for resource utilization.

19.5 CONCLUSION

The proposal is to find the optimal scheduling algorithm for PSO, FCFS, and priority algorithm. The aim of the proposal is to reduce the patient's waiting period and attend them at the earliest, when they are in pain. The idea is to work on selecting appropriate parameters to cater to their needs using the best and fair scheduling algorithm. The parameters used to check the optimality in the current scenario are velocity, speed, and position. This selection is meant to satisfy the patient's needs and requirement in the best possible way. The results show that the performance improvement is noted for PSO when it is compared with the other two selected algorithms. An effectual patient arranging is one which reduces the patient's waiting time for consultation in the hospital, thereby reducing the anxiety of the patient. The major finding of the proposal is to find the best scheduling for selected performance metrics. The metrics considered in this experimentation is the completion time of the process for contending resource and the resource utilization time. The extension of the proposal would be finding minimum make span, Resource load, waiting time for non-sporadic jobs.

KEYWORDS

- **Allocation**
- **Earliest Deadline First**
- **First Come First Serve**
- **Healthcare**
- **Particle Swarm Optimization**
- **Resources**
- **Shortest Job First**

REFERENCES

1. Mohammed, A., & Fahmina, T., (2018). *Power Consumption Analysis in Multi-hop Networks of Mobile Environments.* Springer Nature Singapore Pte Ltd. FTNCT 2018, CCIS 958, 1–12. [Online available]: https://doi.org/10.1007/978-981-13-3804-5_35.
2. Jingjing, H., Muhammad, B., Liping, M., & Dandan, W. (2020). An improved method of particle swarm optimization for path planning of mobile robot. *Hindawi Journal of Control Science and Engineering, 2020,* 12. Article ID 3857894. [Online available] https://doi.org/10.1155/2020/3857894.
3. Fahmina, T., Reshma, N., et al., (2020). *Handover Management Using IEEE 802.11 and IEEE 802.16 Standards in MANETs* (Vol. 12, No. 3, pp. 17–22). SAMRIDDH.
4. Mohit, K., & Sharma, S. C., (2019). PSO-based novel resource scheduling technique to improve QoS parameters in cloud computing. Real-world optimization problems and meta-heuristics. *Neural Computing and Applications* (Vol. 134, p. 16). Springer-Verlag London Ltd., part of Springer Nature.
5. Zhaoyun, S., Liu, B., & Hao, C., (2018). Adaptive particle swarm optimization with population diversity control and its application in tandem blade optimization. *Journals of Mechanical Engineering Science, 233,* 6. Sage.
6. Uma, D., (2018). Prediction system for heart disease using Naive Bayes and particle swarm optimization. *Biomedical Research, 29*(12), 2646–2649.
7. Iman, S., Mohammad, S., & Fatemeh, S., (2013). Various types of particle swarm optimization-based methods for harmonic reduction of cascade multilevel inverters for renewable energy sources. *Engineering Sciences Physics, International Journal of Innovation and Applied Studies, ISSR Journals, 2*(4), 671–681.
8. Grace, M. K. E., & Valarmathi, M. L., (2012). Multi-agent-based patient scheduling using particle – swarm optimization. *Procedia Engineering, 30,* 386–393.
9. Alfi, A., (2011). PSO with adaptive mutation and inertia weight and its application in parameter estimation of dynamic systems. *Acta Automatica Sinica, 37,* 541–549.
10. Zhi-Hui, Z., Jun, Z., Yun, L., & Shu-Hung, C. H., (2009). Adaptive particle swarm optimization. *IEEE Transactions on Systems, Man, and Cybernetics, 39*(6), 1362–1381.

11. Mojtaba, A. K., Hassan, T., Mohammad, T., & Mahdi, A. S. (2009). *Novel Binary Particle Swarm Optimization.* pp.1–12, Intech Open, 2009.
12. Cheng, W. S., Zang, X. Z., Jensen, Z., & Cai, H. G., (2008). *Modified Strategy to Inertia Weight in PSO for Searching Threshold of Otsu Rule.* October 2008.
13. Ying-Nan, Z., Qing-Ni, H., & Hong-Fei, T., (2008). Active target particle swarm optimization. *Concurrency and Computation Practice and Experience, 20*(1), 29–40.
14. Jian, C. Z., Jing, J., & Jian, X. H., (2006). Adaptive particle swarm optimization guided by acceleration information. International Conference on Computational Intelligence and Security, *IEEE Xplore,* 351–355.
15. Kennedy, J., & Eberhart, R., (2002). Particle swarm optimization. *IEEE Xplore,* 1942–1948.

INDEX